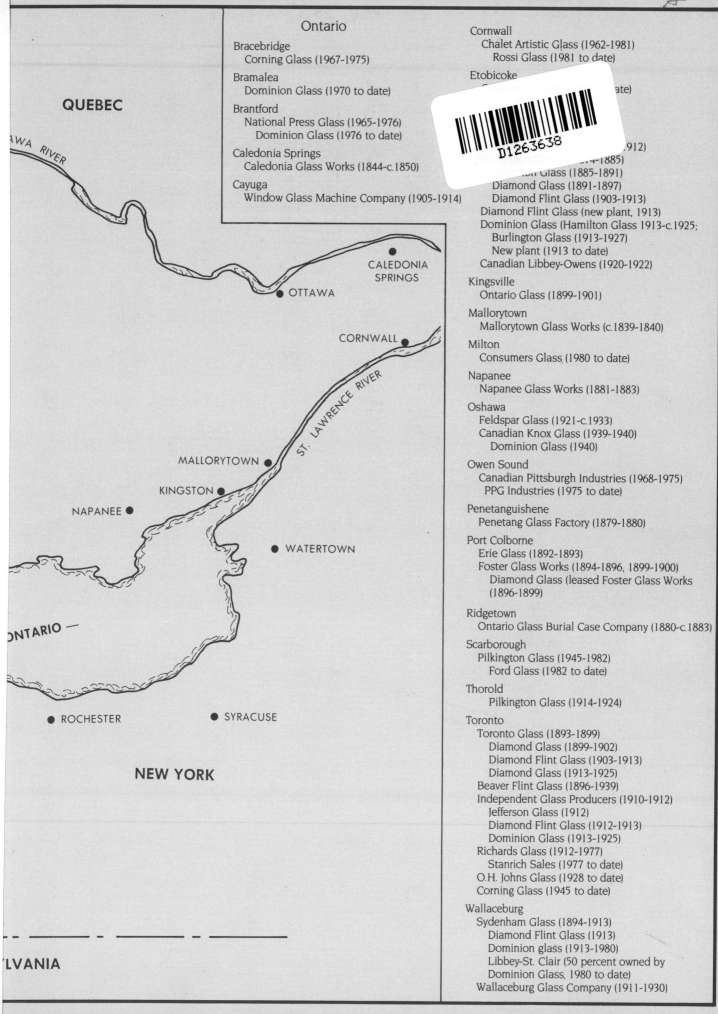

QUEBEC

TAWA RIVER

CALEDONIA SPRINGS

OTTAWA

CORNWALL

ST. LAWRENCE RIVER

MALLORYTOWN

KINGSTON

NAPANEE

WATERTOWN

ONTARIO

ROCHESTER   SYRACUSE

NEW YORK

LVANIA

Ontario

Bracebridge
  Corning Glass (1967-1975)
Bramalea
  Dominion Glass (1970 to date)
Brantford
  National Press Glass (1965-1976)
    Dominion Glass (1976 to date)
Caledonia Springs
  Caledonia Glass Works (1844-c.1850)
Cayuga
  Window Glass Machine Company (1905-1914)

Cornwall
  Chalet Artistic Glass (1962-1981)
    Rossi Glass (1981 to date)
Etobicoke
  C_____ate)

  _____912)
  ____74-1885)
  ___on Glass (1885-1891)
    Diamond Glass (1891-1897)
    Diamond Flint Glass (1903-1913)
  Diamond Flint Glass (new plant, 1913)
  Dominion Glass (Hamilton Glass 1913-c.1925;
    Burlington Glass (1913-1927)
    New plant (1913 to date)
  Canadian Libbey-Owens (1920-1922)
Kingsville
  Ontario Glass (1899-1901)
Mallorytown
  Mallorytown Glass Works (c.1839-1840)
Milton
  Consumers Glass (1980 to date)
Napanee
  Napanee Glass Works (1881-1883)
Oshawa
  Feldspar Glass (1921-c.1933)
  Canadian Knox Glass (1939-1940)
    Dominion Glass (1940)
Owen Sound
  Canadian Pittsburgh Industries (1968-1975)
    PPG Industries (1975 to date)
Penetanguishene
  Penetang Glass Factory (1879-1880)
Port Colborne
  Erie Glass (1892-1893)
  Foster Glass Works (1894-1896, 1899-1900)
    Diamond Glass (leased Foster Glass Works
    (1896-1899)
Ridgetown
  Ontario Glass Burial Case Company (1880-c.1883)
Scarborough
  Pilkington Glass (1945-1982)
    Ford Glass (1982 to date)
Thorold
  Pilkington Glass (1914-1924)
Toronto
  Toronto Glass (1893-1899)
    Diamond Glass (1899-1902)
    Diamond Flint Glass (1903-1913)
    Diamond Glass (1913-1925)
  Beaver Flint Glass (1896-1939)
  Independent Glass Producers (1910-1912)
    Jefferson Glass (1912)
    Diamond Flint Glass (1912-1913)
    Dominion Glass (1913-1925)
  Richards Glass (1912-1977)
    Stanrich Sales (1977 to date)
  O.H. Johns Glass (1928 to date)
  Corning Glass (1945 to date)
Wallaceburg
  Sydenham Glass (1894-1913)
    Diamond Flint Glass (1913)
    Dominion glass (1913-1980)
    Libbey-St. Clair (50 percent owned by
    Dominion Glass, 1980 to date)
  Wallaceburg Glass Company (1911-1930)

GLASS
IN CANADA

GLASS
IN CANADA

by Thomas B. King

THE BOSTON MILLS PRESS

Cover Photo –

1.	insulator	attributed to Foster Brothers, St. Johns, Quebec c.1854-1860
2.	fruit jar	Hamilton Glass Works, Hamilton, Ontario c. 1864-1880
3.	goblet (crown)	Nova Scotia Glass, New Glasgow, Nova Scotia 1881-1890
*4.	breakfast set (maple leaf)	Diamond Glass, Diamond Flint Glass and Dominion Glass, Montreal, Quebec and elsewhere 1890-1920
5.	flower holder (flameworking)	F.H. Johns Glass, Toronto, Ontario 1928-
6.	paperweight (signature T.B. King 1965)	Altaglass, Medicine Hat, Alberta 1950-
7.	commemorative	Canada's first float glass plant, Pilkington Glass, Scarborough, Ontario 1967

* 4A creamer/4B covered sugar bowl/4C spooner/4D covered butter dish

Photograph by Graetz, Montreal.

Canadian Cataloguing in Publication Data

King, Thomas B., 1913-
   Glass in Canada

Bibliography p. 303
Includes index.
ISBN 0-919783-01-5

1. Glass manufacture - Canada - History.
2. Glassware - Canada - History. I. Title.

TP854.C3K56 1986   666'.1'0971   C86-094682-7

© Thomas B. King, 1987

Edited by Noel Hudson
Designed by Gill Stead
Printed by Ampersand, Guelph
Typeset by Lexigraf, Tottenham

Published by:
THE BOSTON MILLS PRESS
132 Main Street
Erin, Ontario
N0B 1T0
(519) 833-2407

American Association
for State and Local History
Award of Merit

Winners of the
Heritage Canada
Communications Award

We wish to acknowledge the financial assistance and encouragement of
the Canada Council, the Ontario Arts Council and
the Office of the Secretary of State.

This book is respectfully dedicated to William and David Yuile, "The Fathers of the Canadian Glass Industry," who, along with their associates, successors and even their competitors in the industry, have established and maintained the high profile that the industry enjoys in the Canadian economy today.

ACKNOWLEDGEMENTS

In researching this history, a great deal of material was reviewed. Perhaps the most valuable material came from individual members of GLASFAX and from its internally published newsletter, so ably edited by Madeleine Thomson, for which I am most grateful.

Among the members who contributed were Douglas and Marion Bird, Alan and Dorothy Bradbeer, Helen Tait Campbell, Newt Coburn, Jean-Pierre and Jacqueline Dion, Janet Holmes, Ken Judges, Jack Kingdon, Joseph Macgillivray, Willa Mercer, Dave Parker, Ailsa Pearson, Mac Provick, Manse Quartermain, David Roberts, Bob Rosewarne, Barbara Lang Rottenberg, Huia Ryder, Hazel Sauer, Wally and Mary Saunders, John Sheeler, Audrey Smith, Mary Smith, Jack Stephenson, Larry Taylor, Judith Tomlin, Julian Toulouse, Ollie Urquhart, Bob and Doris Wentzell, and Frankie Woodrow.

The next group to whom I am greatly indebted are the many glass company personnel whose input and guidance were most useful. They include Lind Ayres, Ewart Blyth, Jack Dent, Angie Fiorentino, Bill Jordan, Peggy Kelly, Bill Sellhorn and Gene Yachetti from Domglas.; Don Kennedy Jr., Aubrey Kingdon and Tom Tinmouth from Consumers Glass; Brian Bezanson and Jan Gube from Ahlstrom; Michael R. Terry, Ford Glass (formerly Pilkington); Douglas Hill from Canadian Libbey-Owens; Jean Peeters from Canadian Pittsburgh Industries; George Williamson from Corning Glass; Earl Myers from Lorraine Glass. Three people supplied information on studio glassblowing: Martin Demaine, Elena Lee and Harvey Littleton.

From government and public institutions, the cooperation of the following are gratefully acknowledged: Neil Forsyth, archivist; Peter Rider, Atlantic provinces historian; Olive Jones, Environment Canada, Ottawa; Brian Young, archivist; F.A. Skinner, assistant deputy registrar of companies, British Columbia; Debbie Trask, assistant curator, and Carol Rosevear, head, library and archives department, New Brunswick Museum; Isabelle McNair, coordinator, Town of Haldimand Public Libraries.

The fourth group of researchers to be acknowledged are those individuals who for one reason or another provided me with detailed information on the companies that operated in their respective locations. They include Stephen Foster, Ontario incorporated companies; John Beswarick Thompson, the Como-Hudson glasshouses; Jack Foster, Foster Brothers, St. Johns, Quebec; Earl Hann, the glasshouses of Oshawa, Ontario; Alan Mann, Wallaceburg, Ontario, glass operations; Francis Vink, Ontario Glass Burial Case Co., Ridgetown, Ontario; John Barclay, Kent Bridge, Ontario, the Beaver jar; Tom Hallenbeck, Toledo, Ohio, the Owens bottlemaking machine.

During the conversion of my research material into manuscript form, I am most grateful to the following people: Justin Battle, former director of public relations, Dominion Glass, and his assistant, Darlene Kreusel Hyde; Don Farrell, director of corporate communications, Consolidated-Bathurst; and Noel Hudson, freelance editor, Guelph, Ontario, for their guidance and suggestions. My thanks also to Louise Dumont and Carole Robertson for typing the manuscript.

In a material sense, my acknowledgements must include the very tangible support afforded me by Bill Turner, chairman of Consolidated-Bathurst, who made it possible for me to enjoy all the amenities needed to carry out my project under ideal conditions. For all the other contributors who I have not acknowledged by name, please accept my thanks for your help and interest.

Finally, I would like to underline the tremendous debt I owe to my wife, Helen Campbell King, who over my first eight years of retirement generously and graciously accepted the full-time work load I adopted, which created considerable absentmindedness on my part.

Westmount, Quebec
1986
                                                                    Thomas B. King

CONTENTS

The purpose of this book is threefold. Firstly, to update already published data, providing further definitive information on the glass industry. Secondly, to broaden the information on containers and tableware. And finally, to introduce data on segments of the Canadian glass industry that have not previously been covered or, at most, have been barely touched upon — such as flat glass, contemporary tableware, commercial glassblowing, studio glassblowing and flameworking.

The first step in recounting the history of Canada's glass industry was taken by the late Gerald Stevens, who in 1953 established that there had been a short-lived glass operation at Mallorytown, in Eastern Ontario, (c.1839-1840). The few articles that he attributed to this location comprised pieces of freeblown tableware and may be seen in the Canadiana Department of the Royal Ontario Museum in Toronto. Eight years later, Mr. Stevens published the first general book on the industry. It was titled *Early Canadian Glass* and covered his research on the better-known glass operations in Canada.

In 1966 Hilda and Kelvin Spence of Como, Quebec, published a well-illustrated book titled A *Guide to Early Canadian Glass*. Among other things, this suggested that glass articles might have been made in Canada during the French regime. Unfortunately, there has been, thus far, no acceptable evidence to substantiate this possibility.

In 1964 Dominion Glass Company, Limited, as part of its contribution to Canada's coming centennial celebrations in 1967, established the Dominion Glass Centennial Research Foundation. With the assistance of Mr. Stevens, a collection of glass articles attributed to Canadian glasshouses was assembled and turned over to the Royal Ontario Museum for display in its Canadiana Department. As an additional contribution to the centennial year program, Dominion Glass retained Mr. Stevens to write a more definitive book on Canada's glass industry. This was published in 1967 as *Canadian Glass c.1825-1925*. Thus the industry's published history was covered in three broad-based books. Together, they represented a good start in the research of Canadian glass. Many questions, however, remained unanswered.

During the next 15 years, the main thrust of research was provided by GLASFAX, a non-profit organization tangibly supported by Dominion Glass and co-ordinated by me. The other co-founders were Newt Coburn of Montreal, who was primarily interested in tableware and related glass objects, and the late Bob Rosewarne of Ottawa, who was a widely recognized expert on the manufacture and identification of bottles. An internal newsletter, edited by Madeleine Thomson in Ottawa, was published about four times a year and served as a vehicle for the exchange of information between members. Some of the material from these newsletters appeared in periodicals dealing with glass and antiques.

The presentation of material in this book is basically chronological, starting with a brief history of glassmaking from its inception in (?) B.C. to the start of operations in Canada c.1839. Chapter 2 first highlights the important contribution made by the glassblowers and their fellow workers, and then briefly covers the transition from glassblowing to machine production. At the end of the chapter, there is a selected list of glassblowers and their company affiliations.

Chapters 3 to 8 chronologically record the unfolding story of the developing Canadian industry from c.1839 to 1966, with the accent on bottles and tableware. To further clarify this development, Chapter 9: Authentication, Attribution and Excavation, deals with the several plant-site digs (excavations) that were carried out in the 1960s and 70s.

With the advent of machine production and the wane of glassblowing for mass production at the beginning of the twentieth century, I deemed it appropriate to record the evolution that took place in the production of tableware and industrial ware in this century. This information is provided in Chapter 10.

Heretofore, very little information has been published on flat glass, a very important segment of the industry. I have covered this classification chronologically in Chapter 11, from its historical beginnings to 1966.

Although the major period covered by the book is from c.1839 to 1966, because its publication is actually 20 years later, I have briefly described what has transpired in the intervening years in Chapter 12.

Fortunately for Canada, the glassblower's skill did not suddenly disappear at the beginning of the twentieth century but was modified to satisfy contemporary demands. In Chapter 13 I have attempted to describe the conversion of lampworking to the more sophisticated flameworking. And, at the same time, I have recorded the development of mechanized tableware production, along with the continuing commercial hand production of tableware and artistic glass, and the rebirth, in the form of studio glassblowing, of the glassblowers' skills in the late 1960s.

The following observations have been included to assist the reader in better interpreting some of the terms I have used and my policy with regard to dates. The three words "bottles," "jars" and "containers" all have one thing in common: they are hollow vessels and are capable of being sealed. Individually, however, they have their own identities. "Bottles" from the very beginning indicated hollow vessels, usually having a narrow opening. With the development of food processing and the need for a wider opening to allow for the bottling of fruit and vegetables, the term "jar" was adopted to identify this new wide-mouth style. At the beginning of the twentieth century, and with the conversion to machine-made bottles, the generic term "containers" was gradually introduced to cover both bottles and jars, the former being further referred to as a narrow-neck or narrow-mouth bottle and the latter as a wide-mouth (WM) jar.

To interpret the use of dates in connection with each glass operation, I have adopted the following policy: the first date indicates the first year in which the operation was recognized as an entity, be it an informal association, partnership or an incorporated company, and regardless of whether it produced glass then or later. The closing date is the date on which the first of the following events occurred: the association ceased to exist; the partnership was dissolved and the operation did not continue under the same name; the incorporated company ceased to produce or was dissolved; or the entity was taken over by another entity.

The terms "flint," "clear" and "colourless" refer to different glass properties. In the nineteenth century the word "flint" was used to differentiate between colourless glass made from ground flints and colourless glass made from the more common soda-lime formula, the latter being referred to as "clear" glass. In the twentieth century, particularly in bottle production, the word "flint" is used to describe colourless glass as opposed to amber, green or blue glass. However, glassblowers continue to use the word "clear" for colourless glass.

As mentioned previously, company histories in chapters 3 to 8 appear in chronological order and cover all types of production except flat glass. However, a few exceptions have been made. Where a company was established to make flat glass but soon converted to bottle production, its history appears in these chapters. Again, where a short-lived flat glass operation occurred in the middle of a group of succeeding companies in one location, in some cases it was included. Where a number of companies operated in succession in a general area (say southwest Ontario), they appear in sequence, even though other companies had started up elsewhere during the period. When one company is referred to in the history of another company, its name is abbreviated for simplicity.

There is a selected glossary of glass terms and a short bibliography. The three appendices cover a chronological list of glass companies and their operating dates; bottle markings and closures; and illustrations of selected pressed glass patterns.

It is my hope that this book will encourage others to take up the task, fill out the story, correct the errors, and find renewed enthusiasm and inspiration for researching Canadian glass artifacts and glassmaking. A knowledge of the past can enrich our present and help to form our perspective on the choices that must be made for the years ahead.

Thomas B. King

CHAPTER 1

A Brief History
of Glassmaking

Story of the Phoenician merchants (A.D. 23-79)
Sand-core Method (1500 B.C.)
Glassblowing (100 B.C.)
Roman period (A.D. 50-450)
Dark Ages (A.D. 450-1250)
Venetian period (A.D. 1250-1650)
Britain (1600s)
America (1608-1855)

Mr. Edward Meigh, in *The Story of the Glass Bottle*, put it this way: "Sixteen hundred million years ago, when the earth's crust solidified and igneous rocks were formed from molten matter, Nature made the first glass in various forms: obsidian, quartz, rock crystal, pumice and other volcanic rocks . . . "[1] Sixteen hundred million years later, when we expose silica sand to temperatures in excess of 2000°F, we create man-made glass. So what's new?

What's new is what man has done over the years to improve on Nature. There appears to be no doubt that primitive man used obsidian from time immemorial. The very nature of obsidian, which is opaque, hard and shalelike in structure, made it an excellent material from which to fashion the necessary tools for survival, such as spearheads, knives and other practical objects. When split in thin layers, the resulting flat, shiny surface could be polished to make a mirror.

Obsidian artifacts have been found in Egypt and Mesopotamia dating back to 3000 B.C. There are deposits of obsidian throughout the world. In North America, there are deposits in Wyoming and Utah. Rock crystal, on the other hand, is clear and hard, and over the centuries has been used to make dishes, simulated jewels and other artworks. It is found in chunks of varying sizes in Europe, South America and China. In modern times, it is hard to distinguish between articles made from it and those fashioned from man-made crystal.

When was glass first man-made? Most authors have referred to the "story" by Pliny the Elder (A.D. 23-79) about a group of Phoenician merchants who, in preparing their evening meal on the shores at the mouth of the river Belus, used blocks of natron (an alkali) to support their cooking vessel over the fire. When the fire burned out, they discovered a clear residue, which was credited with being the first man-made glass. While the story has a nice romantic appeal, it would not be possible for the heat from a bonfire to fuse natron and sand into a glasslike substance because the temperature required to convert sand and other raw materials into molten glass, or metal, as it is often referred to, is in excess of 2000°F.

Of all the explanations that have been given, the most plausible, in my opinion, is that the sand in this region was in fact powdered obsidian. It would then have been possible for the heat from the fire, assisted by the fluxing action of the natron on the sandy particles, to have

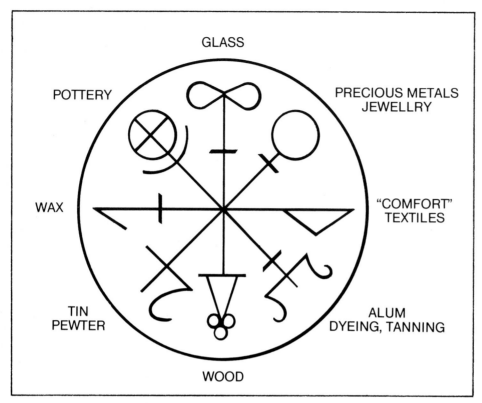

This symbol is composed mainly of signs used in the medieval chemical system. The arrangement is that of the gnostic sun monogram representing the eight corners of the heavens.

Glass vessel made by the sand-core
process.   Courtesy Edward Meigh.

produced a glass residue. Historians tell us that for many centuries before this incident, the sand from these shores was used in Sidon (a chief city in ancient Phoenicia) for making glass.

The first so-called man-made glass was produced in the form of a glaze, which was applied to small stones and other objects. Some of the earliest such objects have been attributed to the Egyptians of about 12000 B.C. Over the centuries, the art expanded to include the glazing of larger objects, such as vases and tiles. It would appear that glassmaking wasn't actually "discovered," but that it was simply developed in various forms and that the regions in which it was most likely to have been developed were those where there was an availability of sand, natron (or other alkali) and wood for fuel — all of which points to Egypt and other parts of North Africa.

The first hollow vessels were made about 1500 B.C. in Egypt by what is known as the sand-core method. A ball of sand of the desired shape was affixed to the end of a metal rod by a piece of cloth tied on with a string. This was then coated with glass, either by dipping it in a crucible of molten glass or by covering it with threads of glass wound around it. When the glass had cooled and solidified, the rod was removed and the loose sand scraped out from the interior. Behold the birth of the bottle (from the Latin *butis*: a dwelling, habitation or vessel).

The most important discovery in the history of glassmaking was the invention of the blowing iron or, as it is now more commonly called, the "blowpipe." Most historians locate its first use at Sidon (now Daida), in Lebanon, about 100 B.C. Using the hollow metal rod, four to six feet in length, had several advantages over the sand-core technique. Probably the most important was the almost infinite number of shapes that could be blown, compared to the pottery-style restrictions of the earlier method.

The greater length of the blowpipe now permitted the glassblower to work with much hotter molten glass. This had the advantage of burning out most of the impurities from the raw materials. It is remarkable that, since this discovery, the method of blowing glass has not radically changed. Indeed, the basic improvement has related to volume, resulting from a conversion to machine production for mass output through the use of compressed air.

The blowpipe breakthrough made glass articles available to people other than royalty and the wealthy, particularly in the areas of Sidon and Alexandria, then the centres of glass-blowing. From the beginning of the Christian era, free- or off-hand blown glass (made without the use of moulds) was used side by side with glass blown in primitive moulds of stone, clay, wood or metal.

The invention of glassblowing, coinciding as it did with the rise of the Roman Empire in the first century A.D., added great impetus to the art of glassmaking. During the 400-year Roman period, two main types of glass evolved, Roman and Egyptian. In considering Roman glass, it is important to realize that this included all the glass made from Afghanistan to Britain.

Generally speaking, Roman glass was light in weight and simple in design. At that time, because they did not know how to make colourless glass, most of it had a green-yellow or green-blue colour due to the iron in the sand. Some bottles were made during this period, but most of the production comprised vases and other utility pieces, many of which were decorated with natural motifs such as shells, fruit, etc. Glasshouses were established throughout the empire, and those communities with an abundance of sand and wood were normally selected as sites.

The Egyptians, on the other hand, were experts in the making of coloured glasses, which they may have considered as reasonable substitutes for their beautiful turquoises, lapis lazuli and other brilliant stones. Their craftsmanship reflected greater technical skills than that of the Romans and included glass mosaics and a marblelike glass which, improved by the Venetians later on, was called *calcedonia*, and which now, as a product of Bohemia, is known as *Schmelzglas*. Wheel engraving was popular, as was the technique of overlaying, which consisted of blowing an article in one colour of glass and then dipping it in a pot of another colour. When the outer layer of glass was cut away in a design, it was known as cameo cutting. An example of this is the world-famous Portland Vase, which has been attributed to the fourth century A.D. and is now in the British Museum in London. Josiah Wedgwood used this design to create his well-known jasper "Wedgwood." Decoration by enamelling was practiced, but to a lesser degree than it would be later on, when the art was more fully developed.

In A.D. 300, when Constantine the Great moved the capital of the Roman Empire to Byzantium and renamed it Constantinople, glassmaking became less traditional and the effects of Greek culture began to be reflected in the new styles. By the mid-seventh century, the Byzantine Empire had almost disappeared, and Mohammed, with his capital in Damascus, established the Islamic Empire. This empire survived until 1402, when Tamerlane sacked Damascus and carried the glassblowers off to Samarkand, south of Tashkent, in what is now the USSR. During the Islamic period, a great deal of glass, including some bottles, was made following the Roman style. Colourful Egyptian mosque lamps were also made at this time.

Turning to the West, we find that from the decline of the Roman Empire in the fifth century, glassmaking fell into a slump until the beginning of the fourteenth century. This has been referred to as the Dark Age of glass. The main reason for this deterioration was the almost continuous fighting, uprisings and invasions, which kept the common people busy just surviving let alone maintaining a trade. Up to the ninth century, very few domestic articles are known to have been made in the area from southern Russia to Spain.

With the death of Charlemagne in 814, Europe began to fall apart. Communications were almost impossible, the fine Roman roads were in disrepair and Roman supremacy at sea was over. Many of the remaining craftsmen moved to Altare, near Genoa, where they reestablished their craft. Left behind in Western Europe were the locally trained people, who continued to make low-quality utility ware, which included vessels, bottles and even window glass. Bottlemaking had the lowest priority.

Until the thirteenth century, little if any glass had been made in Britain, most of the craftsmen having left with the retreating Romans. However, starting in 1226, a number of good glassworkers came to Britain from the Continent and set up shop at Chiddingfold, in the area of Surrey known as the Weald. The availability of sand and wood had much to do with the choice of location.

The first to come was Laurence Vitrearius (Latin for glassmaker) from Normandy. His main production was clear and coloured glass, some of which was commissioned for Westminster Abbey. He also made vessels for domestic use. His son, William le Virir (French for glassmaker), followed about 1300 and specialized in blowing glass vessels, for which he received a Royal Charter. In 1343 the Schurterre family, from France, succeeded to all the glass operations in the Weald, with a John le Alemayne (a German?) arriving seven years later to join them as a selling agent. This latter group also made glass for chapels at Westminster and Windsor. The final chapter of the Wealden industry belongs to a Frenchman by the name of Peytowe, who came to Chiddingfold in 1435, taking over and maintaining control of all glasshouses there for about 100 years.

One of the most glamorous periods in the history of glassmaking followed. It is known as the Venetian period, during which very few bottles were made. Most of the glasshouses had been moved to the island of Murano because of the strict fire regulations in Venice. However, the products from Murano were commonly referred to as Venetian. The period started about A.D. 1250 and reached its peak between 1450-1550. It was the forerunner of a great revival of glassmaking in Europe and Britain. As early as A.D. 600, with the fall of the Roman Empire a fait accompli, Venice had come under the domination of Byzantium and, naturally, reflected its culture.

Until about the middle of the fifteenth century, the Venetians created their beautiful pieces from the soda-lime glass that was traditional for all glassmaking at that time. In 1463 an old, established glassmaking family named Berovieri is credited with having developed *cristallo*, a much better quality glass created by the addition of manganese. This had the effect of masking the greenish and bluish tinge found in conventional glass. The creation of *cristallo* was a definite breakthrough in the history of glassmaking. For decorating, the Venetians developed a white opaque glass, which they called *lattimo*. When this was applied to a piece of glass, it was known as *latticinio*.

Jug by Emile Gallé, 1884.
Musée des Arts Decoratifs, Paris.

Unfortunately, space does not permit a description here of the renaissance of glassmaking in Europe as the result of the influx of Italian glassworkers. Ever since the heyday of the Roman Empire, glass continued to be made, to a greater or lesser degree, in most European countries. However, it is worthy of note that during this renaissance period the most important glass person in Europe was Emile Gallé (1846-1904), in Nancy, France. A master of many skills — potter, artist, glassmaker and decorator — he finally settled on the last one. His inspiration came from the flora and fauna of the French countryside. His techniques included enamelling, overlays, engraving and combinations thereof. One of his pupils, Louis Comfort Tiffany, carried on the Gallé tradition in the United States in the late nineteenth and early twentieth centuries.

It was England whose glass industry directly (and indirectly, through the United States) had the greatest effect on the Canadian glass industry.

According to Mr. Meigh, in *The Story of the Glass Bottle*: ". . . The 17th Century, especially the second half, is a supremely important historical stage in the story of the glass bottle. It was the revival of bottle manufacturing on a large scale as containers of commodities for distribution or storage . . ."

In 1615 the English government, concerned with the rapid depletion by the glass industry of its hardwood stands, enacted "a Royal Declaration Touching Glass" prohibiting the use of wood for the melting process. The best and cheapest energy substitute was coal, developed for use in the glass industry by Thomas Percivall.

One of the first to benefit by this cost-saving adaptation was Sir Robert Mansell, a court favourite who took over the monopoly by letters patent from Verzelini's successors, giving him exclusive glassmaking rights in England and Wales. In the seventeenth century, industrial monopolies were considered a natural and sound commercial practice, accepted throughout the civilized world. Indeed, the practice contributed greatly to the survival of glassmaking. Mansell made all types of glass, including mirrors and window glass. He was responsible for developing coal mining in Newcastle and South Wales just to supply the glass industry. His contemporary archrival in the British Isles was George Hay, an aristocrat also with court connections, who established a thriving glass industry in Scotland, at Wemyss, in Fifeshire. On Hay's death, about 1627, Mansell took over these operations and reigned supreme throughout Britain.

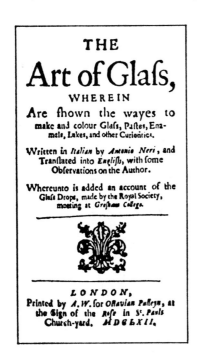

Title page of "The Arts of Glass".
From "The Story of the Glass Bottle" by Edward Meigh courtesy C.E. Ramsden & Co. Ltd.

Charles II came to the throne in 1660, and with him came the Restoration. The whole life and times of England took an upturn. The seventeenth century saw a number of important events occur that would make the glass industry a permanent fixture. The Royal Society, founded in 1645, was incorporated in 1662 and included as members such famous names as Dryden, Pepys, Wren and Newton. In the same year, one of its members, Dr. Christopher Merrett, translated Neri's L'Arte Vetraria into English under the title *The Art of Glass with Observations by the Author*. Coinciding with this great event was the contribution of the Glass Sellers Company, which received its first charter in 1635 under Charles I and had it renewed by Charles II in 1664. As well as being a glass importer, it had the responsibility of seeing that a high level of quality was maintained. It also kept the industry informed on the ever-changing demands of the public. George Villiers, second Duke of Buckingham, was the patron of the industry for 14 years, succeeding Sir Robert Mansell.

Sketches of early glassblowing.

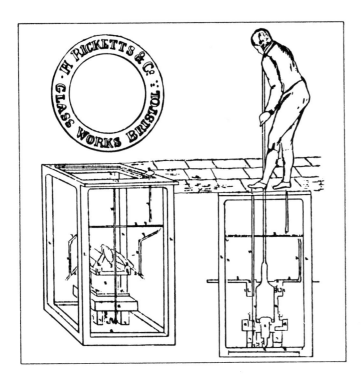

Rickett's design and method of using moulds.

Perhaps the greatest contribution to the industry by the Glass Sellers Company was in 1673, when it engaged George Ravenscroft to carry out research for the development of a better quality of glass than *cristallo*. He was granted a seven-year patent in which to come up with an answer. His first effort was to use English flints ground to powder — hence, the still-used designation "flint" glass for clear glass. Because of its hardness, it required more potash for fusing and also had a crizzling effect. (Crizzling is a breakdown often due to faulty chemistry in colourless glass.) The final solution was the addition of lead oxide in place of some of the potash and the replacement of the flint powder by a better quality of sand. This was the origin of lead glass or, as it is more commonly called, "lead crystal," which continues to be the highest-quality glass today.

The second half of the seventeenth century and the first half of the eighteenth century saw the establishment of bottlemaking on an industrial scale. After the sterility of the Cromwell period, people began to live again under King Charles. The drinking of wine, spirits and beer in excessive quantities became *de rigueur* for all classes. Drunkenness was very common, especially in London, where there were reputed to be 17,000 gin shops. A "gin shop" was one of many names used to indicate a place where alcoholic beverages were consumed. Seventeenth-century bottles tended to be stubby, with short necks, and were made of dark amber or dark green glass. By the end of the seventeenth century and into the eighteenth century, the bottles became cylindrical, first with short necks and later with longer necks. By 1833 there were 126 bottlemaking shops in Britain, and by 1874 the number had increased to 240.

The first attempt to blow larger quantities of bottles in moulds was made by Henry Ricketts of Bristol. In 1821 he took out a patent on the design and method of using moulds:

> . . . by this my sole invention the circumference and diameter of bottles are formed nearly cylindrical and their height determined so as to contain given quantities or proportions of a wine or beer gallon measure with a great degree of regularity or conformity to each other and all the bottles so made after this method present a superior neatness of appearance and regularity of shape for convenient and safe storage which cannot by other means be so well attained.[2]

The bottlemaking industry was now established and would continue to reach new heights of achievement hereafter.

First North American glass blowing attempt, Jamestown, Virginia, 1608.

Over the centuries, it has been popular demand that has set the trend in glassmaking. A rather interesting reversal to this took place in the mid-seventeenth century. The increasing use of bottles in England for beverages created a demand for a better sealing device, or closure. This was solved by the adoption of a tight cork that would fit the inconsistent sizes of the neck openings. Corks remained the dominant closure until late in the nineteenth century.

The glass industry in England suffered a major setback in the eighteenth century with the passing of the Glass Excise Acts of 1745, 1777 and 1787, to raise money for the country's war chest. The taxes lasted for nearly 100 years. The first act taxed flint glass by weight of raw materials used. The main effect of this was the establishment of an English-oriented glass industry in Ireland, where the tax did not apply. Ireland's first glasshouse was set up at Waterford in 1739, but was not very successful. Production was depressed further in 1745, when it was enacted that Irish glass could not be exported. This was remedied when, in the spirit of America's War of Independence, the Irish demanded and finally got free trade. By 1783 the Stourbridge firm of George and William Penrose, and a group of their skilled workers, took over the glasshouse in Waterford that had been limping along since 1739. The Waterford operation lasted until 1851, when it closed its doors for a hundred years.

The consequent lightweighting of glass pieces in England, due to the tax, created an incentive for different decorating techniques. One such technique, enamelling, was further developed by William Beilby and his sister Mary, both of Newcastle, in the period 1760-1778. Although less popular than engraved glass, it was exceptionally well done and lent a new dimension to the pieces.

An important invention was made in France early in the nineteenth century. During the Napoleonic Wars it was found that, for lack of fresh food, the military were victims of scurvy. In 1810 a Parisian by the name of Nicholas Appert invented a sealed cooking process which, in conjunction with a glass bottle and a cork closure, provided food that would remain fresh for a long time. He is considered to be founder of the food processing industry. Appert was also the first to recognize the need for closer co-operation between the bottle manufacturer and the closuremaker when designing a new container.

The first known attempt to make glass in North America, and an unsuccessful one at that, was at Jamestown, Virginia, in 1608. The London Company of Virginia started off with "eight Dutchmen and Poles," but failed almost immediately. It was not until 1739 that Caspar Wistar, a German, established the first successful glasshouse, in Alloyway, South Jersey. Although his main production comprised window glass and bottles, like most striving operators

WHEN	WHAT	WHERE	BY WHOM
1500 B.C.	Sand-core process of making bottles	Egypt, Syria	
100 B.C.	Discovery of blowing glass	Alexandria	
20-500 A.D.	Development of glassmaking	Roman Empire	
500-1250	Dark Age of glass, bottles scarce		
1250-1650	Venice Art Period		
13th C.	Primitive bottles	Britain	
1608	First glass operation in America (unsuccessful)	Virginia	London Company of Virginia
1612	L'Arte Vetraria, book on glass techniques	Italy	Antonia Neri
1650	Development of use of tight cork for closure	Britain	
1662	Translation into English of L'Arte Vetraria	Britain	Dr. Christopher Merrett
17th C.	Upsurge in production of spirits bottles	Britain	
	Development of decanter-style bottle with crests	Britain	
1739	First established glass operation in America	South Jersey	Caspar Wistar
1800-1870	American historical flasks	U.S.A.	Various companies
1826	Formation of New England Bottle Glass Company	Cambridge, Mass.	
1844-c.1848	First established glass operation in Canada	Caledonia Springs, Ontario	
1846-1875	Glassmaking in Como-Hudson area	Quebec	Various companies
1846-1879	Glassmaking in St. Johns area (to eventually become Domglas of today)	Quebec	Various companies
1858	Invention of Mason jar ring & glass lid closure	Philadelphia	John L. Mason
1873	Formation of Illinois Glass Company, now Owens-Illinois Inc.	Alton, Ill.	
1882	First semiautomatic press & blow machine	Pittsburg	Philip Arbogast
1890-1902	Formation of Diamond Glass Company	Montreal	Wm. & David Yuile
1892	Invention of crown finish for pop bottles	Baltimore	Wm. Painter
1896	Improvement on press & blow technique	Wheeling, W. Va.	Charles Blue
1903	Formation of Diamond Flint Glass Company, successor to Diamond Glass Company	Montreal	Grier interests
1903	Invention of stream feeder	U.S.A.	Homer Brooke
1903	Invention of Owens automatic suction & blowing machine	Toledo	M.J. Owens
1911	Invention of gob feeder	Boston	Dr. Karl Peiler
1912	Invention of semiautomatic forming machine	U.S.A.	Frank O'Neill
1913	Formation of Dominion Glass Company, Limited, successor of Diamond Flint Glass Company	Montreal & elsewhere	Public
1916	Invention of semiautomatic forming machine	U.S.A.	James Lynch
1917	Invention of semiautomatic forming machine	U.S.A.	Edward Miller
1917	Formation of Consumers Glass Company, Limited	Montreal	
1920s	Invention of continuous thread closure	U.S.A.	
1925	Invention of Hartford-Empire individual section forming machine	Hartford, Conn.	Henry Ingle
1932	Invention of applied colour lettering (A.C.L.)	U.S.A.	
1933	Development of techniques for lightweighting bottles	U.S.A.	
1951	Invention of the colourant forehearth	U.S.A.	

Highlights of Glass Manufacturing. Taken from a lecture by the author at the University of Toronto, 1977.

he managed to make some tableware for domestic use. His factory eventually closed down in 1780, but during the next 75 years many other glasshouses came and went, making glass in the South Jersey tradition.

The second outstanding glassmaker on the American scene was "Baron" Henry William Stiegel, also a German, who emigrated from Cologne in 1750 and settled near Lancaster, Pennsylvania, where he first established himself as an ironmonger. He eventually started up three glass factories in Pennsylvania, in 1763, 1765 and 1769, the last two being located at Manheim. He made bottles, window glass and tableware. He was called The Baron because he lived in a castlelike mansion, and his arrival at the works each day was signalled by the firing of a cannon. He ended up in debtor's prison in 1795.

The third notable was John Frederick Amelung, who came out to Baltimore, Maryland, from Germany in 1784. With 68 glassworkers and necessary equipment, he opened up a glass-works near Frederick, Md., a year later. Besides the usual bottles and window glass, he made green and white hollowware in an attempt to compete with similar imported items. Unfortunately, his product did not appeal to the public, and he put his plant up for sale in 1795.

In 1818 the New England Glass Company was formed in East Cambridge, Massachusetts, and made bottles, tumblers, and pressed and cut glass. In 1825 Deming Jarves, an agent for this company, started the Boston and Sandwich Glass Company in Sandwich, Mass., where he produced wares similar to those of his former company, as well as a number of Bohemian-style cased and cut glass pieces. In 1826 the New England Glass Company established the New England Bottle Company, which made all types of bottles. After a strike closed down both these companies in 1885, Edward Drummond Libbey, the proprietor of both of them, moved his operations to Toledo, Ohio, where a fresh start was made under the name Libbey Glass Company, and later, the Toledo Glass Company. The main advantage in relocating was the availability of cheaper coal and gas for fuel.

Popularity of the American Historical Flasks, which were made during the turbulent period in the "March of Democracy," from about 1800 to 1870, created a new demand for bottles. There was also a great surge in demand for proprietary and patent medicine bottles during the 1800s, as North Americans went through a long spell of hypochondria and peddlers were in their glory. In many cases, the bottle was worth more than the contents. The period from then until the end of the century, 1903 to be exact, saw the inevitable changeover from manual glassblowing to fully automatic machineblowing of bottles.

FOOTNOTES

[1] Edward Meigh, The Story of the Glass Bottle, (Stoke-on-Trent, England: C.E. Ramsden & Co. Ltd. 1972), p.3.
[2] British patent no. 4623 "Improvement in manufacturing glass bottles," Henry Ricketts, 1821.

CHAPTER 2

Then and Now –
Glassblowing to Machine Production

Dawn of Glassblowing c.100 B.C.
Development Over the Years
Glass Personalities:
The Sephtons, George Gardiner, Donald Lamont
Transition to Machine Production
Selected List of Glassblowers
and the Companies for Which They Worked

From the dawn of glassblowing (about 100 B.C.) and for the next 2,000 years, glass articles were blown either with or without the use of a mould by that paragon of craftsmen, the glorious glassblower. His skill kept him among the leaders in the creative arts. As bottleblowing became more sophisticated, the demand for his work increased. Perhaps the zenith of this centuries-old craft came with the Venetian Art Period (1250-1650), when the scope and skill of the glassblower knew no bounds, It has never since been equalled. It was here, on the Venetian island of Murano, that the glassblowers were recognized as craftsmen *première classe*. In fact, their skills were such a source of profit to the State that they were literally prisoners for life, under penalty of death if caught escaping.

With the decline of glassblowing in the sixteenth and seventeenth centuries and the availability of the new handbook on glass techniques, *L'Arte Vetratria*, published by Italian Antonio Neri in 1612, the glassblowers finally broke their bonds and, armed with this new bible, spread out across Europe and even to Britain.

In France, glassblowers were held in such high esteem that, as early as 1399, they were granted the lowest rank of nobility, *Gentilshommes verriers*, first being restricted to the rank of *ecuyer* and later to *chevalier*. By the seventeenth century, they were exempted from military service.

With the accession of Charles II, England went on a huge binge, and the need for bottles for various spirituous liquors was almost beyond the capacity of the glassblowers — which made them highly valued tradesmen and in great demand. Early in the nineteenth century, the first attempt to produce bottles on a commercial scale was made by Henry Ricketts, whose mechanism was a forerunner of the many mechanical devices that would eventually sound the death knell of the glassblower for bottle production.

Moving to America, with its hard-earned independence in 1776, glassblowers were so much in demand to service the needs of the rapidly growing population that they had to be brought from Europe in great numbers and at great cost. This situation was aggravated by the fact that glassblowers, by tradition, were transients and, once in America, moved from job to job with some frequency. (A selected list of glassblowers appears at the end of the chapter.)

GLASSMAKING TOOLS

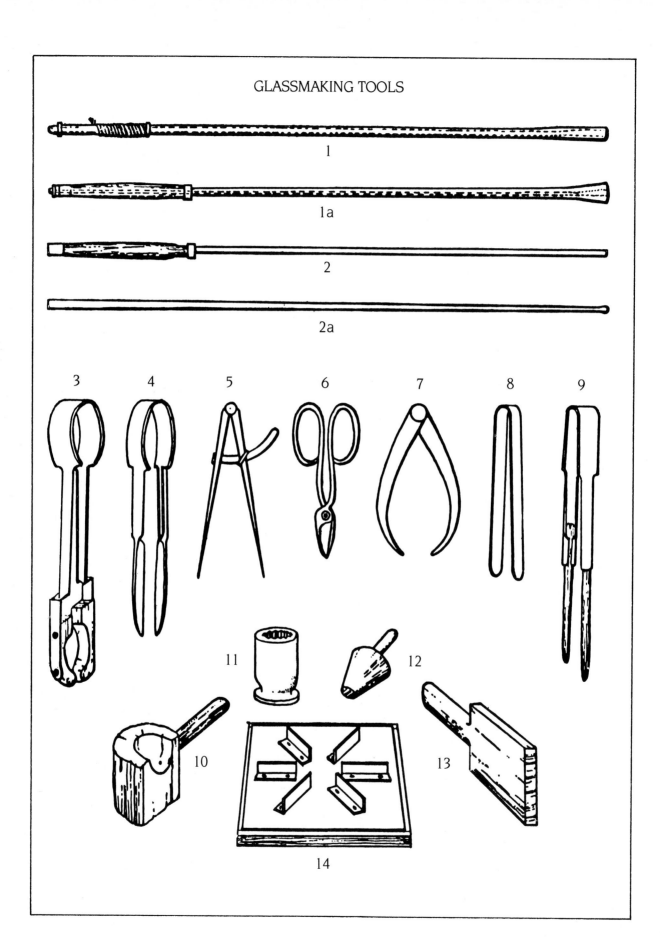

GLOSSARY

Nos. 1 and 1a. Blowpipe, a hollow iron tube wider and thicker at the gathering end than at the blowing end. Blowpipes have been made of brass, bronze and iron and have varied from 2½ feet to 6 feet in length. Today they are from 4 to 6 feet long. Examples shown were drawn from old blowpipes. No. 1, bound with very heavy twine at the mouthpiece end to provide insulation, was used at Coventry, Connecticut; No. 1a, insulated with a wooden sheath at the mouthpiece end, was used at Redwood, New York.

Nos. 2 and 2a. Pontil or punty rod, a hollow or a solid iron rod about the same length as a blowpipe. No. 2, a hollow iron, with one end encased in a wooden sheath, was drawn from a pontil used at Redwood, New York; No. 2a was drawn from a modern pontil. The end on which the gather was secured has a slight bulge. Its principal function is to hold the object during the finishing processes after it has been whetted from the blowpipe.

No. 3 Holding tongs, made of metal with semi-circular wooden ends so designed that when closed the tips form an opening in which the glass may rest without being injured or marked. Used to receive the glass object when it is completed and to carry it to the leer. This type of carrying tool was a 19th century innovation which did not, however, completely replace the forked stick which was used for centuries.

No. 4 Pucellas — one of the three essential tools — a specialized iron tool. With the pucellas all the essential processes of shaping can be accomplished, such as spreading the tops of bowls, diminishing the diameter where a constriction of the body is desired, or elongating and shaping parts such as stems. Eventually, probably after the mid-19th century, steel was used instead of iron. This tool is called steel jack today. The importance of this spring tool is apparent from the blower's name for it — simply, the Tool.

Nos. 5 and 7. Steel compasses and calipers, used in various sizes in measuring the object during manipulation. The compasses are employed in scoring uniform heights on goblets and other vessels; the calipers, the diameters.

No. 6 Shears, used for cutting the glass, which in its plastic state cuts much like soft leather. A large size is usually used to cut off blobs from a gather, as for instance in forming parts such as handles and stems. Small ones, as illustrated, are used to shear away excess glass in shaping a piece.

No. 8. Spring tool, the simplest sort of metal tongs. This tool may be used in pincer work, also in such operations as applying handles.

No. 9. Wood jack, a metal spring tool with wooden prongs which can be replaced when they become too charred for further use. The fact that wood is less likely to mark the surface of glass in its plastic condition probably led to their invention. This tool, we infer, was introduced not long before 1849, for Pellatt speaks of wood tools as ''modern.''

No. 10. Block, made of wood. The block, after being dipped in water to retard charring by the intense heat of the glass metal, is used to give — and aid in retaining — the symmetrical form of a large portion. It is used in the early stages of manipulation.

No. 11. Metal dip mold; part-size open-top one-piece variety used in pattern-molding.

No. 12 Lipper, a small wooden device used sometimes to form a wide lip on a pitcher. Pellatt shows a cylindrical solid of glass used for the same purpose. The small pinched lips found on our early glass pitchers were undoubtedly shaped by the pucellas or tong-like spring tool.

No. 13. Battledore, a wooden paddle used to flatten the bottom of objects.

No. 14. Crimper, wooden base to which short lengths of angle iron radiating from the center have been screwed. The crimper is used to give a crimped or gauffered rim to such pieces as bowls and pitchers. The rim of the piece is presed down upon the upright sides of the angle iron, producing a series of crimps. The one illustrated is modern. However, since gauffering is not modern, it seems logical to conclude that some sililar device must have been used to produce this type of finished edge. Perhaps wooden pieces or small pieces of pipe were affixed to a wooden base.

Courtesy George and Helen Kearin's *American Glass.*

Glassblowers and glassworkers have always been a breed of their own and, from the recognition they received over the years, usually felt they were a cut above the other craftsmen. Being individualists, they were very guarded with their skills. Traditionally, they kept their knowledge in their families and passed it on, boasting about the number of generations their family had been in the glass industry.

Because glassblowers were among the highest-paid craftsmen and always in demand, they were the ones who decided when and under what conditions they would work. In the first quarter of the nineteenth century, in the United States, they usually worked a 12-hour day. Because of the extreme heat to which they were exposed on a daily basis, glasshouses normally shut down from June to September, during which period the blowers took their holidays.

The traditional bottle shop comprised four workers: the gaffer (or foreman), the gatherer, the mould boy and the snapper-up boy. A bottle was made something like this: The gatherer drew a gob of molten glass with his blowpipe from the pot or furnace. While walking to the two-piece hinged mould that was sitting open on the floor, he would give an initial puff into the pipe, which would produce a small bubble or cavity in the gob. He would lower this enlarged gob into the mould, which would then be closed by the mould boy. The gatherer (glassblower) would complete the formation of the bottle by blowing through the blowpipe and forcing the glass out against the sides of the mould. On completion of this action, the mould boy would open the mould and the gatherer would carry the bottle, still on the end of the pipe, to the gaffer, who sat in a chair with arms extending forward to about twice their normal length. At this point, the pipe was cracked off from the bottle, leaving a jagged opening. In order to smooth off this opening and thus complete the bottle, it was necessary to hold the body of the bottle so that the gaffer could "work" the opening.

The earlier method, until about 1860, was to take an iron rod (or pontil rod) about four feet long and attach it to the bottom of the bottle by means of a gob of hot glass. When the pipe was cracked off, the bottle was thus secured on the end of the pontil rod. The rod was then passed to the gaffer, who, while rolling the rod back and forth on the extended chair arms, worked the jagged opening into the desired finished form. During this operation, the bottle often chilled and had to be reheated in a heat chamber known as a "glory hole." This would be done by the worker who handled the pontil rod.

The later method was to enclose the body of the bottle in a snapcase (a metal can on the end of a rod that would hold the bottle while the gaffer worked the finish). In this case, the worker was called a snapper-up boy. Use of the snapcase eliminated the scar (pontil or punty mark) on the bottom — often seen on earlier bottles — which was created when the pontil rod was finally broken off from the base of the finished bottle. After 1870, the shop went to a seven-man team. The new shop consisted of three workers, skilled craftsmen who could either blow or finish and, being equally capable in either task, could be interchanged every 20 minutes. The helpers were a mould boy, who sat on a stool and opened and closed moulds; a cleaner-off or knocker-off, who removed the moile (bits of congealed glass) from the blowpipe; a snapper-up, who held the bottle in the snap and reheated it in the glory hole; and a "carry-in boy," who took the finished bottle to the lehr. (A lehr is a long, oven-like structure through which the finished articles pass on a metal conveyor belt and in which the temperature is reduced from about 1100°F to room temperature. This eliminates an inherent strain in the newly formed piece.) The output by this shop was 138 percent higher than that of a four-man shop.

The following is a personal description of the relationship of the "carry-in boy" to a "shop." It was sent to me in the 1970s by Melville A. Steele, who started at the Toronto Glass Works of Dominion Glass in 1922.

> The glassblower stood on a platform and blew into iron moulds, of which there was two that he used, and operated by what was termed a "snap boy." In other words his duty was to put a clamp around arms extended from the moulds while the bottle was being blown. They all had what was termed a "bust-off finish" and after the mould was opened and the bottle taken from it, it was placed in a metal container about the shape of the bottle but with a long rod. This in turn was inserted into a blast furnace, which we believe was called a "glory hole." The neck

was reheated, and then a tong was used which had a solid bar in the centre and two clamps on the outside the shape of the finish. This in turn was inserted into the neck of the bottle, rolled up and down on a chair, which had two arms, which the metal rod was placed to roll around. After the finish was completed, the bottles were put on a stand and the "carry-in boy" had to put the bottles on their sides, of course, on an affair which was called a "paddle." This consisted of a very long rod and sort of a tray at the end. The bottles were then taken to the lehr and turned over in an upright position to be annealed. The lehrs in those days, I believe, were called Dixon lehrs, which were solid bars or plates about six feet long and approximately three inches wide. At the side of the lehr there was also a rail to start the bottles off by piling to the rail and then working out for a fair distance.

Hundreds of glassworkers contributed, in their own way, to the continuity of the Canadian glass industry. Here are three stories that exemplify this contribution — the Sephtons, George Gardiner and Donald Lamont.

THE SEPHTONS

The Sephtons are a typical example of a glass-oriented family; six family members over three generations served the Canadian industry.

Peter Sephton was born into a glass industry family in Hunslet (near Leeds), Yorkshire, on February 13, 1854. As a glassblower he came to Canada via New York in 1882 and settled in Montreal. He started with Excelsior Glass in Montreal and continued to work for the successor companies — North American Glass, Diamond Glass, Diamond Flint Glass and Dominion Glass. Four of his 14 children became associated with the industry.

The oldest of the four, James Henry, was born in Montreal in 1887. At the age of 14 he started work with Diamond Glass as a machinist. With the advent of the Owens forming machine in 1903, he became the expert in operations. He was the manager of the Hamilton plant of Dominion Glass from 1926 to 1946, after which he moved to the same position at the Pointe St. Charles plant. He retired in 1957 with 56 years of service.

The next son, Peter Willson, born in Montreal in 1893, started to work for his father at an early age. Later he joined his brother Jimmy in Hamilton, in the forming department. He ended his glass career with Consumers Glass and died on April 15, 1967. The third son to be involved was Albert Edward, who was born in 1895 and started with Diamond Flint Glass in Montreal about 1910. There is no record of his activities. He died in 1927.

The final member of this second generation was a daughter, Florence, who was born in Montreal in 1904 and did some drafting work for her father.

Harold James Sephton, son of Jimmy Sephton, represented the third generation. Born in Montreal in 1914, after an engineering education he worked in Dominion's Hamilton plant, where in 1956 he became manager. In 1963 he was moved to head office in Montreal, where he assisted the vice-president, manufacturing, with the day-to-day operations of the company's five plants. In 1968 he was appointed director of manufacturing services. A year later he moved to the United States as a consultant to Midland Glass in that country.

GEORGE GARDINER

The following summary of an interview of George Gardiner, one of Canada's great glass-blowers, illustrates the life and times of a glassblower at the turn of the century. Gardiner began his career at Burlington Glass in Hamilton, Ontario, in 1885 and retired in 1915.

He started at the age of 11, carrying fruit jars to the annealing oven. Twelve years later he became an apprentice glassblower, blowing fruit jars and bottles at night. After five years he became a fully qualified glassblower. The blowers worked in a three-man shop, and in an eight-hour shift turned out about 500 dozen a day, earning from $6 to $10 a day on a piecework basis. The well-established factories used about 60 glassblowers. During lunch hours qualified blowers were allowed to make whimsies (hats, hammers, hatchets, bells, canes, paperweights, etc.). A number of the blowers were known for their skill in making paperweights. These included William McGinnis, George Mullin, Patrick Wickham, George Gardiner, Edward (Nix) Daly, James O'Donnell, Charles McNichol and Patrick Murphy.

One shop, comprising Jim Whittaker and his two sons, left the company and tried to make chimneys in a shop in neighbouring Dundas, but they were not successful. In 1893 three brothers by the name of Foster started a glass factory at Port Colborne, Ontario. Gardiner also worked at Toronto Glass and Sydenham Glass. Blowers made good money but spent it as fast as they made it, betting on sports such as baseball, cockfights, dog fights.

July and August were the traditional holiday months when the factories were shut down.

Gardiner stated that the other glassworks in Hamilton (Hamilton Glass) made fruit jars and bottles. Referring to the latter, some of those made were called twisters. While the bottle was being blown in the mould the blower rotated the pipe, thus eliminating the mould seam . . .[1]

Donald Lamont

DONALD LAMONT

The man who contributed the most to the industry was Donald Lamont, over a 70-year period.

Born in Birmingham, England, on August 24, 1857, of English and Scottish parentage, he began work at the early age of ten in a glass factory as helper to his father, who was a practical glassblower.

It was in 1883 that he came to Canada with his brother and ten other glassworkers, following a visit by an official of the Nova Scotia Glass Company, a newly established firm in New Glasgow, N.S., which was seeking experienced workers.

Three years later he joined the firm of Gill Bros. Acme Glass Co. of Steubenville, Ohio, where he worked for two years as a chimney blower, after which he returned to Canada and again entered the employ of the Nova Scotia Glass Co. In 1893 Mr. Lamont and his brother, with little capital but a great deal of ambition, started a small plant of their own, which operated under the name Lamont Glass Company.

The volume of business increased until in 1899 a four-pot (flint) furnace and one 25-ton tank were in use for the production of bottles, lamps, chimneys, lighting and coloured ware.

In the same year the business was sold to the Diamond Glass Co., and Mr. Lamont was engaged by the firm as superintendent of the green department at their Delorimier plant in Montreal. In 1906 he resigned to take a position with a new glass company which had been formed in Vancouver. This concern, however, went out of business in 1908 and Mr. Lamont went back to the Diamond Glass Company, where he was employed for three years as sales agent for British Columbia. He then resigned to accept a position with Manitoba Glass, whose plant was located at Beausejour. Two years later the plant was purchased by the Dominion Glass Company, as also was the Diamond Glass Co. Mr. Lamont was then transferred to his former position of sales agent, until 1913, when the management built the Redcliff plant in Alberta and Mr. Lamont was privileged to light the first two furnaces to make glass for the Owens machine and hand shops.

It was at this time that Mr. Lamont, of his own choosing, started on what was to be a long career as night superintendent, which position he holds to this day (1937). After a six-year stay in Redcliff he was transferred to the Montreal plant, where he continued as night superintendent, and 12 years ago he was transferred to the Wallaceburg plant.[2]

Evening though was fast approaching. The rapid development of semiautomatic bottle-forming machinery towards the end of the nineteenth century was beginning to challenge the glassblower's supremacy.

The first coffin nail was driven when the blowing skill of the glassblower was replaced by compressed air. This led to the setting aside of the blowpipe in favour of a solid iron rod for carrying to the mould the gather of glass, the correct size of which still required the glassblower's skill. The second nail was the trend to more product-oriented packaging. As merchandisers began to pack more and more of their products in glass, not only was there an increase in the demand for bottles, but there was also a need for bottles of better quality and in which the specifications were rigidly maintained, particularly as to capacity and finish details. This of course would make the filling and capping operation more efficient and less costly and would also guarantee to the end user the quantity advertised.

The actual transition from handblowing to machineblowing began with the invention of the side-lever press in 1820 for certain types of pressed ware, which contributed to product uniformity. The glassblower would deposit a gather of glass in the one- or two-piece mould. The presser would then pull down on a long lever, which would force a plunger into the molten glass and force it out against the sides of the mould, thus forming the piece. The mould would then be opened and the piece removed. Here, the need for the glassblower in making pressed items such as bowls and other similar pieces was eliminated.

In 1847 Joseph Magoun, an American, invented an iron mould which, when improved by the use of chilled iron in 1866, contributed greatly to the quality of the bottle. It also guaranteed at least its outside dimensions and was not dependent on the skill of the gatherer. One improvement followed another in the long trail to fully automatic bottlemaking. In 1865 William Gillinder invented a device which utilized a press-plunger mechanism for forming the top, or rim, of the piece, after which the piece was blown. Eight years later, Thomas B. Atterbury, a Pittsburgh glassmaker, improved on the above by developing a process whereby the pressing and the blowing of a jug could be done in the same mould.

In 1882 Philip Arbogast was the first to adopt and then improve upon the above methods and apply them to bottlemaking by the use of a two-mould technique which, within a greatly refined forming process, is still in use today. The first mould was known as the "parison mould" (from the French *parison*, portion) or commonly called the blank mould. The second was known as the blow mould. The forming technique was really quite simple. The glassblower would deposit a gather of glass in the blank mould, which would then be pressed down by a plunger to create the finish and a solid blank of glass with the general outline of the finished bottle. This blank would then be manually transferred to the blow mould, where the glassblower would convert it into the finished bottle.

In 1886 Ashley, in England, modified the above by using air instead of a plunger to form the blank, a process known as blow-and-blow, which is still used for narrow-mouth bottles, while the press-and-blow process was used for wide-mouth bottles. In 1896 Charles Blue of West Virginia invented a press-and-blow machine with a combined blank and blow mould. Instead of transferring the blank to the blow mould, the blank mould dropped down and the blow mould closed around the suspended blank and formed the bottle. (This was the basis of the Owens forming machine, which was first operated in 1903.)

To keep up with the demand for greater production, the pots in which the glass batch was melted were replaced by large refractory-lined tanks, which in their initial concept could hold enough molten metal for several days. When fully automatic bottlemaking techniques were realized early in the twentieth century, and with higher machine speeds, these tanks — or furnaces, as they were sometimes called — were redesigned to operate continuously by manually, and later automatically, feeding the batch in at the rear end to replace the refined metal that was being converted into bottles at the other end.

The device that finally eliminated the gatherer and his skill was known as a "feeder." At the refining end of the tank was a long, boxlike chamber called a forehearth, through which the glass flowed from the tank. Attached to the end of this was a "feeder" mechanism, which was simply an orifice through which the glass could pour. Various mechanical devices were designed to convert this steady stream of glass into gathers or gobs of glass of uniform size, which would drop into the blank mould on the machine. The consistency of the bottles produced was directly related to the consistency of the sheared-off gobs. To this day, I am of the opinion that the weight, shape and glass consistency of the gob is probably the most critical operation in the whole bottle-forming process, all other things being equal.

The first of many inventors of this type of device was Homer Brooke, an American citizen who had emigrated from Yorkshire in 1849. In 1903 he designed a feeder mechanism that comprised a shearing blade and a cup with a cutting edge. The stream of glass would fill the cup, which in turn would dump the glass into the mould, the quantity being controlled by the action of the shearing blade against the cutting edge of the cup. This action would be repeated when the next mould was in position.

With the successful operation of the Brooke feeder and other similar mechanisms for semiautomatic production, the need for the gatherer's skill was eventually eliminated.

SELECTED LIST OF GLASSBLOWERS AND THE COMPANIES FOR WHICH THEY WORKED

Adams, George HUT
Aikens, Arthur HUT
Albert, D. HUT
Allan, J. SYD
Allen, Harry FGW
Armstrong, A. SYD

Bachus, James SYD
Bachus, Roy SYD
Bard, Andrew HAM SYD
Bard, George A. HAM TOR
Bard, Thomas ERG HAM
Battist, Henry HUT
Behan, Jeremiah HAM TOR
Bennett, Alfred TOR
Berlage, R. SYD
Brodeur, Joseph NAG SYD
Brodeur, Ovilla NAG SYD
Butterman, W. SYD

Cameron, Alexander HUT
Campbell, Henry CGW
Carey, Frank SYD
Charbonneau, R. SYD
Charlton, Joseph HAM
Charlton, Ralph HUT
Chisholm, William HUT
Clish, George HUT
Coley, J.H. STL
Conliffe, Frank SYD
Conway, Michael BUR HAM
Coughlin, W. SYD
Coulter, Curley ONT
Crist Sr., Alfred HAM SYD
Crist, Sam (Cook) EXG HAM SYD
Cummerford, Ed HAM

Daly, Edward (Nix) BUR SYD
Davidson, Andrew CGW
Davidson, James HUT
Dee, Albert Chester HUT
Dolman, Samuel HAM TOR
Donovan, Frank NAG SYD
Douglas, Robert BUR
Doughty, Frank FGW

Falconer, John HUT
Ferry, Bob ONT
Ferry, Tom ONT
Finkbinder, John ERG FGW
Foster, Douglas FGW

Foster, George H. ERG FGW HAM ONT
Foster, G.W. FOB
Foster, H.G. FOB
Foster, John C. FGW HAM TOR
Foster, Joseph FOB
Foster, William FGW HAM ONT
Fraser, Alex LAM
Fraser, D.W. LAM
Furlong, Charles BUR
Furlong, Daniel BUR
Furlong, Moses BUR

Gabile, George OTT
Gaffeny, M. SYD
Gardiner, George BUR SYD TOR
Getzinger, Charles ERG
Gormley, Joseph BUR
Gorry, Ovela CGM NAG
Gray, Robert BUR
Gray, Wm. BUR
Greenwood, Hugh SYD
Griffin, Stephen HAM SYD
Griner, W.B. HAM TOR

Hafner, John HAM
Haggerty, Hugh ERG
Halloran, Pat HAM
Harris, G.E. HAM TOR
Hayes, Wm. J.E. SYD
Herbert, Patrick H. CGC STL
Hockmouth, Henry OTT
Homely, Conrad OTT
Houltin, W. ERG
Humphreys, Edward C. HUT
Humphreys, John HUT HUM

Jacquot, J.B. NAG SYD
Jones, Dan SYD
Jones, Thomas BUR CGC STL
Judson, J. SYD
Judson, Orrin Stewart SYD
Judson, Smiley SYD

Kassner, M. OTT
Kee, William SYD
Knittler, Jerome SYD
Knittler, Joe SYD

Lagrange, Jacob OTT
Lamont, David LAM NSG
Lamont, Donald LAM NSG

LaPierre, Ferdinand NAG
Lauzon, Amedee NAG SYD
Leadbeater, Thomas HUT
Leonard, Albany NAG SYD
Leonard, Arthur NAG SYD
Linn, George SYD
Losch (Loesch), John FGW SYD
Lute, John William CGW

MacGillivray, Joseph H. HUT
Mack, Dennis OTT
Mack, John OTT
Mendell, George MID CON DOM
Menzell, Charles ERG
Middlemiss, Charles LAM NAG SYD
Mooney, J. NAG
Morgan, Harry SYD
Morgan, James FGW
Moynihan, C. BUR HAM
Mullin, George BUR
Murphy, Jos. BUR
Murphy, Thomas BUR SYD TOR
Murray, M. SYD
McArthur, Daniel HUT
McArthur, Peter HUM
McCleary, John SYD
McCleary, W. ERG
McConnell, George STL
McCoull, Thomas HUT
McDonald, Randall HUT
McDonald, Thomas HUT
McEachran, Daniel HUT
McGinnis, William BUR
McIntyre, Eddie SYD
McIntyre, P. SYD
McKay, Rod LAM
McLellan, Simon HUT
McMillan, William SYD
McNaughton, John SYD
McNichol, Charles BUR
McNichol, John BUR TOR
McNichol, Thomas HAM TOR

Nolan, Martin BUR TOR
Norton, Patty ONT

O'Donnell, James BUR
O'Neil, John BUR SYD
O'Neil, Michael HAM

Pace, Alfred HUT

Pancost, Charles FGW HAM
Parker, Amos ONT SYD
Pearson, Thomas HAM
Perkes, John STL
Phillips, Ed BUR
Power, James HUT
Priestland, Harry ERG
Purnell, Wm. ERG

Quinn, M. SYD

Rawson, Ed ERG HAM
Reifsneider, John MAN
Reiter, Fred SYD
Roach, R. BUR
Ross, Roderick HUM NAG NSG
Russelot, L. SYD

Schaaf, E. SYD
Schertz, J. SYD
Schreiber, John MID
Sears, Bob MID
Shannahan, Hugh SYD
Shockley, Doc MID
Smith, Samuel BUR
Smith, Stephen BUR
Squire, Robert STL
Stephenson, William CGC
Stevenson, William FGW HAM
Stoker, Everett ONT
Swan, William ERG

Taylor, H. SYD

Vogel, Louis MAN
Voll, John HAM

Wallace, James SYD
Webster, George SYD
Welser, George ERG
Wickham, Patrick BUR NAG TOR
Winslow, William STL
Wood, William LAM

Yingling, Kibbee MID

COMPANY CODES

BUR Burlington Glass
CGC Canada Glass Company
CGM Canadian Glass Manufacturing
CGW Canada Glass Works
CON Consumers Glass
DIF Diamond Flint Glass
DIG Diamond Glass
DOM Dominion Glass Co. Ltd.
ERG Erie Glass
EXG Excelsior Glass
FGW Foster Glass
FOB Foster Brothers
HAM Hamilton Glass
HUM Humphreys' Glass (Moncton, N.B.)
HUT Humphreys' Glass (Trenton, N.S.)
LAM Lamont Glass
MAN Manitoba Glass
MID Mid-West Glass
NAG North American Glass
NSG Nova Scotia Glass
ONT Ontario Glass
OTT Ottawa Glass
STL Saint Lawrence Glass
SYD Sydenham Glass
TOR Toronto Glass

FOOTNOTES

[1] Taped interview of George Gardiner at his home on October 31, 1958, by Gerald Stevens.
[2] "History of Donald Lamont." Invitation to a banquet in honour of Mr. Lamont's 85th birthday, August 24, 1957, hosted by the Wallaceburg plant of Dominion Glass Company, Limited.

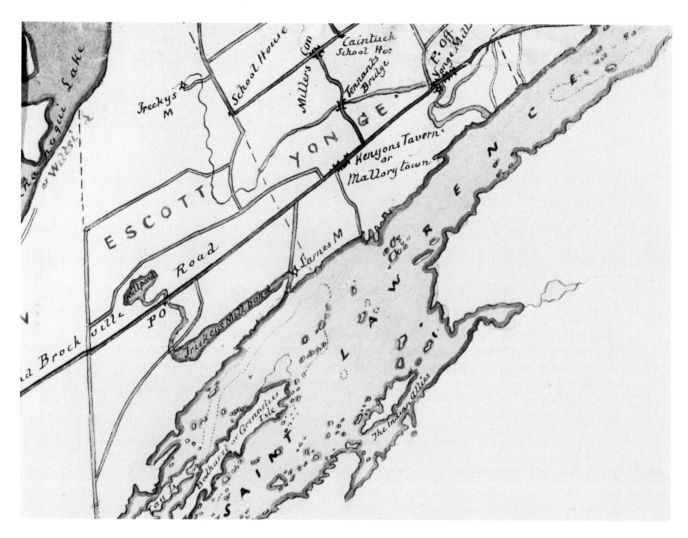

Map showing the location of Mallorytown, Ontario.

National Map Collection, PAC.

CHAPTER 3

Early Canadian
Glasshouses
(c.1839-1878)

Mallorytown Glass Works, Mallorytown, Ontario (c.1839-1840), has the honour of being the first Canadian glass operation

Caledonia Glass Works, Caledonia Springs, Ontario (1844-c.1850)

The four Como-Hudson, Quebec, glasshouses: Masson & Cie., Como (1845-1847); Ottawa Glass Works, Como (1847-1857); British American Glass Works, Como (1857-c.1860); and The Canada Glass Company (Limited), Hudson (1864-1877)

In St. Johns, Quebec, there were two companies making bottles, Canada Glass Works (Foster Brothers) (c.1854-1860) and St. Johns Glass Company (1875-1877)

St. Lawrence Glass Works, Montreal, Quebec (1867-1868), which was incorporated as The Saint Lawrence Glass Company (1868-1873)

In New Brunswick there were three companies: The Saint John Glass Company, Saint John (1872-1873); New Brunswick Crystal Glass Company (Limited), Crouchville (1874-1878); and Courtenay Bay Glass Works, Crouchville (1878)

Hamilton, Ontario, was the site of two very important operations: Hamilton Glass Works (1864-1880), which was incorporated as The Hamilton Glass Company (1880-1898), and Burlington Glass Works (c.1874-1875), whose name was changed to Burlington Glass Company (1875-1885)

The Treaty of Paris, signed in 1763, ceded to Great Britain all territory in the northern part of America that had been developed by the French since Jacques Cartier's landing in La Baie des Chaleurs. Leaders of the new colony were quick to realize the importance of providing the territory with craftsmen to establish the essential trades for survival, such as pottery, building and glassmaking. On November 13, 1685, the Marquis de Denonville, Governor of New France, wrote to the Minister of State of France:

> It is not impossible that one could establish a glassworks in this country; the greatest problem is labour, which makes everything so expensive.[1]

A memorandum from Sieur de Catalogne to the Ministry dated November 7, 1712, reads:

> It is to be hoped that His Majesty will see fit to send to this country all sorts of artisans, especially potters and a glass-blower, and they will find much to keep them busy . . .[2]

In answer to the colonists' pleas, many artisans — brickmakers, tilemakers, potters, weavers and others — were sent out to assist in the development of the colony. Present research, however, has found no evidence of glassware having been made in New France. Many bottles, vials and other common glassware have been excavated by archaeologists in Eastern

Canada. These are similar to the types of ware made in France at the time and presumed to have been imported. This does not rule out the possibility that glass articles were made here, but there has been no evidence to support it.

After the Treaty of Paris, British colonial policy was exactly the opposite of that promoted by its predecessors. It discouraged any local industry that could provide competition for British industry. This was exemplified in a letter from George III to James Murray, Governor of Quebec, in 1763:

> . . . it is Our express will and Pleasure, that you do not, upon pain of OUR highest Displeasure, give your assent to any Law or Laws for setting up any Manufactures and carrying on any Trades which are hurtful and prejudicial to this Kingdom.[3]

The population at that time was somewhere between 65,000 and 70,000. On April 19, 1775, hostilities commenced between American rebels and British troops at Lexington and Concord, near Boston. This was the beginning of a period of transition that would eventually delineate the boundaries of the two sovereign states in North America — the new United States of America and, to the north, British North America, which would become known as Canada in 1867. The Canada Act of 1791 established two provinces, Lower Canada and Upper Canada, separated by the Ottawa River. At the time of its passage, there were approximately 100,000 French and 10,000 English in Lower Canada, and perhaps 20,000 English and a very few French traders and trappers in what became Upper Canada.

Perhaps the first "greening" of the new country to the north was the War of 1812, ostensibly involving England and the United States. Its effect on Canada was, for the duration, to unite the French and the English for mutual self-defense. Unfortunately, the British did not take advantage of this atmosphere, and the antagonism soon returned in the Rebellion of 1837-38, in and around Montreal. This then was the background for the establishment of glassmaking in Canada.

The first house to make glass in Canada was the Mallorytown Glass Works, Mallorytown, Ontario, c.1839.

MALLORYTOWN GLASS WORKS
Mallorytown, Ontario (c.1839-1840)

Credit for establishing the venue of the earliest operating glass factory recorded in Canada must go to the late Gerald Stevens, who had always been interested in Canadiana, including glass. In 1953 he and his wife left Montreal to live in a farmhouse on the outskirts of Mallorytown, about 12 miles west of Brockville.

Mallorytown, Ontario

This is a village numbering about 250 inhabitants. It is situated on the Grand Trunk Railway in the County of Leeds 12 miles west of Brockville, the county town. It derives its name from David Mallory (Daniel Mallory) Sr. who settled here about a century ago and whose numerous progeny occupy a large amount of property in the neighbourhood . . .[4] [1879]

Mr. Stevens' interest in this area may have been triggered by the following extracts from George and Helen McKearin's *American Glass*.

In both the South Jersey and New York pieces more pitchers are found with the lily-pad decoration than any other article. This pitcher and a small bowl with pedestal base . . . are of especial interest because if the history which came with them is correct they were not blown in New York State but in a small glass works in the hamlet of Mallorytown in the Province of Quebec, [sic] about 30 miles from Watertown [N.Y.]. They, with several other pieces, about 20 in all, were purchased about 12 years ago in private homes right in Mallorytown by Harold W. Neff of Utica [N.Y.]. Mr. Neff, who traveled extensively through northern and central New York in his search for glass and other antiques, was told by old residents of the hamlet and the families who inherited these pieces that they were made in a glass works there which was operating at the same time as the Redwood Glass Works near Watertown. On the other hand, we were told by another person who visited Mallorytown a few years ago that he was unable to verify the existence of a local glass house and was told that residents of the village had been employed in the glass works at Redwood. We have since discussed the matter with Mr. Neff, who stated he had revisited Mallorytown, checked the information, and is certain a glass works was located there. Be that as it may, the lily-pad pieces obtained from the old Mallorytown families are similar in colour and technique to the lily-pad pieces blown at Redwood and Redford.

In the 1960s Mr. Stevens wrote two books and a pamphlet, all of which included some information on this factory, its products, years of operation and its owner. In each of these, he made slightly different interpretations of the reference data. Summarizing his several interpretations, Stevens first of all stated that the factory operated from about 1825 (later this was changed to 1839-40). He stated that the owner was Andrew Mallory, which he assumed was the Christian name of A.W. Mallory.

On September 20, 1961, a historical plaque commemorating the pioneer glassworks was unveiled. It reads as follows:

MALLORYTOWN GLASS WORKS

A short distance from this site stood the first glassworks known to have been established in Upper Canada. Although the date at which it began has not been confirmed, it is known to have been in production from 1839 to 1849. Its owner during these years was Andrew W. Mallory, a descendant of the family which founded the community. In the manufacturing process local materials were used including an aquamarine quartz which gave a distinctive colour to the products. The articles produced here included bottles, flasks, glasses and other household wares.

In 1967 John Sheeler, of Toronto, one of Canada's leading researchers of antique Canadian glass, prepared a critique of Stevens' published material.[5] Based on a comparison with his own research, Mr. Sheeler highlighted three corrections that he felt should be made to the published record and the historic plaque:

1) *Dates of Operation*

The only published record of the glass factory was contained in a newspaper article on A.W. Mallory:

... A.W. Mallory, Esq., is a gentleman of great enterprise... He is the son of the late David Mallory and was born in 1819 . . . he has opened and successfully carried on . . . a glass factory during 1839 to '40 which was closed owing to the unreliableness of the foreman . . .

2) *The Name of the Founder*

If the operating dates 1839-1840 are acceptable, then it is plausible that Amasa Mallory, age 20, was the founder. Conversely, the fact that Andrew Mallory could not have reopened or continued the operation of the factory to the winter of 1839/40 is proven by the well-documented facts that he was the son of Daniel Mallory Sr. and was born on July 27, 1780, and died prior to December 29, 1824.

3) *The Raw Materials Used*

There is obviously some confusion as to how the products of Mallorytown received their distinctive aquamarine colouration. According to the plaque, this colour resulted from the use of an aquamarine quartz. That this is not the case can be proven by consulting any work on glass. Authorities consulted agree that all silica contains iron, and it is the iron content of the silica that imparts an aquamarine colour to the finished product. The aquamarine colouration varies in direct proportion to the amount of iron present in the silica. The statement on the plaque dealing with the colour should be clarified.

Mr. Sheeler states:

> The earliest Ontario glass factory, at Mallorytown, was financed by a local businessman and operated in late 1839-early 1840. The few authenticated pieces of glass produced at the factory are obviously in the "South Jersey" tradition. Shortly before this period many workmen from South Jersey had migrated to northern New York State. The possibility that this migration continued into Canada may explain why the products of this small Ontario factory so closely resemble the products of the Redwood, N.Y., factory located just across the St. Lawrence River.[6]

A number of pieces attributed to Mallorytown in the Edith Chown Pierce and Gerald Stevens Collection have been deposited with the Canadiana Department of the Royal Ontario Museum, Toronto. According to Sheeler, no conclusion can be reached concerning the authenticity of these examples of Mallorytown glass, as apparently there is no documentation in support of them available at the museum.

In the opinion of Janet Holmes, curatorial assistant of the Canadiana Department of the Royal Ontario Museum in Toronto, Amasa W. Mallory, founder of Mallorytown Glass Works, was indeed part of the northern migration of workers in the "South Jersey" tradition.

> The glass factory was operated by a glassman who was part of the northern migration of workers in the "South Jersey" tradition that occurred after Caspar Wistar's Salem County, New Jersey, glasshouse closed in 1780 during the American Revolution. Workers from this house traveled into Connecticut and up into northern New York State, establishing small bottle and window glasshouses. There was such a house at Redford, N.Y., just a few miles across the St. Lawrence from Mallorytown. Like its counterparts in New York state, the Mallorytown house was formed to provide bottles and common tablewares for a local market.[7]

Several examples of this style of glassware have found their way into collections at the National Museum of Man (Ottawa), the Royal Ontario Museum (Toronto), and the Gananoque Historic Museum (Gananoque, Ontario). All of them have been traced to the Mallorytown area, but only local tradition serves to promote their claim as Canada's first native manufactured glassware. From the research presented by Mr. Sheeler, there appears to be little doubt that the works operated only during the period 1839-1840.

CALEDONIA GLASS WORKS
Caledonia Springs, Ontario (1844-c.1850)

The glass factory at Caledonia Springs was one of the few Canadian glassworks that was built with an already established and expanding market for its products. It is presently considered to have been the first glassworks to have operated on a commercial basis in Canada.

To put this in context, it is necessary to go back to the early history of the Caledonia Springs. These springs were long known by the Indians, as evidenced by this extract from CANADA: *The Country, its People, Religions, Politics, Rulers and its Apparent Future* by Captain "Mac":

> ... Passing Rigaud Mountain we arrive at Carillon; rapids again occurring here are overcome by means of a lock and a canal 12 miles in length; thence 8 miles by wagon-road, and we arrive at the farfamed Springs, noted from the earliest settlement of the country. It was these Springs formerly called 'Newhenee' that were spoken of by the untutored Gaspé Indians in terms of adoration and reverence to Jacques Cartier upon his arrival at their camp as the 'Life Waters'; and still further upon the Captain General's arrival at Quebec, the chief Donacona urged him forward to the Springs ... It was amid the forests of this country that the Indian tribes placed their dead, and the young warriors brought the ailing and decrepit of their nation to partake of the healing waters ...

From the *Canadian Gazetteer* of 1846, a description of the life and times at the springs in the 1840s presents an overview of the circumstances and surroundings in which the Caledonia Glass Works was established:

CALEDONIA

A village in the township of Caledonia, in the Ottawa District, five miles from the Ottawa River, and nine miles from L'Original. This is the situation of the "Caledonia Springs" which are now generally well known in Canada by reputation at least. There were but two or three houses in the place which were kept for the reception of visitors to the springs, till the property came into the possession of the present proprietor in 1836, who immediately commenced improving the situation, by clearing and building. A large hotel has been built for the reception of visitors, capable of accommodating 150 persons, and a bath house; and a circular railroad has been laid down round the grounds for the amusement of invalids. There are also in the village two churches, stores, saw mill, post-office, a resident physician, three taverns, and other boarding houses, and a small paper called "Life at the Springs," is published weekly. The principal tavern, the "Canada House," is kept by the proprietor of the springs. There are four springs in the place, called the Saline, Sulphur, Gas, and one more lately discovered, called the Intermittent. The Caledonia water is bottled and exported.

The four springs — gas, white sulphur, intermittent and saline — were first publicly noted by the Hon. Alexander Grant, president and administrator of the Upper Canada (Ontario) Assembly from 1805 to 1806, while on a hunting trip. Some 30 years later, another hunter, by the name of Kellogg, sensing the potential value of the waters, built a few cabins to accommodate the increasing number of visitors coming for the "cure." It was quite a trip from Montreal to Caledonia Springs, 85 miles by steamer and stagecoach.

The area was sparsely populated. It was part of the township of Caledonia, and in the period 1842-1845, there were 704 inhabitants, with 1,594 acres under cultivation. In the next five years, the population increased to 956, which included the residents at the springs.

In 1834-35 a syndicate headed by Mr. Lemuel Cushing of Montreal was established to purchase the land and buildings. On March 4, 1837, it was incorporated under the name Caledonia Springs Company. As the fame of its waters spread to the eastern seaboard, and later to Great Britain and Western Europe, agencies were set up in these areas to handle sale of the waters. One such agency was operated by John Winer, a druggist in Hamilton, Ontario, who would later become involved in the Hamilton Glass Works. The season was short, extending but from June 1 to October 1, but before the end of the decade, Mr. William Parker, an American, acquired the sole interest, and he wasted no time in setting up a town plan to include all sorts of activities and facilities catering to the convalescent visitors.

There is no definitive information on the main source of bottles prior to the start of the glassworks, but it would appear that the bottles were made in England. Mr. G.E. Poulin, of Stanstead, Quebec, has a "blob seal" bottle embossed with "Caledonia Springs U.C.," and on the base there is a reference to Ricketts, the well-known English inventor of a bottle-forming machine. During this period, Molson's Brewery in Montreal was known to be importing its bottles from England as well. It is possible that when the Caledonia Glass Works began in 1844, Molson's obtained some of their requirements there.

By 1839 Mr. Parker had overextended himself and he advertised for a partner. This being unsuccessful, he arranged to have a raffle or lottery early in 1840 for 1,000 lots, including the springs and buildings thereon, at $24 each. This gave him a breathing spell.

In 1844 a progress report in *Life at the Springs*, the resort's own newspaper, appeared.

GLASS WORKS AT THE SPRINGS

The new furnace having been completed, a second and most successful attempt has been made at the Caledonia Springs for the manufacture of Glass Bottles, samples of which were exhibited on Tuesday last, which are superior to those generally imported, both in quality and shape.

The workmen declare the materials to be the best they have ever used in any country; and all the ingredients for making glass are procured at, and very near the Springs.

Thus, another improvement has been added to the Springs, which promises to be a greater advantage to the proprietor than anything hitherto attempted.

Mr. Parker will, in the course of a few weeks, be able to try the experiment of making white glass, such as decanters, dishes and tumblers, the latter of which as well as bottles, he will require no small quantity for his own use. We understand the principal ingredients for this kind of ware are to be found a short distance from the Springs.

Go on — Mr. Parker — and while your friends kindly wish you all sorts of good luck (and at the same time exhibit considerable skepticism in nearly all your projects) you must soon arrive at the height of your laudable ambition. In the absence of news, we may speak of curiosities and, among the wonders of this place, the Glass Works, at present, rank the first — being the only thing of the kind in British North America. It is not strange that the men, old women and young children in the neighbourhood throng the place and open their eyes with astonishment at the blaze of this seven-times-heated furnace containing the two immense pots of solid red-hot glass, which is handled with as much familiarity by the workmen with their iron pipes as any old woman would stir up her oatmeal porridge with a spoon, whilst children by the dozens and children of larger growth are seen snatching up little curiosities of glass falling from the pipes, spun out and curled in all manner of shapes, which none but the best of material would hold together to handle and, owing to the superior quality, a trial has been made to melt and blow bottles without potash, which has succeeded beyond all expectations.[8]

Several articles appeared in the newspapers concerning the glassworks and the springs. From the *Montreal Transcript*, December 14, 1844:

A large and valuable bed, or vein, of White Sand has just been discovered in opening a winter road from the Caledonia Springs to the Military Road ending in Lockie and this valuable material is pronounced by the bottle makers at the Springs to be the best kind for the manufacture of White Glass of all descriptions. Should this be the case, it will be a discovery of no small importance to the Glass Works now in operation.

In this same issue was the following advertisement, dated as from 9 May 1846.

BOTTLE BLOWERS WANTED
at the
CALEDONIA SPRINGS

* * *

Two Men Acquainted With
The Manufactury
of
BLACK BOTTLES
Will Find Employment
By Calling At
THE CALEDONIA WATER DEPOT
No. 4, Place d'Armes, MONTREAL.

The *Toronto Globe*, August 19, 1848, said: "The Caledonia Springs are no longer the property of Mr. William Parker. The energetic gentleman some two years ago parted with his interest to Mr. J.L. Wilkinson . . ." Further details of this transaction were recorded by the Bytown *Packet and Weekly Commercial Gazette*, indicating that Parker had sold the property and the springs thereon to Wilkinson for over $44,000, the latter taking over the Governor-General's cottage for his own dwelling. This appears to be the end of Mr. Parker's association with the springs. It is not presently known when the glassworks closed, although this may be related to the advent of a series of glasshouses in the Como-Hudson area, some 40 miles downriver. An ad in the Montreal *Herald* (1850) indicated that the Ottawa Glass Works were prepared to provide hollow glassware, including mineral water bottles. Another glasshouse started up in the St. Johns, Quebec, area around 1854 which could supply bottles as well. This was Canada Glass Works — Foster Brothers.

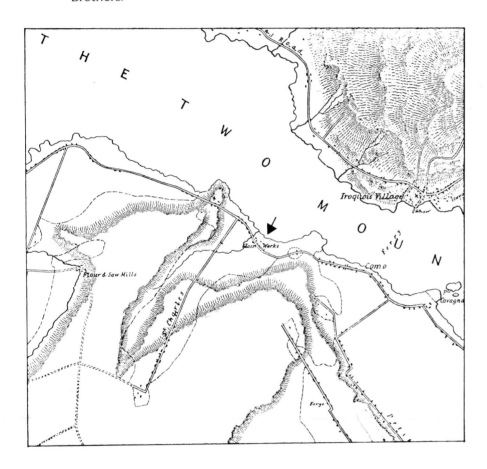

Map showing the location of the Canada Glass Company in Hudson, Quebec.

From the Fortification Surveys, Canada east, 1865-68.

COMO, QUEBEC, OPERATIONS
MASSON ET CIE (1845-1847)

There were four partners in this operation, each of whom pledged to invest ($650) for the establishment and operation of a glass factory. The head of the company, a merchant named Damase Masson, was given the power to manage financial arrangements and, after production had begun, to supervise sales. Another merchant, François-Xavier Desjardins, provided the land (Lot 11) on which the works was to be built and undertook to handle financial arrangements and later to organize local sales. Desjardins was born in St. Benoit and was one of the leading *patriotes* in the Rebellion of 1837-38. The third partner, Jules Brady, was to build the factory and oversee the glassmaking operations. Brady was a contractor by profession. And the fourth, François Coste, was actually the technical member of the partnership. An engineer and a chemist, he would not only supervise the construction of the works but would be responsible for the erection of the furnace and the acquisition of raw materials and supplies.

It has been claimed that the factory was situated on Lot 19 of "La Première Concession Au-Dessus du Fief Cavagnal" in Vaudreuil. For the following reasons, based on Coste's plan, it appears that the site was actually Lot 11:

a) F.-X. Desjardins is noted as owning the land across the Chemin du Roi. In the Seigneurial Register of Vaudreuil, Desjardins is listed as having owned Lot 12 since 1824 and having bought Lot 11 for 300 pounds in 1845. He did not own Lot 19 or any property near it.

b) Below one of the borders of the site shown is the notation "Gouilding ou Golden." Lot 10 which bordered Lot 11 to the east was owned from 1832 until 1847 by Elizabeth Goulding.

c) The bend in the road, shown on the plan, approximates the angle made by the road today as it crosses Lot 11.[9]

There was soon dissension among the partners and, in December, Desjardins withdrew and sold his share to Brady and Coste for $1,300. In return, he was to receive $150 a year for rental of the property. J. Beaudry, of Montreal, replaced him in the partnership. A month later, Coste was accused by Masson and Beaudry of delaying the construction by his frequent absences, going away on trips before even the furnaces had been built. Furthermore, when he failed to pay his share of capital, they began proceedings to remove him from the group. To make matters worse, Brady was threatened with expulsion by Masson and Beaudry if he didn't pay his share.

By mid-1846 several wooden structures, including a polygonal main building over 100 feet in length, had been built. Glassmaking tools were ordered from a Montreal foundry, together with fire bricks for the furnaces and clay to make moulds. This last item would suggest that they planned to make bottles as well as window glass. In March 1847, as a result of all the dissent, Masson and Beaudry sold their interest to Stewart Derbishire, the Queen's Printer in Montreal. Thus ended the saga of Masson & Cie., apparently without having made any glass.

OTTAWA GLASS WORKS/DERBISHIRE AND DESBARATS (1847-1850)

Derbishire soon reorganized the operation as a joint stock company, bringing in his printing associate Georges Desbarats. In April, Brady and Derbishire unsuccessfully petitioned for incorporation under the name "Vaudreuil Glass Factory." By the summer they had hired Peter J. Byrnes, an experienced glassworker from St. Helens Glass Works in England, to run the operation. The fact that Byrnes came from St. Helens would support the idea that the main item of production would be window glass. He hired a number of experienced hands from England and Germany.

Soon after, another potential glass operation took shape in Vaudreuil. On August 14, 1847, Henry Hockmuth purchased Lot 19. It was about an acre in size and was located somewhat west of the Ottawa Glass Works. In the same month Jules Brady, the last of the original partners in the earlier Como operation, withdrew from the Ottawa Glass Works, leaving George Desbarats as a major shareholder. In October 1847 it was reported that ". . . a new glass factory [Ottawa Glass Works] has recently been put in operation in Vaudreuil County by Messrs. Desbarats and Derbishire. This is the second establishment of its kind in Lower Canada, the other being at St. Johns [Canada Glass Works 1845-1851]."[10]

On November 19, 1847, the *Montreal Gazette* stated that the Governor-General, Lord Elgin, had "expressed his admiration of the beautiful samples of glassware produced by this new establishment. . ." On March 9, 1848, a petition was put forward by W.A. Townsend and others seeking incorporation of the Ottawa Glass Company. It was given first reading in the legislature. And in December 1848 Derbishire sold out his share to Desbarats, as well as "all the wood, clay, [soda] ash and other materials, all the houses and animals and all the goodwill."[11]

Returning to the Hockmuth venture, Henry, his brother Sebastian, George Wilhelm Hirsch and Frederick Carl Boden established a partnership which was created to transact "the business of glass manufacturing."

Because of the debts incurred by Hockmuth, Boden bought out Hockmuth's small section of Lot 19 as well as all the buildings for making glass thereon. The original partnership was dissolved on July 26, 1850, and Boden and a new partner, Jean Baptiste Lebert, took over the factory. It is assumed that they had planned to make bottles. No authenticated articles have been found.

OTTAWA GLASS WORKS/BODEN AND LEBERT
(1850-1851)

At the same time that Boden bought out the partnership of the operation on Lot 19, and after Jean Baptiste Lebert became his partner, they bought out the Ottawa Glass Works for 1,500 pounds from Desbarats. A list of the buildings on Lot 11 at the time gives a good description of the operations:

a) Two wooden houses, about sixty feet in length and two storeys high, divided into apartments.
b) A wooden building in which moulds were made.
c) A wooden building with a mill to grind the clay.
d) A divided building, with one section used as a forge and the other as a stable.
e) A shed about 40 feet long.
f) A wooden building containing eight furnaces used to dry wood.
g) The main building, a domed structure about one hundred feet.[12]

Advertisements in the Montreal newspapers of 1848-1850 spoke of regular window glass and double-thick glass equal to the German plate (glass), as well as hollowwares. The following advertisement was run on a regular basis from soon after Boden and Lebert purchased the Ottawa Glass Works until late 1851:

CANADIAN GLASS
SNYDER'S WHARF, VAUDREUIL

Established and operated by Messrs. Boden and Lebert.

The Owners of this establishment are ready to manufacture Mirror Glass and Window Glass of all sizes, hand coloured or tinted, from samples or orders. Oil and Gas Lamps clear, decorated or coloured for Churches, similar to those in European Churches, also for houses, cottages, summer houses and steam boats: Bottles and Vials for Apothecaries, made to order.

ALSO,

Soda Water, Beer, Ginger Ale and other bottles, with or without the name of the bottler.

AND,

Sauce pans or Milk Bottles in regular sizes. All these pieces will be of the best quality and will be sold on the most reasonable terms; the proprietors seek the public's favour and their examination of these articles.

To order or to obtain further information contact the Proprietors at the People's Hotel 206-207 Notre Dame St., Montreal.[13]

Boden and Lebert placed an advertisement in the *Montreal Gazette* which differed somewhat from the French version already noted. The addition of facilities for the manufacture of hollow glass is noteworthy. This suggests that plans had been made to operate the works on Lot 19, originally established by Henry Hockmuth.

Although Boden and Lebert claimed to be ready to manufacture various articles of glass, their success will not be known until a careful archaeological examination of the site is carried out.

OTTAWA GLASS WORKS/PETER J. BYRNES,
(1851-1857)

A year and a half after acquiring the Ottawa Glass Works, Boden and Lebert leased the factory to the gentleman who had managed the works since 1847, P.J. Byrnes. The following notice appeared in the *Montreal Gazette* on June 20, 1851:

> OTTAWA GLASS WORKS
>
> Mr. P.J. Byrnes, formerly of the St. Helens' Glass Works, having LEASED the above GLASS WORKS, has appointed the undersigned his agents for the sale of GLASS manufactured by him.
>
> From MR. BYRNES' long experience in Glass making, and the superior quality of the materials on the ground, an article of WINDOW GLASS equal if not superior to any imported, will be produced. The works are now in full blast, ORDERS for any size and quantity will be executed with despatch.
>
> T.C. Panton & Co.
St. Sacrement Street
Montreal
>
> . . . Having always advocated the support of our native manufacturers, we feel pleasure in noticing the reestablishment of the Ottawa glassworks . . . There are 50 hands employed, and the yield at present is about 4,000 feet of sheet glass per day . . .

The Census of 1851 provides a great deal of information regarding the Ottawa Glass Works:

> The glass works, situated at Point Cavagnal within the limits of this census district, is owned (leased) and operated by Peter G. Byrnes. From information provided by him, the land on which the works is located comprises thirty acres. There are eight buildings crowded together. This works was built and completed in 1847, under the direction of Mr. P.J. Byrnes, the cost was enormous — 11,000 Louis and included enough raw materials for nine months' operation. It was able to produce 30,000 boxes of glass (flat) of 50 square feet. There were 150 workers and 8 horses; there were also 30 horses used to bring in wood and other things. Much of the wood was used in the wood-burning and steam boats, and locomotives of this line. The cost of this work amounted to 500 hours per summer. One could buy glass from this Works as cheaply as from any other similar operation. Mr. Byrnes remarked further that an operation as expensive as this one, in an emerging country, will always suffer from lack of encouragement, the prices were high enough, but the sales were mediocre. Further, that one compares, without regard, our glass with that of the Germans which we are unable to sell in Europe and they are quick to sell us glass of the best quality at a price which makes their glass more available than ours, on the contrary, we do not enjoy this advantage, our sales are small and yet we are obliged to sell at a price almost equal to that of first or second quality glass; this creates great losses (for us). He observed, however, that we had, in return, an obvious advantage, after five years experience in this country and having been a glass worker in England, that the sand available here, which is available in quantity (and which is essential to us) eliminates the 15% (duty) on the best (sand) that one can obtain in England.

The remarkably high estimate of the number of men employed by the industry can only be explained by including those indirectly involved, such as woodcutters, steamboat operators, etc. The various skills included in the 17 workers listed were: glassblowers (6), glasscutters (9), glassmaker batch mixer (1), and glassflattener (1).

Since the establishment of the Ottawa Glass Works, the community had grown apace.

The first post office in the area was established in 1841 at Pointe à Cavagnal. Between October 1853 and July 1854, a second post office was opened in the eastern part of Cavagnal and was named the Ottawa Glass Works Post Office. In 1854 Queen Victoria changed the name Bytown to Ottawa. This created two changes in the local scene. In 1860, probably to avoid confusion, the Ottawa Glass Works Post Office was renamed the Como Post Office, purportedly because of the similarity between the Lake of Two Mountains and Lake Como, in Italy.

In October 1852 the employees of the Ottawa Glass Works unsuccessfully petitioned the Legislative Assembly for a protective tariff on imported window and sheet glass. And during the period 1852-1857, control of the company changed several times, always reverting to Georges Desbarats. By 1855, though, production at the Ottawa Glass Works must have fallen off — if one uses advertisements as a barometer of the works' success — since by that year they had dropped to mere single-line announcements. By 1857 advertisements had ceased altogether, marking the closing of the company.

BRITISH AMERICAN GLASS WORKS (1857-c.1860)

In 1857 a group of New Yorkers — Henry W. Jones, John Dickson and William M. Barclay — leased the Ottawa Glass Works buildings, glassmaking utensils and the use of their land for $4,000. *The Canada Directory* of 1857 listed the British American Glass Works as operating in Vaudreuil County and owned by Henry W. Jones.

In a letter written on August 25 of the same year, Annie Cameron, who lived in the village of Como, wrote:

> . . . Ottawa Glass Works is alive with people . . . I believe they intend to start blowing next month. They are going to have twenty-two glass blowers and besides as many more . . . to attend them . . . They are all Americans . . . and they are the meanest looking lot of men I ever saw . . .

If the writer was correct in stating that the artisans were "all Americans," then there had been a change in personnel, judging by the census of 1851. The tone of the letter clearly implies that a new start was about to be made. Likely, the British American Glass Works had been formed to operate the factory of the Ottawa Glass Works. Because of the relatively recent change of name from Bytown to Ottawa, the name of the glassworks had been changed to avoid confusion, although the name of the district remained unchanged. Nothing is known about the operation of the British American Glass Works. It probably failed in the depression which began in October 1857.

THE CANADA GLASS COMPANY (LIMITED)
Hudson, Quebec (1864-1877)

The first indication of operations at the Hudson site were the words "Glass Works" on an ordinance map. The site for this operation was sold by Alexander MacNaughtan to George Matthews. Johnny MacNaughtan, Alexander's son, later bought back the property, with improvements, for a favourable price. This MacNaughtan area became known as Hudson. Matthews named the area, post office and railroad station in honour of his wife's maiden name. A decree was granted by the Superior Court for Lower Canada to incorporate The Canada Glass Company (Limited) on October 16, 1864. This company was built on Lots 25-26, purchased by Matthews, a wealthy Montreal lithographer who spent his summers in Hudson.

A review of the operations in 1867 gave a clear picture of the ongoing success of the company:

> The Canada Glass Company's Works at Hudson, Province of Quebec, have been established for several years. The operations, which at first were limited to the manufacture of Druggists' Bottles, Telegraph Insulators, etc., have been recently much extended. The first addition made to the articles produced consisted chiefly of chimneys and other lamp-ware. The capital has been increased; a steam engine

The Canada Glass Works at Hudson, Quebec, painted about 1867 by James Duncan.
Reproduction courtesy of John B. Thompson.

Glass workers' houses at the Canada Glass Works, Hudson, Quebec, painted about 1867 by James Duncan.
Reproduction courtesy of John B. Thompson.

has been erected to drive all the machinery, which includes a Crushing-mill, and the manufacture of German Flint Glass is now carried on. The consumption of raw material at the Hudson Works in 1867 included 180,000 lbs. of Borax, and smaller quantities of chemicals for colouring. About 100,000 lbs. of Lime, and 360,000 lbs. of Sand from the company's own property in neighbourhood of works — and the value of the Glass produced was $56,000.[14]

Canadian-produced glass met the demand when imported glass suppliers were cut off by the American Civil War. But it appears that by 1867 the company's sales were falling. It authorized an auction of its products for September 16, offering for sale fruit jars, lamp chimneys and a variety of bottles for beverages, foods, medicines and some industrial lines. A year later, Benjamin Lyman, head of a prominent drug firm, became president.

In 1869 the company was in real trouble. Whereas the shares had had a market value of $100 in 1866, the financial pages now reported that all the shares were paid up, but that dividends were no longer being paid. Market value was $40 to $55.

George Matthews, the former president, died in 1870. By 1871 only 18 men were listed as employees, just two of whom were identified as glassblowers. In 1871 a depression, the bane of industry, started in Canada. *Census of the Canadas* for 1871-1872 indicated that Hudson "had a glass factory." By 1881 there was no mention of it. It would appear to have ceased operations about 1877, when it was last listed in the *Gazetteer*.

Canada Glass Works (Foster Brothers), about 1858.

Courtesy of John Morrill Foster.

CANADA GLASS WORKS (FOSTER BROTHERS)
St. Johns, Quebec (c. 1854-1860)
(Hereafter referred to as Foster Brothers)

With the demise of The Canada Glass Works in 1851, or thereabouts, there were no glass operations in St. Johns until the arrival of Joseph Foster (c. 1854).

According to John Morrill Foster, Joseph "Old Bottle" Foster and two of his sons, George Whitefield (1829-1892) and Charles Wesley (1836-n.d.), went to St. Johns in 1854 to establish a glass factory. Joseph had immigrated to America from England sometime prior to 1824 and located in Keene, New Hampshire, where he was a glassblower with Perry Wheeler & Co. until the firm and its successor went out of business in 1842. He thereupon purchased the remaining assets and set up shop in Stoddard, about 15 miles away. When that failed, in 1844, he tried again with an operation north of the Village of South Stoddard and survived there until 1849, when he went into bankruptcy. His final attempt was in St. Johns.

The Fosters were all individualists and had been brought up in a glassmaking atmosphere. Joseph, born in Preston Pans, near Newcastle, England, had learned his trade in Hartley, at John Carr & Sons Bottle Works. At the age of about 20, he had come to America and married Mary Sanders (Saunders) of Swanzey, New Hampshire. As John Morrill Foster says in his book ". . . Truly, Joseph Foster was quite a remarkable man. He was known as 'Old Bottle Foster' and was reputed to have been able to blow a large demi-john at one blowing. . ."[15] He was not only a glassblower, but a great family man too. He and his wife, Mary, had ten children, six boys and four girls.

Their third son, George Whitefield Foster — named after the famous English Methodist minister George Whitefield — was born in East Cambridge, Massachusetts, on March 26, 1829. He was the last person one would imagine entering the hurley-burley of the glassmaking trade.

45

George Whitefield Foster.
Courtesy of John Morrill Foster.

He had little schooling, ending up with a three-month term at the Newbury Seminary, Newbury, Vermont. At the closing ceremonies, he received a "recommendation" for penmanship. In Stoddard, George proceeded to learn the art of glassblowing.

Stories are legion about glassblowers and their characteristics. Some say they were hardworking, highly skilled but uneducated men. On the other hand, it is hard to believe that they were God-fearing teetotalers. An excerpt from John Foster's book gives an interesting example of the life and times in the eighteenth century.

> There are several legends regarding the origin of the name 'Stoddard Box' or 'The Box' as South Stoddard was known in those days. One legend relates that a certain man at Gibson's Tavern had imbibed too freely and was placed in a box, with air-holes in the cover. The box, as the story goes, was nailed down and sent by the next stage to his wife.[16]

Although this doesn't necessarily relate to glassworkers, the very nature of their work — a ten- to twelve-hour day, six days a week, under intense heat conditions — suggests the need for some re-moisturizing of the body.

The Foster's sixth child was Charles Wesley. He was born in Keene, New Hampshire, on February 28, 1834, and at the age of 20 became the cornerstone of the St. Johns operation.

The address for Foster Brothers in the 1857-1858 *Canada Directory* was the same as shown for the earlier Canada Glass Works — between Dormaray/Albert (now Collin) and St. Jean (now Mercier), south of the railway. Under the new management, flat glass production was replaced by bottles, jugs, insulators, etc.

A third brother, Henry Gilman Foster (1827-n.d.), was also there for a short time. As was the wont of glassblowers, they were very transient. According to the records, both George and Henry had moved to the Granite Glass Works by 1856, leaving Charles to run the show in St. Johns. Also moving to St. Johns, probably in 1854, were their mother and father and two sisters, Ellen and Mary Ann, both of whom married in Canada. Mary Ann Foster Gillespie remained in St. Johns. Her grandson, Willie (William G.) Campbell, was interviewed there by W.N. Coburn, who reported his visit in the first GLASFAX seminar newsletter in June 1971.

An elongated (torpedo-shaped) soda water bottle embossed with FOSTER BROTHERS ST. JOHNS C.E.   Courtesy of the Royal Ontario Museum.

Canada Glass Works,

FOSTER, BROTHERS,

MANUFACTURERS OF

Black, Green, & Flint Glass

BOTTLES OF EVERY DESCRIPTION:

Such as Wines, Ginger Beers, Porters, Inks, Flasks, Snuffs, Vials, Medicine Bottles, Pitchers, Jugs, Willow Covered Demijohns, Telegraph Insulators, Pickle Jars; also Candy and Preserve Jars, including all kinds of Glass Ware made at such Establishments. Also, constantly on hand, different kinds of Lanterns.

ST. JOHNS, C.E.

GEO. W. FOSTER.   CHAs. W. FOSTER.

N.B.---Particular attention given to Private Moulds.

Newspaper advertisement.   Courtesy of John Morrill Foster.

According to several entries in George's 1856 diary, letters were received from Charles in St. Johns periodically and it was clear that he was managing – Canada Glass Works (Foster Brothers) there. Charles was next mentioned as being in Stoddard in 1861, where he blew glass for his brother, who had started up the New Granite Glass Works in the winter of 1860-1861. Again there was a hiatus in glassmaking in St. Johns, this time for 15 years. Charles returned to work in the newly formed St. Johns Glass Company in 1875. The works was situated on a new site about a block to the west of Foster Brothers' operations and adjacent to the railway. This would appear to indicate that Foster Brothers did not operate in St. Johns after 1860.

I am indebted to John Morrill Foster, great-grandson of Joseph "Old Bottle" Foster (1801-1863), for making available many of the documents that recorded the Foster family's contribution to the North American glass industry. John M. Foster is a fourth-generation glassman. More recently, this information has been supplemented by the research done on the glasshouses of St. Johns by Mr. & Mrs. W.N. Coburn of GLASFAX.

ST. JOHNS GLASS COMPANY
St. Johns, Quebec (1875-1877)

Fifteen years after Foster Brothers closed their doors in 1860, a group of local citizens decided to reopen the plant. Letters patent were issued in the name St. Johns Glass Company, with James MacPherson, merchant, Alexis Bertrand, merchant, and Henry Gillespie, builder, all of St. Johns, as the first directors. Further evidence of the existence of this company appeared in *The News and Frontier Advocate*, September 8, 1876:

. . . Among the other buildings being erected in St. Johns this fall is a windmill, which is a building in a vacant lot northwest of the glass factory . . .

The fact that Charles W. Foster was one of the petitioners supports the idea that he was actively involved in the operations, probably as manager. In 1876 Canadian Patent No. 5,925 was issued to Foster for a "Glass Melting Furnace." This would be known as the "Foster Tank Furnace."

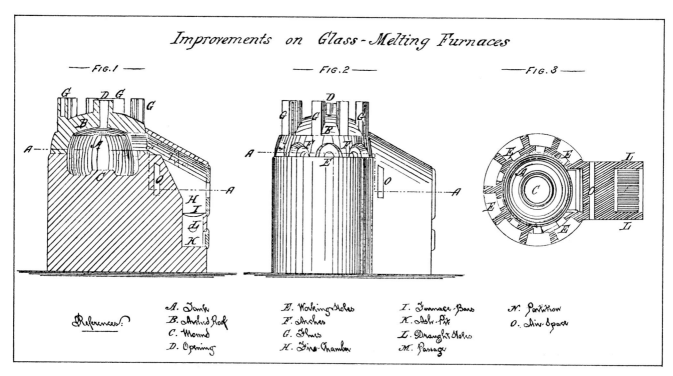

Improvements on Glass-Melting Furnaces

References:
A. Tank
B. Arched Roof
C. Mound
D. Opening
E. Working Holes
F. Arches
G. Flues
H. Fire Chamber
I. Furnace-Bars
K. Ash-Pit
L. Draught Holes
M. Passage
N. Partition
O. Air-Space

"Foster Tank Furnace", patent 1876.

The patent for this invention covered certain "new and useful improvements on glass melting furnaces" consisting "in the arrangement in the tank of a mound, in forming an opening in the roof of the tank, an air space between the fire and the tank." The opening in the roof could be plugged or opened as desired to allow greater control of the draught, while a hanging bridge located in the air space between the fire and the tank would prevent cinders or other waste from spoiling the glass. The new style furnace was installed in the St. Johns Glass factory and used there until 1880.[17]

The land on which the factory was to be built was on the south side of the railroad and a few blocks northwest of Foster Brothers' location. It comprised some 10,000 square feet, bounded by Reine St. (Bouthilier), Albert St. (Collin), George St. and the railroad.

The works must have been in operation at least by June 1876, as evidenced by the following extract from *The News and Frontier Advocate*, June 16, 1876:

> ... We regret to learn that the St. Johns Glass Co. has had to stop work for a week or so in consequence of getting out of sand. It is supposed that the boat which was bringing the sand was wrecked on the Atlantic coast.
> The Company we hope to work again in a few days...

No record has been found of the product mix, but it has been assumed that they made bottles and possibly some insulators. A number of claims were issued against the property in 1877, and on July 25, 1877, the company closed. Two of the major creditors, William and David Yuile, Commissioned Merchants of Montreal, took over the assets of the company in their own names on April 1, 1878, for $2,200 owed them. No money changed hands.

They had the works back in operation the following spring, as reported by *The News and Frontier Advocate*, May 21, 1879:

> ... The new kiln to be built by the St. Johns Glass Co. will be entirely of clay, and will effect a great saving of fuel. The work will be done under the supervision of Mr. C. Foster, the patentee of the kiln, and will be finished, it is expected, in four

or five weeks time. The clay used is from Germany and is very expensive. It cost $40 per ton.

In April 1879 the Yuile brothers incorporated the operation under the name The Excelsior Glass Company. It was later noted in the newspaper that Mr. James MacPherson, 41-2 St. James St., St. Johns — presumably the same James Macpherson who was a director of St. Johns Glass — had leased the extensive premises, which he was converting into a hay-pressing establishment, and would be prepared to buy loose and baled hay. This was the end of glass-making in St. Johns.

On July 7, 1880, Registry entry #11913 ordered the sale of the two lots, 699-700 (earlier numbered all of lot 333 and parts of lots 332 and 334), to the new company, Excelsior Glass. On November 15, 1883, a month before Excelsior Glass was reorganized under the name The North American Glass Company, Excelsior Glass, represented by shareholder William V. Lawrence, resold the two St. Johns lots to the Yuiles, who retained them until October 30, 1906, when they sold them to the Grand Trunk Railway of Canada for $600.

ST. LAWRENCE GLASS WORKS (1867-1868)
THE SAINT LAWRENCE GLASS COMPANY (1868-1873)
Montreal, Quebec

In 1866 the Fenians, a rebel group across the border, banded themselves together to invade the emerging nation to the north; the United States refused to renew the Reciprocity Treaty of 1854; and the Commercial Bank in Montreal failed. Despite all these setbacks, leaders continued to emerge. One such man was Dr. S.J. Lyman, owner of Lyman Brothers & Co., a druggist who was a cousin of Benjamin Lyman, the president of The Canada Glass Company (Limited) in Hudson, Quebec. Like his cousin, Dr. Lyman needed a domestic supplier of bottles. In 1867 he founded a partnership under the name St. Lawrence Glass Works with William Workman, first president of The Montreal City & District Savings Bank (1846) and mayor of Montreal (1868). His other two partners were Peter Redpath of Redpath Sugar and C.A. Delisle of Delisle Brothers and McGill, hardware merchants. Workman's bank provided the financing.

The works was located in Coteau St. Augustine, which lay just outside of the then existing City of Montreal limits. It was described as a village of St. Henri, seigneury of Montreal, County of Hochelaga, District of Montreal, and adjoining the city limits. The village contained a rolling mill, a glass factory (St. Lawrence Glass Works) and a tannery. Serviced by the Grand Trunk Railway, the population was about 5,000.

The works is first listed in Lovell's *Montreal Directory* of 1868 and lists the office at 383 St. Paul St. (subsequently renumbered 124-126 St. Paul St.) in Montreal. On a copy of Bishop's *New Map of Montreal*, dated 1867, there was an added notation which showed the works outside of the Montreal city limits. A Montreal Evaluation Roll for St. Henri, dated 1864, listed the purchase of 20 lots, numbers 475 to 496 inclusive, on Albert St., by Messrs. Workman & C.A. Delisle for $30,700. In the Provincial Deeds Registry Office, a 1915 map was found to include the lot numbers for the area. This located the 20 lots as lying between Dominion St. on the east, Vinet St. on the west, Delisle St. on the south, and Albert St. on the north. This area, in the southeast corner of the CNR right of way and Atwater Avenue, is now occupied by a low-rent housing project.

Although the company was not incorporated until 1868, the opening ceremonies took place on October 22, 1867. From the *Montreal Gazette* of that date:

> The works were not quite in readiness to commence the manufacture, some of the preparations having taken longer time than was expected, but there was sufficient ready to show those who had never seen it before, the mystery of glass blowing, and it is an exceedingly interesting process. When these works are in full operation we will endeavour to furnish a description.
>
> After examining the building and the works, so far as completed, the visitors gathered to a champagne lunch provided in one part of the factory . . .

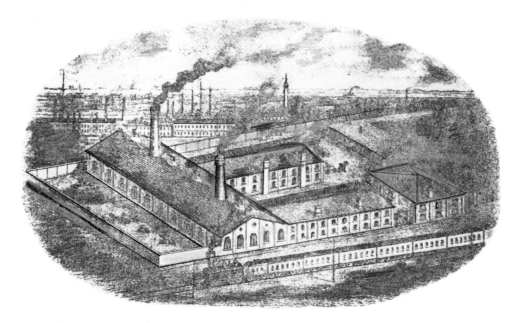

St. Lawrence Glass Works.

Here followed many complimentary remarks and the information that these were the first works of the same extent that had been erected in the vicinity of the city. There had once been smaller works in operation which had not been successful, which he did not name and for causes he did not describe . . . More toasts . . .

Mr. A. McKeand Cochrane, Secretary of the firm, briefly returned thanks, stating some of the causes which had led to the delay mentioned above . . . More compliments, etc., proposing the health of Dr. S.J. Lyman, the originator of the company, to which he replied and referred in complimentary terms to the Hudson company on the Ottawa — the pioneers in the manufacture of green glass. He said the St. Lawrence Glass Company would only make flint glass. He proposed the health of the Superintendent, Mr. Eddington [Egginton], who, he said, had experience both in Germany and in the United States. Mr. Eddington [Egginton] replied, expressing his devotion to glass manufacture, saying it "was the only thing he saw clearly through."

The works was incorporated under the name The Saint Lawrence Glass Company. The first directors were William Workman, president; Peter Redpath, of Redpath Sugar; William MacDonald, an honourary director of the bank; Alexander Maurice Delisle, a director of the bank (1849-1880); and Anthony McKeand Cochrane, secretary, who had held the same position in the Canada Glass Co. The manager of the company was Enoch Egginton, an Englishman from Birmingham, who had come out to America some years previously to run the Portland Glass Co., in Portland, Maine. According to Elizabeth Collard:

Even the factory had the advantage of being designed by one of the most prominent architects of the day: J.W. Hopkins, later a charter member of the Royal Canadian Academy. A contemporary description, published in July 1867 while construction was in progress, gives an idea of what Hopkins planned. The buildings were to cover an area of approximately 300 by 160 feet, arranged on three sides of an oblong. The foundations were to be of stone, the structure brick, the height two storeys. The account continues:

At the northwest angle will be a building 53 ft. square, which will be appropriated to pot room, laboratory, and superintendent's offices. Adjoining this will be an entrance gate on Albert Street, 20 feet wide, in line with which will be another building 102 x 38 feet, containing storage rooms for moulds and presses, blacksmiths' shop, engine and mill rooms. Adjoining and at right angles we have next a large furnace house . . . with a chimney in the centre, 16 feet in diameter at the base, and 75 feet high . . . On the third side of the yard, facing the entrance, will be another large building . . . which will be appropriated to cullet mixing rooms, packing rooms, etc . . . Such is the commencement of an enterprise in Montreal . . . which . . . carries success on the very fact of it . . . The estimated work force was 200 hands. [18]

A description of the works appeared in *The Montreal Witness* newspaper on January 3, 1868:

. . . eight pot furnace — two shops were engaged on different kinds of lamp chimneys — he applies a circular measure to ascertain that the bottom of the chimney is the right gauge . . . the boy takes it away . . . to a glory-hole . . . and after it has been heated, it is brought back and the top is finished . . . on the previous day, these shops had completed seventy-five dozen chimneys . . . they were working three moves of five hours each . . . Another shop was making phials . . . a third shop was engaged in the finest works of all, namely blown goblets . . . The whole was then returned to a glory-hole, heated and then polished and then sent to an annealing oven for about twenty-four hours . . . The ware is carefully packed in barrels . . . In this room, Mr. Egginton showed us a sugar [sic] dish . . . One of the long buildings for the mixing of the (raw) materials . . . and the annealing and packing of the ware . . . the other is devoted to the manufacture of the moulds for every different pattern of ware . . . and to grinding clay for the pots . . . They are of a peculiar shape, measuring about three feet every way sitting flat on the ground, but circular in every other direction, with an opening at the front in top, covered with a pent roof, calash-fashion . . . There is one peculiarity about this process of pot-making which deserves notice. The clay, after being properly mixed, has to be trodden by men for weeks . . .

The following articles were advertised in advance of the opening of the works, which was located on Albert St., with sales office at 388 St. Paul St., in Montreal: coal oil lamps, lamp chimneys, lamp shades, glass shades, tableware sets and industrial ware. Before the end of the year, they advertised "Real Flint Glass" much superior to the "Lime-Glass or German-Flint Chimneys" usually sold in Canada.

Starting on October 24, 1867, the following advertisement appeared for some time in the *Toronto Globe*:

BROKEN CRYSTAL WANTED

by the
St. Lawrence Glass Company
388 St. Paul St., Montreal

Broken glass, or "cullet," as it's known, when added to the batch reduces the amount of energy required to convert the raw materials into molten metal.

The work force numbered approximately 75, including five glassblowers. Enoch Egginton was the first manager, from 1867 to 1868, but resigned due to ill health and died in 1869, at the age of 42. His brother Oliver took over and was last listed as manager in 1873. However, in Lovell's *Montreal Directory* for the years 1872-73, 1878-79, 1880-81, and 1887-88, Joseph Augustin Egginton, son of Oliver Egginton, was listed as a glasscutter at a factory operating under the name Ornamental Glass Works at 363 St. Lawrence (1872-73), and 519 Lagauchetiere for all the other entries. No glass was actually made there, only embellished.

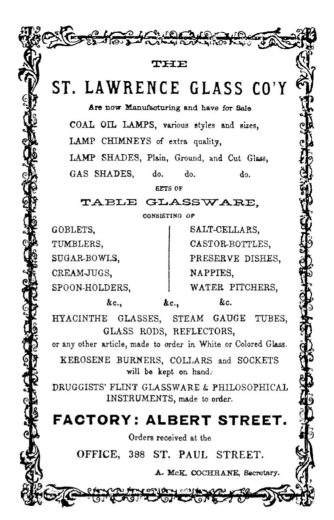

THE

ST. LAWRENCE GLASS CO'Y

Are now Manufacturing and have for Sale

COAL OIL LAMPS, various styles and sizes,

LAMP CHIMNEYS of extra quality,

LAMP SHADES, Plain, Ground, and Cut Glass,

GAS SHADES, do. do. do.

SETS OF

TABLE GLASSWARE,

CONSISTING OF

GOBLETS,	SALT-CELLARS,
TUMBLERS,	CASTOR-BOTTLES,
SUGAR-BOWLS,	PRESERVE DISHES,
CREAM-JUGS,	NAPPIES,
SPOON-HOLDERS,	WATER PITCHERS,
&c., &c.,	&c.

HYACINTHE GLASSES, STEAM GAUGE TUBES, GLASS RODS, REFLECTORS,

or any other article, made to order in White or Colored Glass.

KEROSENE BURNERS, COLLARS and SOCKETS will be kept on hand.

DRUGGISTS' FLINT GLASSWARE & PHILOSOPHICAL INSTRUMENTS, made to order.

FACTORY: ALBERT STREET.

Orders received at the

OFFICE, 388 ST. PAUL STREET.

A. McK. COCHRANE, Secretary.

Advertisement for St. Lawrence Glass which appeared in McAlpines Directory for Nova Scotia, 1868-69 issue.
PAC.

A Mr. M. Ladyatt was then shown as manager. No further entries in the Montreal directories have been found and it is presumed that the factory closed down in 1873.

In the fall of 1873 a bad depression hit the United States and spilled over into Canada. It lasted for five years and really set the economy back on its heels. Three years later, Mr. Workman decided to convert the works into a pottery operation. From the Quebec *Official Gazette*, January 5, 1877:

> The directors of the pottery included William Workman and A.M. Delisle (the two who had owned the property on which the St. Lawrence Glass factory was built) . . . under the name of the Montreal Porcelain Co., but the pottery began work as the West End Dresden Pottery. It expired as the Stafford Pottery, after a total lifespan about equal to that of the St. Lawrence Glass Co.

A limited "dig" took place over the Labour Day weekend in 1970 and involved Newt Coburn, John Sheeler, Peter Behn, Olive Wilson, Audrey Smith, Elsie Angus and several other members of GLASFAX.[19]

NEW BRUNSWICK GLASSHOUSES IN THE NINETEENTH CENTURY

Very little information is available on the glass industry in New Brunswick in the nineteenth century. Three companies were established in the area of Saint John: The Saint John Glass Company (1872-1873), New Brunswick Crystal Glass Company (Limited) (1874-1878), and the Courtenay Bay Glass Works (1878).

James Christie

THE SAINT JOHN GLASS COMPANY
Saint John, New Brunswick (1872-1873)

The following is a synopsis of an article prepared for the New Brunswick Museum by the Acting Art Curator, the late Mrs. Huia G. Ryder:

On June 16, 1872, an L-shaped property, with a 25-foot frontage on Brook St., was transferred from James Christie, M.D., and Gilbert R. Pugsley to The Saint John Glass Company for $600. The transfer included the existing buildings and a railroad siding. On April 19, 1873, George W. Fletcher brought suit against the company for $234. At the same time, a Trust Deed was set up in the name of Alexander Christie and John Ferguson for the purpose of selling all the joint stock and property of the company to the said parties, who are also large creditors, in trust for all creditors, to sell all estate and effects of the company, and to pay Daniel A. Pugsley the sum of $106.60 for wages due him. The trust deed was signed by James Christie, M.D., a director, and Gilbert Pugsley, the company secretary . . .

Mrs. Ryder went on to say:

We have found no advertisements to prove glass was ever made in this factory. One interesting article is the water bottle pictured on our cover. This bottle was purchased by this writer about 1942 at an auction for twenty-five cents and given away by her fifteen years later. It was hastily taken back after finding the records linking Dr. Christie's name with the glassworks. The engraving reads "James Christie M.D., St. John N.B., Canada", the man who owned the land and sold it to the company of which he became director. We do not claim this bottle was made at the St. John Glass Company [sic] factory but the age, style and type of glass is right for 1873-74.[20]

Mr. Mansell Quartermain, GLASFAX, in an address to its first seminar, was still inclined to agree with Mrs. Ryder that " . . . it is doubtful that the company was a working glasshouse."

On December 22, 1873, the company was sold at public auction to J.S. Blois de Veber for $230.

NEW BRUNSWICK CRYSTAL GLASS COMPANY (LIMITED)
Crouchville, New Brunswick (1874-1878)

There is a lack of authority in establishing the legal name of this company. In the handwritten letters patent, it is referred to as "New Brunswick Crystal Glass Company." In the Statutes of New Brunswick for 1874, p.292, the following appears:

Passed April 8th, 1874, an Act to incorporate the New Brunswick Crystal Glass Company (Ltd.), their Associates etc., are hereby constituted a body politic and corporate by the name of New Brunswick Crystal Glass Company and by that name shall have a common seal, sue and be sued, etc., etc., as well as to manufacture glass, crystal and glassware of all kinds and descriptions.

The following has been extracted from the findings of Huia G. Ryder:

. . . The Company directors were James Domville M.P., John E. Turnbul (sic), John Holshead, Alex McDermott, John Roop, James B. Forbes, James Hawkes, John Ross and Richard Davis . . .

The Roe and Colby Atlas of 1875, plate 78, locates the Glass Works on Little River Road in Crouchville, now [1962] known as East St. John. The buildings are large and spread out along behind the beach at the head of Courtenay Bay . . . according to Mr. Cusack, a stained glass window worker, the Company manufactured window glass and bottles. They made the window glass with blowpipes but they used local sand which was of poor quality. The glass was found not to be of fine enough quality for house windows but was used in greenhouses, etc. [In support of this kind of production, the fact that Richard Davis was a Director of the Company strongly indicates that flat glass was part of the product mix. In Chapter II – Flat Glass, Mr. Davis' name will appear as a promoter or management person in several glass companies] . . . Bottles of various kinds were made possibly for aerated water as several of these have been found bearing the names of such local firms as James Ready, Fairville, Simeon Jones, John Nash, etc. . .

We have noted with interest the continuity of dates between the two last-named factories. The St. John Glass Factory was sold in December 1873 for $1230. The N.B. Crystal Glass Company was incorporated in April of 1874. The first-named factory property was resold in December 1874, at a loss of $730. It would appear that the glassmaking equipment was removed from the premises after the sale and probably formed the basis of the N.B. Crystal Glass Company in Crouchville. This would account for the large drop in the value of the Brook Street property. It would also indicate that any glass made in the Brook Street works was blown glass . . . glass was manufactured here until 1878, at which time the factory burned down. [21]

In the summer of 1965, while returning from a trip to Nova Scotia, Gerald Stevens and his wife contacted Mrs. Ryder, who showed them the glass company site, which had then become a parking lot for a garage. Some cullet and shards were collected, and, as a result, Mr. Lloyd Muir, Curator of History at the New Brunswick Museum, arranged a preliminary but extensive dig in September 1965. The shards were sent to the Royal Ontario Museum in Toronto for study.

Mansell Quartermain, in an address to the first GLASFAX seminar, stated in part:

. . . The New Brunswick Crystal Glass Company (Limited) is a different story from that of St. John Glass Co. in that "lumps" of glass have been found in the area. Verbal reports were given to Mrs. Ryder that window glass and bottles were made there, as well as lamp chimneys. The R. Chalmers' *Report on the Surface Geology of Southern New Brunswick*, dated 1888, states that glass works were erected at Courtenay Bay some years ago and the coarser grades of glass were manufactured from the sands occurring there . . . [22]

In January 1880, the *Toronto Globe* reported on the visit of Sir Leonard Tilley, in his capacity as finance minister, to Saint John. Quoting from a correspondent of the newspaper, dateline Saint John, New Brunswick, December 22, 1879:

> ... the few factories there were for him to visit were not only not better, but worse off for the tariff which he had framed, avowedly for their benefit ... why did he not visit the glassworks, also closed since the National Party commenced its baleful operations? I hear, the Manager, Richard Davis is starting a glass factory in a distant city – Penetanguishene ... [See Chapter II, Flat Glass, Penetang Glass Factory.]

COURTENAY BAY GLASS WORKS
Crouchville, New Brunswick (1878)

One of the directors of the New Brunswick Crystal works was Richard Davis, an American entrepreneur who would later become identified with establishing flat glass operations. Shortly after that company had been closed by a fire, early in 1878, Davis bought it, and after making repairs he intended to commence operations in about six weeks. He renamed it the Courtenay Bay Glass Works.

In February, 29 Pittsburgh glassblowers and tending boys left for Saint John, N.B. A month later it was reported that the works (New Brunswick Crystal) had been leased by a new firm (Courtenay Bay Glass Works) and placed under the superintendence of Mr. Grey of Philadelphia. Operations apparently commenced that same month, because it was reported that the glassworks shut down on April 8, after having been in production for several weeks. There is no record of its having starting up again.

In June 1878 the following notices appeared in *The Daily Telegraph*:

COURTENAY BAY GLASS WORKS
BY AUCTION

There will be sold at public auction, on Saturday, the 22nd inst. at 12 o'clock noon, at Chubb's Corner:–

The Leasehold Land, with Buildings thereon, known as the Courtenay Bay Glass Works, situated on *Red Head Road*, Parish of Simonds, together with all machinery, etc., therein. These Works have cost upwards of $50,000, and are well adapted for glass or other manufacturing purposes.

W.A. Lockhart, Auctioneer.

The Courtenay Bay Glass Works, advertised for sale in another column, will be sold tomorrow, at 12 o'clock at Chubb's Corner.

At noon today, Mr. W.A. Lockhart sold the Courtenay Bay Glass Work for $1,250 to John McAllister.

This was the first example of a number of incidents that would be directly connected with Mr. Davis.[23]

The next glass operations in New Brunswick would be in Moncton, where Humphreys' Glass Works, formerly of Trenton, Nova Scotia, moved in 1917 and became incorporated under the name Humphreys' Glass, Limited.

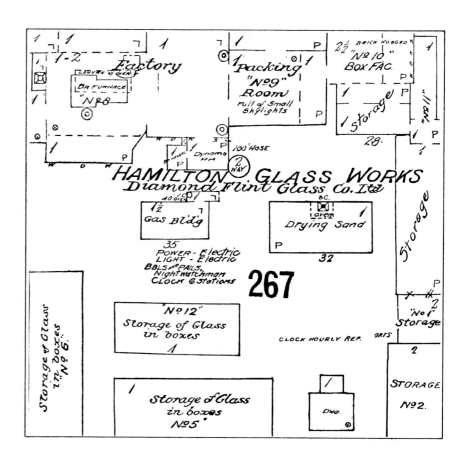

Hamilton Glass Works, 1898.
Fire Underwriters Plan.

HAMILTON GLASSHOUSES

If a Canadian Glass Hall of Fame is ever established — Hamilton, Ontario, would be the logical location, having the honour of being the Canadian city with the longest period of glass manufacturing. With the exception of eight years, from 1898-1906, glass products have been made there since about 1864.

Two companies operated there as independents in the nineteenth century before being taken over by the newly formed Diamond Glass Company (Limited) in 1891 — Hamilton Glass Works (1864-1880), which was incorporated as The Hamilton Glass Company in 1880, and the Burlington Glass Works (c.1874-1875). Their partnership became known as the Burlington Glass Company for the rest of its existence. It became a subsidiary of Hamilton Glass in 1885.

In the decade prior to the establishment of the Hamilton Glass Works, conditions in Hamilton had had their ups and downs. By 1858 the population of the city had reached almost 25,000. This rapid expansion brought about a spree of overspending, until the city was on the verge of bankruptcy. The depression which followed was one of the worst in the city's history. Whole blocks of houses stood unoccupied, and for several years not one new house was put up. Every branch of trade was paralyzed and did not return to normal until the outbreak of the American Civil War in 1861. By 1863 the population stood at 19,000.

HAMILTON GLASS WORKS (1864-1880)

The establishment of this company was the culmination of a series of events that started 35 years earlier. In 1829 John Winer settled in Hamilton and, within a year, established himself as a druggist. In 1857 he was joined by Lyman Moore. The firm was listed as wholesale and retail chemists and druggists. Lucien H. Brooks acted as a traveller for the firm. In the history of the Caledonia Glass Works (earlier in this chapter), one of the agents authorized to sell Caledonia Springs water is listed as "Mr. Winer, Druggist, Hamilton." Presumably the same Mr. Winer.

George H. *Rutherford* (1837-1916).

By 1862 Winer, Moore & Co. had been replaced by J. Winer & Co., wholesale chemists and druggists, the owners of which were J. Winer and George Rutherford. Lyman Moore had purchased the retail side of the business and set up his own shop. In the *Canada Directory* for 1857-58, George Rutherford rated only one line: ". . . bookkeeper, resident in Hamilton . . ."

By this time, three of the four key people — Winer, Moore and Rutherford — who were eventually responsible for the establishment and operation of Hamilton Glass were well acquainted with each other and plied the same trade. This would provide a ready and captive market for a glassworks, but they needed a glassmaker. This deficiency was made up by Nathan B. Gatchell.

Gatchell was born in Upper Canada in 1829. At the age of 21, he married Mary J. Utmann and, six years later, moved to Lancaster, N.Y., where he became a partner in the Lancaster Glass Works. The works burned down in 1859, and he was no longer listed as a partner in 1863. He must have returned to Canada, because the following entry appeared in *Mitchell's Hamilton Directory* 1865-1866:

> *Hamilton Glass Works* — These works have been lately established by Gatchell, Moore & Co. It is the only factory of its kind in Western Canada (Ontario) and there is no doubt from the experience of some members of the firm, and the abundance of capital at command, that success will be kept in constant employment. [At the bottom of the title page, the *Directory* gave the year as 1864.]

This was the first mention of the Hamilton Glass Works and indicates that it was in operation in 1864, and presumably Gatchell was the glassmaker. The choice of Gatchell suggests that, up to this point, the needs of the druggists and chemists in Hamilton had been supplied by Lancaster. The names of the other two partners, Winer and Rutherford, are not mentioned, but it has been assumed that they were party to the hiring of Gatchell.

The works was located close to Hamilton harbour and the Great Western Railway, both of which facilitated the handling of incoming raw materials and outgoing finished ware. The works was referred to as the "Green House," a term used to indicate that the finished products would have a light green tinge to them, as the result of the iron in the sand. This colour appears in the bottles and industrial production. On the other hand the "Flint House" (Burlington Glass Works), which at its peak specialized in nonbottle production, produced a better and colourless glass for its tableware.

In the *Canada Directory* for the same period, it was stated that the George E. Tuckett & Co. (this should have read George E. Tuckett & John Billings, partners) were the proprietors of the Hamilton Glass Works. Which was correct? It is highly probable that they were both correct. In the early directories, although most of the information provided was generally accurate, the period to which it referred was never too clearly indicated and was often arbitrary.

In Peter R. Austin's address to the Head-of-The-Lake Historical Society on March 11, 1955, the following statement appeared:

> . . . In 1865, in conjunction with John Winer, Lyman Moore, George Rutherford and John Billings, he [Tuckett] bought the newly formed Hamilton Glass Work at Hughson and Warren. We are told by *The Herald* on February 4, 1899 . . . A short experience in this line sufficed to dissatisfy Mr. Tuckett, and coming home from Toronto one day, he threw his samples into Lake Ontario and that was the last of the glass business [for him] . . .

The share of the works that Tuckett and Billings acquired would therefore appear to be only that owned by Gatchell, as, according to Donald C. Keller of the Lancaster Historical Society, Gatchell was again active in Lancaster (N.Y.) in 1866. Why Gatchell pulled out of the venture is unknown. The thought that he might have been just a technical advisor during construction is inconsistent with the fact that the company initially bore his name. Perhaps this was purely an attempt to establish an instant reputation for the new company based on Gatchell's experience in Lancaster. This evidence, however, does not prove that he did not become involved in the Hamilton Glass Works with every expectation of being part of the ongoing operation. It merely raises a doubt.

Tuckett and Billings, having sold out their interests, returned to the tobacco business in 1856. The new group, Rutherford & Co., was made up of Winer, Moore, Rutherford and partner-manager Lucien Henry Brooks. The *Hamilton Spectator*, March 29, 1867, reported:

> During the past winter, Messrs. Rutherford & Co. have been manufacturing and are now introducing to the trade a universally saleable article of domestic use in the shape of a preserve bottle known as the "Home Fruit Jar." They are fitted either with the latest stoppers or with corks, which are cheaper but not so convenient. Pamphlets and priced samples can be seen at Messrs. Brown and Gillespie's trade sale on Wednesday. Some idea of the extent of business done at the Hamilton Glass Work may be gathered from the fact that they give employment to about sixty-five persons, the weekly wages amounting to over $700.00 a week. The monthly production of the Works is about $6,000.00 and we are glad to learn that this season, the demand will be in excess of the supply.

By the early 1880s Winer had retired from business, but his firm eventually became the basis of the National Drug Co. Brooks was still managing the Hamilton Glass Works, in partnership with Rutherford and Moore.

THE HAMILTON GLASS COMPANY (1880-1898)

On January 14, 1880, the Hamilton Glass Works was incorporated under Ontario law and became The Hamilton Glass Company. Rutherford was the president and Moore was vice-president and managing director. Brooks was the manager of the works and Winer was a director.

Ten years after the Hamilton Glass Works started, the Burlington Glass Works set up shop a few blocks away. The following description of The Hamilton Glass Company in the mid-1880s appeared in *Industries of Canada 1886*:

THE HAMILTON GLASS COMPANY:
Office and Works, 309 Hughson Street North

Chief amongst the glass manufacturers of Canada is the Hamilton Glass Company, the trade of which was established thirty years ago by George E. Tuckett & Co., and subsequently carried on by Rutherford & Co. until a stock company was formed, being composed of Messrs. J. Winer, George E. Rutherford, Lyman Moore and Mrs. (sic) L.H. Brooks. Mr. George Rutherford is President, and Mr. Lyman Moore, Vice-President and acting Manager. The Hamilton Glass Company manufacture all kinds of green and coloured glass bottles, telegraph insulators, etc., and have facilities for turning out bottles of any style whatever. The works are very extensive and cover an entire block, extending from Hughson Street to James Street, and from Picton Street to Macauley Street. One hundred and fifty hands are employed, men and boys, and a seven-pot furnace (and five-pot furnace which is now idle) is used to its utmost capacity. The departments embraced are: moulding shop, batch room — where the ingredients are mixed up — colouring room, a large stone pot house, soda ash room, carpenter's shop, blacksmith's shop, packing house and store-room. The trade enjoyed by this Company extends over the whole of the Dominion, and supplies all the wholesale druggists in Canada with their patent medicine bottles, etc. This immense trade is conducted without any travellers whatever, a significant fact, which proves that the Hamilton Glass Company met the wants of the trade in every sense of the word. Moreover, the trade is constantly increasing, and it is said by those who know that the Hamilton Glass Company do the largest amount of shipping from the city of any manufacturing concern in Hamilton.

In 1885 the Hamilton Glass Company bought out its competitor, Burlington Glass Works. Although Burlington would eventually become a "flint house" which produced noncontainer ware, it had originally started to manufacture flint bottles to capture some of the local trade. This competition in bottleware no doubt generated the takeover. Hamilton Glass now had a fast hold in the flint glass container area, which complemented their regular production of amber and green bottles, mason jars (including the Rutherford Gem), prescription bottles and insulators.

In November 1889 Moore went before the Tax Appeal Court in Hamilton, objecting to the assessment placed on the Hamilton and Burlington factories. Proving perhaps that the welfare of the glass industry in the city was a matter of some public concern, the *Spectator* saw fit to print the following remarks by Moore on the occasion:

It appears to me that you want to assess us on our capital stock (instead of personal property on which assessment was supposed to be based). Our assessment is increased this year by $15,000.00. We have a chance to get out of town at a profit, and we may go if our assessment is increased year by year. Here we pay wages to a large number of men and boys and you want to drive us out of town.

Whether or not there actually was a plan to relocate elsewhere may never be known. There is little doubt, however, that the proprietors were seriously considering the liquidation of their holdings. Within two years time, the facilities of both companies had been sold to The Diamond Glass Company (Limited). George Rutherford, who had been running both operations, was made a director of Diamond Glass. This information on the takeover came to light in a *Spectator* report of the fire at the Burlington works on September 7, 1892:

... The factory (Burlington) is owned by the Diamond Glass Company, a Montreal syndicate, which purchased both the Burlington and Hamilton glass works a little over a year ago...

Truth is sometimes stranger than fiction. David Parker, an active member in the early years of GLASFAX, recounts this true story which demonstrates the real spirit of a glass researcher.

"No Dot" Crown Fruit Jar

The Darling Fruit Jar

The Gem Rutherford & Co. with blow back

Hamilton Glass Works Fruit Jars

Bogarders Shooting Balls made by
Rutherford & Co.

Dalley's Ink Bottles

Drawings by Jack Kingdon of products of Hamilton Glass Company indicated by shards found on the property in 1970-71.

This unbelievable but true story began in the spring of sixty-six (Nineteen sixty-six, that is).

While digging an old glass dump site in Dundas, Ontario, a bottle of considerable rarity was unearthed by me. I am one of the many bottle diggers in this area. The description of it is as follows: a cobalt blue, blob top, iron pontilled, soda water bottle.

The embossing "PILGRIM & CO., HAMILTON" made it one of the much prized bottles of my collection and the few collectors that I know have Pilgrims, treasure them greatly!

I have neglected to add one point about this beauty on the minus side of the ledger. It was split almost entirely in two when found. I found the half with the embossing on it and almost cried when I found the back half missing! The break travelled from just below the neck, through the C. down through the iron pontil, and back to the point below the neck.

Needless to say, I scoured that dump from top to bottom for the other half, but never found it.

Now for four and one half years, I showed this half to many collectors always lamenting the fact of its incompleteness. I felt this bottle was one of my best on account of its colour (deep blue) and its iron pontil (circa 1850).

The story now shifts to the diggings of one Jack Kingdon of Dundas, Ontario. Jack, a machinist by day, but a very active bottle digger on weekends, with his wife Alma, were digging their first glass site of the year on April 12, 1970. Uncovered on that outing was a cobalt blue piece of glass with half an iron pontil mark on the base. The piece might have been discarded by an ordinary bottle digger (if there is an *ordinary bottle digger*), but Jack had seen my half of the blue Pilgrim approximately six months previously and had a mental picture of it. This shows how alert some of these bottle diggers can be!! On his piece there was a single "o".

After a few days I received a phone call from Jack, asking me to assist him in some research that we had been working on. I was also asked to bring along my Blue Pilgrim. Thinking a comparison of colours was the reason for the request, I brought the piece along and was asked to show it. Upon perusing the embossing with the missing "o" in "Co." Jack made the announcement — he had the other piece. Thanks to a very keen-eyed glass collector, I have the Pilgrim intact now.

I am sure this story will keep me talking for quite some time. I might add, if you ever dig *just part* of a bottle, and have heard this story, do not throw it away. Maybe after four years or so, it might turn up – stranger things have happened![24]

The Hamilton Glass Company plant was shut down in 1898, with personnel and equipment being transferred to the recently formed (1893) Toronto Glass Company (Limited). The story of The Hamilton Glass Company is continued in Chapter 5 – Consolidation 1903-1913.

BURLINGTON GLASS WORKS (c. 1874-1875)
Hamilton, Ontario

The next glass company to operate in Hamilton was the Burlington Glass Works. This was one of the most unique glass operations in Canada in the nineteenth century and, during its peak years, in the whole of North America. For its diversity of products, range of colours, and its innovative operating and decorating techniques, it was truly a company *sans pareil*. From the quantity and diversity of pattern glass shards found on the site, I have presumed that such patterns must be attributable to the Burlington operation, if not authenticated. I am unable to accept the alternative that the majority of shards, representing patterns from many American glass companies, could have come to Hamilton in the form of cullet, which is normally in the form of crushed glass.

Ruins of the Burlington Glass Works, Hamilton, Ontario.
From *"Canadian Glass & Early Canadian Glass"* by Gerald Stevens, courtesy of Lloyd Bruce.

It operated as a partnership, with changes in partners, until its takeover by the Hamilton Glass Company in 1885. In 1891, along with its parent company, it became part of the Diamond Glass Company (Limited) and, 12 years later, a subsidiary of Diamond Flint Glass Company Limited. The plant was shut down in 1897. Its counterpart in the twentieth century was Dominion Glass Company, Limited, which took over Diamond Flint in 1913. Dominion Glass has enjoyed the same broad diversification and innovative approach, and has been the leader in the Canadian glass industry since its incorporation.

What prompted the establishment of a second glass factory in Hamilton at this time? It is my opinion that the Burlington Glass Works was set up for the same reason as the successful Hamilton Glass operation, i.e. to provide glassware locally for the marketing of specific products. Like so many other great companies, it had humble beginnings. On December 29, 1873, Edward Roberts Kent, proprietor of E.R. Kent & Co., a glass distribution firm, and the Myles brothers, Alfred and Charles, coal merchants, formed a partnership to manufacture and market glassware. The plant was built a few blocks northwest of Hamilton Glass, on the east side of MacNab St., on the shores of Burlington Bay. In the fall of 1874 the first batch was melted. According to the *Hamilton Spectator*, early production included lead glass for lamps, lamp chimneys and globes and soda-lime glass for bottles and containers.

BURLINGTON GLASS COMPANY
(1875-1885)

In May 1875 John Neil Tarbox of the Wanzer Sewing Machine Company bought out the Myles brothers' interests. On May 18 Kent and Tarbox formed a partnership registered in the name of the Burlington Glass Company. Tarbox must have been an engineer with some knowledge of the glass industry because he was a co-inventor of four glass-oriented processes, all of which were patented. This partnership obviously provided some glass know-how. The plant was enlarged and improved and alterations were made to the furnace. The decade of the 1870s was one of economic instability, not only in Canada, but throughout the Western world. Fluctuations began in 1873, and by 1875 a full-scale depression gripped the country. It worsened steadily until 1879, when the economy started to recover. To add to the problem, the decline in the cost of raw materials did not keep pace with the decline in finished goods prices. Even an increase in the Canadian tariff from 15 percent in 1874 to 17½ percent in 1878 gave little relief to the Canadian glass industry. In 1879, under the national policy, the tariff was raised to 30 percent. A further fact that created higher-priced goods in Canada was Canada's smaller population, 3,689,000 compared to the 40,000,000 living in the United States. This would close many companies in Canada, and Burlington Glass was no exception.

The following description, written by Christopher S. Peters, a long-term employee of the Hamilton Glass Company, is attributed to the Burlington Glass Company a few years prior to its takeover by Hamilton Glass in 1885:

> The 'Flint House' was a pot furnace, coal fired, and made milk bottles, prescriptions, lamps, lamp chimneys, lantern globes, and round candy jars, mostly all screw top ware which was blown with a bust-off and ground. Joe Guerin ran the grinding machine and took care of all the bust-off ware, large and small.
>
> They also made some pressed ware such as candy jar stoppers, whiskey flask stoppers, and they pressed in opal several different sizes of McLarens cheese jars which I believe are still made at the present time.
>
> Glory holes and Lehrs were oil fired, and all packing was done in straw. The selectors had to know their stuff, the glass blowers seeing to this, and as supervisors of the packers they registered 100%.
>
> The factory shut down some time on the 24th of May and re-opened again on the 1st of October.
>
> The writer has often thought how things have changed in the past 35 years. In days gone by the Blacksmith Shop was all important, and the Machine Shop was the 'tail of the dog'. In these days of mechanized machine production, conditions are reversed.

On December 22, 1876, the partnership of Kent and Tarbox, under the name Burlington Glass Company, was dissolved. In October of the following year, the remaining partner, Tarbox, declared bankruptcy and the company passed into the control of the Consolidated Bank of Canada. William Godkin Beach, who had been active in the Canadian Manufacturers' Association for many years as a strong advocate of higher tariffs to protect the Canadian glass industry, blamed the Americans and was quoted in the *Hamilton Spectator*, January 14, 1878, as saying:

> When the former proprietor [Tarbox] was compelled to suspend and go into insolvency, the prices had been reduced forty percent below what they were when the factory started. Immediately upon the closing of the works there was an upward tendency in prices; the end had been accomplished; the Canadian rival had been crushed and the temptation to slaughter American glassware in Canada no longer existed.

In July 1878 the company was reestablished by Murray A. Kerr, a local wholesaler and retailer of coal oil and lamps, located at 71 King St. W. Mr. Beach was hired to manage the plant, which position he occupied until 1881, when he moved to the newly formed Nova Scotia Glass Company (Limited). Kerr carried on alone until 1884, when he was joined by George R.

Secord. With the increase in tariff protection in 1879 to 30 percent, the company prospered. This partnership ended a year later with the death of Secord in October. Before the end of the year, Kerr sold the works to the Hamilton Glass Company for $20,000.

This sale was followed by a fire two weeks later, the fourth in the company's history. The *Hamilton Spectator*, December 14, 1885:

> One of those disastrous fires which fortunately are of rare occurrence in Hamilton took place Saturday night. A few minutes after 7 o'clock, Mr. Harry Lee, clerk at the Burlington Glass Works discovered fire in a warehouse on Zealand's wharf. The fire department was quickly telephoned to and responded promptly, but during the few minutes it took to make the run of over a mile, the flames had made such headway that there was no hope of saving that portion of the building in which the fire originated.
>
> The steamer Acadia was lying in the slip broadside dock. The burning building was not eight feet away, and the side of the steamer was already scorched and blistered. A hundred ready hands assisted in pushing her out of the slip, and she was kept off until safely beyond all danger. About $21,000 worth of glassware was lost in the wharf fire.

During the next few years, the company employed about 150 men and had an average annual production of $120,000.

On August 10, 1891, Hamilton Glass sold its two plants, with their diversified capabilities, to the Diamond Glass Company (Limited) of Montreal. By 1897, with new semiautomatic forming equipment being introduced, the operation became obsolete and was closed down. Although Burlington Glass was still listed in the directories until 1909, according to the local tax rolls it ceased to be a taxpayer in 1897. The property was sold by Dominion Glass Company, Limited to the City of Hamilton in June 1927 for $5,000.

TECHNIQUES AND PRODUCTS

Although Burlington Glass has always been considered to be the most diversified and innovative glass operation of its time in Canada, the lack of catalogs and advertisements have made it difficult to substantiate this assumption. Gerald Stevens, in his two books, *Early Canadian Glass* and *Canadian Glass c.1825-1925*, went to great lengths to describe the unique diversity of this company, as the result of his personal research and a number of interviews with former employees.

They used all the methods of making glass by nonmechanical means — blowing into a mould, off-hand (without the use of a mould) and pressing (side-lever press). One product developed was the seamless bottle. This technique could be used for round bottles only. The glassblower, while blowing the bottle in the mould, would rotate the blowpipe, thus eliminating the vertical mould seam. These bottles can be identified by very faint horizontal striations on the body of the bottle.

Types of decorating included acid-etching, cutting, sandblasting, and probably some hand-painting (a forerunner to Applied Colour Lettering).[25] The colours they produced or experimented with were legion. From clear glass right through the spectrum — red, orange, yellow, green, blue, indigo and violet, and shades thereof. Various colours of opalescent glass from milk-white through blue to purple were tried.

The products also included a vast range of styles. The company was originally established to get in on the expanding use of bottles for marketing products, including prescription ware, milks, soft drinks and alcoholic beverages. It was also involved in such industrial products as lamps, lamp chimneys, lamp shades and a number of household items. It was not until the early 1880s, and the subsequent takeover by Hamilton Glass in 1885, that a myriad of tableware shapes and patterns were developed, the majority of the latter having been copied from American patterns and, in many cases, given Canadian names.

On Saturday, November 7, 1970, a plaque to commemorate the Burlington Glass Works was unveiled at the corner of Burlington and MacNab streets in Hamilton. The plaque inscription reads as follows:

The unveiling of the provincial historical plaque commemorating the Burlington Glass Works, November 7, 1970. From left to right are: Mr. Gerald Stevens, noted author of numerous works on Canadian glass, Miss L. M. Shaw, President of the Head-of-the-Lake Historical Society, Mr. J. Sheeler, authority on Canadian Glass, His Worship V. Copps, Mayor/City of Hamilton, Mr. William M. McCullough, Alderman, City of Hamilton.

THE BURLINGTON GLASS WORKS 1874

The Burlington Glass Works, formerly situated here, was one of the most important 19th century glass houses in Canada in terms of the variety and quality of its production. From 1874 to about 1897 skilled artisans produced lamps, tablewares and containers. Glass-production techniques included free-blowing, mould-blowing and pressing in a mould. Pot furnaces produced several different types of glass in a wide range of colours. Glasswares were decorated by cutting, painting, sand-blasting, acid-etching and wheel-engraving. Archaeological excavations in 1966 and 1969 established the layout of the works and authenticated and enlarged previous knowledge of its output.

FOOTNOTES

[1] Hilda Spence and Kelvin Spence, A *Guide to Early Canadian Glass*, (Toronto: Longmans, 1966), p. 13.

[2] Ibid. p. 13.

[3] Adam Shortt and Arthur B. Doughty, *Documents Relating to the Constitutional History of Canada*, Seasonal paper, no. 18, (Ottawa: King's Printer 1918), p. 63.

[4] *Our Cheerful Friend*, vol. VII, no. IV, (April 1, 1879).

[5] John R. Sheeler, "Mallorytown Glass Factory 1839-1840," GLASFAX *Newsletter*, vol. 1, no. 5, (October 1967), p. 2.

[6] John R. Sheeler, "Glass in Canada: Its History and Study," p. 31. Presented to OMA-ROM seminar in Toronto, November 1977.

[7] Janet Holmes, "Glass and the Glass Industry," *The Book of Canadian Antiques*, ed. Donald B. Webster, (Toronto: McGraw-Hill Ryerson, 1974), p. 268.

[8] O. Urquhart, "Life at the Springs & The Caledonia Glass Works," GLASFAX *Newsletter*, (May 1973), p. 12.

[9] John Beswarick Thompson, "The Glass Industry of Vaudreuil County," GLASFAX *Newsletter*, (June 1973), p. 9.

[10] Thompson, p. 13.

[11] Ibid. p. 13.

[12] Ibid. p. 14.

[13] Ibid. pp. 16, 17.

[14] Statements relating to trade, navigation, mining, etc. for 1867 cited in Gerald Stevens' *Canadian Glass c.1825-1925*, (Toronto: Ryerson, 1967), pp. 41, 42.

[15] John Morrill Foster, *Old Bottle Foster and His Glass-Making Descendants*, (Fort Wayne, Indiana: Keefer Printing Company, 1972), p. 14.

[16] Ibid. pp. 12, 14.

[17] Department of Justice, Patents Branch, "Improvements in Glass Melting Tank Furnaces." Patent no. 5925 (Ottawa: 1876).

[18] Elizabeth Collard, "The St. Lawrence Glass Co. Glasshouse to Pottery," *Canadian Collector*, (September 1970), pp. 12, 13.

[19] See Chapter 9 Authentication, Attribution and Excavations, "The Saint Lawrence Glass Company.

[20] Huia Ryder, *Art Bulletin*, The New Brunswick Museum Art Department, Vol. VI, no. 3, (March 1962), p. 2.

[21] Huia Ryder, pp. 2, 3.

[22] Mansell Quartermain, "Maritime Glass Houses," GLASFAX *Newsletter*, vol. 5, no. VI, (June 1971), p. 97.

[23] See Chapter 11, "Penetang Glass Factory" and "Napanee Glass Works."

[24] David Parker, "Pilgrim Bottle Reunited After Many Years Separation," GLASFAX *Newsletter*.

[25] See Appendix 2, Bottle Markings and Closures, "A.C.L."

CHAPTER 4

The Establishment of the Canadian Glass Industry on a Permanent Basis (1878-1902)

The Yuile Brothers, "Fathers of the Canadian Glass Industry"
The Yuile-King Family Tree
The Excelsior Glass Company, St. Johns, Quebec (1879-1880),
and Montreal, Quebec (1880-1883)
The North American Glass Company, Montreal, Quebec (1883-1890)
Three glass companies in Nova Scotia: The Nova Scotia Glass Company (Limited), New Glasgow
(1881-1890); Lamont Glass Company, Trenton (1890-1897); and Humphreys' Glass
Company, Trenton (1890-1917), which was incorporated as Humphreys' Glass, Limited,
Moncton, New Brunswick (1917-1920)
The Montreal Bottle and Glass Company, Montreal (1887)
The First Conglomerate in Canada
The Diamond Glass Company, (Limited), Montreal (1890-1902)
The Toronto Glass Company (Limited), Toronto (1893-1899)
The First Glass Operation in Montreal
Three of the four companies in Montreal had the words Dominion Glass in their names
Dominion Glass Company (early) (c.1886-1894), a partnership, was incorporated as Dominion Glass
Company (1894-1896) and became The Dominion Glass Company (Limited) (1896-1897)
In Southern Ontario, The Erie Glass Company of Canada (Limited) (1892-1893) and Foster
Glass Works (1894-1900), Port Colborne, Ontario
The Ontario Glass Company Limited, Kingsville (1899-1901)
In Wallaceburg, The Wallaceburg Glass Works Company (Limited) (1893) and The Sydenham
Glass Company of Wallaceburg (Limited) (1894-1913)
The Ontario Glass Burial Case Company (Limited), Ridgetown (1880-c.1883)

THE YUILE BROTHERS:
FATHERS OF THE CANADIAN GLASS INDUSTRY

William Yuile (1845-1925) and his younger brother David (1846-1909), sons of William Pollock Yuile of Helensburg, Scotland, came to Canada with their family about 1857 and settled in Ingersoll, Ontario. They moved to Montreal in the 1870s and set up an office and warehouse at 479-481 St. Paul Street. The brothers first became involved in the glass industry when they took over the bankrupt St. Johns Glass Co., St. Johns, Quebec, in 1878, for monies owed them. After refurbishment, that company's plant was back in operation in 1879 under the name Excelsior Glass Company. In 1880 they moved the operation into Montreal.

William Yuile   David Yuile

This modest beginning started an unbroken chain of glass companies which exist today as Domglas Inc. and Consumers Glass Company, Limited, the leaders in the Canadian glass industry. And thus did the Yuiles earn the title of "Fathers of the Canadian Glass Industry," being responsible, in the period 1878-1902, for establishing the Canadian glass industry on a permanent basis. William Yuile ceased to be active after 1902. However, David continued and became the first president of Diamond Flint Glass Company Limited in 1903, where he served in that capacity until his death in 1909.

From 1878 to 1978, when I retired as corporate secretary of Domglas Inc., one or more members of the closely related Yuile and King families were involved on a continuous basis in the Canadian glass industry, with a combined 224 years of service. The following family tree indicates the years of service for each individual.

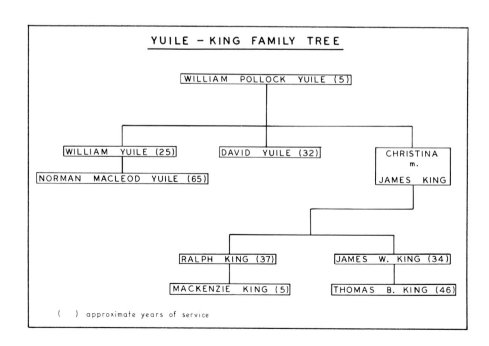

THE EXCELSIOR GLASS COMPANY
St. Johns, Quebec (1879-1880)
Montreal, Quebec (1880-1883)

In April 1879 the Yuile brothers, who had acquired the St. Johns Glass Company a year earlier, incorporated the operation under the name The Excelsior Glass Company. On May 23, 1879, *The News and Frontier Advocate* reported:

> . . . The new kiln to be built by the St. John Glass Co. [Excelsior Glass] will be entirely of clay, and will effect a great saving of fuel.
> The work will be done under the supervision of Mr. C. Foster, the patentee of the kiln, and will be finished, it is expected, in four or five weeks time. The clay used is from Germany and is very expensive. It costs $40 per ton . . .

In a letter dated April 1944 from Joe Jones, a former glassblower in St. Johns, to Eddie Davies, manager of Dominion Glass's Wallaceburg plant at that time, the following appears:

> . . . It was the early part of December 1879 that my father moved from Glassboro, New Jersey to St. Johns, Quebec. I was then 15 years old, and of course went to work in the factory. It was at that time operated by the Yuile Bros. (William and David) who had taken over the plant from a person by name Charles Foster, who built the tank, and it was known as the Foster tank, and consisted of nine ring holes. There were four cast ring shops, two insulator presses (the old hand press style) and three glory hole shops, of which I carried in on two of them. It was there I met some blowers who at some time had worked at Hudson, and I believe they learned to blow there as their relatives, the old folks, were on farms there, and these men were the descendants. The plant at St. Johns was managed by a man by the name William Borland, and the office clerk was an Ed. Sawyer. I must say two nice fellows and all liked them. The boss packer was a man by name John Farnham. The working staff was from the States, South Jersey, and a couple who at one time worked at Hudson.

The company made a general line of bottles and fruit jars. On February 2, 1880, the Yuiles purchased in their own name part of Lot 1495, St. Mary's Ward, Montreal. Prior to this move to Montreal, the local press regularly reported the competition between St. Johns and Iberville, the neighbouring city, both offering incentives to try to keep the Yuiles' operation and its glassworkers from moving to Montreal.

From *The News and Frontier Advocate* (St. Johns, Quebec):

March 12, 1800

The Committee of the Town Council in the matter of the proposed aid to the Glass Factory is still negotiating – so we understand – with favourable indications.

That our city fathers may be able to come to terms with the Messrs. Yuille [Yuile] is "a consummation devoutly to be wished for."

We believe we are within the mark when we say that a factory employing 200 hands and paying good wages would be worth as much to the town in one year as the bonus asked for.

April 2, 1880

Iberville has offered to the Messrs. Yuille [Yuile] $6,000 bonus and a site, if they will put their glass factory on that side of the river.

Plucky Iberville! You should put to blush the shilly-shallying of our timid and half-hearted corporation.

If our luke-warm corporation fails to have those amendments to an act of incorporation 'put through' in time for the meeting of the Legislature, then the negotiations with the Messrs. Yuille [Yuile] must of necessity fall to the ground, and the glass factory will be forever lost to St. Johns.

But some of our city fathers act as though this was just what they were aiming at. If they had their way they would eventually wipe out all taxes — and all tax-payers too.

In spite of these offers, it would appear that the Yuiles had already made up their minds to move to Montreal. From *The Observer*, Cowansville, Quebec, March 25, 1880:

... Considerable rivalry is felt here for the site of the Glass Factory. As the furnaces, owing to the intense and continuous fires kept up night and day, do not last more than about a year, the present one will not be fit to use but for two or three months more at the farthest. It was the intention of Messrs. Guiles (Yuiles) to remove the works to Montreal when they rebuilt, and for this they had, so report goes, procured land in the eastern part of the City. To prevent the removal of works so important to a town like St. Johns — works, in which now, some two hundred persons are employed, and with the new and enlarged arrangements which it is said are soon to be entered upon, many more must be engaged the coming year, the Council have made an offer of five thousand dollars and a suitable site whereupon to build the factory. But the Council of the spirited little town of Iberville, just across the river, have also made an offer and that in advance of St. Johns they propose a donation of six thousand dollars, and the land as much may be needed, and in any place, on waste land that may be chosen. The competition is spirited, and it is a pity that both places cannot be accommodated.

By 1881 the address of the office in Montreal was listed as 503 Mignonne Street, corner Parthenais Street, on part of the plant site.

Again from Mr. Jones's letter:

The new building was on Parthenais Street. There were two furnaces, one for flint and the other for green. There were also some presses and bottle shops. At that time, these shops were connected with the A.F.W.U. [American Flint Workers Union]. Later that department became amalgamated with what is known as the G.B.B.A. [Glass Bottle Blowers Association]. On the Green Tank the output was mostly bottles, and under the management of Mr. [William Fletcher] Borland and the office clerk, Mr. [Edward] Sawyer.

Mr. [Jean Victor Christophe Frederic] Herdt, who had come to Montreal from France [Baccarat] with his family had become manager of the flint department, with his son Henry as office clerk. As time went on, Mr. Borland retired on account of poor health and Mr. Herdt Sr. took charge of flint and green. The flint department was made up of workers from the States, and the green made up of some of those who worked at St. Johns, and others from the States.

I forgot to mention the two brothers who worked at St. Johns Excelsior Glass Co. and one of them you know, was Cook Crist and his brother Eugene. I feel sure that Cook Crist went to work at Wallaceburg when it was known as the Sydenham Glass Co. 1894-1913. The last I heard of his brother he was working at Baltimore, Md. In the meantime, there was a pot furnace in operation on Mignonne Street (five pots). A fire broke out I believe in 1885 which destroyed most everything some time in May of that year; only the pot furnace was left standing. I am not sure, but I think it only ran for a couple of years. During the vacation season the Company built a tank in its place which ran remarkably well, and the men made good wages...

The company continued to produce fruit jars, prescription ware and some pressed ware. By 1883 their thriving business required refinancing. At the end of 1883 they reorganized under the name The North American Glass Company, retaining the same site.

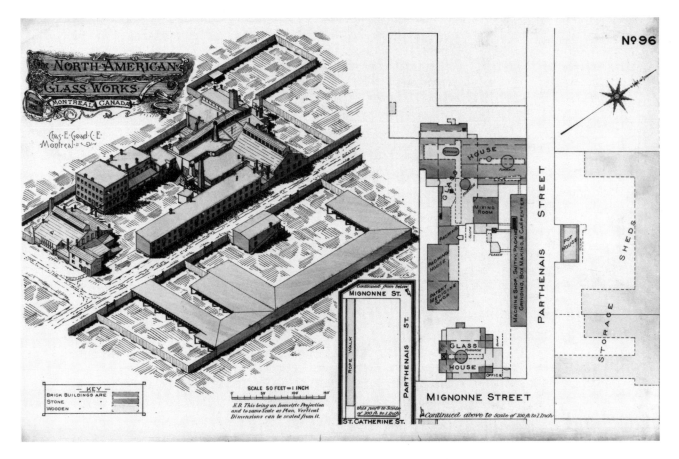

Plan and Isometric drawing of the North American Glass Works of Montreal.   National Map Collection PAC.

THE NORTH AMERICAN GLASS COMPANY
Montreal, Quebec, (1883-1890)

The Yuiles' success in the glass industry continued. Using Excelsior Glass as a base for reorganization, they incorporated a new company under the name The North American Glass Company, with a Quebec charter. Their capital had been increased by five hundred percent. William Yuile continued to manage the company and David Williamson was hired as secretary-treasurer.

The Yuiles acquired additional property to handle the expansion in business. From the *City of Montreal Atlas* of 1881, revised to 1890, it would appear that the property now comprised parts of lots 1479, 1480, 1494 and 1495. As previously, the properties were bought in the name of Messrs. William and David Yuile. By 1890 the office was listed as at 503 Mignonne Street (later de Montigny, now de Maisonneuve). The operation appears to have been a very substantial one. These additional lands were on the east side of the original property.

In order to improve the quality of the glass and broaden the product mix, the Yuiles brought in some experienced glassblowers from England and France. In a letter from glassblower Joe Jones to Eddie Davies dated April 1944, Jones wrote:

> . . . I forgot to mention that one year when the old plant was in operation . . . the Yuile brothers brought some workers to Montreal from England, and Jimmy Sephton's father was one of them. Jimmy came to work in the new plant and snapped up for me and his father. Later on Jimmy ran the finishing machine for us; and as time went on he went to the Machine Shop as an apprentice, and finally became head machinist, and now in 1944 as you know, he is in charge at Hamilton . . .

The Yuiles also brought out from France Jean Victor Christophe Francis Herdt, an experienced glassblower who had worked at the Baccarat works. Herdt became manager of the flint (nonbottle) department and his son Henry became the office clerk. When a Mr. Borland, who operated the green bottle department, resigned because of poor health, Herdt took charge of both departments. The flint department was made up of workers from the States, and the green department by some of those who had worked at St. Johns and others from the States.

Under the Herdts, the tableware operations gained impetus and, as the result of an informal "dig" in 1973,[1] a number of patterns would be attributed to these operations on this recently acquired land. The North American name would continue for 12 years, at which time Diamond Glass would be reorganized under the name Diamond Flint Glass Company Limited.

Further space was required and the company acquired property which extended to Delorimier Avenue on the west side. A new plant was erected, with three tanks under one roof and a flint furnace adjoining, and equipped with more modern machinery and lehrs instead of ovens.

Douglas and Marion Bird, authors of A *Century of Antique Canadian Fruit Jars*, have identified three specific types of fruit jars with the North American Glass Company operation. They are the NAGC monogram, with a "Boyd"-type cap, handblown with ground lip two-part mould, and a Crown "bulge" fruit jar, the bulge appearing just under the upper cross, zinc ring on outer seal glass lid, handblown two-part mould. The third one, Crown "ring," is the same as the second except the crown emblem has a ring under top cross. They also made a general line of bottles and lamp chimneys.

In 1890 North American Glass Company became the base of the newly incorporated Diamond Glass Company (Limited), the first of three conglomerates that would dominate the Canadian glass container industry. In the meantime, there would be several other companies that would start as independents and eventually be taken over by Diamond Glass between 1890-1902. No dissolution date has been found for this company.

THE GLASSHOUSES OF NOVA SCOTIA

Nova Scotia, which entered into Confederation along with New Brunswick, Quebec and Ontario on July 1, 1867, has been credited with three operating glasshouses in the nineteenth century, all located on the border between Trenton and New Glasgow. (The area was part of New Glasgow until 1890, when it became incorporated into Trenton.)

The first glasshouse was The Nova Scotia Glass Company Limited, New Glasgow. It was established in 1881 to make tableware and industrial ware, all of which, with the exception of lamps and chimneys, had heretofore been imported. It might be noted that Burlington Glass (c.1874-1885), in Hamilton, Ontario, started to specialize in the production of tableware at this time. In 1890 Nova Scotia Glass was taken over by The Diamond Glass Company (Limited) of Montreal and operated for two years. The other two glasshouses in the Trenton area were established nine years later: Lamont Glass Company (1890-1897), which made all types of glassware — bottles, tableware and industrial ware — and Humphreys' Glass Company (1890-1917), which specialized in making bottles and some industrial ware.

THE NOVA SCOTIA GLASS COMPANY (LIMITED)
New Glasgow, Nova Scotia (1881-1890)

Of the three glass companies that operated in Nova Scotia in the nineteenth century, Nova Scotia Glass has to be the most interesting one. Whereas Lamont and Humphreys concentrated on bottles and some industrial ware, Nova Scotia Glass specialized in tableware. In fact, Nova Scotia Glass and Burlington Glass, in Hamilton, rivaled each other in the diversity of their product mix in the 1880s. Why New Glasgow, Nova Scotia, of all places? It would appear that William Godkin Beach, manager of the Burlington Glass Company from 1878 to 1881, felt that there was a ready market for glassware in the maritime provinces, then being serviced by glass companies in the United States. The following excerpt from the *Eastern Chronicle* explains the reason for selecting New Glasgow:

Nova Scotia Glass Company. Detail from a birds eye view of "New Glasgow,, Nova Scotia, 1889".

Nova Scotia Museum Collection.

A letter from a correspondent in the Eastern Chronicle of March 31, 1881, states that he had noticed in the previous issue . . . an item to the effect that a gentleman from Hamilton visited Pictou a few days ago and had about decided to establish a glass factory there. This correspondent thinks that that information is not quite correct, as he has before him a letter on the subject from Mr. Beach, the Hamilton gentleman referred to, saying that he had not decided on any town as yet, but that the choice lay between Pictou, New Glasgow, Truro and Halifax, (all were towns or cities situated in Nova Scotia) and that the place offering the best inducements and advantages would be chosen. According to those statements, he adds, New Glasgow (Trenton) will certainly be chosen because it possesses advantages for any amount of heavy manufacturing, and especially glass manufacturing . . . with which . . . other places . . . cannot . . . compare . . . New Glasgow possesses . . . cheap fuel, a supply of suitable sand and good shipping facilities.

Pictou was also a strong contender, but, due to lack of shipping facilities, had to be dropped.

Events moved quickly. In April the following prospectus appeared in the *Eastern Chronicle*:

It is proposed to establish a glass company at Trenton for the manufacture of glassware such as tumblers, goblets, and all kinds of glassware for general use, kerosene lamps and chimneys. There is ample work for a company of this kind in Canada, as in 1879 and 1880, $240,000 worth of these goods were imported from the United States and further there is none of the goods proposed to be made, at present manufactured in Canada except lamps and chimneys. Provisional Directors are Andrew Walker, merchant; James Eastwood, jeweller; Graham Fraser, Nova Scotia Forge Company; P.A. MacGregor of R. MacGregor and Co., and Adam C. Bell, M.M.P., chemist and druggist. Capital stock about $100,000 divided into 10,000 shares of $10.00 were put up for sale and have been taken up in the area. Mr. W.G. Beach of Hamilton, Ontario, has been engaged as manager of the plant.

The works was erected on a site donated by Mr. Harry Townsend, on the right bank of Smelt Brook, beside the Inter-Colonial Railway, from which a siding ran to the plant. In July a wooden building with a chimney was erected. Mould-making machinery was imported. Soon afterwards, the components for a glassmaking furnace, costing $8,000, were imported from Pittsburgh, Pennsylvania. The sources of raw materials were as follows: sand, Berwick, Massachusetts; soda, England; manganese and arsenic, United States; lime, local. Coal, the energy component, came from the nearby Acadia Coal Mines.

The company obtained a Canadian charter and the works came on stream in September, under the management of William Godkin Beach. Beach started off with 15 "shops" making lamp chimneys and one making lantern globes. These were the bread and butter items of this type of operation. A "shop" comprised two men and a boy. One shop could produce 600 chimneys per day.

It soon became evident that they were going to specialize in tableware, probably to emulate the highly successful Burlington Glass operation in Hamilton. During the period of Nova Scotia Glass's independence (1881-1890), the value of manufactured ware on hand ranged from $10,000 to $30,000. By 1884, $3,000 had been spent on new equipment and the 17 new workers from Ohio brought the work force up to one hundred men and boys, with a weekly payroll of $1,600.

The following comments have been extracted from a write-up on The Nova Scotia Glass Company Limited in the *Morning Chronicle*, January 31, 1885:

GLASS MAKING

A Look Through the Factory at New Glasgow

"Our sales during the year past were from $90,000 to $100,000,00," said the manager W.G. Beach of the Nova Scotia glass factory at New Glasgow the other day to a Chronicle reporter. "We have difficulties to contend with, which we will not outgrow till the country gets larger. If we had more capital we might do better. But I suppose we must creep before we can walk."

"Are you working full time now?" asked the reporter.

"We haven't quite as many men making tableware as we would like. We're just manufacturing at present in all lines to meet the demand. Our busy season is about all over now till along in the spring. Almost all our employees are on piece-work."

"What particular line are you doing most in?"

"Lamp chimneys is what we started on and make a specialty of and we claim that our chimneys are ahead of anything else on the continent. We commenced making cruet bottles about a month ago . . ."

"How many hands do you employ?"

"We have 130 — men and boys — on the payroll at present."

"There any truth in the rumor that the shares of the company are being gradually concentrated in the hands of a few?"

"Nothing that I know of. There were only twenty shares changed hands since this time last year."

"Where do you sell most of your goods?"

"Our principal shipments are to Quebec, Montreal and Toronto. We send our manufactures right into Hamilton, where they sell in competition with the glass made there. The trade of the Maritime Provinces is comparatively small. We haven't enough population down here."

"How many other glass factories are there in the Dominion?"

"The principal one is in Hamilton. The others — one or two — are small concerns. There is one in Montreal, whose principal business is fruit jars and bottles. We don't do anything in those yet. Would you like to take a look through the factory?

"These men are cutting [designs in] pressed ware. The articles come up to them plain and they ornament them with those fancy designs and lines by holding them against these revolving stones which cut the lines into them gradually by using sand and oil on the stones. The stone is called 'Cragleith,' as it comes from a quarry of that name in Scotland. It is a very hard stone, yet not too close in grain — not like flint or that. Most all the cutting is done by piece-work; we find it more satisfactory. Our cutters are mostly Bohemians. We got some of them out on purpose, and they liked it so well that they sent for some of their friends, who came out on their own responsibility, and we found work for most of them. They are very steady, industrious fellows as a rule. Here are some butter dishes and fine glassware being ornamented. This (going to another part of the floor) is our latest design in an ornamental crimp for chimney tops. The old Canadian style of crimp-top chimneys had only ten crimps. Last season's had twenty and this style has forty — quite fine, you see, but I think ours is prettier than the American. Here is one of each; compare them!"

"What makes that difference in the ring of the glass?" asked the reporter.

"The American is lead glass, rather a more mellow ring than ours, which you notice is sharp. Ours is lime glass.

"This is our moulding [mould] shop. We make all our own mouldings and need to keep such a quantity that that is where the principal expense is. These are for tumblers, of which we make twenty-one different styles. Here they are pressing goblets. You see he pours a quantity of the molten glass into the mould, the stamp comes down and presses it into shape. In a second it is hard enough to retain its form and is lifted from the mould and set for half a minute before these cold air pipes, when a boy carries it over to the other furnace to be purified. The glass is a little thick and smoky — that is all. Placing it in the furnace a moment to heat it is again taken out and polished over simply with a wooden stick which makes it quite clear. Then it is taken off by the boys to the annealing furnace, where all the other new ware is placed. The annealing furnace is hot only at one end, and being placed on pans the goods are shoved through which tempers them, and are taken out cold at the other end and sent to the sorting and packing rooms.

"Here they are making pepper and vinegar cruets. A workman takes a small quantity of molten glass on the end of his blow-pipe and, after getting a little air into it by skillfully twisting it around while blowing through it, places it in the mould which the operator immediately closes. The blower blows the mould full of the glass and knocks off the top. The pipe is then passed over to a boy to be cleansed of the cooling glass remaining on the end of it, and the cruet is taken from the mould to be polished and the mouth finished to fit the stopper, after which it is sent up to the cutters for ornamentation. This is the only place in the Dominion for this line of work."

"Does it take much wind to blow the articles into the moulds?"

"No, it's more knack than anything else — like playing a wind instrument. An inexperienced person could not do it properly. It's something like blowing soap bubbles, you see. Of course for heavy work sometimes it takes powerful lungs.

"At this furnace they are making chimneys. They simply blow them out, mould them by rolling on a board, open the end and size that with a compass-like tool and knock off the other end, after which it is sent to a further furnace to be heated and crimped. The chimneys have to be all the same size, and sometimes the men miss it. These men are all Bohemians.

75

"The furnaces are of different sizes — this for instance, is what we call a 13 pot one, because it accommodates 13 pots of glass. The pots are large and made of clay and remain in the furnace all the time, the molten glass being gradually ladled out of them till empty. We just put the raw materials in the pot, with the refuse glass [cullet] to be used over. Each pot has a capacity of about 1½ tons, but we usually put in only about 2000 lbs. A potful takes about 24 hours to melt ready to work up again. We use two kinds of glass — one for pressed ware and the other for lamp-chimneys, and the result is we make a very much better chimney than ever. The raw material we use we import largely from England.

"The preparing room here is solely devoted to the mixing of the [batch] materials. Our sand is in various qualities. This fine white stuff comes from Boston and would pass for sugar to look at it. It is used for pressed ware. This browner quality, coarser, comes from Belgium, imported direct, and is used for chimneys. It requires less flux to melt it, which is quite a consideration in making glass. The nearer the material is to the pure silica and the less chemicals it requires, the better glass is the result. The soda we use is of the highest test — what is known as 58 degrees, and gives the best satisfaction. These men are constantly employed sifting and mixing the materials in the required proportions. The glass sand found in America comes from Massachusetts and south of Pittsburgh, Pennsylvania. In making chimneys the colour of the glass is not so much an object so that [as long as] it is clear and free from cords and blemishes, but in pressed ware colour is the prime object, and consequently we couldn't make decent pressed ware from the same quality of sand we use for chimneys."

"That is where you draw the colour line in glass making," said the reporter.

"Yes; and the colour line in this case is very rigid."

"We are gradually employing more native talent and getting the boys acquainted with the business. When we first started we had a number of American operatives, but they were almost, without exception, dissolute and great spendthrifts; while they would make $20 to $24 per week, before the week was half done their money would be all gone. The foreigners here save money, and I believe will make good citizens.

"From the annealing department the goods go to the washing and packing rooms where they are all examined, picked over and sorted. The lamps, of which you see we make quite a variety, are also finished with collars, etc., ready for use.

"Here in the chimney room we have women wrapping and packing. Our specialties in chimneys are each separately wrapped in tissue paper and labelled with our trade mark. Our two principal specialties outside of the ordinary crimps are the 'Salamander,' with the straight sides, and the 'Quaker flint,' with the plain curved top, which latter are taking quite a trade. We have lately had a special line in chimneys for electric burner lamps. We also make lantern globes of various styles, locomotive head-light chimneys — for which we have had large orders from the Grand Trunk, and make in especial designs for the I.C.R. [Inter-Colonial Railway]. There is scarcely a carload of chimneys outside of the ordinary crimp sold in the Maritime Provinces because the merchants don't take the trouble to keep and won't introduce them. A steam elevator carries the goods from the sorting and packing rooms upstairs to the store rooms. You see we have particular facilities for shipping, with railway tracks each side of the factory and water communication within a stone's throw."

"What do you do with your 'seconds'?" [second quality]

"Ship them almost solely to Quebec City and Montreal, where they sell as readily as 'firsts'. But there is really not so much difference as some people imagine.

Here, for instance, is a 'second' simply because the top of it is slightly crooked, and here is another because there happens to be a cord or lump on the side."

"We would have had that factory built in Pictou town if we had had a railway communication," said a prominent Pictonian to the reporter. "When Mr. Beach, of Hamilton, the promoter of the enterprise, came down here prospecting for a suitable place for a factory, he was met on the train by one of our townsmen and brought here. His chief object was to get a site where cheap coal could be produced as that is the essential for the cheap manufacture of glass. Up in Hamilton they cannot get coal sufficiently cheap to spend much of it on their annealing department and their glass is consequently inferior. Here they get all the coal they want — black from the mines — for fifty cents a ton. Mr. Beach was very much pleased with Pictou and our superior shipping facilities etc., but as New Glasgow has the advantage of us in railway facilities and the people took hold of the project and put their capital in it, we were left. That was the chief start of New Glasgow."

In 1886 the factory turned out a new, beautifully designed set of diamond flint crystal ware. In order to accommodate the increasing production of new tableware patterns that were being created, it was necessary to curtail chimney production.

At the end of December 1889 the company paid a seven-percent dividend and held plant material and stock worth $89,891.28, with a capitalization of $50,000. Despite its apparent prosperity, high freight rates to the markets in Western Canada and increased taxation finally took their toll. In March 1890 the company disposed of its assets to the incorporated Diamond Glass Company (Limited), a conglomerate based in Montreal. Mr. Beach, company manager, was also moved to Montreal, where he worked under superintendent Herdt.

It would appear that Diamond Glass in Montreal (The Glass Combine) worked hard at the elimination of competition. The *Eastern Chronicle*, May 24, 1884, reported an interesting discussion which had taken place in Parliament a few days earlier, using the following headlines:

HOW THE GLASS COMBINE MANAGED TO CLOSE DOWN THE NOVA SCOTIA GLASS FACTORY AT TRENTON, TO KEEP UP PRICES:

The Iniquitous Effects of Protection Shown up in Parliament by Mr. Fraser (Member of Parliament for Guysborough County) and Others.

The article then went on to tell of the changes to be made in taxation on glass and listed items which would be subject to tax:

Glass carboys, and demijohns, empty or filled bottles and decanters, flasks and phials, glass jars and glass balls, and cut, pressed or molded glass tableware, 30 per cent advalorem. The result of this change is equivalent all round to about 8 per cent (increase in price). Insulators of all kinds and lamps, including arc and incandescent; lamp chimneys, sidelights, headlights, lamps, gaslight and electric light shades and globes.

Nova Scotia Glass was levelled by a tragic fire on August 25, 1899.

Due to the fact that there were three separate glass operations on the Trenton site, and that the land has been worked over since their demise, it is difficult to accurately attribute glass shards to specific companies. As a general guide, however, the majority of the tableware and lamp shards must have been made by Nova Scotia Glass, whereas the bottle and chimney shards, unless otherwise identified, could have been made at Humphreys' or Lamont Glass.

Nova Scotia Glass was dissolved in November 1924.

LAMONT GLASS COMPANY
Trenton, Nova Scotia (1890-1897)

Donald Lamont may not be well known to Canadian glass researchers and historians, but as his story unfolds in this history of the Canadian glass industry, it will be seen that he was one of the most important and probably the most travelled glassworker in Canada. During his career, from 1883 to the late 1930s, he held managerial positions in seven different glass companies.[2]

In 1883, along with his brother David and ten other glassworkers, he was brought out from Birmingham, England, by Nova Scotia Glass, where he served two stints as a glassblower — 1883 to 1886 and 1888 to 1890. The urge to start his own works was strong enough for him to set up an experimental shop with his brothers, David and Henry, on a small farm about two miles below Trenton, in a section known as Little Egypt or Egypt Road. Their original objective was to specialize in coloured glassware, but their product mix was eventually dictated by market demand. Apparently satisfied with their pilot operation, Donald and David purchased a lot adjoining Nova Scotia Glass and set up a small operation, which they named the Lamont Glass Company.

McAlpine's Nova Scotia Directory ran an advertisement from 1890 to 1897 which read:

David Lamont	Henry Lamont	Donald Lamont
	LAMONT GLASS WORKS	
	– Manufacturers of –	
	A general Line of Blown and Cut Glassware	
	Green and Flint Bottles of all Kinds	
	Cut Door Lights a Specialty	
	Trenton, New Glasgow, N.S.	

Despite the advertising, their best product was lamp chimneys for railways and lighthouses. In fact, within a year, their business had increased sufficiently that they enlarged their furnace to four times its original capacity and expected to replace Nova Scotia Glass as the leading glass company. This ambition was realized by 1893, and for the next two years, shipments of glass in barrels were maintained at a high level. Their production now included blown and cut glassware, green and flint bottles of all kinds, battery and fruit jars, insulators, gas and electric globes, and lamp shades in all styles — plain, coloured and decorated. Included in their work force were the three Lamont brothers and William F. MacDonald, responsible for making up the batches of raw materials. MacDonald had served in the same capacity with Nova Scotia Glass in the 80s.

During this period, the trend towards using private moulds was on the rise. Normally, customers would order a plain unembellished bottle for their particular need, be it whiskey; soda water or something for the drug trade. The first improvement on this was a bottle whose mould could accept a plate on which was cut the name of the customer and any other useful information. This was most common in druggists' ware, using a flat-sided bottle known as a "panel" bottle. This principle would later be adapted to milk bottles and other types of ware common to many customers in the same trade. The next phase was the availability of private moulds, in which case a customer would determine the shape of the bottle — the embossing (lettering and/or design) would appear thereon and the customer would, of course, enjoy its exclusive use. This was really considered to be an advertising gimmick.

As in the case of Nova Scotia Glass, Big Brother (Diamond Glass) had had its overpowering effect on the Lamont operation as well. This, coupled with high freight rates to the marketing centres of Quebec and Ontario, led to the takeover of Lamont Glass by Diamond Glass. According to Gerald Stevens, ". . . The Lamont Factory appears to have done well until, on April 1st, 1898, they leased their works to the Diamond Glass Company."[3] On the other hand, the late George MacLaren stated, ". . . The Lamont brothers struggled on for a few years until absorbed by The Diamond Glass Company of Montreal."[4] Regardless of whether Diamond Glass leased the works or took it over, the Lamont brothers were retained to operate it.

In 1899, when fire struck Nova Scotia Glass, one of its warehouses, which contained the accumulated stock of the Lamont brothers, was also destroyed, thus bringing to an end the second of the three operations in the Trenton area. The third one was the independent Humphreys' Glass Company, which moved its operations to Moncton, New Brunswick, in 1917. The Lamonts' plant site was sold to Bailey-Underwood, manufacturers of farm machinery, with the stipulation "that it was not to be used for a glassworks."[5] The sale price was $1,150. Donald Lamont's story continues in Montreal, where he worked for Diamond Glass's operation (the former North American Glass Company).

Humphreys Glass Company Ltd., 1890.
From "*Nova Scotia Glass*" by George MacLaren courtesy Nova Scotia Museum.

HUMPHREYS' GLASS COMPANY
Trenton, Nova Scotia (1890-1917)

HUMPHREYS' GLASS, LIMITED
Moncton, New Brunswick (1917-1920)

The third glassworks to be operated in Trenton was Humphreys' Glass Company, which was formed by John (Jock) Humphreys, assisted by four of his brothers: Edward, Edgar, Benjamin and Ephraim. It was a highly successful independent operation throughout its 30 years. Its principal product was bottles, but it also made some industrial ware, including lamps and chimneys.

The promoter of the partnership was Jock, who had previously gone to Pittsburgh to learn the trade of glassblowing. On his return, he started an experimental shop in the back yard of their home on Main Street. Each of the brothers brought their own skills to the operation: Edward, glassblowing; Edgar, glass finishing; Benjamin, maintenance; and Ephraim, office management. Apparently satisfied with their ability to make glass on a small scale, they built modern works near The Nova Scotia Glass Company Limited operation.

The first works was erected in 1890 in Trenton. At the height of production, there were six bottle shops, with two working a night shift, and six chimney shops, with three working a night shift. At this time, Humphreys' employed about 75 people.

The following description by Joseph H. MacGillivray provides a clear picture of how lamp chimneys were made:

> . . . Making lamp chimneys was an entirely different kind of work. Lamp chimneys were free blown — no mould was used. The glassblower did not blow hard. It was more like blowing a soap bubble. A larger, longer blowing iron was used. It was about the size of broom handle with a knob on the end. When the glassblower finished blowing, he had on the end of his blowing iron what looked like a large electric light bulb with a little knob on the bottom. He then sat in a finisher's chair to complete the job with a hand tool. Both the top and bottom of a lamp chimney were re-heated to finish. The glass was blown and hardened quickly, so it had to be re-heated to form the base, and again on the top for the crimp. Blowing lamp chimneys and blowing bottles were two entirely different trades. There was as much difference as there is between bricklaying and carpenter work in the building trades . . .
>
> . . . A lamp chimney shop was made up of three people. A gatherer, who took a gather of glass out of the furnace, walked to a marver where he rolled and shaped the glass, blew one puff of air into it and passed it to the glassblower to complete, except for the crimp on the top. When the glassblower separated the lamp chimney from the blowing iron, it was picked up by the crimper, the neck re-heated, and pressed into the crimping machine, which operated and looked like a machineshop lathe . . .[6]

Until the advent of Humphreys' and the Lamont Glass Company in 1890, all bottles used in the area had been imported from such American firms as Whitall & Tatum Co., New York; Burgess & Sons, Philadelphia; Whitney Foster & Co., Boston. In the last quarter of the nineteenth century, whiskey and rum were imported in barrels and then bottled. Soft drinks were beginning to be popular, with such names as Bear River Cherries, Peach Cream Nectar, Blood Orange and Sarsaparilla Blood Purifier. The bottlers included:

Felix J. Quinn, Halifax
Whalen & Ferguson, Halifax
William Donovan, Halifax
Francis Drake, New Glasgow
Wilson & Sullivan, Halifax
Bigelow & Hood, Truro and Halifax
Amherst Mineral Water Company

Crystal Spring Ltd., Truro
Givin's, Moncton, N.B.
Atlantic Mineral Water Company, Halifax
Havelock Mineral Spring Co., Ltd., N.B.
Standard Soda Water Company, Yarmouth
Enterprise Bottling Company, Fredericton, N.B.
Cumberland Beverage Co., Springhill, N.S.[7]

The majority of the bottles used by these customers had a patent stopper or cap closure and used the system of having a private metal plate made with their company name and trademark imprinted on it. When the manufacturer inserted it in the mould, the plate produced an embossed bottle (a bottle with raised lettering and/or a design). Bottle production peaked at 1,200 to 1,500 a day. From MacGillivray's "Recollections":

> When a boy started to work in a glass factory, he usually started as a carry-over boy, as I did. He carried the finished, still-hot bottles to the lear on a long-handled paddle, carrying four pop bottles, fewer larger bottles and more smaller ones at a trip. The next higher-up position was snap-up boy and then to mould boy. It took me about two years to reach the mould boy position. It was next to the glassblower position and was desirable because a mould boy could sit on a stool at his work.
>
> The work period in the glass factory was nine hours starting at 7 A.M. with a 15 minute recess at 9:30, an hour for lunch at noon, another recess at 3 o'clock and the shift ended at 5 P.M. In those days most factory employees worked a 10-hour day, from 7 A.M. to 6 P.M., so glassblowing was considered a choice type of trade with income above the factory or steel plant worker. A glassblower could own a

George McLaren left,
John MacGillivray right.
Photograph by Wamboldt-Waterfield Photography,
Halifax, Nova Scotia.

nice 8- or 10-room house, drive a high-stepping horse and buggy and a high-back sleigh in winter with a real buffalo robe, silver-plated jingle bells and fancy do-dads on his horse's harness. Yes sir! He was right up there with the professional people.

During lunch hour and recess, the boys would get an old blowing iron and practice working with the glass. Their first big effort would be to get a gather of glass on the blowing iron and get it out of the pot to the marver before it would drop off the blowing iron onto the floor. To keep the glass from dropping to the floor, the glassblower had to keep the blowing iron and glass in continuous motion. After a time, the boy would learn to control the hot glass so that he could blow a sort of bubble. The first ones would not be perfectly round and might burst like a soap bubble. After a time, however, he would learn to make a perfectly round ball that he could take home. It was a big event in the life of a boy when he could take home and show his parents a ball or globe that he had made himself. Later as he progressed towards becoming a glassblower, he would learn to make glass chain, canes and other whimseys.

It usually took four years or more to learn the glassblowing trade, but I made it in about three and a half years. My brother and I were the last ones to learn the trade at Humphreys. He died over 20 years ago, and I believe I am the last one of the Humphrey glassblowers living now [1971]. All the others were much older and most of them would be over 100 if living.

Humphreys made a very large number of Minard's linament bottles. They had two moulds and a shop of two glassblowers, who worked almost continually on them.

Many bottles made for these companies have been found, but few of them can be authenticated to Humphreys' or Lamont. However, as far as Humphreys' is concerned:

... among their largest customers were the Minard's Linament Company, who took 300,000 bottles at a time; L. H. Packard's Shoe Dressing; Harvard Bottling Company, Fraser Thornton & Company, Cookhire, Quebec, which received carload lots; and James Roue, as well as the leading liquor dealers of Halifax and Saint John, and all the ginger all and beverage companies . . . [8]

The main batch materials came from the following locations: soda ash, manganese, karolyte and powdered blue from England, sand from the U.S.A., and local limestone. Energy was provided by a gas producer, which converted slack coal into gas. The cast iron moulds were machined from cast iron blanks.

In 1902 a fire destroyed the works, but a new one was soon erected at the end of Glass Street. From MacGillivray's "Recollections":

... The new plant was about 400 feet long by about 50 feet wide, and was a steel frame plant with corrugated sheet iron on the sides. The glass furnace was in the centre of the plant, with the gas producers, three in line, in the north end. Gas was produced from slack coal, and was piped into the furnace through vents near the top. The glass furnace holding about 75 tons of glass near the west wall of the plant, with the front and glass pots facing south and curving around to the east side where the lamp chimney shops were located. The bottle shops were in the south end of the plant. Leading off in an eastern angle from the south end of the main plant. There were three smaller wooden buildings all joined together for the lear (lehr) sorting room, packing room, mould room and office ... Later, about 1912, a new concrete building was built for a machine shop and mould room to the east and near the centre of the main plant. At this time Ephraim Humphreys was General Manager and Paymaster. He did the office work with one clerk as assistant. Ben Sr., the oldest of the Humphreys brothers, was plant Manager, assisted by his son Forrest. Edgar was a bottle finisher and his son Ben Jr. was a bottle blower. John Humphreys (Jock) was an expert bottle blower and could make any size bottle or jar.

The company's operations went through three phases. At the outset, in 1890, it comprised a partnership of the five Humphreys brothers. In 1914 *MacAlpine's Directory of Nova Scotia* reported that there were 44 men on the payroll, including the following officers, directors and managers:

president	—	J.M. (Jock) Humphreys
director	—	Edgar T. Humphreys
director	—	Edward C. Humphreys
cashier acct.	—	William D. McKay
stenographer	—	Robert G. Humphreys
general manager	—	Ephraim M. Humphreys
foreman	—	Benjamin Humphreys

Of the 37 workers, 12 were glassblowers.

The fact that the directory recorded that there was a president and two directors would suggest that the partnership had been converted into an incorporated company by 1914. This appears to have been phase two. The following quote supports this assumption:

In a letter received from Mr. R.W. Hewson, Q.C., of Moncton [New Brunswick] the story [of Humphreys' Glass Company] continues. The three Humphrey [sic] brothers came to Moncton in 1915 and incorporated their company and collected considerable capital from businessmen in this city [Moncton].[9]

In 1917 the Humphreys decided to move their operations to Moncton, New Brunswick, to take advantage of the more fuel-efficient natural gas. Hence, the third and final phase began. Two newspaper reports tell the story.

From the *Eastern Chronicle*, June 29, 1917:

TRENTON LOSES INDUSTRY

It would appear that the Town of Trenton is likely to lose the glass manufacturing industry carried on there by Messrs. Humphreys. The plant is to be moved to Moncton. Several reasons are ascribed for the change, but the chief is the cheap-

ness of natural gas for fuel. Almost since Trenton first appeared on the map, the Humphreys family have been identified with and have formed a respectable number in the population. Their removal to Moncton will be learned with much regret, not at the loss the County will sustain from an industrial point of view, but the loss in citizenship caused by the several brothers and their families (moving) to the New Brunswick railway center. We can only wish that their future operations will be crowned with success and that the people of the New Brunswick City will be good to them.

The *New Glasgow News*, October 15, 1917, further reported:

Mr. E.H. Humphreys returned home from Moncton on Saturday last. Tenders for the new glass factory at Moncton are called for, and early in November the new building will be completed. The building will be 45' x 90'. The personnel of the new Humphreys Glass Company recently formed is as follows: President, J.M. Humphreys; Vice-President, L.H. Humphreys; Secretary-Treasurer, E.H. Humphreys. Mr. Humphreys says that Moncton is a busy place just now. There are upwards of 200 new houses in the course of erection.

HUMPHREYS' GLASS, LIMITED (1917-1920)
Moncton, New Brunswick

In actual fact, Humphreys' Glass Company was not incorporated until 1917 under the name of Humphreys' Glass, Limited, with its chief place of business in the City of Moncton. There is obviously a conflict of information. In my opinion, it is conceivable that the Humphreys did not, on the spur of the moment, move their operation to Moncton in 1917 just because natural gas was available. It is quite possible that, as in the case of most expanding companies, public financing was necessary. If, at the same time (1914), it can be established that natural gas was available in Moncton, is it not reasonable to assume that they would seek outside financing in the area in which the new works was to operate? In the same vein, is it not possible that the Humphreys set up a "paper" company with the names of the directors and officers in a prospectus, as is often done to attract public financing?

In 1919 gas rates for commercial users were increased by about 50 percent, thus making the use of gas prohibitive. By 1920 Humphreys' Glass, Limited had closed down for good.

According to George MacLaren, it was assumed that lamp chimneys and lantern globes formed most of the stock. The elimination of bottles from the product mix was caused by the availability of mass-produced bottles from semi-automatic and automatic bottle-forming machines at Diamond Flint Glass Company Limited in 1907 and its successor, Dominion Glass Company, Limited, in 1913.

A number of "digs" took place in the Trenton area, details of which will be covered in Chapter 9.

THE MONTREAL BOTTLE AND GLASS COMPANY
Montreal, Quebec (1887)

This company was incorporated ". . . for the manufacture and sale of glass bottles and other glassware in all its branches . . ." No other action appears to have been taken.

THE DIAMOND GLASS COMPANY, (LIMITED)
Montreal, Quebec (1890-1902)

In 1878 the Yuile brothers, William and David, took over the bankrupt St. Johns Glass Company, in St. Johns, Quebec, for monies owed them. A year later, they formed The Excelsior Glass Company and moved it to Montreal in 1880. In 1883 they reorganized the company under the name The North American Glass Company. In 1890, in a second reorganization, they changed the name to The Diamond Glass Company (Limited). This would be the first of three successive companies (excluding flat glass operations) that would play the leading role in the Canadian glass industry for the next one hundred years, as they carried out a continuing program of taking over independent operations which offered a threat of competition. The successors were Diamond Flint Glass Company Limited (1903-1913) and Dominion Glass Company, Limited (from 1913).

It should be noted that the company produced no glass in its own name, with the exception of a monogrammed fruit jar. It really acted as a controlling operation for North American Glass, the company it succeeded, and the other companies it acquired during its period of operations.

The Yuile brothers continued to control the business and were joined by David Williamson; Ralph King, a distant cousin of the Yuile brothers; and John Watt, a brother-in-law of Ralph King. They operated out of the same offices as their predecessor. Starting with North American Glass and following through the seven other companies they acquired, each of these companies, on takeover, would retain its name but would be considered a subsidiary or works of Diamond Glass.

During its lifetime, Diamond Glass took over:

The North American Glass Company, Montreal, Quebec 1890-1902
Nova Scotia Glass Company, (New Glasgow) Trenton, Nova Scotia 1890-1890
Hamilton Glass Company, Hamilton, Ontario 1891-1898
*Burlington Glass Company, Hamilton, Ontario 1891-1892
Foster Glass Works, Port Colborne, Ontario (leased) 1896-1899
Lamont Glass Company, New Glasgow, Nova Scotia 1897-1899
The Dominion Glass Company (Limited), Montreal, Quebec 1897-1898
The Toronto Glass Company (Limited), Toronto, Ontario 1899-1902

*subsidiary of Hamilton Glass Company.

Diamond Glass was originally incorporated under federal charter on June 27, 1890, but for some unknown reason the charter was cancelled on June 30 and a new charter was issued on August 6. North American Glass was used as the "flagship" of Diamond Glass's fleet of operating companies. With the acquisition of additional land on the west side of the original site and fronting on Delorimier Avenue, the Montreal operation took off. Over the next 35 years this plant would be the training ground for future management throughout the succeeding companies. Such names as James W. King, Thomas Bassett and Eddie Davies will appear in the story of Dominion Glass Company, Limited.

In the same year that Diamond Glass took over North American Glass (1890), Diamond Glass bought out The Nova Scotia Glass Company Limited, in Trenton, Nova Scotia, and continued to operate it with an infusion of new moulds for tableware production until 1892.

In 1891 Diamond Glass, with its rapidly expanding operations, found that some refinancing would be necessary. Supplementary letters patent were issued to increase the capital from $10,000 to $500,000. That same year, Diamond acquired Hamilton Glass and its subsidiary, Burlington Glass, which had been operating since 1864 and 1875, respectively. Hamilton Glass had been primarily a bottlemaking operation, with some industrial ware. Burlington Glass had started off as a competing "bottle shop," but had started in 1885 to develop as a leading tableware producer. They were closed in 1898 and 1892, respectively.

With the takeover of Hamilton Glass in 1891, that operation must have thrived, because in 1896, in seeking increased capacity in that area, Diamond Glass leased Foster Glass Works, a bottle operation in Port Colborne, Ontario, for three years, presumably under the direction of its Hamilton Glass subsidiary, from 1896 to its shutdown in 1898. A year later, Diamond went after the very successful Lamont Glass, in Trenton, Nova Scotia. The takeover took place in 1897, with the Lamonts continuing to operate the plant. William Yuile was appointed president.

In the meantime, Diamond Glass had competition literally on its doorstep. The Dominion Glass Company (Limited), which had reorganized the original Dominion Glass Company in 1896, operated a few blocks east of Diamond Glass's operations in Montreal. This competition was eliminated by a formal takeover of the assets and liabilities of Dominion Glass on November 16, 1897, retroactive to the standing of the books at July 1, 1897.

With the closing of the Hamilton Works of Diamond Glass in 1898, Diamond had no acknowledged operations in Ontario, although it has been assumed that by that time they controlled Toronto Glass. In my opinion, Diamond Glass had been party to the splinter group that had spawned Toronto Glass out of the Hamilton Glass works to test the waters. Apparently, with the successful operation in Toronto, they rectified the situation by taking over Toronto Glass in 1899. J.C. Malcolmson retired as manager in Toronto and was replaced by John Watt. In 1903 the plant would become the Toronto Works of Diamond Flint Glass.

In the decade of the nineties, a mechanical revolution was taking place in the glass industry. Both in England and the United States, numerous inventions were being introduced with the broad intention of providing mechanical means of both gathering the gobs of glass and blowing the bottles.[10] This revolution apparently convinced Diamond Glass that it would be necessary to reorganize the company in order to compete profitably in this new method of production. The conversion involved George A. Grier, a lumber merchant from Montreal and a shareholder of Diamond Glass, who, on September 23, 1902:

> . . . offered to purchase from the said Diamond Glass Company (Limited) the whole of the assets and business of the said Company for the price or sum of one million one hundred and seventeen thousand nine hundred and fifty dollars payable to wit, six hundred thousand in six per cent first mortgage coupon bonds to be the total issue of first mortgage bonds on the property of the Company to be formed (Diamond Flint Glass) and five hundred and seventeen thousand nine hundred and fifty dollars in cash . . .[11]

It appears obvious that the whole reorganization had been prearranged, because members of the Grier family were active in the new company (Diamond Flint Glass). The directors of Diamond Glass approved the deal on December 23, 1902, and recommended it to the shareholders on January 14, 1903. With their approval, the deal was consummated on March 24, 1903, and involved the entire assets of Diamond Glass, which comprised the nonoperating Hamilton Glass, its burned-out subsidiary, Burlington Glass, and the Toronto Glass Works.

The company was dissolved in November 1924.

THE TORONTO GLASS COMPANY (LIMITED)
Toronto, Ontario (1893-1899)

Toronto's first glass operation was started by four glassworkers from the Burlington Glass Works in Hamilton: William Barrett Griner, glassblower; William Keegan, glass melter; Herbert Henry Malcolmson, mould maker; and John Clarke Malcolmson, superintendent. Ontario letters patent were issued on September 15, 1893, and the first directors were J.C. Malcolmson, W.B. Griner and George Morris, an interested Hamilton businessman. The site was on the south side of Blair St. (now Sudbury), at the corner of Abell (now Dovercourt Road).

Operations were started in 1894 and were built around a single day-and-night tank, known as the Green House (for bottle production). The tank was coal-fired and the finished ware was annealed in wood-fired ovens. Starting in the early stages, some pressed ware was made.

The Annual Return for December 31, 1895, provides some interesting information:

Directors:	David Williamson, Montreal	
	John Watt, Hamilton	
	Ralph King, Hamilton	
Shareholders:	Ralph King, in trust	$100
	John Watt, in trust	10,600
	David Williamson, in trust	100
	David Yuile	100
	William Yuile	10,700

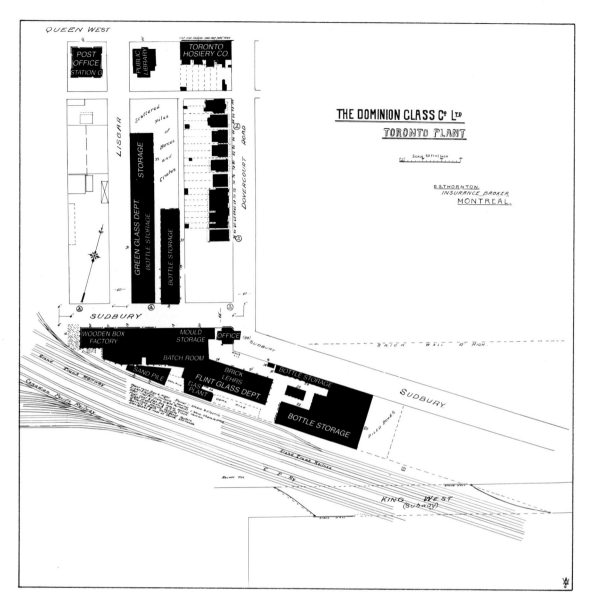

Insurance plan of the Toronto plant of Dominion Glass Company Limited.

Directors David Williamson and John Watt were also directors of Diamond Glass, of which Hamilton Glass was a subsidiary, and Ralph King was manager at Burlington Glass, also controlled by Diamond Glass. The five shareholders were all part of the management of Diamond Glass. It can only be concluded that if Diamond Glass didn't sponsor the splinter group that started Toronto Glass, they had certainly established control within a year of its first operations.

During the period 1897-1898, another furnace, this time a flint tank (for nonbottle ware) was set up in the east half of the property. The gas for firing the furnace was produced on the premises from coal. Continuous belt lehrs with a mechanical intermittent drive were used to anneal the finished ware. Production included fruit jars, round pickle bottles, various styles of flasks, electric oil bottles, panels and a great variety of patent medicine bottles. Much of this prescription ware was made by hand. They used a standard plate mould into which was inserted the nameplate for each individual customer. This was a very simple operation and here and elsewhere has produced thousands of similar bottles, each showing the wording from the customer's individual plate. Platemaking was a full-time job for a letter-cutter in the mould shop.

Griner was not only a well-qualified glassblower, but was an expert flameworker (lamp-worker) as well. He and several members of his family have been credited with turning out quantities of flamework.

The *Toronto Directory* for 1897 includes the following names of significant workers at Toronto Glass, together with entries from directories in the other locations in which they worked:

John Watt, president	(Hamilton, 1889)
John C. Malcolmson, gaffer	(Hamilton, 1889)
Wm. F. Chapman, clerk	
W.B. Griner, blower	(Hamilton, 1889)
Thomas Murphy, blower	(Hamilton, 1899)
Patrick Wickham, blower	(Hamilton, 1895, 1897, Montreal, 1899)

The last return on file is stamped by the Provincial Secretary's Department on March 27, 1899, indicating that shareholdings had not changed since the return of December 31, 1898. As on December 31, 1898, John Watt was president and Messrs. Williamson and Ralph King were still directors. Watt's address is shown as 610 King Street E., Hamilton; David Williamson's is c/o Diamond Glass Co., Montreal; and King's is c/o Toronto Glass Co., Toronto.

On October 17, 1899, by deed and bill of sale, The Toronto Glass Company (Limited) was acquired by The Diamond Glass Company (Limited) for a consideration of $19,423.31, and became the Toronto Works of Diamond Glass.

DOMINION GLASS

The name Dominion Glass has been the subject of some confusion among glass researchers. There is now acceptable evidence that the name Dominion Glass was used to identify four different but closely related glass operations. The first one was a partnership Dominion Glass Company, from about 1886 to 1894. This partnership was then incorporated as a company in the name of Dominion Glass Company, 1894-1896.

The same original group, with additional members, then bought out the former company and incorporated it under the name The Dominion Glass Company (Limited), 1896-1897, to provide a broader base for future expansion. This was achieved by increasing their capital from $20,000 to $490,000. A year later, they were taken over by The Diamond Glass Company (Limited) of Montreal.

The fourth operation involving the name Dominion Glass occurred in 1913, when The Diamond Flint Glass Company (Limited) was taken over by the newly formed Dominion Glass Company, Limited (1913-1976). This company is now Domglas Inc.

DOMINION GLASS COMPANY
Montreal, Quebec (c.1886-1894)

This company was established about 1886 by the Barsalou family, who enjoyed a controlling interest. Their principal occupation appears to have been as J. Barsalou and Company, soap merchants. The fact that both operations used potash may not have been coincidental.

For whatever reason, the company was incorporated under the same name on October 22, 1894. The first directors were Henry Hogan, hotel keeper; John Stirling, accountant; Dr. J. Gustave Laviolette, physician; Joseph Barsalou, auctioneer — all of Montreal — and Henry P. Schnelback, glass manufacturer, from Steubenville, Ohio. The officers were Joseph Barsalou, president; the Hon. Alphonse Desjardins, vice-president; and John Stirling, secretary-treasurer. John Stirling worked for the successor companies of Dominion Glass and retired in the position of treasurer with Dominion Glass Company, Limited in 1930.

From its inception, the factory was located on Lot 615, which was bounded by Dorion Street (formerly Shaw), the old Protestant Military Burial Ground (Lot 635, now called Le Parc des Veterans), Lafontaine Street, and de Montigny (now de Maisonneuve). The head office was located at the corner of Papineau Road and Lafontaine Street. Logan Street was homologated, but not put through at that time.

This was a bottle operation managed by Henry Schnelback. One of the glassblowers was Richard Witt, a career man who had been born in Schlesweig-Holstein, Germany, about 1857, and had come to Canada via the United States, then to the Burlington Glass Company in 1888. Five years later, he was blowing at Dominion Glass Company. While there he made, as a summer holiday exercise, a glass model of Montreal's famous Notre Dame Cathedral.

Dominion Glass Company must have been doing well, as they decided to reorganize it, apparently to broaden its operations. Dominion Glass Company was dissolved on December 17, 1977.

THE DOMINION GLASS COMPANY (LIMITED)
Montreal, Quebec (1896-1897)

The second reorganization of the Barsalou's glass operations took place on July 17, 1896, when by federal charter the company's name was changed from Dominion Glass Company to the above. Although the capital was reduced from $50,000 to $20,000, it was anticipated that the new company would be better able to generate additional capital when it was needed to expand operations.

The directors and officers were: Joseph Barsalou, director & president; Hon. Alphonse Desjardins, director & vice-president; Maurice Barsalou, managing director; Henry Hogan, director; Dr. J.G. Laviolette, director; H.P. Schnelback, superintendent of works; John Stirling, secretary-treasurer.

An agreement between Dominion Glass Company and The Dominion Glass Company (Limited) was ratified on October 29, and conveyed the assets from the former company to the new company for $129,000, payable in cash and shares in the new company; it also took over a balance of payment of $10,500 owing to Mr. Schnelback and renewed an agreement with George H. Snyder, traveller, to pay him $500 a year while employed by the company. The above arrangements became effective when the planned increase in capital was ratified. Supplementary letters patent were issued on December 22, 1896, authorizing 4,700 additional shares of $100 each, bringing the authorized capital to $490,000.

At the 1897 annual meeting, held in October, J.O. Gravel replaced the late Joseph Barsalou as a director and Hon. Alphonse Desjardins replaced him as president. Dr. Laviolette became vice-president and Maurice Barsalou, managing director.

Success had not only been sweet, but it also attracted the attention of The Diamond Glass Company (Limited) (1890-1902), the first of three conglomerates, which had already taken over a number of independent companies and who now set its sights on this company. On November 16, 1897, Diamond Glass took over Dominion Glass by distribution of 1,180 shares in the new company to the shareholders of the former company. In addition, Schnelback received 30 shares and George Snyder received five shares.

At a special general meeting on January 21, 1898, the board was reconstituted as follows: William Yuile, director and president; Maurice Barsalou, director and vice-president; Geo. H. Perley, director; A. Lumsden, director; D. Williamson, director. At the last special general meeting, George Rutherford and John Watt replaced Maurice Barsalou and A. Lumsden for the ensuing year. At the same time, it was agreed that the company had practically ceased to operate and that the directors should be instructed to appoint no paid officers, with the exception of the secretary-treasurer. No date has been found for the dissolution of the company.

THE ERIE GLASS COMPANY OF CANADA (LIMITED)
Port Colborne, Ontario (1892-1893)

Port Colborne owes its existence to the establishment of the Welland Canal, which provides a navigable link between Lake Ontario and Lake Erie. This canal, finished in 1829, extended from Lake Ontario only as far as Port Robinson, on the Welland River. From there, the boats followed the Welland River to Chippawa, and then, via the Niagara River, south to Lake

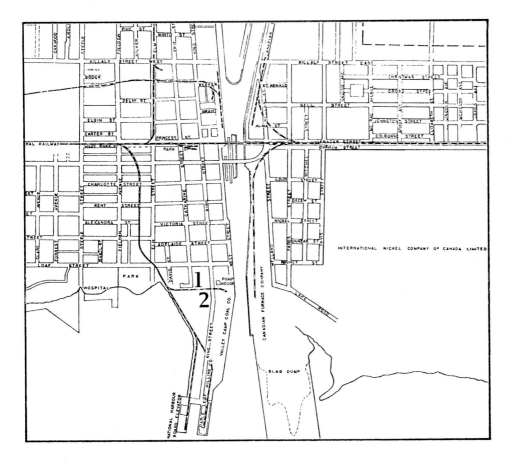

Erie. With increased traffic, it was decided to continue the canal right through to Lake Erie. A little village called Gravelly Bay (because of the amount of gravel on the beach) came into being at the southern terminus of the canal. And in 1834 William Merritt purchased the land around this village, had it surveyed into village lots, and named it Port Colborne, after the governor of Upper Canada, Sir John Colborne.

The selection of this area for a glass operation was obviously based on the discovery of the availability of natural gas. In 1891 the town council of Port Colborne, mesmerized to some degree by this bonanza, and counting on the excellent rail and water facilities for shipping, established a program to attract industry by offering free land, free fuel and a tax exemption for ten years in return for the establishment of an industry which would guarantee to employ not less than one hundred people.

The organization of a glass company started in July 1891 under the name Humberstone Glass Works Company, with a capital of $30,000. In its formative period, two names were considered for the company, the Lake Erie Glass Works Company of Port Colborne (Limited) and the Ontario Glass Company of Port Colborne. The factory was situated on a piece of government property just north of the Lakeview Mills, a grist mill operated by the Knoll brothers, Herman and Charles. The property was bounded by Mill Street, Welland Street, Huron Street, and the Welland Railway siding. The widening of the canal has erased all of these streets, with the exception of Welland Street. This places the factory on property now (1981) shared by the Dwor Company scrapyard and the Hardrock Paving Co. This site was confirmed by Arthur Knoll, son of Herman Knoll, and Murton Chambers, who has boyhood memories of the factory and who started his own glass career in the Foster Glass Works, which operated in Port Colborne from 1894-1900.

A delegation of Port Colborne citizens went to Pittsburgh, Pennsylvania, then the centre of American glass technology, to seek information about establishing factories in general and glass factories specifically. There was great enthusiasm when they reported back. Many of the villagers were willing to buy stock in such a company.

In November 1891 James Lydiatt of Toronto, subsequent manager of the glassworks, appeared on the scene. He was listed as operating a real estate and insurance business and had two sons, James Jr. and George. (It is my opinion that this was the same George Lydiatt who first appeared on the Canadian glass scene as a director of The Sydenham Glass Company of Wallaceburg (Limited) in 1910.

During his visit, Lydiatt found that the lime — which is extensively used in glass production — was suitable. The sand available in the area contained 75 percent silica, which was also satisfactory. Lydiatt was confident that the common black beer bottle could be manufactured here to advantage, although such bottles had not as yet been made in this country, owing to the low price at which other countries turned them out.

Lydiatt was very ambitious. Not satisfied with the already generous inducements, he requested a bonus of $10,000. Since, by law the village could not grant a bonus greater than ten percent of its annual taxation (at that time under $4,000), a compromise was reached by enacting a bonus bylaw on April 4, 1892 to raise the sum of $4,500 for the purpose of aiding the Erie Glass Company. It defined how the bonus should be paid and, in return, the company was required to be incorporated on or before October 1, 1892, (the company received a Canadian charter on September 26, 1892). It was also required, "within thirty days of October 1, 1892, to erect a suitable factory or building in said Village of Port Colborne, sufficient to operate one or more furnaces with capacity at least equal to that of one ten pot furnace . . . and on or before the said date the said factory shall be in actual operation . . . and shall employ not less than fifty men and boys . . . for the term of ten years, except during the months of June, July and August . . . and expend not less than $20,000 per annum in payment of wages . . ."[12]

What a challenge for Lydiatt and his fellow directors and officers: John M. Faircloth (president), co-owner of Faircloth Bros. Wallpaper & Decorating, Toronto; James Lydiatt (managing director), real estate & insurance agent, Toronto; J.E. Neville (secretary-treasurer), owned the city Drug Store, Deutsche Apotheke, Berlin (renamed Kitchener in 1916); Thomas F. White (director), partner with his father-in-law in Cronmiller & White Brewers on Welland St., south of the glass company plant site; Wm. David Burn (director), banker, Toronto.

June 21, 1892, was a banner day for the village. Excavations were started on the staked-out land and contracts were awarded for the carpentry and masonry work. The main building was to have stone and brick foundations. Dominion Day was chosen for the laying of the cornerstone.

During the week of July 24, James Lydiatt moved his family from Toronto and the completion of the factory roof was signalled by the raising of a Union Jack. Early in October, glassblowers began to arrive in town, including George Foster from Hamilton, who later started up his own Foster Glass Works (1894). A Mr. Clark arrived from Indiana to operate the furnace. The pots were lowered into position on October 10 and the gas regulator arrived on the 12th. The first glass was drawn on Thursday, October 13, thus satisfying the requirements of the bonus bylaw by being operational within 30 days of October 1, 1892.

A partial list of workers at the factory included: James E. Lydiatt, manager, Toronto, Ontario; Robert Hunter, under-manager, St. Helens, England; George H. Foster, foreman blower; Wm. Brenton, machinist, Hamilton, Ontario; Newell Bateman, blacksmith, New Jersey; John Carroll, furnace, New Jersey; Charles W. Foster, gatherer, Balmoral, Manitoba; together with 22 blowers and gatherers. Of these names, we have already mentioned George Foster as the subsequent founder of the Foster Glass Works in Port Colborne. The *History of Humberstone Township* states he was in partnership with two brothers, Douglas and William. This would seem to preclude the Charles W. Foster mentioned in the above list. The other name of particular interest is that of Wm. Brenton. Brenton was employed by the Burlington Glass Company and articles have been found with his name embossed on the base. This raises the interesting possibility that some of Erie's products might similarly carry his signature if he were employed as a mouldmaker.

A *Tribune* reporter made some remarks pertinent to the two English blowers, namely Howson and Purnell, who were having union difficulties. He said, "Two English blowers who came here to work in the Erie Glass Works are prevented from doing so by the laws of the American Glassblowers' Union, although they are willing to join the Association and it costs a

The Erie Glass Company of Canada. Second factory building, 1893.

snug sum too — $105.00. It seems pretty tough when an English mechanic is prevented from working in an English country by an American organization!" Another account, in the *Welland Tribune*, indicates that the union meetings were held weekly and well attended. The union problems affected another area, as well, as we read in the November 4, 1892, *Tribune*:

> The glassblowers juvenile brigade of helpers struck for higher wages on Monday and almost paralyzed business for a time. The few who returned to work were hooted at by the 'unionists' lads, and manager Lydiatt was compelled to appeal to the Magistrate and Chief of Police Greenwood for protection.

Finally an agreement was reached, the boys to get $2.50 a week, as before, but without any lost time. The work force had increased to above 75, but by December there was a need for more blowers. A group of glassblowers from Hamilton came to see the wonders of glass being made using natural gas and were most impressed. The year ended optimistically, with glassblowers coming and going as was their wont.

Early in the new year, 1893, unrest among the workers increased. Although blaming it on faulty construction and equipment, it was really felt that they were not happy with management. Then disaster struck on the evening of February 4, 1893, when the glassworks burned to the ground. The loss was estimated at $20,000, half of which was covered by insurance. The loss of $700 in weekly payroll was felt by the villagers.

At a directors' meeting, it was decided that the factory should be rebuilt as quickly as possible. In March the stockholders approved the rebuilding and authorized, if necessary, the issuance of additional stock to carry on the company successfully, with the stipulation, however, that a committee be appointed to look into the affairs and finances of the company and prepare a report. Hints of dissatisfaction with the management were still prevalent. By the end of March, the glassblowers were returning to town and the factory neared completion. The glass factory resumed operations on Monday, April 3. The weekly payroll was $900. Salaries for officers amounted to $21 per day. However, the works was still in serious trouble, as reported in the *Welland Telegraph* on June 9, 1893:

. . . The extent of the financial difficulties of the Erie Glass Company became public when the sheriff took possession on June 12/93 on behalf of Thomas F. White, a director and shareholder, who had backed the company's note for some $10,000.00 and paid it. A writ had been issued in this matter to recover the money earlier the previous month, but without result. At the end of the week, the sheriff gave up possession when a settlement was reached.

A letter from the Erie Glass Company's solicitor, J.E. Hansford, Toronto, appeared in the *Welland Telegraph* on July 7/93 demanding an apology for "false and defamatory" statements made in their reporting concerning the company. When asked by the editor to be more specific, another lengthy letter appeared the following week which branded as false all rumors of mismanagement at the factory. It stated there were no judgements against the company — all obligations were met as they fell due and future prospects were bright. The financial difficulties had all been caused by Mr. White's precipitate action in paying the said note, which they maintained had been renewable.

On July 28, 1893, in a public letter to the editor of the *Telegraph*, White replied to the above allegation. Since he owned $2,500 worth of stock, it would not be to his best interest to undermine the company. He had endorsed the note in question before his confidence in his co-directors had been destroyed and had only instituted suit after repeated failures on their part to carry out their promises. He had never agreed to sign a renewal of the note, as they had intimated. Letters from Dickinson & Suess and other contractors appeared in the same new column — all listing amounts of several hundreds of dollars owed them by the Erie Glass Company. Also reported was the first annual meeting of the Erie Glass Company in Toronto. The financial statement listed a loss of $5,126.97 on the past year's trading, plus a loss from the fire of $4,910.00 — or a total loss of capital, to date, of $10,036.97.

The factory was kept operating in a limited way during June, finishing orders for jars and lids, packing glassware and straightening up things in general. Most of the glassblowers had left the village and, when the factory closed at the end of June for the summer, it was destined never to reopen.

In August Mr. T. White and Dr. J.B. Neff offered for sale 55 shares in the Erie Glass Company at 50 cents on the dollar. Two weeks later it was reported there were no buyers. The factory did not open September 1st, the normal date to resume operations, and although there seemed to be hopes of beginning at a later date, more glassblowers left town. From the *Welland Tribune*, October 6, 1893:

> JUDICIAL SALE — The glass factory property of the Erie Glass Company is advertised for sale in today's *Tribune*, October, 1893 by legal process on Judgement obtained in favor of Dickinson and Suess. The sale takes place on Nov. 3rd at 12 o'clock noon.

The *Tribune* reported the sale had been cancelled and that the premises had been mortgaged to meet the judgement against the company. This later proved to be only a temporary reprieve, as on November 10, 1893, the *Tribune* reported: "the sheriff again took possession of the factory the previous week, on behalf of one John Damp, who has a chattel mortgage on the factory for something over $2,000." Other writs were out against the company.

A meeting of the stockholders was held in Toronto on November 28, 1893, and a demand made on the directors for their resignations. All but one or two complied willingly, and the others were forced to resign. It is a surprising fact that at this meeting of the stockholders there was but one Toronto man legally entitled to vote! The others were in arrears on stock and were thus disqualified. The remainder carried on and elected the following new board of directors: president, J.R. Wright, Toronto; secretary-treasurer, John Rowe, Berlin; directors: W.H. Bowlby and J.E. Neville, Berlin; T.F. White and Jno. D. Kinnard, Port Colborne; Mr. O'Hearn, Hamilton. The amount of stock necessary to qualify was reduced from 25 shares to ten shares. The principal subscribers were: J.M. Faircloth, Toronto, $10,000; Jas. Lydiatt, Port Colborne, $9,000; W.D. Burn, Toronto, $8,000; W.H. Bowlby, Berlin, $4,000; J.J. Eaton, Toronto, $3,500; B.E.

McKens(z)ie, Toronto, $3,000. Two other subscribers, John Lowden ($2500) and Robert W. Lowden ($500), later established Independent Glass Producers, Limited, in Toronto, in 1910.

The new board met at once and looked carefully over the company's affairs, finding the liabilities so large that nothing remained but for the company to be liquidated. On December 29, 1893, the *Tribune* reported that "the date for the reopening of the factory seems as far off as ever, to the very great regret of our businessmen and citizens, generally. That the winter will be a hard one is admitted on all sides; with the factory closed, it will be double felt here."

The company was dissolved in November 1924.

FOSTER GLASS WORKS
Port Colborne, Ontario (1894-1900)

There was a hiatus in glassmaking in Port Colborne from the summer of 1893 until the fall of 1894. The combination of a devastating fire in February 1893 and the shareholders' lack of confidence in James Lydiatt, the promoter and manager, had been too much for its survival and, consequently, Erie Glass passed into history by way of a judicial sale.

From the ashes the phoenix arose in the persons of George H. Foster and John Finkbinder, two highly qualified glassblowers.

George Foster had originally worked in the Hamilton Glass branch of The Diamond Glass Company (Limited) and, during the company's existence, he would be joined by other members of the Foster family — brothers John C. and William, and later, William's son Douglas, all of whom had been trained in Hamilton. The site chosen for their works, approximately one-fifth of an acre in size, was again outside Port Colborne, adjoining Reeb's lime kiln on Lot 33, Humberstone Township, one mile west of Port Colborne.

By November 1894 they were in full operation. The local newspapers spoke of a broad product mix, from conical ink wells to gallon jugs, with the accent on fruit jars.

The following write-up in the *Welland Tribune*, November 23, 1894, gives a clear picture of the operation:

The location of this factory is on the line between Humberstone and Wainfleet, and might aptly be christened *Limestone City*.

THE GLASS FACTORY
"Great oaks from acorns grow," is an old saying and a true one; and after seeing all we could see and hearing all we could hear in connection with the latest venture in glass making in this field, we have a firm belief that the industry has this time come to stay.

In face of the disastrous failure of the Erie Glass Company at Port Colborne, it was indeed plucky for Mr. George Foster to place his money and hopes of future success in a like venture so near to the scene of the Erie wreck. Did we say "a like venture?" Then we be pardoned. It is not a like venture. True, both factories were built for the purpose of making glass, but their management is as widely different as winter is from summer. There are no princely paid officers or expensive city offices; all are practical workers, no drones. Mr. Foster and his brothers and employees are stripped for work, and as each day is told of, hundreds of glittering glass jars are piled up as the product of their labor. At present two blowers are steadily at work making fruit jars, and in all nine or ten hands find employment about the factory, turning out from 60 dozen to 200 or 400 dozen per day, according to the size and style of the article in hand.

The furnace and ovens are wholly different from those of the defunct factory at Port Colborne. The furnace is a continuous tank in two compartments. It holds ten tons of glass, and as the material is constantly fed at one end the melted glass is taken by the blowers' irons at the other. The system is far in advance of the old style pot.

Three large brick ovens give ample room for the annealing process. During our visit on Friday last one of these ovens was being filled, another was cooling and the contents of the third were being removed — and so it goes, one group following the other systematically.

At present the grinding room for smoothing off the rough tops of the fruit jars, after being bust off from the blowpipe, is situated some little distance from the main factory, so as to utilize steam from Reeb's adjacent lime works, but with continued success the buildings will be enlarged by another season and the departments still more compactly arranged.

Although very busy, Mr. Foster kindly and courteously explained to the *Tribune* representative the process of glassmaking and demonstrated it by the rapid manufacture of an "Ideal" fruit jar — a clear and handsome article very similar to those made in the city of Hamilton, and for which there is ample sale. After a while glass bottles will be manufactured as well as the jars. Experts say the class of goods turned out are No. 1 in every aspect. The sand is procured from Ohio and Pennsylvania and the soda ash from Liverpool, England.

In March 1896 a petition was circulated asking that a public meeting be convened to consider the advisability of inducing Mr. Foster to move his works into town, on the complaint heard that it was so far from town (one mile!) that it was difficult to get blowers to work there. Stonebridge was also believed to be trying to wean the glassworks away from their present location. At the ensuing public meeting, Mr. Foster declared himself as not being adverse to the request, but in fact was in favour of the idea. The matter was clarified when it was determined that the factory owner was expecting to receive a large cash bonus in return for his willingness to move into town. In this case, the principle "once bitten, twice shy" was the determining factor and the idea was shelved for the time being.

While all this was taking place, Messrs. Reeb had bought 60 tons of gas pipe. The gas was going somewhere. Was it possible that the old glassworks was going to be reestablished and, if so, was Diamond Glass in Hamilton looking for added capacity? This question would be clearly answered before the end of the year.

Sometime prior to June 24, 1897, the Reeb brothers (owners of the lime kiln) promised to supply gas to John Losch (who had arrived from Brooklyn in January 1896 to work at Fosters) should he start a glass factory in Port Colborne. Losch had secured the smelting works with an eye to the glass business. The Diamond Glass Company, who had leased the Foster works, did not relish the idea of competition and notified Reeb Bros. that, should they supply Losch with gas, they (Diamond Glass Co.) would cease taking gas from them. Diamond Glass Co. then leased some six farms west of the village and secured options on four others. It was rumoured that a contract had been let for the drilling of several wells for Diamond. However, this never came about, and John Losch and his son went to Wallaceburg on September 1, 1897, to work in the Sydenham Glass factory.

This then was the reason the Reebs ordered so much gas pipe. Diamond Glass had leased the Foster Glass Works for three years (1896-1899) and controlled its production until 1898 through its plant in Hamilton, formerly The Hamilton Glass Company.

During the week of August 13, 1897, there was an explosion at Reeb's lime kiln, which left the glassworks partly wrecked. Lightning was considered to be the cause. Permission was granted by Diamond Glass to rebuild the factory and, by mid-November, they were back in production.

In January 1898 George Lydiatt turned up again, this time to find out whether the town would provide a gas supply so that he could start a glass factory to make lamp chimneys. His request was turned down.

From time to time, the newspapers mentioned the various lines that were being produced. These included Crown fruit jars — pints 50 cents a dozen, quarts 60 cents a dozen and half gallons 80 cents a dozen. Table lamps were also made at prices ranging from 20 cents to $8. The tank alternated between flint, (clear) amber and green.

The Diamond Glass lease expired in 1899 and the Fosters once more became independent. The following figures, extracted from Diamond Glass records, indicate the operating results for the three years that the works were controlled by them: wages, $36,917; materials,

$24,241; expenses, $4,580; profits $22,264; production, $86,288; sales, $105,683.

Before the end of the year, the question of the company moving into town was again raised. Foster indicated that it would cost $1,200 and an adequate supply of gas would have to be guaranteed. Not only was the $1,200 not raised, but there now appeared to be a shortage of gas in the area generally. The Fosters remained at the lime kiln.

The new campaign (period of operation) started on November 16, 1899. Because of the shortage of gas, the company began experimenting with new techniques. They used slack coal, which was more expensive but gave splendid results at first. The furnace, as rebuilt, had two fireplaces in the back end. These were in the form of two chutes, which were fed from a platform near the top of the furnace and emptied into a large ash pit below. The bottom of the chute was protected by grates. When the furnace was fired, a brilliant bed of coals was made at the bottom of the chute, over the grates. The chute was then filled with slack coal and the heat from below drew the gas out of the coal as it passed through. As the fuel grew red it was shoved down to the grates and more was added above. Thus the process continued. Underneath the furnace was a hot air flue, which met the gas just as it entered the body of the furnace. The heat generated passed through the entire length of the furnace, and as the gas was consumed it was passed off in vapour through three chimneys.

The furnace proper was divided by a wall, the front end being called the working end and the back, the melting end. The two were connected by a passage in the bottom of the furnace. The sand, soda and lime — materials used in making the glass — were dumped into the furnace through an opening in the side of the melting end. As the material melted, it sank to the bottom, ran through the opening to the working end, and found its own level. At this end were several openings where the blowers stood and drew the glass out in thick chunks on the ends of their blowpipes. Difficulties arose as soon as the furnace was opened. When the blowers began work, they found that the glass was not viscous enough to work, so the Fosters added two small heaters to the working end to keep the furnace at the proper temperature. These worked in the same way that the larger fires did, and gave satisfactory results. The furnace held many tons of glass and consumed a batch (2,000 pounds of material) every six hours. It required two and a half tons of coal every 24 hours to maintain the heat.

Blowing was commenced near mid-November 1899. There were two furnaces in the factory, although only one was in use at the start. They had six large ovens, where the bottles were annealed after being taken from the moulds. The ovens were heated by coal or coke, and the bottles remained in the ovens three days. There were 25 to 30 employees. The wares turned out were of great variety and of good material. Moulds for bottles ranged from a tiny ink bottle to a gallon jug. The moulds cost from $15 to $100 each. At the end of December 1899, the Fosters were still having trouble with their heating. With the wind blowing, the furnaces worked all right, but on a dull day the draft was not sufficient to keep the fire hot enough. In January 1900 they were compelled to change back to natural gas. The only changes required were to make holes for the burners.

In the period from November 1899 to January 22, 1900, they turned out about 800 gross of fruit jars, as well as many other types of bottles. Lamp chimneys, tumblers and tableware, made from a better quality of glass by adding some lead oxide, were also produced. There were about 30 hands, with annual wages of from $10,000 to $12,000. But by May it was impossible to maintain production. Boys were offered $3 a week and could not be found at that price. The works started its summer break on June 18, 1900, never to reopen. Reeb Sr. purchased the plant from the Fosters that same month. There was talk of Foster moving the plant to Hamilton and Reeb carrying on the factory in the future, but neither came about.

In September 1900 George Foster left for Kingsville, Ontario, where he took charge of The Ontario Glass Company Limited. In December John Foster and his family moved to Toronto, where he had taken a position in The Toronto Glass Company (Limited), which was the Toronto plant of The Diamond Glass Company (Limited). William Foster went to Kingsville, and then Wallaceburg — The Sydenham Glass Company of Wallaceburg (Limited).

THE ONTARIO GLASS COMPANY LIMITED
Kingsville, Ontario (1899-1901)

The establishment of this company has been attributed to the discovery of natural gas in the area. However, its survival, even for only three years, may have been possible for an entirely different reason.

During the last decade of the nineteenth century, an industrial revolution was taking place in the American glass industry. Slowly but surely, semiautomatic and automatic machines were replacing the gatherer and the blower. One of the inventors in this field was an American, Frank O'Neill, whose particular interest was a machine for blowing bottles. His chief competitor was Edward Miller, also an American. O'Neill moved to Kingsville about the turn of the century and filed an application for a Canadian patent on July 31, 1900. The patent was issued on April 19, 1901. This was for "certain new and useful improvements in machines for manufacturing glassware to provide an improved mechanism for measuring and delivering molten glass to the moulds . . ." He was subsequently issued under Patent No. 73,425. George H. Foster, who had moved to Kingsville from Foster Glass Works in Port Colborne, was a witness to the signing of the application.

The Ontario Glass Company Limited was incorporated on November 29, 1899. It is the contention of John Sheeler, GLASFAX, that Frank O'Neill moved to Kingsville to avoid interference and/or pirating of his ideas by his inventive competitors in the United States.

At the directors' meeting following the first general meeting of shareholders, the following directors and officers were elected and appointed: Dr. H.W. Walker, director, president; George W. Burkhart, manager director, vice-president; W.A. Smith, director, secretary-treasurer; H.S. Warwick, director; J.H. Reaper, director.

The property consisted of five and one-half acres located on Lot 25, Division 1, Town of Kingsville. There was a main building and a detached office. Warehouses were to the north of the property. A continuous furnace of 50 tons capacity was used with side regenerators (ovenlike affairs that preheated the air to be mixed with the natural gas prior to combustion). There was a machine and mould shop in the charge of J.H. Reaper. Charles Corson, assisted by Amos Broadwell, ran the powerhouse and blacksmith shop.

The blowers were arranged in three main shops. Each shop could turn about 40 gross per shift of nine hours, or something over 6,000 bottles. The factory ran night and day. The day shift ran from 7 a.m. to 5 p.m., and the night shift from 5 p.m. to 3 a.m. Workers on the two shifts alternated weekly. All bottle and pressed ware production was made by the glassblowers, with the exception of wide-mouth jars and fruit jars. These were made on a machine, presumably O'Neill's, which was run by compressed air. About 150 were employed when two tanks were operating, and the men belonged to the Green Glass Workers Association, Local No. 71.

According to the *Kingsville Reporter*, 23 November 1899, ". . . the Works will be devoted to the manufacture of bottles and druggists' sundries, carboys, insulators, battery jars, pickle and fruit jars . . ." How many of these actual lines were made may never be known. For many years, the famous Beaver Jar was attributed to The Beaver Flint Glass Company of Toronto (Limited). However, John C. Barclay, citing his research on Ontario Glass and Sydenham Glass, states in a letter to me dated December 12, 1982:

There are (3) companies that have been credited with making BEAVER jars.

1) GERALD STEVENS in his book EARLY CANADIAN GLASS states that between the years 1898-1900 Beaver jars were produced in Toronto at the BEAVER FLINT GLASS CO. He just says they were made there, he really doesn't show any physical evidence in the form of shards or a catalogue or first hand reports. So until some real concrete evidence is found I do not list this company as a maker of Beaver jars. Although the evidence may be found.

2) Excavation on the site of the ONTARIO GLASS CO. has produced shards of the BEAVER jar in large numbers. Also the glass lid attributed to the Beaver. So here we find some real evidence of manufacture.

This small bottle marked Mayell's Eclipse was made in the Kingsville factory and is filled with sand used in the plant.

Photograph courtesy of the Royal Ontario Museum, gift of William Stephanoff.

3) I did quite a bit of research in Wallaceburg and local historians there confirmed BEAVER jars were made in Wallaceburg. Since then I ran across the ends of several shipping crates which I illustrate in my book. John Moore's ends to be specific. Which states that Beaver jars were produced by the SYDENHAM GLASS CO. OF WALLACE-BURG, ONT.

So in my book I say that Beaver jars were produced at the SYDENHAM GLASS CO. and the ONTARIO GLASS CO. And I also state Beaver jars were also supposed to be made in Toronto at the BEAVER FLINT GLASS CO. but until some real evidence is found I am very skeptical that jars were made there.

To support the statement in #2 above, it has been recorded that D.A. Gordon, managing director of Sydenham Glass of Wallaceburg, Ontario, bought Ontario Glass by mortgage sale on August 6, 1901. Item #3 above is self-authenticating.

Production started some time after May 1900, a date supported by an item from the *Wallaceburg News*, May 29, 1900: ". . . a few of our glassblowers continue to change places between W'Burg and Kingsville in order to give them a start and will return in short time . . ." In the November 23, 1899, edition of the *Kingsville Recorder*, a cut appears of a Monarch jar. However, controversy has arisen over the actual maker of this jar. According to Rick Harrison, GLASFAX, who has done considerable research on the subject, this jar was never produced in Kingsville, due to the delay in obtaining a patent. He states that the embossed capital "M" in the circle stands for Ernst R. Meyer of Detroit, Michigan. Dr. J.H. Toulouse states that Patent No. 643,908 was issued to Ernst R. Meyer on February 20, 1900, for a fruit jar called The Victor. It was issued on a new concept in sealing, in which fingers along the upper and lower edges of a horizontal band pulled lid and jar together when the band was clamped in place. This appears to be consistent with the sealing technique on the Monarch jar shown. Mr. Harrison is of the opinion that, because of the delay in the patent grant, Ontario Glass probably gave up the contract to make it. Harrison then goes on to say that Meyer went to Detroit and had the jar produced in that vicinity. The name of the jar was later changed to Victor — first sold by Meyers for Fruit Jar Co. of Detroit and later changed to Victor Jar Company. A Monarch jar with "PATENTED 1899" on it was found and may be a variant of the Victor jar.

By 1901 the company was in financial trouble. It had to take out mortgages on the property. The first one, in January 1900, was for $4,000 (Sidney A. King). The next one, in April 1900, was for $10,000 (D.A. Gordon, managing director of Sydenham Glass). In 1901 Gordon was shown as the owner of Ontario Glass in the tax rolls.

Production stopped on August 6, 1901. In 1902 there was a transfer of ownership from Gordon to Conklin Planing Mills Limited. In 1903 Gordon took over King's mortgage. The contributing factors to the demise of the company were increases in the prices of raw materials, a bad fire, and the last blow was that the gas wells started to produce less. Finally, they became flooded with salt water from below the field. Men and machinery were transferred to Sydenham. In a letter dated August 24, 1904, written by Gordon to the president and officers of Sydenham Glass, the following sentence appears: ". . . The value of the plant removed here from Kingsville has also been reduced by $1,300. . ."

No record has been found of the actual dissolution date of the company.

THE WALLACEBURG, ONTARIO, GLASS OPERATIONS

As early as 1891 discussions were taking place on how to set up a glass factory in Wallaceburg. The first attempt, The Wallaceburg Glass Works Company (Limited), was incorporated in 1893 but never actually materialized. A year later, The Sydenham Glass Company of Wallaceburg (Limited) was incorporated, and it was producing glass by the fall of 1895. A third company was The Wallaceburg Glass Company Limited.

THE WALLACEBURG GLASS WORKS COMPANY (LIMITED) (1893)

The company received an Ontario charter ". . . for the purposes and objects following, that is to say — (a) to acquire a site and to erect thereon buildings and furnaces suitable for the manufacturer of glass and (b) to manufacture and sell glass under the name of The Wallaceburg Glass Works Company Limited." But the operation was stillborn. This fact surfaced when the third Wallaceburg glass operation, The Wallaceburg Glass Company Limited, was applying for its charter. The government was concerned that the name chosen by the petitioners was in possible conflict with the already chartered Wallaceburg Glass Works. To clarify the matter, Dr. George Mitchell submitted the following affidavit on May 19, 1911:

> ". . . that the Wallaceburg Glass Works was never organized, did not carry on any work and had not existed for the past twelve years . . ."[12]

Dr. Mitchell became one of the leaders in the establishment and operation of Sydenham Glass. The Wallaceburg Glass Works was dissolved on May 1, 1961, for not having filed regular annual returns.

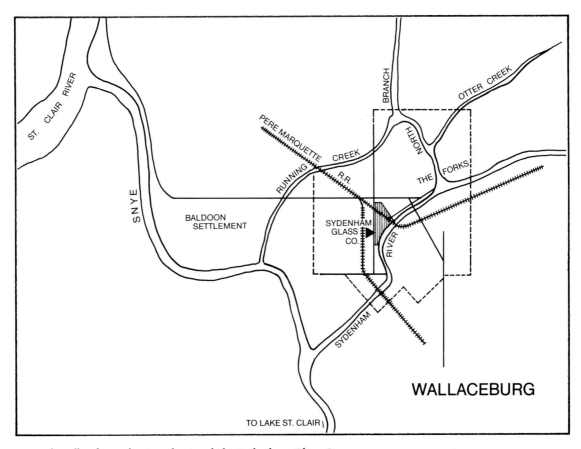

Map of Wallaceburg showing the site of the Sydenham Glass Company.

THE SYDENHAM GLASS COMPANY OF WALLACEBURG (LIMITED)
Wallaceburg, Ontario (1894-1913)

In 1875 the Village of Wallaceburg became the Town of Wallaceburg. The industry of the community had been built around lumbering and associated industries — barrel staves and shipbuilding. Wallaceburg was a deep water port, having access to the Great Lakes system via the Sydenham and Snye rivers.

The idea of establishing a glass factory in Wallaceburg has been credited to Thomas Harrison, a local jeweller, and Capt. William Taylor, two natives of England who had been neighbours there, near a glass factory. The latter was impressed by the vast quantities of sand lining the navigable waters. Experiments in glassmaking were carried on at the rear of Harrison's jeweller's shop. Although the local sand was not considered suitable for making glass on a commercial basis, they found that suitable sand was available in the United States. As a result, a public meeting was held on March 11, 1891, at which the idea of establishing a glassworks was presented. Much enthusiasm was shown and financial support promised. The company received its charter on November 7, 1894.

The "sparkplug" behind this company was Captain James Wynand Steinhoff, a leading citizen who spearheaded establishment of the glass factory. He was born in St. Thomas, Ontario, on October 1, 1834. Five years after his family settled in Wallaceburg, Steinhoff, at the age of 21, ventured into the shipbuilding business. In 1856 he served as master of the *Islander*, a passenger vessel, and with his newly earned papers he was thereafter referred to as "Capt. Steinhoff." After establishment of a barrel hoops firm, he set up the banking firm of Steinhoff and Lillie. In 1896 he established a flax mill. He died in 1921 at the age of 87.

Original Sydenham Glass Factory, 1893.

If Capt. Steinhoff was the "sparkplug," then David Alexander Gordon, managing director, was the "engine" that kept it going for 19 years. He was a nephew of Capt. Steinhoff and a partner in the cooperage firm. David Alexander Gordon was born in 1858 and was the first member of another "glass family" that would involve four descendants over three generations. He died on March 17, 1919, at Braithwaite, Louisiana.

The site chosen for the works was on the north side of the Sydenham River, adjacent to the Pere Marquette Railway bridge. It was known as the Patterson Mill site and was purchased from the Bank of Montreal.

Again Richard Davis appeared on the scene. This was the fifth glass operation to which his name has been linked. On October 6, 1894, an agreement was signed between Richard Davis and Sydenham Glass whereby Davis would purchase 200 shares of Sydenham stock and would erect the plant. Although he became a shareholder on November 17, 1894, extant records so far only indicate that he was engaged as a "highly recommended tank engineer" from Indiana to build the first glass tank. The following news item takes up the story:

> . . . the new glass works at Wallaceburg, Ontario, are nearing completion. It is expected that they will be in operation about the 15th of April. The building and plant has been erected at a cost of about $30,000.00, and employment will be given to about 700 hands. The machinery is all of the most modern styles, and it is claimed that the company will turn out glass at a lower cost than at any other place in Canada. Mr. J.W. Steinhoff is the President of the Company . . .[13]

While the furnace was under construction, the rest of the factory was built apace. A crew from the Erie and Huron Railroad arranged to build a siding from the Pere Marquette line, and Mr. S.R. Smythe from Pittsburgh erected the gas producers. The *Wallaceburg News and Herald* of June 7, 1895, described the works as follows:

Wallaceburg Chimney Shop, about 1908.　　　　　　　　　Courtesy of Dominion Glass Archives.

. . . The main building is 70' x 100' with a circular roof, the top of which is 65' from the ground. On the east side is a wing 40' x 100'. There are two wings to the west 100' x 30', each standing at right angles to the main building. Between these is the engine room 24' x 30'. At the north end of the main building are the annealing ovens 20' x 100'. In the main building is the great glass tank and a portion of the gas producers. The tank was built of fire-brick, iron, and cement. The tank was 16' x 45'.

In those days, before the advent of automatic glassmaking machinery — which would eventually depose the reigning glassblowers — the most important part of a glass factory was the glass furnace, in which the raw materials were melted. The following quotation, from the *Wallaceburg Herald*, May 24, 1895, is an example of this recognition:

A pleasing event took place at the glass works, when the great glass tank received its name. The brickwork of the arch was just nearing completion when Captain J.W. Steinhoff, President of the company, entered the building, accompanied by his niece, Miss Eva Kelly, who mounted a ladder with the Union Jack in her hand, which she unfurled and placed on the arch. She then drove the key brick of the arch and said 'I name this tank the "Nonpariel" and trust the works with which it is connected may prove a lasting success to those who are identified with it, and that it may be of great benefit to our town, as well as the Province in general.'

This was a continuous tank and was only the second of its kind on this continent. It was first developed by the Germans about 1880. (Miss Kelly's wish of trust has certainly come true. Whereas Hamilton is the city in which glass has been produced for the longest time — since 1864 — Sydenham Glass and its successor Dominion Glass are credited with the longest continuous glass operation in Canada on the same site, from 1895 to date. This record, coupled with the fact that its products were shipped across the land and also that it was the town's largest employer, earned the community the name "Glasstown of Canada.")

Actual glass production started on September 6, 1895. Then came the rush of glass-blowers from all parts of North America.

The first large shipment of glass went to Nonsuch Mfg. Company in Toronto during the week of September 20, 1895. A month later, Sydenham shipped $15,000 worth of patent medicine bottles to Scott & Bowne in New York — indicating that Sydenham Glass was being recognized as a reliable glass company. In January of 1896, 15,000 fruit jars were shipped to Victoria, B.C., probably by rail.

The company was so successful that it increased its capital from $100,000 in 1896 to $300,000 in 1903. Dividends on the preferred were paid as follows: up to 1905, eight percent; 1905-1910, six percent; 1910-1912, nine percent; and in 1912, two dividends of five percent each.

In the spring of 1896 Sydenham purchased a number of freight cars for their own use. Larger and larger shipments were being made. On the resumption of blowing in the fall, after the summer break, they started with an amber tank (for bottles) and later changed to green. For the ten months ending June 30, 1896, they produced $130,000 worth of glass. In 1897 a second tank was built, and both ran full out. The company turned out more and more glass, for which there appeared to be a ready market. According to Dr. Julian Toulouse, Sydenham's production during the period 1894-1913 included the following fruit jars: Crown, Gem New Gem and Wallaceburg Gem.[14] The company was now one of the largest glassworks in the country, if not *the* largest, employing several hundred workers. During one week in March, 16 carloads were shipped.

In order to expand, the company purchased several acres of land across the street during the summer break of 1898, on which they built another factory for the manufacture of flint (clear) glass. Their total land area was now about 25 acres. The new flint house for fancy ware was started in the fall with about 100 hands. Richard Witt, who had been a glassblower at Dominion Glass Company in Montreal, was hired as manager, and he remained until 1905, when he moved to Philadelphia.

In 1900 oil lamps were being replaced by electricity. Mr. S.E. Carr, of the company, patented an incandescent globe which contained prisms increasing the light. Just about this time, the Ontario Glass Co. was started up in Kingsville, near Windsor, by some of the glass-blowers formerly at Foster Glass Works in Port Colborne. Two Sydenham glassblowers, Amos Parker and Tony Lacourse, went to Kingsville to help them in May 1900.

On February 20, 1901, the main building, a wing and the moulding shop were levelled by fire. There was little delay in getting everything back in working order.

Included in the minutes of the ninth annual meeting, held on August 27, 1903, the report by managing director D.A. Gordon indicated the happy state of affairs:

> . . . we think it is a matter of congratulation that we have passed through the best year in our history . . . we have in the past been taking stock in at its full value. Last year we wrote off 3% extra, and this year 2% additional, making in all 5% . . . in 1897, our liabilities exceeded our assets by over $51,000. To this sum should be added all our loss and interest charges paid on $35,000 worth of poor ware, which we had on hand at that time . . . For the first time in our history, we show a surplus not including plant . . . amounting to $4,551.80 . . . it does show that the Company now has sufficient assets to pay all its liabilities out of stock and book debts on hand and leave the plant entirely clear. Owing to the increase in the size of the plant and the volume of business done, it was deemed necessary to increase our capital stock to the extent of $150,000 . . .

A year later, at the next annual meeting, a vast improvement in the company was depicted in the managing director's report:

> The statement of the affairs of the company herewith presented show a net profit for the year of $13,708.61 . . . After having exhausted every available effort to get

Beaver fruit jar made by the Sydenham Glass Company Wallaceburg, Ontario.

Railroad rates reduced, we were compelled to make an appeal to the Railroad Commission, and are pleased to report that the decision . . . orders the Railroad companies to reduce our rates by about one-third . . .

Mention has already been made of the company's operation of its own freight cars on the railroads. In 1908 bylaw 59 was approved by the shareholders:

. . . that application be made forthwith to the Provincial government for such powers as will enable the said Company to own and operate vessels and steamships, and also act as general traders . . .

No indication has been found that the company took advantage of these powers.

The product mix now comprised bottles, lamp and lantern chimneys, lantern globes, fruit jars and tumblers (probably blown). Flint (clear), amber and green glass was produced. During the period of independence of the company, there appears to be no evidence that any tableware was made on a commercial basis. However, many whimseys were made, including glass hats, wig stands, swords, canes, drapes, hatchets, hammers, animals, birds, pipes and paperweights.

The following item appeared in the *Wallaceburg News* on January 13, 1910:

Jan. 13: Irwin P. Doolittle died in Toronto of gas asphyxia, 96 Beverley Street, Toronto. He was a one time millionaire peach-grower — poor speculations broke him. He lived in W'Burg some years previously. He was interested while here in the introduction and manufacture of the Doolittle fruit jar placed on the market by the Sydenham Glass Co. . . .

There is some question as to whether the "Doolittle" fruit jar was made in Wallaceburg. Toulouse, in his book *Fruit Jars*, described a Doolittle fruit jar as follows:

DOOLITTLE
Circa 1901
Glass lid held by two spring clips permanently mounted on the lid, and tightening by rotating to bring an arm under a finished ledge. Handmade wide-mouth round, pressed laid-on-ring, in flint. Front: 'DOOLITTLE'
Lid: 'Doolittle,' in script with patent dates in a circle: Jan. 2, 1900, Dec. 3, 1901, and Dec. 24, 1901
Maker unknown
Due to the wide mouth, pints are very squat shaped.

The end of Sydenham's independence was in sight. As early as 1906 a committee comprising H. Munderloh, D.A. Gordon, John Scott and J.W. Steinhoff had been appointed "to deal with the question of sale of the plant, said Committee to report to the directors before any definite action be taken . . ." At this point, Henry Munderloh, a director of Diamond Flint in Montreal, had already been a director of Sydenham for eight years and had accumulated the majority of the shares of the company, presumably for Diamond Flint.

Diamond Flint Glass executed an agreement with the Toledo Machine Co. of Toledo, Ohio, (makers of the Owens Automatic Suction and Bottle Forming machine) in 1908 to carry on Owens machine operations at the Canadian Glass Manufacturing Co. in Montreal, over which Diamond had effective control. Through that company, by rental agreement, it would operate Owens machines at Hamilton Glass and Sydenham Glass.

At a special general meeting of the shareholders of Sydenham Glass held on April 26, 1913, the following motion was approved:

Moved by W.H. Mitchell, seconded by W. Heap that the Company be, and it is hereby authorized to sell or dispose of the undertaking of The Sydenham Glass Co. of Wallaceburg (Limited) (including all the assets, rights, credits, goodwill, claims and demands of the Company of any and every kind) to the Diamond Flint Glass Co. (Ltd.) for 8000 paid-up shares of the common stock of the Diamond Flint Glass Co. Ltd. representing a proper or face value of $800,000.00 or such lesser number of shares of stock as to the Directors of The Sydenham Glass Co. of Wallaceburg Limited may seem proper or advisable, and upon such terms and conditions as the said Directors may seem available and expedient.

This was subsequently finalized by an agreement signed by Sydenham Glass and Diamond Flint Glass on May 22, 1913.

On May 15, 1913, when Dominion Glass Company Limited acquired the assets of Diamond Flint Glass, Sydenham Glass became the Wallaceburg plant of Dominion Glass.

When it was decided to convert Wallaceburg to tableware production only in 1975, it became the St. Clair Division of Dominion Glass. In 1978 it became a separate company, Libbey-St. Clair Inc., a joint venture between Dominion Glass and Libbey Glass Co. of Toledo, Ohio.

Sydenham Glass was dissolved on April 6, 1964.

The following is a list of directors and officers of The Sydenham Glass Company of Wallaceburg (Limited).

	DIRECTOR	OFFICER
J.W. Steinhoff	1894-1911	president 1894-1908
Dr. Geo. Mitchell	1894-1902	vice-president 1894-1902
D.A. Gordon	1894-1913	managing director 1896-1898
John H. Fraser	1894	
John Scott	1894-1908	vice-president 1903-1908
Harvey Morris	1894	
Harry Martin	1894	

DIRECTOR		OFFICER
A.G. Laird		secretary-treasurer 1894-1896
J.W. De C. O'Grady	1895	
J.C. Shaw	1895-1911	
John Cooper	1895-1909	
Thos. Harrison, Jr.		acting secretary-treasurer 1896
R.T. Riddell	1896-1897	
T.B. Dundas		secretary-treasurer 1897-1912
Henry Munderloh	1898-1913	
John E. Gordon	1903-1911	assistant manager 1908-1910
		manager 1910
George Lydiatt	1910-1911	
G.A. Grier	1912-1913	
A.H. Grier	1912	
N.M. Yuile	1912	
T.B. Dundas	1913	

THE ONTARIO GLASS BURIAL CASE COMPANY (LIMITED)
Ridgetown, Ontario (1880-c. 1883)

ONTARIO GLASS BURIAL CASE CO., RIDGETOWN, ONT.

Manufacturers of the celebrated patent Metallic Glass Burial Case, warranted perfectly airtight. They are handsomely trimmed on the inside with fine silk and satin drapery, which shows through the glass sides, relieving this casket of the dark and sombre appearance of all others and costing no more than good wooden caskets.[15]

This advertisement first appeared in 1880 and continued for several years. In the letters patent, the petitioners stated that their application was for "... the manufacture and sale of glass and iron burial cases..." This would suggest that the company belonged to the secondary glass industry (i.e. the fabrication of an article from preformed glass). To support this theory, it was customary in those days, and for many years afterwards, for the local furniture maker in small towns to not only make the wooden caskets, but also to serve as the undertaker for the area. Also, in the letters patent, there is an indication that the first-named petitioner, Joseph Askins, manufacturer, was the inventor of the burial case: "... The amount paid in by the said Joseph Askins has been paid in by transfer of Patent..."

During this period of industrial development in Canada, small towns and cities provided incentives to attract new businesses. Ridgetown was no exception. It attracted a foundry, a canning factory and a pork packing factory, as well as the burial case company.

On October 18, 1881, the town council passed two bylaws on behalf of the company. The first one provided a loan to the company in the form of interest-free debentures in the amount of $5,000 (5 x $1,000) for a ten-year period, repayable $1,000 a year, starting with the sixth year. At the same meeting, they approved a bylaw exempting the company from municipal taxes for a ten-year period, from January 1, 1882. On December 5, 1881, by supplementary letters patent, the company doubled their capital to $50,000 (5,000 x $100).

The factory was built directly across the street from the broom factory, which was located on Lots 47-48, Plan 77, Ward 1. The first officers were John P. McKinlay, president; Thomas Schlenker, treasurer; and Ransom Pierce, manager. No information has surfaced on the operations of the company, but it must have been unprofitable, because in the January 26, 1883, edition of the *Rondeau News*, published in Blenheim, Ontario, the following appeared:

> ... The Ontario Glass Burial Case Company of Ridgetown has merged into the Ontario Casket Company and resumed business again...

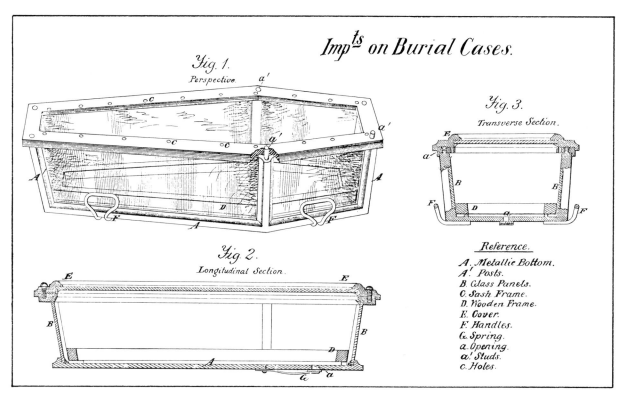

Patent drawings for the Glass Burial Case.

The new directors were John P. McKinlay, James Watson (son of Zenas Watson), Charles E, Scane, Charles Baker, Thomas Schlenker and William Pennale. the directors of the merged operations weer all involved in the original company, with the exception of William Pennale.

In 1885 a financial report of the company was prepared for the town council indicating that the securities were not sufficient to support the loan. On May 26, 1885, a bylaw was passed relieving the company of its debt. The company subsequently failed and moved to London, Ontario, for a new start. The building was taken over for an apple-drying operation.

FOOTNOTES

[1] See Chapter 9 Authentication, Attribution and Excavations, "Delorimier Avenue Glasshouses."
[2] See Chapter 2 Then and Now – Glassblowing to Machine Production
[3] Gerald Stevens, *Canadian Glass c. 1825-1925* (Toronto: The Ryerson Press 1967).
[4] George MacLaren, *Nova Scotia Glass* (Halifax: Nova Scotia Museum. Occasional paper no. 4, Historical series No. 1, 1965), p. 10.
[5] "Nova Scotia Glass Houses," GLASFAX *Newsletter*, vol. V, no. VI, (June 1971), pp. 81, 82.
[6] Joseph H. MacGillivray, "Recollections of the Glass Works at Trenton, Nova Scotia," GLASFAX *Newsletter*, vol. V, no. 4, (April 1971), p. 3.
[7] MacLaren, pp. 11, 13.
[8] MacLaren, p. 19.
[9] *Nova Scotia Museum Newsletter*, ed. Elizabeth Whealey, vol. 2, no. 3, (April 1958), p. 52.
[10] See Chapter 2.
[11] Extract from minutes of directors' meeting of Diamond Flint Glass Company Limited held on December 23, 1902.
[12] Letter to Ontario government
[13] *The Canadian Manufacturer*, (Toronto: The Canadian Manufacturers Association, March 1895).
[14] Julian H. Toulouse, *Fruit Jars*, (Don Mills: Thomas Nelson & Sons Canada Limited, 1969) p. 521.
[15] O. Urquhart, GLASFAX *Newsletter*, (September 1972), p. 19.

CHAPTER 5

Consolidation
(1903-1913)

Diamond Flint Glass Company Limited, Toronto (1903-1913), the second conglomerate and successor to Diamond Glass

The Canadian Glass Manufacturing Company (Limited), Montreal (1905-1913), set up by Diamond Flint Glass to handle that company's automatic bottlemaking operations

In the West: Crystal Glass Company, Limited, Sapperton, British Columbia (1906-c. 1908);

The Manitoba Glass Manufacturing Company, Limited, Beausejour, Manitoba (1907-1912); Alberta Glass Company Limited, Medicine Hat, Alberta (1911)

Welland Glass Manufacturing Company Limited, Welland, Ontario (1909)

DIAMOND FLINT GLASS COMPANY LIMITED
Toronto, Ontario, and elsewhere (1903-1913)

An event of major importance in the glass industry took place in Toledo, Ohio, in 1902. Michael J. Owens, a glassblower who along with E.D. Libbey had invented many mechanical contrivances for blowing glass, invented the Owens Automatic Suction and Bottle Forming machine while in the employ of the Toledo Glass Co. The machine rotated clockwise like a merry-go-round and overlapped a saucerlike revolving pot which rotated counterclockwise. The machine would suck up a gob of molten glass from the pot into the blank mould, where the neck would be finished and a small cavity made in the gob. The gob was then transferred to the blow mould, where the bottle was completed by use of compressed air. The machine was designed for mass production and was adaptable to moulds that could make one, two or three bottles simultaneously. As was recorded in the history of Diamond Glass, a syndicate headed by shareholder George A. Grier purchased that company for $1,938,309.78 with the intention of starting up a new company, presumably to get in on the ground floor of this revolutionary new method of mechanical production.

As a result, Diamond Flint Glass was incorporated. Its facilities comprised the offices and works of Diamond Glass (formerly North American Glass) in Montreal, Toronto Glass and the two nonoperating plants in Hamilton, Hamilton Glass and Burlington Glass. This takeover also signalled the changing of the guard. William Yuile had ceased to be active in the industry, but his son, Norman MacLeod "Mac" Yuile, who began his career in 1899 with Diamond Glass, was getting established in glass and related industries. (He completed 65 years of service in 1964, as a director of Dominion Glass, the successor company.) Three new glass-oriented families became involved in this company. The King brothers, Ralph and James Watt King, were cousins of Mac Yuile and played important roles in Diamond Flint and Dominion Glass. In a similar manner, George Arthur Grier of Montreal and his sons, George W. Grier, Arthur Harold Grier and Charles Brockwell Grier, were also involved. The third family was the Gordons, from

Michael J. Owens   Edward D. Libbey

Wallaceburg, Ontario. David Alexander Gordon was first involved with Sydenham Glass in 1894 and became a director of Diamond Flint in 1911. His son, John E. Gordon, also a director of Sydenham, later became a director of Independent Glass. Several other Gordons were involved in the industry.

Beaumont Shepherd of Montreal was the first president, but was replaced six months later by David Yuile. After six months as vice-president, George Wardrope was replaced by Frank Ross. The other original directors were David Williamson (managing director) and John Watt, both from Diamond Glass, George W. Grier and Frank W. Ross.

As soon as the dust had settled, the directors addressed themselves to the reorganization of their facilities, with plans to accommodate both hand shops and automatic production for bottlemaking. In March 1905 it was decided to refurbish the Hamilton plant by the erection of a glass furnace similar to the one at Toronto Glass, which would supply glass for two of the new Owens bottle-forming machines. Hand shop operations were continued in Montreal and Toronto.

In the fall of 1905 a new company was established in Montreal, The Canadian Glass Manufacturing Company (Limited). It is my opinion that it was set up by Diamond Flint Glass to anchor the mechanical bottle production (Owens) operations while maintaining the hand operations and overall control of both types of operations. As part of the agreement, with regard to the changeover from Diamond Glass to Diamond Flint Glass, a $600,000 ten-year first mortgage bond was issued and, at the same time, it was decided that instead of the $500,000 being issued as preference stock, $100,000 of it would be issued as common stock.

On February 8, 1906, the directors decided that as soon as the Hamilton furnace was ready for use, they would lease it to Canadian Glass for $4,000 per annum, for eventual Owens machine operations. Later in the year, Hamilton Glass was back in operation. The following comments are from an in-house article by Ernie Larner, an electrician who started to work in Hamilton on the reopening:

> . . . J.W. King, Manager, Geo Inglis, Office Manager, Percey Winn, Office Boy, Mr. Jacobs, Production Superintendent . . . Charlie Havers (just back from the South

The Owens fifteen arm "AQ" bottle machine, 1914.　　　　Courtesy of Owens-Illinois.

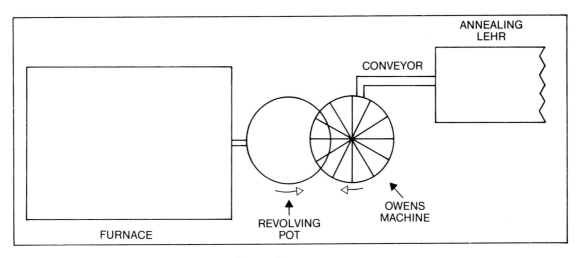

Flow chart for Owens Automatic Bottle Machine production.

African War, and we certainly heard about it), Denny Bennett, who had first won a Boston Marathon . . . Mike Hudecki (just over) learned the Owens machine and the English language at the same time . . . labourers in Batch Dept. worked 11 or 13 hours . . . Fuel for the furnace was natural gas. Earl "Jep" Jepson, came around to read the meters. He eventually became the Dominion Glass representative in Winnipeg . . . Furnaces usually lasted about eleven months and then were tapped into an iron pan full of water. "Trip" Havers fell into this tank when pulling the glass through it and was nearly boiled alive . . .

Regarding the production, we started off with a bang. Between the help we had and the glass turned out, we had a mountain of cullet in the yard in no time. I am not sure what colour we were after. We had green, dark green, black green and flint at times. We used the colour that was suitable at the time. It seemed to me it

The six arm "A" type Owens machine.
Courtesy of Owens-Illinois.

was seldom clear of seeds, etc., but perhaps the public was not so particular or as well educated to the fine points of a bottle to criticize too much, and as long as it had only one opening and did not leak, it was good enough to use.

The ware was carried from the machine to the lehr on paddles with long handles — four to six bottles at a time, depending upon the size and weight. With the help we seemed to get, we lost plenty trying to get them into lehr doors and kept the cullet wheeler busy to the yard pile. Also, a large amount of bottles were lost at the fire finisher on the machine when the bottles left the mould on the machine, it fell into a funnel over a three hole fire-pot, in a pit lower than the machine. The bottles fell into the funnel suspended by springs (neck down) into a permanent tube over the "Glory Hole," and from there to a cage on a circular table which moved in time with the machine over the burner holes on top of same, to fire finish the tops.

The lehrs were of the pan type, with pans the full width of the lehr. The pan was emptied in the Packing Room and brought to the front to be hooked onto the carrier chains, the lehr being pulled out by a clutch (manually operated) in the Packing Room in the drive of a motor running continuously.

. . . Natural gas was very erratic then, especially in the winter, so the producer gas house would be put in operation . . . The steam boiler was operated mostly in the winter by a variety of firemen off the boats, idle during the freeze-up, and a real drunken lot. There were no certificates needed by that lot. They'd lose steam for want of cleaning until the gas house hollered, and then they cleaned the fire and tubes, etc. and fired up until the stack was red to the top. It was a good job, it was located in the open, but it still may have been responsible for the fire which burned down the factory in May of 1912, as at these times sparks flew all over the yard . . .

110

Glass bust of Michael J. Owens.
Collection of the author.

We still had trouble with help and steady production on the machines. When they decided they needed a rest they all took a holiday and shut the plant down, or some mysterious break occurred on the machines. After one particular accident occurred repeatedly a watch was put on the roof of the factory over the machines, and they were caught pulling out pins on plungers and breaking the arms off . . . As mentioned before, this all helped to make plenty of cullet but the little brought in from outside never seemed to get any particular inspection except for any large lumps of iron or bottle tops that the shoveller would care to throw out in handling it. Consequently, more arsenic, manganese, etc. would be added until it turned dull and brown, then more cullet until it would go to a darker colour. We used a lot of brown sand from back over the (Hamilton) Mountain; also a lot of Belgium sand that came over in empty ships as ballast . . .

The works at Montreal and Toronto continued to work hand shops and some pressed ware, but were not involved in the new Owens process, which the company would start using in 1908, at Canadian Glass, Hamilton Glass and Sydenham Glass. At the same time, the beginning of a number of changes in key personnel took place. Henri Jonas, one of the three original directors, resigned. Norman MacLeod "Mac" Yuile, who had started with Diamond Glass in 1899, was appointed assistant manager of the Montreal works under David Williamson; and, because of Williamson's ill health in 1907, Yuile replaced him as manager.

The game plan and the relationship between Diamond Flint Glass and Canadian Glass began to emerge. In September 1905 Henry Herdt, on behalf of Diamond Flint Glass, assigned a rights agreement to Canadian Glass. In my opinion, Henry Herdt had been empowered by Diamond Flint Glass to obtain the exclusive Canadian rights for the Owens machine. This action supported the establishment of Canadian Glass in the same month.

On June 29, 1906, a licence agreement from Toledo Glass Company to Canadian Glass Company was signed for Owens operations. On February 14, 1908, Diamond Flint Glass signed an agreement with Canadian Glass and Sydenham Glass for Owens operations at these two companies. On April 4, 1908, these other agreements were executed: agreement between Toledo Glass and Canadian Glass; assignment from Toledo Glass to Canadian Glass; and agreement between Sydenham Glass and Canadian Glass.

To summarize, Diamond Flint obtained the exclusive Canadian rights to the Owens machine, assigned them to Canadian Glass, who in turn made arrangements for Sydenham Glass (now controlled by Diamond Flint) to use the Owens machine. Canadian Glass would be responsible for the Owens operation on behalf of Diamond Flint Glass. It was reported to the directors on September 16, 1908, that the company had loaned a total of $204,189.52 to Canadian Glass.

At a subsequent directors' meeting in the same year, John Watt was asked to make the best possible deal to obtain a Canadian licence to make the Schram Automatic Sealer — when the lid was pressed down, it automatically sealed the container. Although no agreement has been found, in Toulouse's book, *Fruit Jars*,[1] he states that the SCHRAM was also licenced in Canada.

By 1911 the relationship between Canadian Glass and Sydenham Glass to Diamond Flint was so close, through both shareholders and directors, that Diamond Flint deemed it advisable to purchase the shares of the other two companies as follows: all of the shares of Sydenham would be exchanged for fully paid-up shares of Diamond Flint on the basis of two Diamond shares for each Sydenham share; all of the shares of Canadian Glass would be exchanged for fully paid-up shares of Diamond Flint on the basis of four Diamond shares for each Canadian Glass share.

To finance these acquisitions, Diamond Flint obtained supplementary letters patent on October 24, 1911, increasing its capital from $1,600,000 to $3,500,000 and, at the same time, received authority to issue bonds of $600,000.

The year 1912 was a busy one for Diamond Flint Glass, and before it was over, the telltale signs of a further reorganization were in the air. In February Donald Lamont, who had been sales agent for the company in British Columbia for three years, decided to leave. Mr. Flock, Sydenham Glass's representative out west, was considered for the job. In March another $30,000 was allocated to the new Hamilton plant (which was being sponsored by Canadian Glass), bringing the total up to $180,000. In May it was agreed to recommend to the directors of Canadian Glass that the company proceed with the erection of a second furnace and two more machines in Hamilton, and that another be installed in Montreal. It was finally decided to proceed with the bond issue in May, and the Sun Life Assurance Co. was awarded the underwriting at 96 percent. The last piece of business for the directors before the summer hiatus was the authorization to spend $20,000 to purchase a suitable piece of land in the Winnipeg area as a site for a glass factory. A gauge of the year's activity is reflected in the authorization of an increase in the capital of the company from $3,500,000 to $4,000,000. A further $70,000 was paid out by Toronto Glass to the Hamilton works. G.A. Grier was appointed to represent Diamond Flint Glass at all Canadian Glass meetings.

Up until now, no real consideration had been given to establishing a plant west of the lakehead. There were two small companies that tried to make a go of it but were short-lived, Manitoba Glass and Crystal Glass. In March Mr. Munderloh reported to the directors that the Town of Medicine Hat, Alberta, had offered the usual carrots to try to persuade the company to establish there — with a refundable deposit of $500 if the plant was erected within two years.

For the past five years, the company had had some competition in Toronto from Independent Glass Producers, which had been started by the Lowden family and which catered mainly to the pharmaceutical trade. By 1912 they were in financial trouble, and D.A. Gordon, one of the company's directors, started conversations with Independent.

Diamond Flint Glass, like its predecessor Diamond Glass, was always concerned with competition. In order to acquire Independent, Munderloh of Diamond Flint, in an apparently prearranged plan, had earlier in the year obtained control of Independent. He then sold Independent to Diamond Flint for $110,000 cash and 240 paid-up shares of Diamond, said shares to be issued as soon as authority to increase the capital stock of the company be received (supplementary letters patent were issued to Diamond on October 10, 1912, increasing the capital stock to $4,000,000). Munderloh, on behalf of the proposed Jefferson Glass Company, Limited (the new name under which the former Independent Glass would operate), purchased from Diamond Flint the assets of Independent Glass in exchange for 1,600 fully paid-up shares of Jefferson Glass, on the further condition that Diamond Flint purchase 395 shares of Jefferson stock. This was approved by Diamond on September 24, 1912. Thus another pearl was added to Diamond's necklace.

The scene now moved west where, in Manitoba, Diamond Flint Glass acquired Manitoba Glass at Beausejour by an agreement dated September 28, 1912. The land was purchased for $10,000 cash, the factory and plant to be paid for by a mutually acceptable cash sum. Redcliff, near Medicine Hat, Alberta, offered free gas and land. The company decided to accept the offer and proceeded with the erection of a plant, now the Redcliff plant of Domglas. This, of course, cancelled the arrangement in Medicine Hat.

On May 13, 1912, Richards Glass was incorporated and became a distributor for some of the company's pharmaceutical products in Toronto. On behalf of Diamond, Mac Yuile purchased 51 shares of the 100 outstanding shares of Richards Glass.

The level of business had now reached such proportions that it was deemed necessary to establish a committee regarding prices and sales of goods. The committee, which was to meet as required, comprised Munderloh, Watt and Ralph King, representing Toronto and Hamilton; N.M. Yuile and A.H. Grier, son of G.A. Grier, representing the two Montreal operations; and D.A. Gordon and George Lydiatt, representing Wallaceburg. The Toronto works was authorized to lend the new Jefferson Glass Company up to $40,000 as required.

Taking a leaf out of the Canadian Glass's book on employee relations, Diamond Flint Glass directors passed a resolution whereby $60,000, out of the sum of $133,500 set aside out of the undivided profits of the company, be paid to the employees, either as a bonus or in satisfaction or in lieu of the obligation entered into by the company to pay them stock as part of their salary, over a five-year period, subject to their continuing in the company's employment. The remaining $73,500 was only to be used to assist employees to complete the purchases of common shares.

In March 1913 the president reported on a verbal offer that he had received for the purchase of shares, assets and business of the company, to which the directors agreed to recommend acceptance if the offer was made in writing. At the same time, it was agreed that a formal appraisal be made of the value of the properties and plants of the company, together with that of Canadian Glass and Sydenham Glass. The Toronto works was authorized to put out on account of Hamilton construction the sum of $25,000.

Concern had been expressed by some of the directors over the fact that, although the registered office of the company was in Ontario, most of its meetings were held in Montreal for the sake of expediency. On April 4, 1913, Bylaw 35 was passed by the directors, validating all the actions that had been taken at these meetings. This bylaw was subsequently confirmed at a special general meeting held on April 18.

The approval of Bylaw 36 provided for the purchase of Canadian Glass and Sydenham Glass, and for the sale of this company to C. Meredith & Co., as per their offer of April 3, 1913, for the following consideration ($5,308,000), payable as follows:

> ... $3,672,000 in cash and $1,636,000 in paid-up common shares of the par value of $100 each of a company to be incorporated under the name of "Canadian Glass Corporation, Limited" or such other name as the undersigned may determine [the new name was Dominion Glass Company, Limited][2].

Meredith & Co.'s offer was accepted on May 13, 1913.

BY-LAW NO. 36

A By-law to provide for the purchase of the undertakings of the Sydenham Glass Company Limited and the Canadian Glass Manufacturing Company Limited and for the sale of this company, passed the 4th April 1913.

The Directors of the Diamond Flint Glass Company Limited hereby enact (as a By-law of the company) as follows,–

1. The Company is hereby authorized to purchase the undertakings (including the assets, stocks, shares, rights and credits of the companies) of the Sydenham Glass Company of Wallaceburg, Limited, and the Canadian Glass Manufacturing Company Limited, or any part thereof, on such terms as to the Directors of this Company may seem proper, and for consideration either of stock in this Company (either Preference or Common) or of cash or otherwise as to the Directors may seem advisable.

2. That the Company is hereby authorized to sell and dispose of the undertakings of the Company or any part thereof for such price or consideration and upon such term as the Directors may think fit and particularly for shares or stock of a Company having objects altogether or in part similar to those of this Company, or for cash or other consideration.

3. That the Company is hereby authorized, if the Directors see fit, to sell and dispose of the undertakings of the Company, including those being purchased from the Sydenham Glass Company Limited and the Canadian Glass Manufacturing Company Limited, upon the terms set forth in the offer of C. Meredith & Co. Limited dated the 3rd day of April 1913 now submitted to this Company with such modifications as may be deemed advisable.

[Minutes of meeting of directors of Diamond Flint Glass Company Limited held the 13th day of May 1913. Present: G.A. Grier, president, in the chair, D.A. Gordon, F.W. Ross, N.M. Yuile and A.H. Grier.]

A letter from Messrs. C. Meredith & Co. was read amending their offer to purchase the assets of this company, and after discussion it was moved by D.A. Gordon, seconded by F.W. Ross and carried unanimously that the amended offer be accepted and that the president be requested to notify C. Meredith & Company, Limited to that effect.

At a directors' meeting on May 29, 1913, approval was given to National Trust Company with regard to the retirement and redemption of the $600,000 bond issue, dated January 1, 1913. As this company was the owner of all the shares of Sydenham Glass, with the distribution of the 8,000 Diamond Flint shares to the Sydenham shareholders, it would become both debtor and creditor and, as a result, cancelled its obligation to issue these shares.

Bylaw 39, a bylaw for the sale of the undertaking of Diamond Flint Glass as a going concern, was ratified on May 23, 1913, whereby the company, having acquired the assets of Canadian Glass and Sydenham Glass, agreed to accept the purchase offer of C. Meredith & Co.

Bylaw 40 provided that the cash and shares of Dominion Glass Company, Limited, received from C. Meredith & Co., were distributed as follows:

1) Each holder of preferred shares of Diamond Flint Glass, on transferring his preferred shares to The Royal Trust Company, as trustee for C. Meredith & Co., received in exchange for each preferred share so deposited $100 in cash plus 7 percent interest from April 1, 1913.
2) Each holder of common shares of Diamond Flint Glass, on transferring his common shares to The Royal Trust Company, as trustee for C. Meredith & Co., received in exchange for each common share so deposited $100 in cash and 50 percent of the par value of each such share.

The land and buildings conveyed to C. Meredith & Co., which would be the basis of Dominion Glass Company, Limited's assets, were:

a) Those acquired by Diamond Flint Glass from Diamond Glass in 1902:
Diamond Glass in Montreal
Toronto Glass Works
Hamilton Glass and its subsidiary
Burlington Glass (nonoperating)

b) Those acquired by Diamond Flint Glass during its period of operation:
Manitoba Glass, Beausejour, Manitoba
Canadian Glass, Montreal, Quebec
Sydenham Glass, Wallaceburg, Ontario

c) Plants under construction in:
Hamilton, Ontario (Chapple St.)
Redcliff, Alberta

d) 87½-percent interest in Jefferson Glass, formerly Independent Glass producers, Toronto (Carlaw Ave.)

The company's charter was dissolved on February 27, 1928.

The following is a list of officers of the Diamond Flint Glass Company Limited:

Feb. 25, 1903	Henry J. Wright	Director-President
Feb. 25, 1903	John Payne	Director
Feb. 25, 1903	Richard Credicott	Director
Feb. 25, 1903	William J. Gilchrist	Director
Feb. 25, 1903	Henry Toynbee	Director
Feb. 25, 1903	David Yuile	Secretary-Treasurer
Mar. 11, 1903	Beaumont Shepherd	Director-President
Mar. 11, 1903	Alexander McGregor	Director-Secy-Treasurer
Mar. 11, 1903	Richard T. Heneker	Director
Mar. 11, 1903	George Wardrope	Director
Mar. 24, 1903	George Wardrope	Director-Vice-President
Mar. 26, 1903	David Williamson	Managing Director
Mar. 26, 1903	David Yuile	Director
Mar. 26, 1903	George W. Grier	Director
Mar. 26, 1903	Frank W. Ross	Director
Sept. 23, 1903	David Yuile	Director-President
Sept. 23, 1903	Frank Ross	Director-Vice-President
Sept. 23, 1903	John Watt	Director
Feb. 21, 1908	G.A. Grier	Director
Sept. 16, 1909	G.A. Grier	Director-President
Sept. 16, 1909	H. Munderloh	Director
Sept. 15, 1910	N.M. Yuile	Director
Sept. 15, 1910	A.H. Grier	Director
Nov. 21, 1911	D.A. Gordon	Director

THE CANADIAN GLASS MANUFACTURING COMPANY (LIMITED)
Montreal, Quebec (1905-1913)

Two years after Diamond Flint Glass was incorporated to take over the Diamond Glass operation, a new company was established in Montreal. Canadian Glass received a federal charter in 1905 and set up its plant in Pte. St. Charles, in the west end of Montreal, bordering on the City of Verdun. The site was on the south side of Wellington St., at the foot of Charlevoix. Shortly thereafter, they acquired the adjacent (defunct) Montreal Water Works land and buildings.
At the outset, it had all the appearances of being an independent operation. Two of the three directors, H. Jonas and A.R. Oughtred, were not openly connected with Diamond Flint Glass. However, the third director, Henry D. Herdt, was a definite link between the two com-

panies. A further link, although of short duration, was the appointment of Charles B. Grier, son of George A. Grier, a director and officer of Diamond Flint Glass, as Canadian Glass's first secretary-treasurer. Herdt had started with Diamond Glass, carried on with its successor, Diamond Flint Glass, and was now going to continue, supervising the manufacturing operations of Canadian Glass. This appointment surely indicates that, if Canadian Glass was not a wholly-owned subsidiary of Diamond Flint Glass, the latter company must have had a definite interest. As the story unfolds, it will become apparent that Henry Herdt was the key figure behind the whole exercise and that Diamond Flint Glass would achieve its objective of exclusive Canadian rights for the Owens Automatic Forming Machine through the establishment and operation of this company.

Oughtred was elected president and, after Charles Grier's short stint as secretary-treasurer, John Stirling, who had started with the old Dominion Glass Company, became the secretary-treasurer for the duration of the company. Specifications for a glass tank and equipment, prepared by the Dixon Company of Pittsburgh, Pennsylvania, were presented by Herdt and approved.

Little has been recorded about the operation of the company for the next three years. Even in the directors' minutes, consecutively numbered, nothing is recorded between December 1906 and November 1908. It appears that all decisions made on behalf of the company were handled by the directors of Diamond Flint Glass during this period. In 1907 the following appeared in the directors' minutes of Diamond Flint Glass:

> . . . It was thought by our Directors better to work with the Canadian Glass Manufacturing Co., and your Directors have verbally rented to the Company, the Hamilton Glass Works at a rent of $4,000 per annum. They have already loaned to that Company as per statements the sum of $146,000 on 25 June . . .

Again, referring to the directors' minutes of Diamond Flint Glass, it can be seen that a committee comprised of Messrs. G.A. Grier and N.M. Yuile had been negotiating an agreement with Henry Munderloh & Co., principal shareholder of Sydenham Glass, to lease the factories of Diamond Flint Glass to Canadian Glass. As a result, an agreement between Diamond Flint Glass, Canadian Glass, Sydenham Glass and Munderloh & Co., dated February 14, 1908, was signed by Diamond Flint Glass.

In November 1908 the directors enacted Bylaw 6, authorizing the issue of 20-year six-percent first mortgage bonds amounting to $200,000. Although ratified by a shareholders' meeting held on November 19, 1908, it was only activated by the directors in March 1910. At the adjourned meeting on the same day in November 1908, 200 shares were allotted to some 25 employees throughout the company, the principal recipients and their allotments were:

D. Williamson 36	Frank W. Ross 18
Geo. A. Grier 36	Frank Ross 16
David Yuile 17	H. Munderloh 25
John Watt 18	

In January 1909 D.A. Gordon of Sydenham Glass and his wife, Rose, were allotted 13 and 12 shares, respectively, of the 250 authorized shares. Two hundred and twenty-five had been issued to employees of Diamond Flint Glass and their subsidiaries. At the shareholders' meeting held on February 28, 1909, the following Diamond Flint Glass directors were elected directors of Canadian Glass: D. Yuile, F. Ross, G.A. Grier, F.W. Ross, J. Watt and H. Munderloh, together with Henry Herdt, who would become a director of Diamond Flint Glass in 1912. At the following directors' meeting, David Yuile was appointed president and Frank Ross vice-president. Henry Herdt was appointed manager of the Montreal plant and J.W. King was appointed manager of the reopened Hamilton Glass plant of Diamond Flint Glass. Starting with a general meeting of shareholders, held on February 28, 1909, all future directors' and shareholders' meetings were held at the offices of Diamond Flint Glass.

At a directors' meeting in 1910 a report by Messrs. Jenkins and Hardy relating to Diamond Flint Glass, Sydenham Glass and Canadian Glass was presented in what would turn out to be the first overt step in the reorganization of these companies (i.e. the incorporation of Dominion Glass Company, Limited in 1913). A dividend of ten percent on the capital of the company was declared payable forthwith.

The next step was the acquisition in January 1911 of a parcel of land in the east end of Hamilton. In September it was decided to proceed with the construction of a plant thereon, the specifications for which would be prepared by John Watt and J.W. King, the cost, excluding land, not to exceed $105,000. Frank Ross, one of the directors, offered to lend the company up to $100,000 if needed. At the directors' meeting on November 21, 1911, an employees' bonus plan was set up, which would be continued for the remainder of the company's existence as a subsidiary of Diamond Flint Glass. The first bonus was $50 per share for shareholders of record of November 1. Subsequently, eight bonus payments were made, in increments totalling $12,500 each, to shareholders in proportion to their holdings.

In Hamilton a siding agreement was executed with the Toronto, Hamilton & Buffalo Railway for installation on the south side of the new plant. In September 1912 a further sum of $100,000 for completion of the Hamilton plant, including the installation of a sprinkler system, was approved. At the same meeting, it was agreed that the clauses dealing with the leasing of plants, commissions on sales, and distribution of profits between Diamond Flint Glass, Canadian Glass and Sydenham Glass be cancelled on July 1, 1911.

In December 1912 the directors approved the sum of $75,000 for the construction of buildings and the installation of two more bottle-blowing machines at the company's Montreal plant. That same month the directors set aside a sum of $47,500 out of the undivided profits of the company to be used for the granting of bonuses to employees or for carrying out the company's obligations under its employee contracts to give stock of Diamond Flint Glass as part of their salaries. Of the said sum, $20,000 was paid as a cash bonus, the remaining $27,500 was used to assist employees to purchase common shares of Diamond Flint Glass.

In May 1913 Bylaw 27 was passed by the directors, authorizing the sale of the company to Diamond Flint Glass ". . . for the consideration of one dollar and further considerations . . ." effective April 1, 1913. This bylaw was approved and sanctioned at a special general meeting held on May 13, 1913. This ended the operational life of this company under the name The Canadian Glass Manufacturing Company (Limited). The continuing story of this plant will be found in the Diamond Flint Glass history.

In May 1941, at a special general meeting of Canadian Glass, at which all the directors (viz: T.W. Bassett, J.H. Crowe, J.E. Glithero, W. McKibbin, M. Offer, D.J. Ross and J. Wallace) were present, Special Bylaw AA, a bylaw to submit the company's charter for cancellation, was passed and subsequently approved and sanctioned. The effective date of the surrender of the charter was October 2, 1941.

The following is a list of officers of the Canadian Glass Mfg. Co. Ltd.:

Oct. 2, 1905	Allan R. Oughtred	Director-President
Oct. 2, 1905	Henry D. Herdt	Director-Genl. Superintendent
Oct. 2, 1905	Henri Jonas	Director
Oct. 2, 1905	Charles B. Grier	Secretary-Treasurer
Dec. 21, 1906	John Stirling	Secretary-Treasurer
Feb. 23, 1909	D. Yuile	Director-President
Feb. 23, 1909	Frank Ross	Director-Vice President
Feb. 23, 1909	Geo. A. Grier	Director
Feb. 23, 1909	Frank W. Ross	Director
Feb. 23, 1909	John Watt	Director
Feb. 23, 1909	Henry Munderloh	Director
Feb. 23, 1909	Henry D. Herdt	Director
Sept. 16, 1909	Frank Ross	Director-President

Sept. 16, 1909	Geo. A. Grier	Director-Vice President
Sept. 16, 1909	Geo. W. Grier	Director
May 13, 1913	Geo. A. Grier	Director-President
May 13, 1913	Henry Herdt	Director-Vice President
May 13, 1913	N.M. Yuile	Director
May 13, 1913	A.H. Grier	Director
May 13, 1913	John Stirling	Director
May 13, 1913	William Laurie	Director
May 22, 1941	T.W. Bassett	Director-President
May 22, 1941	James Crowe	Director
May 22, 1941	J. Eric Glithero	Director
May 22, 1941	William McKibbin	Director
May 22, 1941	Mervyn Offer	Director-Secretary
May 22, 1941	Donald J. Ross	Director
May 22, 1941	John Wallace	Director

CRYSTAL GLASS COMPANY, LIMITED
Sapperton, British Columbia (1906-c.1908)

The venue of the first documented glasshouse in British Columbia was at Sapperton, a suburb of New Westminster. The town was named after the "sappers," as army engineers were referred to at that time. A formation of Royal Engineers, under the command of Col. Richard Moody, had come out from England to help build New Westminster, which was declared the capital of British Columbia on February 14, 1859. During the establishment of this settlement, it was referred to as "Queensborough." On May 5, 1859, Queen Victoria named it New Westminster, and it is often referred to as the Royal City of New Westminster. Victoria replaced New Westminster as the provincial capital on May 25, 1868.

According to an article by the late Julian H. Toulouse, ". . .There was an earlier glass activity than Crystal in New Westminster, but we have no details of it . . ."[3] In an article by Alan and Dorothy Bradbeer, GLASFAX, the following appears:

> . . . shortly after 1900 a syndicate, involving various brewing, bottling and canning interests, was formed with the intention of purchasing premises on the Fraser River at Sapperton for the site of the glasswork . . .[4]

It would appear that the syndicate referred to was the Vancouver Glass Works Syndicate. No evidence has been found, however, that it ever operated under that name. On May 9, 1906, an agreement was made between Arthur G. Thynne and Richard Byron Johnson, representing the above-named syndicate, and with Herbert Lockwood as trustee for the above, to be incorporated as Crystal Glass Company, Limited. The prime objective was:

> . . . To acquire and take over the assets, property, options, and contracts of the Vancouver Glass Works Syndicate, in the Province of British Columbia, and to adopt and carry into effect, either with or without modification, the agreement set out in the Articles of Association registered herewith . . .[5]

The purchase price was $41,000, made up of $16,000 in paid-up shares in the new company and $25,000 cash.

A memorandum and Articles of Association of Crystal Glass were signed on June 4, 1906. The Crystal Glass Company, Limited was incorporated by a Certificate of Incorporation dated June 14, 1906. The facility they acquired had belonged to the Automatic Can Company, which had a property with a 500-foot frontage on the Fraser River. The address was shown as 772 Brunette St.

Two views of the Automatic Can Company later to become the Crystal Glass Company. In the top photo it appears in the middle of the far shore and in the bottom photo on the far right.

Photographs courtesy of the Vancouver Public Library and the New Westminster Public Library.

In a letter to the Bradbeers in 1966, the late Major J.S. Matthews, archivist for the City of Vancouver, described a trip he had taken "about 1908" from Vancouver to New Westminster by tram.

"... at New Westminster I hired a buggy and horse, at some Westminster livery stable; and drove myself east beyond the Penitentiary, to the brewery on the Coquitlam Road, and I think about half a mile beyond the Penitentiary, turned south towards the river over a corduroy road to a shed where they were making glass. I may not be correct as to detail of location; it was somewhere out there... There was a furnace, and it was in full blast ... I did see some molted (sic) glass poked out on the end of an iron bar; they stuck the bar in for me, it seems from memory." It was his impression that the glassworks ceased operation because of lack of sand, due perhaps to the loss of a ship carrying the sand from Belgium. The furnaces cooled down and, to quote Matthews, ("that was the end of it"). However, although sand was being imported from Belgium, it was planned to utilize the silica deposits in the Fraser Valley at Sumas for making sand.[6]

The facilities comprised two corrugated-iron buildings of 200 feet by 90 feet each, together with an engine and boiler room and wharves on the river front. The operation was run by the famous Donald Lamont, who had left the Montreal operation of Diamond Flint Glass in 1906 to take over the management of Crystal Glass. One of his first decisions was to put a layer of cement over the wooden floors to reduce the hazard of fire from spilled molten glass. A machine shop was set up for the manufacture and repair of moulds, and a continuous tank furnace was built with six rings for flintware, with about 100 workers. Hand production was to include beers, sodas, minerals, wines and brandies, while fruit jars and wide-mouth ware were made on a press machine capable of turning out 3,500 bottles in a nine-hour shift. In those days, Lamont was lucky to have an agreement with the owners for his services, stipulating an annual salary of $2,500, payable 75 percent in cash and the remainder in fully paid-up shares of the company.

As will be seen, it took over a year to get the factory in operation. This was partially due to the great distance from the eastern United States, whence most of the melting and forming equipment came.

The July 6, 1907, issue of New Westminster's *Royal Columbian* stated:

> . . . The fires will be lighted in the glass furnaces about the middle of next week and glass will be produced towards the latter end of the month . . .

On July 26 the *Columbian* reported . . . that light wood fires had been started in the furnaces, and when all was ready the gas from the large gas manufacturing plant in an adjacent building would be turned on and the manufacture of glass would be started. Glassblowers from Montreal and Wallaceburg were expected to arrive in time to start blowing bottles. Special moulds were being made in the machine shop for Vancouver Breweries Ltd., a distillery in New Westminster . . .

The Crystal Glass Company was represented at the Provincial Exhibition, held that autumn in New Westminster, as described in the October 4 edition of the *Columbian*:

> A glistening array of crystal under a blaze of electricity attracts visitors to the Crystal Glass Works Limited . . . Against a background of crystal canes of all shapes and forms a pyramid of bottles is arranged, surmounted by a gilded ball of glass. A display of jars and bottles ranging from fruit jars to flasks and medicine bottles of every size, forms this feature . . . This is the first exhibit made by this firm, it having been in existence in the city for a period of about 2 months only. The daily output of fruit jars is about 2,500, while the same number of beer bottles is daily turned out.

The first directors and officers were:

E. Cook	president
Captain N.M. Garland	vice-president
C.J. Peter	director
R. Martin	director
W. Baird	director
The Rev. J.S. Henderson	secretary-treasurer

In 1908 Mr. Horner was secretary-treasurer. At its peak, it is estimated that the company turned out between 150,000 and 200,000 bottles a month, besides quantities of lamp chimneys, insulators and other industrial ware.

In February 1908 an extraordinary meeting was held for the purpose of raising more money by increasing capitalization. This apparently did not happen and the works closed down in the same year. The company, like so many others, was short-lived. In a letter dated January 6, 1912, from W.B. Ferrie, manager of Canada Life Insurance Company in Vancouver, and one of the original incorporators, to D. Whiteside, Registrar of Joint Stock Companies, Victoria, Ferrie stated:

> Your favour of 29th ult. in reference to Crystal Glass Company, Limited, received. I beg to say that this Company has been out of existence for the last three or four years.

The company was officially dissolved on August 25, 1912. Lamont returned to the employ of Diamond Flint Glass and was their sales representative for British Columbia from 1908-1911.

Manitoba Glass Factory, Beausejour, Manitoba between 1909-1911.   Photograph by J. Reifschneider.

THE MANITOBA GLASS MANUFACTURING COMPANY, LIMITED
Beausejour, Manitoba (1907-1912)

... At Beausejour, a road streaks north to the summer resorts on the east shore of Lake Winnipeg, where the huge waves crash in over the gravel. Grand and Victoria Beaches are quiet residential colonies, rather than amusement beaches. Beausejour was named by the French, who had found it a pleasant camping-ground. The name has stayed with the settlement which grew up. Beyond the neat town with its white houses, its trees and its grain elevators, the road crosses Brokenhead River, once Manitoba's eastern boundary. A tourist park beside the winding river looks charming, promising "un beau sejour" to anyone who stops there. Poplar and ash trees on the banks lean over to see themselves reflected in the quiet water...[7]

This was the setting for Manitoba's first glass factory. It all started in 1905, when a group of Polish residents, headed by Joseph Keilbach, found sand suitable for glassmaking on the edge of the town. Clay for making the pots was imported from Germany and an experimental outdoor operation was started, using wood for melting the batch. The first products were bottles in amber and aqua, and the old pastime of the glassblowers, making whimseys, was practiced.

Within a year, they were sufficiently satisfied that glassmaking was feasible, and so proceeded to set up a regular glassworks on 20 acres of land. The foundation of the works was built of wood. The superstructure was made of local brick and wood. Firebrick for the glass melting furnace was brought in from St. Louis, Missouri. Production of regular amber and aqua bottles was augmented by lamp and lantern chimneys. The principal market for this ware was Winnipeg, some 40 miles to the southwest.

Encouraged by their initial success, Joseph Keilbach, Gustave Boelm, Edward Keilbach, Carl Keilbach, all farmers, and Joseph Wenwoski, a mechanic, all of Beausejour, petitioned the Province of Manitoba in 1907 to ussue letters patent in the name of The Manitoba Glass Manufacturing Company, Limited. This was granted on January 23, 1907. The first directors were Joesph Keilbach, Gustave Boelm and Edward Keilbach. (This operation is sometimes incorrectly referred to as the Beausejour Glass Works.) The foundation of the first works is still in evidence (1967).

Two years later, much larger and more substantial buildings were erected. The foundations were of brick and concrete, with the upper part constructed of sheet iron over steel framing.[8] The remains of the foundations are still identifiable — although somewhat in disarray due to people seeking usable brick. The source of energy for melting was gas, produced on the site from coal. The main stack, to handle the gases generated in the melting furnace, was 120 feet tall. The company operated on a two- or three-shift basis. At its peak of production, from 1908-1913, this factory, along with the earlier one, employed 350 to 400 men and boys. The names of a number of workers brought out from Poland to operate the new works have been recorded and include Adolph Opye, Konarowski and Joseph Wenwoski, a master craftsman who ran the operations. According to Louis Vogel, who started to work there in 1911 at the age of 13, there were six shops in each of the factories, employing some 250 people. Men, boys and girls were employed in grinding off the rough tops of the fruit jars so that a proper seal could be obtained.

The furnaces were about 20 feet in diameter and eight feet high. They were made of firebrick from St. Louis and had gas jets mounted high up inside so that the flames were directed down onto the molten glass. They were capable of generating a heat of 2,000° F, which is somewhat less than the current practice of maintaining the furnace heat at around 2,700° F.

The Polish and German glassblowers were soon replaced by Americans from Chicago, Illinois, and Terre Haute, Indiana. The Americans introduced a new type of blowpipe, which had a conical end, as compared to the straight pipes used by the Poles, and was capable of picking up more glass in a gather. Although most production including lantern and lamp chimneys was handblown, towards the end of the company's period of operation an automatic bottlemaking machine was installed to make a small size of bottle. However, Mac Provick, GLASFAX, indicates in his article that, from the shards found on the site, milk bottles and fruit jars were also machine-made. A few pressed fruit jar lids were also found. The product mix included beers, sodas and prescription bottles, with the emphasis on the number and variety of prescriptions, from 20cc and up. Patent medicines, machine oils and ink bottles were identified from the shards that have been excavated.

According to local residents, and the recovery of shards, beer bottles were made for several breweries in Winnipeg. Shards were also found embossed with trademarks from Victoria and Vancouver. Such production can be attributed but not authenticated to this company, as it could quite possibly have been purchased as cullet (broken glass, a normal ingredient in glassmaking). Most of the soft drink bottle shards were bright green with a crown finish. Embossings included the well-known bottlers, Blackwoods and E.L. Drewry, both of Winnipeg. Round-threaded ink bottles were found in quantity, having been made for the Reliance Ink Company of Winnipeg.

By 1910 the old guard had been replaced by a new group of directors and officers. In 1911 the Hon. Douglas C. Cameron, Lieutenant-Governor of Manitoba and later knighted, was president and John C. McGavin of Winnipeg, a director and secretary, was treasurer. In the same year V.S. Bartners and J.C. Misgades had short terms running the operation before it was taken over by Donald Lamont, who had come out from the old Montreal plant of Diamond Flint Glass to take charge for the remainder of the operating period. They were now operating five bottlemaking machines — a Miller, an O'Neill and three Teeple Johnsons. In order to support this continuous increase in production activity, it was necessary to create additional capital. In 1910 the capital was increased to $300,000 and a year later to $1,000,000. In 1912 the company marked $400,000 of the capitalization as preference shares.

A broad range of drug and prescription shards were found, mostly in flint (clear) glass, but some in pale green. Embossed on shards found in the shambles were the Western Sewing Machine Co., Winnipeg, and the Rawleigh Medicine Co. emblem, with the words "W.T. Raleigh Medicine Company Winnipeg." Parts of spirits bottles, including one of the "Shoo-Fly" style, were found, but can only be attributed to the company pending further conclusive evidence. Douglas Bird attributes the Acme Seal fruit jar to Manitoba Glass.

It is my opinion that Donald Lamont's move to Manitoba Glass in 1911 was arranged by Diamond Flint Glass, perhaps by mutual consent of the two companies, to see the lay of the land. It seems history was repeating itself. Since joining Diamond Glass in Montreal about 1897, after his own company had been taken over, wherever Lamont went — or more likely, was sent — after that, Diamond Glass, and later Diamond Flint Glass, took over that operation and either operated it for a short period or closed it down.

Manitoba Glass continued to operate independently and successfully during the period 1907-1912. On September 28, 1912, an agreement was signed between Manitoba Glass and Diamond Flint Glass for the takeover of the former company by October 1, 1912. In essence, the land was to be sold for $10,000 and the remainder of assets to be sold for a price to be determined by mutual consent or, failing that, at a price to be established by the American Appraisal Company. In the end, with an appraised value of $97,957.29 as a starting point, the transaction was completed by an agreement dated March 8, 1913, amending the agreement of September 28, 1912, whereby Diamond Flint Glass paid Manitoba Glass $107,500 as the full purchase price of all the said lands, factories, equipment, chattels, materials, supplies and cullet, but not the manufactured stock, the property of the vendor. A third document between the two companies, dated March 19, 1913, gave Diamond Flint Glass the option of acquiring an additional (from one to 20) acreage by no later than September 28, 1914, for the price of $1,000 per acre, cash.

The plant did not operate after the spring of 1913.

ALBERTA GLASS COMPANY LIMITED
Medicine Hat, Alberta (1911)

Many years ago, so the story goes, there was a great battle between the Cree and the Blackfoot on the bank of a southern Alberta river. The Cree fought valiantly until their medicine man deserted them — losing his headdress in midstream as he fled to the safety of the opposite shore. Believing this to be a bad omen, the Cree put down their weapons and were massacred by the Blackfoot. The site of this tragedy was called "SAAMIS," an Indian word meaning "medicine man's hat." Years later, in 1882, when the Royal North West Mounted Police and the Canadian Pacific Railway roadbuilders settled the area, the Indian name was translated and shortened to Medicine Hat.

Thirty years after its establishment in 1883, Medicine Hat had a population of 15,000 and was enjoying a land boom. The Canadian Pacific Railway was the biggest employer, with 650 on the payroll. Why would Medicine Hat have been chosen for the location of a glass factory? It would appear that it offered the three ingredients necessary for the operation of a manufacturing company: cheap land, plentiful natural gas and good public transportation for inbound raw materials and outbound finished goods.

The company was promoted by Mr. A.E. Cross, president and manager of the Calgary Brewing and Malting Company, some 150 miles to the northwest, who was seeking a local supply of bottles for his brewing operation. Together with Mr. F. Allan, manager of Western Agencies and Development Company, Limited, and J.W. Davidson, president of Crown Lumber Company, both of Calgary, Cross made an application for a charter for a glass company. The certificate of incorporation is rather interesting. It was incorporated under the Ordinance of the North-West Territories, but was signed by the Registrar of Joint Stock Companies of the Province of Alberta.

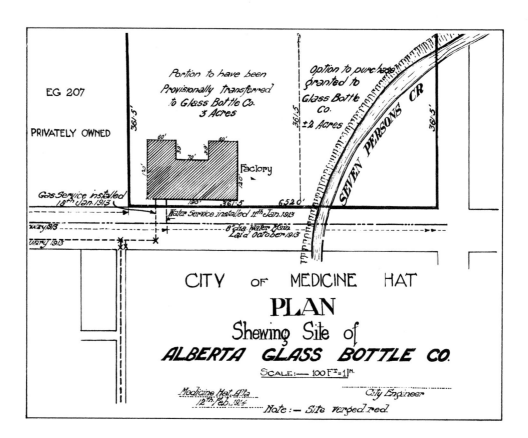

Site of the
Alberta Glass Company,
Medicine Hat Alberta.

The plant was located on approximately three acres of land, at the corner of Medalta Avenue and Pottery Street. This facility was never completed. In a report by G. Percy Cole, technical engineer of Dominion Glass, addressed to Mr. Herdt, superintendent of works for Dominion, April 19, 1917, he states in part:

> . . . The plant was never finished or operated, although the buildings themselves may be said to be practically completed. A hand furnace of quite liberal proportions comprises the only installation, no lehrs or other equipment having ever been installed . . . .

In my opinion, the fact that Diamond Flint Glass had already started to build a glass factory in nearby Redcliff was the deciding factor in the abandonment of the Medicine Hat project by its promoters. To support this, Dominion Glass, the successor to Diamond Flint Glass, reimbursed Cross and his associates in the amount of $1,149.60 to defray the cost of the incorporation fees. As the plant never operated, its entire history is included in this chapter.

In 1916 the municipality seized the property for back taxes. In 1917 Dominion Glass purchased the plant for $7,500. In 1920 the buildings, which had been leased to the Saskatchewan Bridge and Iron Company, were destroyed by fire. The amount of $7,000 insurance was considered to be adequate to cover the loss. Finally, in 1927, the property was sold to Medalta Potteries Limited for $1,000 by deed of transfer. The company was dissolved on December 15, 1927.

WELLAND GLASS MANUFACTURING COMPANY LIMITED
Welland, Ontario (1909)

This company was incorporated "To manufacture, sell and deal in all kinds of glass and all articles made from glass or of which glass shall form a part." No other action appears to have been taken.

FOOTNOTES

[1] Julian H. Toulouse, *Fruit Jars*, (Don Mills: Thomas Nelson & Sons Canada Limited (1969), p. 277.
[2] Extract from Bylaw 36 of Diamond Flint Glass Company Limited approved at a directors' meeting held on May 13, 1913.
[3] Julian H. Toulouse, "Bottle Makers of the Pacific Northwest," GLASFAX *Newsletter*, (1973), p. 16.
[4] Alan Bradbeer and Dorothy Bradbeer, "British Columbia's First Glass Factory — The Crystal Glass Company," *Canadian Collector*, (May/June 1976), pp. 104-06.
[5] Memorandum of Association of Crystal Glass Company Limited, para. 3(a) June 4, 1906.
[6] Alan Bradbeer and Dorothy Bradbeer, p. 105.
[7] Lyn Harrington, *Manitoba Roundabout*, (Toronto: Ryerson Press 1951), p. 71.
[8] A.M. Provick, "Beausejour Glass Works," *Canadian Collector*, (January 1967), pp. 7-10.

Dominion Glass Company, Redcliff works, Redcliff, Alberta.   Photograph courtesy Dominion Glass Company.

Perfect Seal fruit jars at back of lehrs, New Wallaceburg factory, 1916.
Photograph courtesy of Dominion Glass Company.

CHAPTER 6

The Canadian Glass Industry Comes of Age (1913-1925)

Dominion Glass Company, Limited, Montreal (1913-1976), a reorganization of Diamond Flint Glass, was the third conglomerate and, on incorporation, took over and operated the latter company's plants on Delorimier Avenue and in Pte. St. Charles in Montreal, Jefferson Glass and Toronto Glass in Toronto, and Sydenham Glass in Wallaceburg, Ontario. As well, it took over the shut-down plants in Hamilton, Hamilton Glass and Burlington Glass, and began construction of two new plants in Hamilton and Redcliff, Alberta. Three personalities in the company: Mervyn Offer, Jim Mackenzie and Mac Yuile. The Owens and other automatic bottlemaking machines. Discussions with other glass companies. Sale of Toronto Glass and Burlington Glass Properties.

Consumers Glass Company, Limited (1917-1925) was the first successful glass producer on the site in Ville St. Pierre, Quebec, following the unsuccessful attempts of a splinter group from Diamond Flint Glass on Delorimier Avenue to start a new operation, firstly under the name Atlas Glass Works, Limited (1912-1914) and its successor, the Premier Glass Company of Canada, Limited (1914-1917)

The Victoria Glass and Bottle Company, Limited, Victoria, British Columbia (1914-c.1915)

Canada Flint Glass Company, Limited, Toronto, Ontario (1919), which did not operate

Feldspar Glass Limited, Oshawa, Ontario (1921-c.1933)

THE INDUSTRY COMES OF AGE (1913-1925)

The two principal manufacturers of glass containers in Canada in the twentieth century were Dominion Glass Company, Limited, which started in 1913, and Consumers Glass Company Limited, which started four years later.

DOMINION GLASS COMPANY, LIMITED[1] (1913-1976)
Montreal, Quebec, and elsewhere

Dominion Glass was not a new company but simply the latest name for a specific group of glass operations that had been established by the Yuile brothers in 1878. Like its predecessor, Diamond Flint Glass, Dominion was on the planning board for several years before its actual establishment. By 1910 it was obvious that the trend to machine production was here to stay. In 1911 Diamond Flint Glass purchased all shares of Canadian Glass Manufacturing Glass Co. and Sydenham Glass. It then owned or controlled every operating bottlemaking company in Canada, with the exception of Humphreys' Glass Co., in Moncton, N.B. In 1912 Diamond

Wallaceburg Chimney Machines and tank, Green Factory, 1916.

Photograph courtesy of Dominion Glass Company.

Hartford #28 tumbler machine.
Photograph courtesy of Dominion
Glass Company.

Dramatic photograph of the Dominion Glass Company, Redcliff plant, Redcliff Alberta.
Photograph courtesy
Dominion Glass Company.

Flint Glass built new plants for machine production in Hamilton, Ontario, and Redcliff, Alberta. Early in 1913, it acquired control (87½ percent) of Jefferson Glass Co. in Toronto by bailing them out of a cash crisis.[2]

The reorganization of Diamond Flint Glass into a new company was rather devious and well planned in advance. Part of the consideration for which C. Meredith & Co. bought the assets of that company and acquired Canadian Glass and Sydenham Glass was that a new company would be formed under the name Canadian Glass Corporation, or such other name as Meredith & Co. might determine. The name turned out to be Dominion Glass Company, Limited. The actual sale of Diamond Flint Glass was completed June 12, 1913, a month after Dominion Glass was incorporated.

Dominion Glass obtained a federal charter on May 15, 1913, and started with a capital of $8,000,000. Additional capital was raised by the issue of a 20-year six-percent Sinking Fund Trust Mortgage Gold Bond in the aggregate of $3,000,000. Dominion took over the head office of Diamond Flint at the plant site, later renting temporary space in the Royal Trust Company building on Place d'Armes. It moved uptown in 1918 to occupy several floors in the Guarantee Company of North America building, at the top of Beaver Hall Hill, until that building was demolished in 1967.

The operating facilities acquired from Diamond Flint, with their new designations, were as follows:

Diamond Flint (Montreal)	— Delorimier
Canadian Glass (Montreal)	— Pte. St. Charles
Jefferson Glass (Toronto)	— Jefferson until 1922 and then Carlaw
Toronto Glass	— Parkdale
Hamilton Glass	— Old James St. property
Hamilton (new) (under construction)	— Hamilton
Sydenham Glass	— Wallaceburg
Redcliff, Alberta (new) (under construction)	— Redcliff

James R. Mackenzie
Photograph by Hubert Beckett.

Sales offices continued to be located in Montreal, Toronto, Winnipeg and Vancouver. With the exception of George A. Grier, who was retained as president during the formative years, there was a new slate of directors and officers to better represent the broader interests of the company. Of the nine original directors, five were from Montreal, one from Quebec City, one from Wallaceburg, Ontario, and two from England.

The day-to-day management of the company was left to the executive committee (changed to officer's committee in 1915), whose liaison with the plants was carried out by the superintendent of works, Henry Herdt. In a similar manner, the head office managers dealt with their opposite numbers at the plants and regional sales offices.

Every industry has had its quota of personalities, and the glass industry was no exception. Many of them were members of multi-generation glass families. Here, I have selected three Dominion Glass employees, with a combined service of 162 years, who, in my opinion, contributed more to the ongoing success of the company than any other three employees.

The foremost of the trio was Mervyn "M.O." Offer. A shy Englishman, Offer had come out to Canada with Noel Buch in 1910 to establish Lloyds' first brokerage in Montreal, Matthews, Wrightson. Of medium height and balding, he was easily recognizable, having a forbidding appearance and bushy eyebrows (these he tweaked on the slightest provocation). Offer was appointed secretary of Dominion Glass on its incorporation. This position he held, with other duties from time to time as treasurer and controller, until his retirement as secretary in 1945. He was then elected a director and served until his death in 1955. In 42 years of service, he enjoyed a position of authority and respect well beyond his appointed position and provided a focus of continuity for succeeding groups of directors and officers. I was taken under Offer's wing for training when I joined the company in 1932.

In the manufacturing division of the company, James Robertson "J.R.M." Mackenzie was by far the most travelled person, having managed or acted as a consultant at Pte. St. Charles, Toronto, Hamilton, Wallaceburg and Redcliff. He finally became vice-president of manufacturing at head office. Jim was a director of the company from 1964 to 1967. He was born in Sarnia, Ontario, in 1897. He retired in 1967 and lived in Hamilton, Ontario, until his death in 1984. He told me this story in an interview:

> I started working at Hamilton Factory in October of 1915, nailing lids on wooden boxes after the bottles had been packed. The rate of pay was 16 cents per hour for 12 hours during the day and 13 at night, and there were no coffee breaks. I progressed to the job of carrying bottles on a paddle into the lehr, which was a hot

job and was always hard to fill. There was a shortage of men and positions were hard to fill, as I said before, so I was moved up front. Mike Hudecki showed me how to run the Owens AE bottle machine.

In 1916 I quit to join the army. In 1917, when I came back, jobs were scarce but I was able to rejoin Dominion Glass, Hamilton Factory, as a machine operator, operating an AR machine. I remained at Hamilton Factory until 1925, when I was transferred to Montreal to work as a superintendent under Horace Morin, who was the manager at that time.

In 1926 I was transferred to Toronto to work for the sales department as a customer troubleshooter. From Toronto to Wallaceburg was my next transfer, as I had Owens experience and they needed men to operate this machine, which was producing beer bottles for the bootleg trade.

I spent 16 years at Redcliff, with my first major job being to survey and report as to whether the factory should stay in Redcliff or go to Vancouver. I discovered that what was selling was natural gas at glass bottle prices, so my report recommended that the plant stay in Redcliff as there was no "free" gas in Vancouver.

In 1946 I was transferred to Hamilton as factory manager, taking the place of Jimmy Sephton, who was transferred to Pointe St. Charles, replacing Horace Morin, who was retiring.

While in Hamilton I made plans to turn the factory around during the ten years which I spent at that location. In 1957 I was transferred back to Montreal (head office) to take charge of manufacturing. I stayed there until 1967, when I retired after 52 years of service.

Norman MacLeod "Mac" Yuile on far right, at a reception, 1959.
Photograph by Richard Arless Associates.

The third man was Norman MacLeod "Mac" Yuile, son of William Yuile, one of the two Yuile brothers who, in 1878, founded the Canadian glass dynasty that would become Dominion Glass in 1913. Mac started his glass career in 1899 on Delorimier Ave., in Montreal, when it was the Diamond Glass Company. He continued on when it became Diamond Flint Glass and ended up with Dominion Glass. In 1906 he became assistant manager of the Diamond Flint plant in Montreal, and a year later became manager. In 1910 he was elected to the board of Diamond Flint Glass and was on the operating committee. He was on the Canadian Glass Manufacturing Company board for the year 1913, but resigned on being appointed sales manager of Dominion Glass. He was also responsible for the company's interests in Jefferson

Glass. In 1924 he resigned as sales manager in order to take a more active part in Cassidys Limited, which his family controlled. Cassidys was the main distributor for the company's non-bottle production. Shortly thereafter, he became a director of Dominion Glass, which position he held until his death in 1964. His service to the company totalled 65 years. Mac, like his close friend M.O., was quite shy, a surprising trait for a very successful sales executive.

The long-term objective was to gradually concentrate all the hand and specialty production at the Wallaceburg plant while still retaining at that plant sufficient machine production of bottles to serve the western Ontario market. This transition was completed about 1925 with the termination of production at Delorimier and Parkdale. Jefferson, which became a fully-owned subsidiary of Dominion in 1916, became known as the Carlaw plant in 1922 and ceased production about ten years later.

Since the early part of the twentieth century, automatic and semiautomatic bottlemaking machines have been slowly eliminating the glassblower from the production of bottles. The semiautomatic machines, which later became fully automatic, were generically known as feeder machines and included such names as O'Neill, Lynch and Miller. Whereas the Owens machine sucked up its gob of glass from the revolving pot, the gobs for the feeder machines were sheared off from a steady stream of molten glass that emanated from a mechanism known as a feeder — which was on the end of a long enclosed trough, through which the glass moved from the furnace. The feeder machines were energized by compressed air, as opposed to the Owens machine, which operated by electricity. Until about 1945, when both of these types of machines were phased out by the introduction of the new Hartford Empire individual section machine, the Owens machine was the principal production unit at Pte. St. Charles and Hamilton, whereas the various types of feeder machines were concentrated in Hamilton and Wallaceburg. Redcliff started with hand production but moved to feeder operations later on.

The success of these machines indicated the need to rearrange the company's operations into two separate types of production — mass machine production and specialized hand production. This dictated the following breakdown by plants:

MACHINE PRODUCTION	HAND PRODUCTION
Pte. St. Charles	Delorimier
Hamilton	Parkdale
Wallaceburg (bottles)	Jefferson (Carlaw)
Redcliff	Wallaceburg (other)

The company had just settled down when World War I broke out in the summer of 1914. It wasn't long before production capacity exceeded demand. In the directors' annual report dated 16 December 1914, the following statements reflected the war's effect on the company's operations:

> Having in view the general contraction of trade during the year . . . It is yet too early to express a definite opinion as to the effect of prevailing conditions upon the operations of the current year but it is feared that a further contraction of trade must be anticipated . . . .

As more and more key personnel answered the call to the colours, plant managers were concerned about the status of service reservists. Until a public announcement was made, the directors decided that the dependents of any of the company's regular employees who went on active service would be looked after, with a review every six months. A.H. Grier of head office and W.A. Hossie from the Winnipeg sales office were among those who first saw active service. In 1916 Jos. Cauliez of Pointe St. Charles joined the tricolour of France. Due to the uncertain supply and demand situation during the war, management started to set up a simple form of production scheduling for all the plants to best utilize their capacities and capabilities. Although it had been planned to concentrate the mass production of bottles at the three Owens-equipped plants — Pte. St. Charles, Hamilton and Wallaceburg — it was not always feasible to do so. As a result, it was necessary to transfer the moulds from plant to plant to best accommodate the production schedule. Because of the war, imports of Belgian window glass ceased. Serious consideration was given to the idea of setting up a flat glass production line in the Redcliff plant, but the idea was shelved in 1915. The company then considered the idea of exporting glass products to England because of its wartime restrictions on production. Mr. Lydiatt, the manager at Redcliff, went to England and reported back that it would not be feasible because of low prices there and the high cost of shipping. The year closed with the company still operating under capacity and with the expectation of worse to come.

Carried over from the old hand shop days, when the plants operated from October to the following June, was the term "fire." Thus the "fire" of 1914-1915 represented the period of operations starting early in October and ending in the following June. Comparative figures for the "fires" of 1914-15 and 1913-14 clearly indicated the effect on the company as the war progressed, and the fact that Owens mass production had been reduced:

	1914/15	1913/14	Difference
Glass Packed in lbs.	54,608,789	89,105,590	38.7%
Mfg. Cost per lb Cents	2,750	2,511	9.9%
Ware Mfd. Sale Price	2,063,249	3,285,786	37.2%
Mfg. Cost to Sale Price	72.8%	68.09%	4.7%
Lbs. of Glass per $ of S.P.	26.4	27.1	.7 lbs.
Owens Machine Ware Mfd.	876,832 (42.5%)	1,616,231 (49.2%)	46%
Other Ware Mfd.	1,186,437 (57.5%)	1,669,555 (50.8%)	29%

When the company obtained the exclusive Canadian rights for Owens machine production, a clause in the agreement precluded the company from exporting Owens-made ware to any country in which an exclusive had been granted. As an example, no Owens ware could be exported to Japan because such an agreement had been granted to a glass company in that country; and vice versa, Japan could not export Owens ware into Canada. England, however, was an exception. Although it had an agreement, due to wartime restrictions on production there, the company was able to negotiate an arrangement through George A. Alexander of London whereby Canadian glassware could be exported to England in the same way that the United States could export to England.

The product mix of hand, semiautomatic and automatic ware was growing by leaps and bounds and it was deemed advisable to set up a centralized mould record system and a sample room at head office.

Another casualty of the war was the cutting off of some major raw materials supplied from overseas. This necessitated the finding of new sources in Canada and the United States. One supply of sand was found in Melocheville, Quebec, where a deposit was leased for five years at $500 per annum, with a maximum draw of 10,000 tons per year. For manganese dioxide, much of which came from Russia, there was a different solution. It was replaced by selenium, which was available in both Canada and the United States. Its use in the glass industry is almost contradictory:

> Metallic selenium is used in the glass industry as a colorizer for various types of ruby, pink, and amber glass, and as a decolorizer in flint, or so-called water-white glass. As a decolorizer, selenium has now practically displaced manganese dioxide. Some of its advantages are that it does not burn out so readily; higher heat in the annealing furnaces, or lehrs, does not produce an intensified colour; and, after it is once incorporated in the glass, probably in colloidal suspension, it is retained permanently, provided a temperature of above 2,600° F. is not reached.
>
> Due to its powerful action, very small amounts are required to offset the greenish tint produced by the iron impurity contained in the raw materials of the batch, one ounce per ton of sand being the average quantity used. The colour produced is even better and more stable than that with manganese, and it does not change appreciably when the finished bottles are stored in the sun for long periods.[3]

When Dominion was established, there were two inactive independent companies: Manitoba Glass in Beausejour, Manitoba, which Diamond Flint had acquired in 1912, and the unfinished Alberta Glass in Medicine Hat, Alberta. In May 1914 Diamond Flint transferred Manitoba Glass to Dominion, who eventually disposed of it. In 1915 Dominion acquired the remaining 12½ percent outstanding interest in Jefferson Glass for $50,000 from Jefferson Glass in West Virginia.

Despite the company's healthy operating position in 1915, it is surprising to find that it still had outstanding loans on its books in the amount of $319,002.53 from some of its directors and shareholders. By July 1, 1917, $168,000 of these loans had been retired.

In 1916 the officers' committee was renamed the officers' executive committee. Its first chairman, A.H. Grier, president of the company, also established and assumed the new title of general manager, which title continued to be used until 1967, when a senior management group was established.

With the advent of machine production, glass melting furnaces replaced the former clay pots. Up until 1917, the clay blocks for these furnaces were ordered from such suppliers as the H.L. Dixon Company in Pittsburgh, Pennsylvania. In 1917 a clay block plant was set up at Wallaceburg to make the blocks for some of the smaller furnaces. Frank Carey, a tank builder, was in charge of this plant until his retirement in 1943.

The first common stock dividend of one percent was declared in August 1918. After five years of consideration, the company's securities were listed on the Montreal Stock Exchange on January 24, 1918. The dividend was increased to 1½ percent in 1920 and 1¾ percent in 1922.

At the directors' organizational meeting, following the annual general meeting in 1918, Sir Charles Gordon requested that he be relieved of his duties as president, owing to his additional duties in connection with the British War Mission in Washington and the expectation of his being called to Ottawa frequently during the ensuing year. But due to the fact that Abner Kingman, the vice-president, was expected to be abroad on war service much of the coming year, it was decided that Sir Charles remain as president and that William McMaster replace Abner Kingman as vice-president for one year. (In fact, he retained this position until his death on May 5, 1930, when his son, Ross H. McMaster, replaced him.)

Discussions took place in 1919-1920 with Consumers Glass, incorporated in 1917, on the subject of Dominion Glass buying their capital stock. Talks broke off when Dominion's directors deemed the terms to be excessive.

In May 1920 Ralph King retired after serving for 25 years in various managerial positions in Diamond Glass, Diamond Flint Glass and Dominion Glass. His last appointment was plant manager of Toronto (Parkdale). He was also responsible for the overall supervision of the Hamilton plant, at which his brother James was local manager. He was retained as a consultant and appointed to the board of directors. At the same time, and with the permission of the board, he was responsible for establishing Canadian Libbey-Owens Sheet Glass Company in Hamilton.

With the resignation of Ralph King, there was a realignment of duties in Ontario at the beginning of 1921. James W. King became plant manager in Hamilton. Donald D. Gordon, son of the late D.A. Gordon, became manager at Wallaceburg.

With sales for 1921 of $6,682,801.17, Mr. Yuile, the sales manager, was finding it difficult to coordinate the marketing effort. To correct this situation, a divisional sales office was set up at Parkdale under the direction of T.B. Dundas in January 1921. In November an eastern sales office was established at head office in Montreal under Mr. F.E. Johns. Both Dundas and Johns would report to Yuile. A much closer relationship was then established between Yuile, Herdt (general superintendent) and Dundas in Toronto.

The year 1921 started out with a curtailment of production throughout the company. The market was soft and sales were off about 17 percent from the previous year. Reflecting the recession that was taking place, a general reduction in wages and salaries of from 10 to 20 percent was effected. Short-lived discussions took place re the possibility of Corning Glass Works of Corning, N.Y., buying an interest in the company in order to manufacture some of its products in Canada, but nothing came of it.

In the same year, a new production technique became available to the company. Up until now, the moulds on the Owens machines were single moulds, i.e. there was a single bottle-forming cavity in each mould. A double cavity mould had now been developed for some of these machines, and thus two bottles could be made at the same time. There were great cost advantages to this set-up.

In order to speed up communications between various branches of the company, private telegraph wires were used between Montreal and Toronto (Parkdale), and Toronto and Hamilton.

An example of the type of competition the company was facing from imports can be seen in a minute of the executive officers' committee of April 1922:

B.C. COMPETITION

Reported that considerable British Columbia milk bottle business as being lost to the San Francisco [California] factory [Pacific Coast Glass Works] due particularly to the cheap water rates of 60 cents and the convenience of shipping L.C.L. [less than carload]. The water rates from Europe via Panama were also reported to be very advantageous and doubtless there would be a further loss of business unless something could be done with the rail rates [in Canada]. Mr. Yuile undertook to consider the best manner of approaching the Canadian Pacific Railway for a considerable reduction of the rail rate . . . .

A month later, Yuile reported that the CPR had been seen and their tentative support obtained for a reduction on rates on milks to the Coast. The Rate Committee now had an application before them for a dollar rate to the Coast.

One of the main reasons for selecting Redcliff, Alberta, as the site of the plant that would handle glass requirements in the West was the abundant supply of natural gas, some of which came from wells on the company's property. In December 1922 the company purchased all the issued shares and the bonds of the Canadian Western Power & Fuel Co. Limited at a price of $300,000. Shortly thereafter, CWP&F supplied some of Calgary's gas requirements.

Dominion Glass, from its earliest predecessor in 1878 to today, has always been a truly Canadian company, as the statistics for 1925 would suggest:

Reporting as follows regarding distribution of shareholders in December last:

	Preferred Stock	Common Stock
Total issued	26,000 shares	42,500 shares
Held in United Kingdom	2,734 shares	1,129 shares
No. of Holders in U.K.	104	43
Largest Holding in U.K.	259 shares	250 shares
Held in U.S.A. & abroad	738 shares	619 shares
No. of Holders in U.S.A. etc.	37	28
Largest Holding in U.S.A. etc.	58 shares	75 shares

During the first five years of the company's operations, it was difficult for the sales organization to match the production capacity of the company's plants. In the period under review (1913-1925), sales almost exactly doubled themselves, $3,227,632 in 1913 to $6,473,169 twelve years later.

For several years the company had been working towards centralization of its operations by selling off surplus land and, at the same time, enlarging plant sites where necessary. Following this policy, part of the Parkdale property was sold in April 1925. In June of the same year, the old Burlington Glass site in Hamilton was sold for $20,000. And in September, that portion of Parkdale north of Sudbury St. was sold to Toronto Hosiery Co. for $60,000.

CONSUMERS GLASS COMPANY, LIMITED
Ville St. Pierre, Quebec

The other large Canadian bottle manufacturer was Consumers Glass Company, Limited, which was started in 1917, taking over an unfinished glass factory that had been under construction since 1912. That was the year Atlas Glass Works, Limited had been started by a splinter group from Diamond Flint Glass. In 1914, with the advent of World War I, it ran out of funds and declared bankruptcy. Undaunted, two of the leaders formed a syndicate to carry on. This was done under the name The Premier Glass Company of Canada, Limited. By 1917, when it was almost ready to produce glass, Premier went into liquidation. Consumers Glass was formed to buy its assets.

ATLAS GLASS WORKS, LIMITED
Town of St. Pierre (Ville St. Pierre), Quebec (1912-1914)

The years 1911-1913 were important ones in the history of the Canadian glass industry. Diamond Flint Glass was in the process of acquiring most of the independent companies, which culminated in the creation of Dominion Glass in 1913. At the same time, a threat to its monopoly was quietly developing.

In 1911 Lymans Ltd., well-established druggists in Montreal and one of Diamond Flint's regular customers, made inquiries of the H.L. Dixon Company, Pittsburgh, Pennsylvania, glasshouse specialists, about the cost of establishing a glass factory in Canada. They estimated that to produce from $300,000 to $500,000 worth of glass products per year, it would require two tank furnaces, eight lehrs, and one mould oven (for preheating the moulds), at an approximate cost of $25,000. In addition, if producer gas was used to heat the furnaces, an additional $10,000 would be required. A year later, David Pugh, general manager of Diamond and said to have ambitions of his own, teamed up with O.J. Klein, a recent arrival from Payne Brothers, a well-established glassmaker in England, to consider the same idea. Was this just a coincidence?

I believe it was more than that. It is highly plausible that Lymans may not have been entirely happy with the monopolistic attitude of Diamond Flint and therefore was seeking an alternative supplier. What would be more natural than to encourage Pugh, a qualified glass technician, to spearhead such a project?

Be that as it may, Atlas Glass received a federal charter on August 16, 1912, with its head office in Montreal and the plant to be built in what is now Ville St. Pierre, a municipality on the western edge of Montreal. The regular remission of taxes for ten years was provided by the town council, provided the company operated for at least 40 weeks a year. O.L. Brunelle was elected president, J. Whitesell secretary-treasurer, and David Pugh manager.

Atlas was to be a hand and press shop, with two furnaces and four double lehrs for production of bottles and pressed ware. Construction continued until the outbreak of World War I in 1914, when the company went bankrupt. It appears that Klein was still enthusiastic because, in the same year, he promoted a new company, Premier Glass, to take over the assets of Atlas.

THE PREMIER GLASS COMPANY OF CANADA, LIMITED
Ville St. Pierre, Quebec (1914-1917)

It would appear that O.J. Klein, who had been associated with David Pugh of Diamond Flint Glass in setting up Atlas Glass, had already anticipated the impending bankruptcy of that company, because in 1913 he had a new project under way.

In that year he formed the Primus Syndicate, hoping to raise $825,000 through stock issued in the United States, Canada and England. Primus would use some of that money to buy from Klein various contracts he had pulled together in the previous 12 months. These included a deal with Payne Brothers to allow its name to be used in connection with the prospectus to supply all the skilled labour needed to start the new factory; Canadian rights for the new Severin glassmaking machine, invented a year earlier in Strassburg and capable of producing six bottles every 55 seconds without hand labour; offers by three communities to provide free land and special tax deals if Klein would locate his new glassworks in their town; and a deal to buy the land and nearly finished plant of the now bankrupt Atlas Glass Works for $170,000 in bonds and $72,000 in cash.

The package proved attractive enough for Klein to raise at least some of the money. In May 1914 Primus Syndicate sold the various assets it had acquired from Klein to the new Premier Glass Company for $1,405,000.

Premier Glass was incorporated by federal charter on May 9, 1914, with a capital of $3,000,000. The group behind this venture included Mr. Prind Bernier and His Worship J.H. Lebeuf, Mayor of Ville St. Pierre. The prospectus listed the Honourable Sir Douglas C. Cameron, K.C.M.G., Lieutenant-Governor of Manitoba, as president.

The appointment of Cameron as president brought some reaction from the recently formed Dominion Glass. When Diamond Flint Glass took over Manitoba Glass in 1910, Cameron was Manitoba's president. Article 10 of the agreement stated in part ". . . It is also understood and agreed that the present directors and officers (of Manitoba Glass) shall not in the future acquire or hold any interest in any other glass company manufacturing competing lines of glassware in the Dominion of Canada . . ." Dominion Glass inherited this stipulation when it took over Diamond Flint Glass in 1913.

Klein was vice-president and general manager, and other directors included: Henry Timmis, president of The Canada Jewellers and The Raymond Cement Products Company; C.E. Vidricaire, a banker; the Honourable George A. Simard, a member of the Quebec Legislature; and Henri Jonas.

Housing workmen was a problem in Montreal in those days, so the new company promised to build workmen's homes "of fire proof construction, of artistic architecture, and with all conveniences" near the Ville St. Pierre plant and sell them to workers.

David Pugh became works manager. Payne Brothers provided an assistant works manager and foreman. Others actively involved with Klein at the time were Henri Jonas and Arthur Lyman. The Canadian works were to become, as far as possible, a replica of the English factories, producing a quality of glass never before attained in Canada.

Premier got further than Atlas. At the Ville St. Pierre property, it installed lehrs, bottle machines (an Olean three-plunger, an O'Neill semiautomatic, and a Miller improved), and a jar machine (the Cox Improved semiautomatic); it also obtained the exclusive Canadian rights to the Williamstown narrow-mouth bottle machine for prescription ware, but it never completed the fire walls of the two continuous melting furnaces.

The Ville St. Pierre council, under Mayor Lebeuf, was helpful. In June 1914 it lent Premier $50,000 at 6½ percent. As security for the loan, Premier put up $60,000 worth of its own debentures, part of a $300,000 issue.

The necessary equipment for glass production had been assembled, right down to milk bottle moulds, gaffers' chairs, mould racks and a snap carrier. All that was needed to get production under way was to finish the furnaces, about $16,000 worth of work. It didn't happen.

Klein's proposition had been to reissue Premier Glass Company bonds to the old bond-holders of Atlas Glass and to take over all of the unfinished contracts of Atlas and pay the full amount for having them completed, and also pay about 50 cents on the dollar to the creditors of Atlas. His proposition was accepted by the liquidators and the bond transfer was made. Klein used Primus in an attempt to sell stock in England to get working capital.

As all of the original Atlas Glass bonds had not been sold, they were transferred to Klein for Premier bonds, $50,000 of which were subscribed for by the town of Ville St. Pierre. In an effort to get his hands on the money subscribed by the town before it was due, Klein sold this $50,000 for $37,500 to a firm of bankers in Montreal. A certain portion of the money received went to the Primus Syndicate, or O.J. Klein. The balance was used for some work at the plant, as also was the money received from the English subscriptions.

The English sales of stock did not move very fast and, with rumours of war in 1914, it dropped off almost completely, leaving Klein without any money to fully equip the plant or for working capital. About March or April 1915, the company was on the rocks completely, but Klein kept struggling with it until it was again thrown into liquidation. On March 14, 1917, the Ville St. Pierre council turned over its Premier Glass debentures to the liquidators. That was the end of the road for Premier. A new company was formed to buy its assets.

The year 1917 was Canada's Golden Jubilee, but in many ways it was no time for celebration. A country of eight million people spread across a continent of 4,000 miles. That year, in order to bolster Canada's war effort, Prime Minister Borden proposed conscription. He was vigorously supported by English-speaking and many ethnic communities, but vehemently fought by nationalists in Quebec.

Canada had been slowly industrializing before the war, largely to make the rails and rolling stock for its 40,000 miles of railroad and to build ships to service its export markets. Munitions were the biggest material contribution. In 630 munitions factories, 300,000 workers produced 66 million shells, and 3,000 military aeroplanes were built for war use. Yet, even in 1917, there was an uneasiness to the industrial boom. The government had to rescue the Canadian Northern, Grand Trunk, and Intercolonial railroads, putting them under government ownership as Canadian National Railways. Income taxes were introduced for the first time. Men and a significant number of women were attracted to the new production-line factories, which were slowly but inexorably replacing the traditional unit-organized "shops." From Ontario westward, women had a vote. And that other instrument that would bring thousands of women into the workforce — the typewriter — was coming into common use. Although cars were still only for the well-to-do, trucks were becoming common on the city streets. It was in this environment that Consumers Glass was launched in 1917. There was a new feeling of confidence abroad, which would last for 12 years.

CONSUMERS GLASS COMPANY, LIMITED
Montreal, Quebec (1917-1925)

Consumers received a federal charter on October 4, 1917, with a capitalization of $1,000,000. Its first act was to purchase the 668,000 square feet of land in Ville St. Pierre, along with the buildings, machines and other assets of Premier Glass for $850,000. Henri Jonas, formerly a director of Premier, joined the board and, as part of the deal, provided the new company with $150,000 in working capital.

The assets acquired included two unfinished 25-ton continuous tank furnaces, one O'Neill semiautomatic bottle machine, one Olean three-plunger bottle machine and one Cox improved semiautomatic jar machine. The list of the moulds purchased indicated that the product mix was intended to include quart milks, quart and pint beers, club-shaped quarts, pint and half-pint sodas, and prescription ware from half-ounce to 16 ounces.

Directors elected were Frank P. Jones, Henri Jonas, Arthur Lyman, Murray Williams and J.A. Kilpatrick. Mr. Jones, the first president, represented Canada Cement Company, which had the controlling interest. David Pugh, who had left Diamond Flint Glass to establish Atlas Glass five years earlier, started as superintendent for Consumers, but returned shortly to England before going to Australia. He was replaced by Joe Kilahear (who had also worked for Atlas). Kilahear, in turn, brought in Antonio Laurendeau, then 45, who had started at the age of 11 with Barsalou Glass (c.1883) and worked for Diamond Glass (1890-1902) and Dominion Glass (1913-1917). Laurendeau then asked his 18-year-old son Joe, who worked at Dominion Glass, to coax other workers to join Consumers — with the result that Joe was fired and joined his father at Consumers.

During the winter of 1917-1918, Kilahear, the two Laurendeaus and three other men spent long hours getting the plant ready to start production. Their day began at 4:30 a.m., walking to work along Sherbrooke Street West. There was neither heat nor electricity in the plant, so they carried oil lamps as they finished the furnaces and built the crate factory. The work force gradually expanded. Ronald Croke was hired to take charge of the machine shop and eventually became superintendent. Others who succeeded him in this position were Paddy Whelan and Arthur Rouleau. John Joseph Olson, from Dominion Glass, worked at Consumers for 34 years, a typical long-service career man in the glass induatry. R.S. Skinner was brought in as general manager.

August 15, 1918, was the great day. The first bottle was produced and the company was in operation. The furnace, with a daily pull of 22 tons, supplied three bottle-forming machines on each side and had four ports through which the glass was drawn for the hand shops. The six machines were three O'Neill Noboys, an O'Neill semiautomatic, an Olean and a Cox Improved. In addition there was a side-lever press. The Cox mainly turned out Mason and Peerless fruit jars, while the hand shops made pharmaceutical ware. The side-lever press, operated by a huge man, Billy Graham, produced tableware and tumblers. The press was discontinued in the 1920s, except for occasional production of ash trays and coasters.

Commercial production was of course augmented by whimseys, made for fun and a little pocket money by the glassblowers. Using a small experimental tank in the basement, a number of glassblowers, including Gordon Williams, Ernest La Pierre, Gerard Ouellette, Jim Dillon and Eddie O'Brien, produced an assortment of drapes (glass chains), hats, hatchets, crossed swords, cuff links and sock darners. An especially ambitious effort was a 66-foot multi-coloured chain carrying mercury-amber balls which looked like gold.

The work pattern was 40 minutes on, 20 minutes off. By the 1930s this became 50 minutes on and ten minutes off. Blowers worked a nine-hour day, from seven to five with an hour for lunch. Boys worked an eight-hour day. The plant closed from noon Saturday to seven Monday morning. The maintenance people, such as furnace men and gas men and those looking after the lehrs, worked an 84-hour week because a constant temperature had to be maintained.

Wages for most of the workers were 45 cents an hour, but blowers on piecework earned better than $8 a day, and occasionally might make $25 a day when making something as complicated as a bird cage feeder. Gordon Williams, a gatherer, set a record by producing 574 dozen (6,888) painkiller bottles in an eight-hour shift. Compared to the production on a machine of 500 dozen bottles in a similar time period, this attests to the ability of the worker.

There were two tanks operating in 1919. Tank #1 was divided in such a way that it produced amber glass on one side and green on the other. Tank #2 produced only flint (clear) glass. Billy Graham continued to produce his tableware on the side-lever press.

The Ville St. Pierre council granted the company the same exemptions that it offered to Atlas Glass back in 1912: a ten-year exemption from all municipal taxes provided that the company hired at least half its employees from the local area and paid them at least as much as it paid any brought in from outside.

The year 1919 was one of optimism and expansion. Capital expenditures of $75,000 were incurred and included extension of its waresheds, a new office, punch tumbler equipment, four O'Neill Noboys, two side-lever presses, a glazer for tumblers, an automatic conveyor from the machine to the lehrs, and $17,000 worth of new moulds. A half-million-dollar modernization program was started with the H.L. Dixon Company to upgrade the batch handling and furnace and gas producer equipment. A bond issue was planned to cover these expenses.

Alas, despite all the enthusiasm, the company lost $60,000. Some key personnel changes were made: Norman Hesler, who had been brought in from Canada Cement as treasurer, was appointed general manager; Frank Fernie became treasurer; Kilahear, superintendent of works; and R.S. Skinner, vice president of sales.

This was the beginning of the low point in Consumers' history. The fact that Dominion Glass had acquired from Diamond Flint Glass the exclusive Canadian rights to the Owens automatic bottle-forming machine and other glass production equipment left Consumers no choice but to use whatever other equipment was available. There were even discussions with Dominion Glass in December 1919 to see whether they might be interested in negotiating the purchase of Consumers' capital stock. Perhaps it was fortunate that this did not take place, because continuing domestic competition better served the Canadian glass industry and made it stronger than if an American or English company had set up a subsidiary to compete with Dominion.

The modernization program was pretty well carried out in 1920. However, there were serious difficulties in the forming area. The only bottle-forming machines available to Consumers were of the "feeder" type. To compound their difficulties, Dominion had the Canadian rights for the Hartford feeder, considered to be the most efficient.

Despite these setbacks, Consumers carried on. To their benefit, Miller forming machines became available (Dominion's exclusive rights had lapsed) and the addition of three of these machines — the JP, JPM and JPS for wide-mouth ware such as fruit jars — improved the production efficiency.

To solve the problem of finding an efficient feeder, Mr. Hesler turned to Federal Glass in Columbus, Ohio, which made tumblers and tableware. They acquired a number of them and it took over a year to get them running efficiently. The real losers were the gatherers, whose function was replaced by the feeder device.

Hesler designed a trademark for the company in the form of an inverted triangle, containing the letter C. This was registered on October 8, 1920. The officers were relieved to see a profit figure of $80,000 for the year.

The year 1921 brought continuing problems. Their forming machines were in a bad state of repair and in some cases no longer efficient. To correct this situation, the company employed Joseph Ardurer from Sapulpa, Oklahoma, to repair the glass machinery and look after the mould equipment. Some of the proper parts for the feeders were still outstanding. The annealing lehrs were inefficient and even the source of coal for the gas producers had to be changed from a local supplier to one as far away as Ohio. By September 1921 the company had spent over $700,000 on alterations and additions, with still more improvements to be made to the furnace. This had all been too much for Mr. Hesler, who went on sick leave in December. Mr. Jones closed the plant with the intent of reopening it in February 1922.

The factory actually reopened on February 6, operating two hand shops and five machines. In an apparent effort to maintain better control of the operation, the factory employed seven assistant foremen, nine shift foremen, nine factory machinists and flowmen, three lehrmen, five engineers and firemen, three tankmen, and six men to operate the gas producers. It was still also necessary to employ many boys (ages 13 and 14) as carry-in boys to carry the finished ware to the lehrs and snap-up boys, who held the bottle in a snapcase after it had been snapped off from the blowpipe.

One of these carry-in boys was George S. Mendell, who joined Consumers in 1922. He then became a gatherer, supplying gobs of glass to a semiautomatic O'Neill bottle machine. Later on, he worked 12 hours a night, seven nights a week, producing seven- and eight-inch bowls and four-to-eight-inch nappies with a swirl pattern halfway up their sides. Mendell eventually transferred to Dominion Glass, after leaving Consumers to assist a glass machine company install new machines at Manitoba Glass in Beausejour.

To indicate the variety of batch formulas that were being used to produce quality glass, Consumers experimented with various formulas. The H.L. Dixon favourite: sand 1,000 lbs., soda 400 lbs., lime 120 lbs., cullet 500 lbs. The D.O. Cunningham Glass formula: wet sand 1,050 lbs., soda ash 380 lbs., limestone 240 lbs., cullet 500 lbs. Turner Brothers: dry sand 1,800 lbs., soda 790 lbs., limestone 195 lbs., cullet 1,000 lbs. And finally, Graham Glass: sand 1,000 lbs., soda 380 lbs., lime 100 lbs., cullet 533 lbs. — and one ounce decolourizer! The bottle machines were still giving a great deal of trouble. Hesler was sent to the United States to hire someone who fully understood the O'Neills and automatic feeders. When this newcomer failed to solve the problems, Hesler resigned, frustrated and exhausted. He was replaced by A.W. Cameron.

Like Dominion Glass, Consumers in its formative years had its V.I.P.s. The first of these was Frank P. Jones. He was born in Brockville, Ontario, in 1869 and was a graduate of Royal Military College in Kingston, Ontario. In 1884 he joined the Nova Scotia Steel and Coal Company in Sydney, Nova Scotia, and then moved to Dominion Iron and Steel Company, where he eventually became general manager.

Max Aitken (later Lord Beaverbrook) convinced Jones to become general manager of the newly formed Canada Cement Company (1909), in which Aitken had an interest. By 1921 Jones had become president as well as general manager. His personality commanded attention and respect. He had unbounded energy, stamina, drive, and generally dominated all situations. He had a prolific imagination, but at times his ideas required a great deal of modification. Dominion Glass had the exclusive Canadian rights to the Miller jar and tumbler machines. This made it almost impossible for Consumers to compete in the product lines produced by these machines. To get around this, Jones arranged with the Whitall-Tatum Glass Company in Millville, New

Jersey, to buy two Miller J8 telescopic jar machines and one Miller J8 tumbler press machine, and then had them reconsigned to Consumers. By the time Miller and Dominion learned of this, it was too late to take any action. (Unfortunately, one of the jar machines was totally unsatisfactory and it was suspected that it had been a second-hand machine.)

Making cement was not enough challenge for Jones' enthusiasm. In 1913 he formed the Canadian Venezuela Iron Ore Company in Imataca, Venezuela. As another example of his aggressiveness, in 1917 Canada Cement took on a contract to manufacture artillery shells. Other Canadian companies had taken very lucrative contracts from the Canadian Munitions Board to supply shells at 70 cents or 79 cents each. When Jones offered to provide them at 55 cents each, the Munitions Board didn't believe it. He finally went to England and got a contract to supply 100,000 complete shells and to do the machine work on a further 50,000 shell blanks. This resulted in the Canadian Munitions Board cancelling the other orders they had placed, then re-letting them to the same firms at the new price. The Cement Company made a modest profit.

About 1918 he convinced Canada Cement to buy a majority interest in Consumers Glass. Large sums of money were advanced by Canada Cement to modernize and rebuild the glass company. Through the hard work of such men as E.J. Brunning, C.G. Kemp, and George Milne, the plant was put on a paying basis.

Ernie Brunning was the key to this rebuilding program. Brunning was born in England in 1890 and trained as an electrical engineer. He came to Canada in 1910 and, from 1912 to 1917, plied his skill with Canada Cement. He then worked in an American munitions plant before returning to England. Coming back to Canada in June 1923, he worked for an engineering company that was commissioned by Frank Jones to take a look at Consumers. He was then appointed assistant to Ray Goddard, the general manager of Consumers, and never looked back. He was elected director, vice-president and general manager in 1939, also Director-General of Munitions. He received the OBE in 1943 and CBE in 1946. He resigned in 1960 and died in 1967.

By 1923 the company's product mix included some 400 items, ranging from a half-ounce Rex Oval and a two-ounce Vaseline jar up to a half-gallon Safety Seal fruit jar. Moulds for the following products were on hand: castor oil, olive oil, cod liver oil, household ammonia, petrolatum, corn cure, sodas, beers, whiskies, pickles and vinegar. The list included a number of customers and their made-to-order items: Castoria, Lepage glue, Lavoris, Waterman ink, Orange Deelight, Schwartz, Boron, Florida Water, Woodbury's liniment, Rexall, Pinkham, Three-in-One, Sultana, Blacking, Absorbine, Norway Pine, Listerine, Pinex, Italian Balm and Carters Mucilage. The company also hand-pressed tumblers with a zig-zag design around the body for Crosse and Blackwell.

Three more Lynch forming machines were purchased and $10,000 worth of Lynch moulds. Henri Jonas resigned as a director and vice-president and was replaced by Arthur Lyman.

To settle a hassle over evaluation that started in 1922, the company and the town made a new 20-year tax agreement in 1924. The company renounced the remaining five years of its 1919 tax exemption; the town then evaluated Consumers' property for tax purposes at $600,000 (property $80,000, machinery $200,000, buildings $320,000) for the next 20 years, no matter how Consumers expanded. Ray S. Goddard replaced A.W. Cameron as works manager on the latter's retirement. George Milne was secretary-treasurer. Canada Cement held 5,468 shares.

By 1925 production had become more efficient and diversified. The variety of closures (the type of device that is used to seal a filled bottle) included the following: C.T. (Continuous Thread), Goldy, Duplex, #3, #4, #5 cork, anchor, crown, special combination and amerseal.

THE VICTORIA GLASS AND BOTTLE COMPANY, LIMITED
Victoria, British Columbia (1914-c.1915)

In May 1913 Walter LeDain set up a small experimental glass factory called the Victoria Glass and Bottle Company. It was situated on Crease Avenue, off Carey Road, in the Municipality of Saanich.

LeDain had brought out from England a reliable foreman and a few glass blowers. A three-and-a-half-ton coal-fired furnace was erected in a corrugated-iron single-floor building with a cement floor, and a continuous lehr was installed. When fully operational it worked three shifts of eight hours each. The going rates were: glassblowers $4 per day, firemen $75 a month, and boys $1 a day. It was situated next to the Victoria and Sydney Railroad. Due to lack of capital, LeDain was forced to use cullet in place of the usual batch materials. The largest customer was the Hudson's Bay Company in Victoria and Vancouver, who purchased flat whiskey flasks in various sizes.

At the end of the first year, the auditor's report showed the following costs: factory site $1,100; building $2,154; tools, moulds, etc. $455; labour $1,067; cullet, chemicals and material $169; fuel $413; and sundries $159. This was too much of a financial burden for LeDain to carry. With the help of four others, including Harold Victor Pratt, manager of wine and spirits at the Hudson's Bay store in Victoria, the Victoria Glass and Bottle Company, Limited was incorporated with a British Columbia charter on July 23, 1914. It had a capital of $25,000 and its head office in Vancouver. It was expected to be fully operational by the fall. However, this was not to be. World War I started and money that might otherwise have been invested in the company was used to purchase Victory bonds.

The last listing in the local directory was in 1915, where LeDain was shown as manager of a glassworks and a hotel keeper. In 1917 he was a munitions worker. On September 4, 1920, the lands assessed in the name of the Victoria Glass and Bottle Works were sold for taxes by the Corporation of the District of Saanich. The charter was cancelled on February 23, 1922.

CANADA FLINT GLASS COMPANY, LIMITED
Toronto, Ontario (1919)

The company received an Ontario charter on May 23, 1919, to manufacture glassware. It never got started, however, and in 1930 the following memo was sent to the companies branch in Toronto:

Companies Branch,   September 5th, 1930.

Re: Canada Flint Glass Company, Limited. #16276.

Mr. T. Rolph, Barrister, informed Inspector Moorby that he incorporated the company which never operated. The charter was handed to Officers whose present location is unknown.

Office of Controller of Revenue.

The provincial secretary dissolved the company on January 9, 1961.

FELDSPAR GLASS LIMITED
Oshawa, Ontario (1921-c.1933)

Oshawa, home of General Motors of Canada, with a population of 115,000 (1982), is situated on the north shore of Lake Ontario, about 28 miles east of Toronto.

Feldspar Glass appears to have had a tenuous and spread-out existence. It received an Ontario charter in 1921 with a capital of $1,000,000. The company planned to make glass, using feldspar rather than sand as the main raw material. There appears to be some (yet to be discovered) link between the company and the supplier of its principal raw material, feldspar, in Perth, Ontario. The prospectus issued on May 30, 1925, stated in part: "... Incorporated under the Ontario Companies Act, (Feldspar Glass) is subject to the Provisions of the Act relating to Mining Companies..."

In 1922 the company purchased just over four acres of land from General Motors on the northeast corner of Adelaide and Ritson. This adjoined a railway siding and, by agreement with the municipality, cars would be brought to the factory from all main lines free of charge. In 1923 and again in 1925, mortgages of $15,000 and $20,000, respectively, were arranged with a solicitor, W.J. McCallum of Toronto, who became company president in 1925.

Between its incorporation in 1921 and the issue of a prospectus in 1925, McCallum and his associates seem to have obtained control of the company. A one-storey building had been erected. The fire-proof building had a solid concrete foundation, with walls of cement blocks, concrete floors and iron window frames. It housed a continuous electric melting furnace and a 75-foot continuous electric annealing lehr, in conjunction with a feeder-type bottlemaking machine. In 1933 the only bottlemaking machine on the premises was a Lynch "R" machine.

There were two innovations peculiar to this plant's operations. Firstly, they planned to use feldspar instead of sand as the main raw material in the batch, claiming that one hundred pounds of feldspar could be converted into one hundred pounds of glass. This assumption appears to ignore the fact that there is a normal shrinkage factor of 15 percent in converting raw materials into molten glass. Secondly, they had obtained the Canadian rights to a collector for the purpose of collecting the potash from the fumes of the melting feldspar. They expected that this would yield a profit, as this by-product "is very valuable in the manufacture of special soaps, fertilizers and various chemicals for which there is a constant and growing demand . . . ."

A balance sheet included in the prospectus showed that 60,445 preference and 488,580 common shares had been issued. Of the latter, 285,000 shares had been issued to Allan Gravel, Kitchener, Ontario, for the exclusive rights to the electric tank furnace and an electric pot furnace. W.T. Symons, a farmer and one of the petitioners for incorporation, received 200,000 common shares and 15,000 preference shares for the exclusive Canadian rights to the collector mentioned above.

No indication has been found that the plant operated on a regular basis over the next seven years. In 1933 George Mendell, a top production specialist from Dominion Glass, visited the plant and reported as follows:

> The plant was located about two miles east of General Motors' main factory at that time.
>
> The owner (Manager) was a German by the name of Mayer and stated he had started the first glass factory in Ville St. Pierre, P.Q., where Consumers Glass Company Limited was then located. He obviously was referring to Atlas Glass Works (1912-1914) and/or Premier Glass Company of Canada Limited (1914-1917), because Consumers Glass took over all assets of Premier Glass in 1917.
>
> Mr. Mayer stated he had to get out of the company (Atlas or Premier) after the 1914 war was started because of his nationality. The Oshawa plant contained a continuous melting electric furnace about 18 feet long and 12 feet wide.
>
> Only one glass machine, a Lynch "R" was in the plant. They had an order for the 7 oz. ribbed Orange Crush bottle in flint glass but were not successful in making it because the glass was a poor colour, nearly opaque. It is said this was partly due to red feldspar being used in the batch.
>
> The lehr was electrically heated and controlled automatically.

Around about 1940 Dominion Glass acquired the land and buildings of the defunct company, probably for back taxes. In 1943 Bert Macklin, an engineer from Dominion Glass, was sent to Oshawa to dispose of the assets. The following comments are taken from a write-up he prepared for me:

> . . . Mr. Offer (Secretary) asked me to go down to Oshawa and clean up a couple of glass plants. [The other was Canadian Knox Glass.]
>
> I was to send anything useful up to one of our plants and dispose of the rest . . . This first (Feldspar) was in North East Oshawa and consisted of one factory building with a small loading platform and a railway siding . . . There was a small pile of greenish cullet in the yard but no containers. No moulds, no machine shop . . . Just one small machine so old in design that I could not name it. [This was probably the Lynch 'R' referred to by George Mendell] . . . The furnace was electric . . . They had no idea how much electricity was needed . . . they had bought a couple of 750 KW transformers which had burned out right away . . . they had had several fires . . . They then got another transformer with four times the capacity,

but apparently ran out of money . . . and did not make any bottles . . . I never heard the name of the person or persons involved nor the name of any company. I was instructed to clean it up and use my own name and in no case was the name Dominion Glass to appear . . . It was finally sold in my name . . . I dealt with a lawyer, but I suspected that General Motors was behind him and, of course, I was right as, after the sale, it became a General Motors Parking Lot . . . I believe it was sold for back taxes and the sale would be registered in my name . . . .

The company was dissolved on September 26, 1955.

FOOTNOTES

[1] Domglas Ltd./Domglas Ltee. (1976-1978); Domglas Inc. (1978 to date).
[2] See Chapter 10, Tableware and Industrial Ware in the Twentieth Century.
[3] I.L. Sills, "Minerals and Mineral Products used in the Glass Industry," Toronto 1933.

CHAPTER 7

The Troubled Years
(1926-1945)

The Depression (1929-1933)
World War II (1939-1945)
Dominion Glass (1926-1945): ½ Million Miles of Trucking Between
Hamilton and Toronto; A Fish Story; Operators' Strike at Hamilton;
H-E "IS" Machine; NAAFI Beers; Borosilicate Glass
Consumers Glass (1926-1945): Feeder Machines; Benefit Plans;
A Flier in England; Frank Jones' Bequest
Mid-West Glass Company Limited, Winnipeg, Manitoba (1928-1930)
Canadian Knox Glass Company, Limited, Oshawa, Ontario (1939-1940),
A subsidiary of Knox Glass Company, Knox, Pennsylvania

THE TROUBLED YEARS (1926-1945)

DOMINION GLASS

Now that the manufacturing and sales operations had been reorganized on a more efficient basis, it was necessary to review the management group. In January 1926 the directors decided that the head office staff organization had become depleted. As a result, James W. King, manager of the Hamilton plant, was appointed assistant general manager and was instructed "... to take up the duties of this position without delay, moving his headquarters to Montreal as soon as that could be conveniently and safely arranged..."[1] He was also given a standing invitation to attend all board meetings.

At the October meeting, a letter of resignation from Harold Grier, general manager, was accepted, and J.W. King was appointed acting general manager. He was requested to "consider and take up with the president and vice-president the question of effecting economies in the running of the company, this included consideration of salaries... the directors having an annual saving of $50,000 in view..."[2]

In the 1926 annual report, the following extract highlighted one of the increasing production problems:

"Particular efforts are being made to cope with the problems which have arisen in the past few years due to increased calls for variety in manufacturing and a feeling of uncertainty as to demand..."

This was reflected in the 1926 mould inventory.

The inventory was made of all the moulds in storage, giving their stock number, capacities of bottles, names of bottles, product, whether made by hand or, if not, the type of machine. Although there is no indication of how old some of these moulds were, from the number of items made by hand, there has to be an assumption that many of them predated the advent of semiautomatic and automatic bottlemaking machines in the first decade of the twentieth century. All production fell into one of two categories — SSL (Standard Stock Lines), which were available to all customers, and MTO (Made to Order), which were for the exclusive use of specific customers. In the latter case, the cost of the moulds was charged to the customer, who in turn received a partial or total rebate, according to the quantities he purchased within certain time limits. The company undertook to maintain the moulds in good working order. The list included approximately 5,000 moulds and 500 names of MTO customers.

The following machines were listed: Owens AR, AN, AE, AN-AR, AQ, Olean, O'Neill, Miller, side-lever press, Lynch, Insulator Machine, Lynch O, Teeple-Johnson, Air-Head (semi-automatic), and Miller rotary press.

The names of the products by which the bottles were listed included some interesting ones: Truss panel, Shoofly flask, Egg Soda, (probably indicated the shape of the bottle), Suppository, Dr. Bells' Medical Wonder, Bereaulls Hair Butter, Braley's Shooting Syrup, Weakness Cure, Bricks Tasteless Large, Fucomorrhum, Down's Elixir, Love's Lotus Liniment, Dysentry Cordial, Mother Graves Worm Syrup, Stearns Coffin-Shape Packer, Square Toothpaste.

To give an indication of the wide variety of items made by the company — other than bottles, tableware, lamps and lantern globes — the following items appeared: fire extinguishers, battery jars, votive cups, bird seed cups, nose cups, lightning rod balls, fishing floats, candy jars, stoppers, kitchen jars, furniture shoes, stove shoes, stove door plates, vigil lights, door knobs, percolator tops, fish bowls, headlight lenses, dental cuspidor bowls and trays, ice cream sandwich holders, bird feeders, pipe holders, prisms, vault lights, bird baths, tobacco jars and insulators.

The ups and down of the Canadian economy were clearly reflected in the manufacturing and sales divisions of the company. In 1926, with the change in general management, a five-year plan of selling off inactive property was implemented.

The next four years were ones of advancement and change. Production increased from 75,000 tons in 1926 to 94,000 tons in 1929, sales from $6,800,000 to $7,600,000. Despite this picture of well-being, the cash position in 1927 seemed to belie it:

Notes discounted at the bank	$450,000
Present overdraft	approx. 243,000
Net requirements to April 1	approx. 60,000
Dividends	119,875
	$872,875

From 1927 to 1940 a total of 18 feeder-type machines were installed in the four main factories in Montreal, Hamilton, Wallaceburg and Redcliff.

In November 1928 the company sold Richards Glass, which it had acquired in 1913, to J.P. Richards for $111,600. This became one of the company's most important distributors of its pharmaceutical ware, one of its main lines being Rigo Ovals.

Also in 1928, the old Burlington Glass (McNab St.) property was sold to the City of Hamilton for use as a playground. In the next 15 months, surplus acreage was sold at Manitoba Glass in Beausejour and at the former Jefferson Glass operation on Carlaw Avenue in Toronto.

It was now becoming apparent that steps would have to be taken to augment the western manufacturing facilities (at Redcliff) in order to satisfy the demand for bottles in British Columbia and compete cost-wise with imports from the western United States. The addition of two automatic forming machines, ancillary equipment and a wareshed, at a cost of $57,500, was approved in May 1928.

For most Canadians 1929 was a traumatic year. The economy had risen very rapidly and all types of investors, both professionals and amateurs, were selling the shirts off their backs in the expectation of becoming instant millionaires. Then came the fateful Tuesday, October 29. The bottom fell out of the market and literally thousands of Canadians took a financial beating. The economy took a nose-dive and many companies were in trouble, if not bankrupt. But surprisingly enough, the company did not bottom out until 1933-1934, probably because its strength was the very nature of its business — that of supplying ordinary glassware for everyday use. The following data graphically illustrates this situation:

Fiscal	Production (tons)	Sales ($)	Net Profit ($)
1928	75,973	7,699,403	129,412
1929	94,177	7,563,450	124,713
1930	70,817	6,706,258	27,309
1931	60,888	5,535,101	loss (105,005)
1932	59,618	5,106,761	loss (95,603)
1933	53,499	4,694,804	loss (146,123)
1934	64,773	5,311,207	8,472

The esteem in which Mr. Offer, the secretary, was held by the directors was evidenced by the fact that on his advice the level of capital improvement was maintained when the economy was soft and prices were depressed. As the following table shows, the level of capital cost additions, which mainly represented improvements to and augmentation of plant and equipment, remained reasonably high in relation to the state of the economy:

Capital Cost Additions

Fiscal year	($000s)
1928	205
1929	252
1930	85
1931	406
1932	87
1933	89
1934	69

The directors' annual report dated 3 December 1929 did not mention the crash but simply said, "There was some decline in business during the latter part of the year . . ."

The company had many long-service and trained employees, some dating back to the eras of Diamond Glass (1890-1902) and Diamond Flint Glass (1903-1913). It was therefore to the credit of the company that, during one of Canada's worst depressions, it rewarded such employees and identified their interests with those of the company, as closely as possible, by establishing an employees benefit scheme in 1930. The amount of money provided by the company was to be redetermined from time to time by the directors.

In the summer of 1930 J.W. King suffered a serious accident, which curtailed his normal activities until his death in April 1937.

By 1931 the first effects of the Depression were reflected in the reduction of general and office salaries by five to ten percent. A similar reduction was made in regular weekly factory wages, retiring allowances, and standing fees payable to directors.

In order to provide some manoeuverability at Pte. St. Charles (Montreal), 190,000 sq. ft. of land was purchased by auction from the City of Montreal for some $150,000. At about the same time, the company suffered its largest fire loss to date ($94,554) as the result of a fire at this plant on January 1, 1931. It was fully insured.

At the annual general meeting in December 1931, the president announced that a scheme of improvement had been approved by the directors for the Pointe St. Charles plant, this improvement by way of the acquisition of further property (purchased from Canadian National Railways) and the upgrading of the operational facilities at the plant at an estimated cost of $237,000.

Despite the Depression, sales in the Toronto area were increasing. With no manufacturing facilities there, the majority of the ware had to be produced in Hamilton. As a result, a fleet of trucks was established in Hamilton, in 1932, to deliver door-to-door to customers in Toronto. This

J.W. *King* (1875-1937).
Photograph by
Blank and Stoller, Montreal.

was the beginning of a unique transportation saga which continued for many years. The daily round trip, six days a week, including deliveries in the Toronto area, covered about one hundred miles, 90 miles of which were on the old, bumpy, concrete two-lane Highway No. 2 between the cities. Records indicate that these trucks travelled well over half a million miles in this operation.

As already indicated, 1933 was the low point for the company in the Depression period. It was also, unfortunately, the year in which the outstanding Twenty Year Gold bonds had to be redeemed. To add to this burden, the premium on American funds was 12.72 percent, which meant that for the $60,000 U.S. required to redeem U.S. holdings, an additional $7,632 had to be paid. In April the second reduction in salaries and allowances was effected, another five to ten percent.

At the annual meeting the president observed that ". . . apart from the non-recurring charges incidental to the redemption of the company's First Mortgage bonds, the profits for the year fell short of the dividends paid on the common shares by the amount of $80,832.84. In spite of this, and having regard to the sound liquid position enjoyed by the company, your directors felt justified in maintaining the dividends throughout the year . . ."

The mid-thirties was a period of innovation and improved efficiency. From the mechanical unloading and storing of raw materials, right through to the storing of the finished goods in the warehouse, mechanical devices were being implemented that would help to offset the ever-increasing labour costs. Warehousing operations were a good example. With the advent of lift trucks and the use of pallets, storing costs per ton were reduced and more ware could be stored per cubic foot than in the past, when ware had been piled by hand.

Up until this time, the majority of the regular standard bottleware was being mass-produced on the Owens machine. However, with the development of certain lines, such as milks, it was determined that it would be advantageous to install additional feeder-type forming machines, which were more efficient for the production of special lines of ware. Even a single-mould machine, made in Belgium and called a Roirant, was installed to make gallon jugs. Two other machines of this type were purchased, but they were not efficient enough to justify ordering more of them.

By 1935 cartons were rapidly replacing wooden cases for storing and shipping, particularly for food and beverage ware. Customers were recognizing the advantages of receiving clean ware as provided by this new packaging. Advertising of the bottler's product on the carton was an additional advantage. To support this trend, it was necessary to build additional weatherproof warehouses in Pte. St. Charles and Hamilton, the plants that produced these lines of ware.

The period 1934-1939 was one of improved returns. The net profit in 1939 was $200,922, compared to $8,472 in 1934.

One of the interesting personalities in the company at this time was Horace Morin, who had been manager of the Pte. St. Charles plant since 1912. A self-made man, he had come up through the ranks, having started in the old Diamond Flint plant in Montreal. As an old-style manager, he believed that in his position he should be able to do any job in the plant better than the incumbent. He would go to the plant around seven, six days a week, and often on Sundays. Changing into a set of old, dirty work clothes, he would prowl through the working areas for most of the day watching how each employee did his job. If he didn't like what he saw, he would brusquely push the man aside and show him how to do it, with much vigour and gesticulation. Knowing the character of the man, it is highly probable that he also adopted this style of "personal" management so that the gentlemen at head office could not reach him during business hours. To add to the problem, Mr. Morin up to this point would not have a secretary. As a result, most of the correspondence and calls between the plant and head office fell to the lot of Donald Addie, the superintendent.

Head office finally put its foot down and insisted that Morin hire a secretary. When the first applicant, Annie Murphy — who was just as stubborn as Morin — turned up, he fled to the factory and could not be found for the rest of the day. The interviewing of Annie Murphy was left to me. I had been working there for several months, introducing the company's new cost system to the recently appointed cost accountant. Murphy was eventually hired and, as a result, Morin spent even more of his time out in the plant. What little time he took off for lunch, he often spent fishing at the land-end of the recently acquired Montreal Water Works intake.

Summertime is always a busy time for glass companies, particularly those that supply the beverage and food packer industries. The Hamilton plant was a typical example. In the spring and summer it was the company's principal producer of soft drink, beer and food packer bottles for central Ontario, the company's largest market.

In the summer of 1936, during a particularly hot spell of weather, the machine operators in the forming department decided to walk off the job. If it had been at any other time, the company could have rescheduled the production to another plant, but not in summer and not at Hamilton. To solve the problem, they decided to use about a dozen operators and assistant operators from Montreal's Pte. St. Charles plant until the situation returned to normal. At that time I was working as an apprentice in that department. I was told to take charge of the project, get the men, move them to Hamilton and look after their welfare for the duration.

A whole sleeping car was reserved for the overnight journey, and the group, mostly unilingually French, turned up at the old Bonaventure Station some hours before the train was to leave, others at the last minute. They were so excited. Some of them said that they had never been more than 100 miles from home, and maybe only one or two had been on a sleeper before. They turned up in various states of attire and certainly with mixed baggage — some had bulging suitcases, others had string-wrapped cartons. It was wishful thinking that they would settle down after a while. No chance. Many of them stayed up most of the night playing cards and exchanging stories.

On arrival the next morning in Hamilton, the train was met by a large tractor and trailer truck, the exterior of which was completely covered with a protective wire screen. When the truck approached the plant, the reason for this was obvious. Outside the plant gates, at the foot of Chapple Street, were some 100 demonstrators (few of whom turned out to be company employees). Going at a fair speed, with horn at full blast, the truck drove through showers of stones and other objects thrown at it. The gates were opened just long enough for the truck to pass through and were then promptly closed and locked.

Thomas W. Bassett (1891-1959).
Photograph by
William Notman & Son, Montreal.

Arrangements had been made to partition off part of the second-floor cafeteria for the men's living quarters, where they soon made themselves at home. The Hamilton forming foreman then broke them down into three eight-hour work shifts. It was soon realized that in the excitement of getting ready for the trip some of them had not brought complete pairs of boots, were short of socks and extra sets of the heavy winter underwear that were necessary to protect them from the excessive heat to which they would be exposed (between 110 and 120 degrees Fahrenheit). These were procured during the first day and things settled down. The next requirement was a supply of picture postcards to send back to Montreal. During their stay, they must have sent over 200 — and judging from the addresses, they were not always sent home. The operators' dispute was settled in less than two weeks and the group returned to Montreal, tired but happy.

In the fall of 1936 J.W. King had a stroke while attending a glass convention in Atlantic City; he never recovered. He died on April 29, 1937, with 30 years of service. Owing to his prolonged absence, Mr. Bassett, manager at the Wallaceburg plant, was appointed acting general manager and subsequently general manager in October 1937. Mr. T.B. Dundas, general sales manager, filled the vacancy on the board.

The first fully automated raw materials (Batch) handling system was installed in Hamilton in 1937 at a cost of over $110,000, with annual savings estimated at $25,000. The other plants were similarly modernized. For many years the energy for melting the batch was natural or producer gas. In 1938 the Pte. St. Charles furnaces were converted to use Bunker "C" oil, at a cost of $33,000, with the ability to revert to gas in an emergency.

September 1939 and World War II. There was no immediate effect on the company, although a number of employees, including myself, went on Active Service. In the meantime Sir Charles Gordon, who had been president since 1916, died and was replaced by La Monte J. Belnap of Consolidated Paper Co. In November T.W. Bassett was appointed vice-president and general manager and was elected to the board. Capital Expenditure Allowance regulations were instituted under the Income War Tax Act.

The Hartford Empire Individual Six Section Forming Machine introduced in 1939.

In the same year, a breakthrough was made with the introduction of an entirely new concept in bottle forming. The new machine was known as the Hartford Empire Individual Section Forming Machine (H-E I.S. for short.) The main advantage of this machine over the Owens and feeder-type machines was that each of the four bottlemaking sections (now available in ten sections) operated entirely independently of the others. This meant that one or more sections could be deactivated for whatever cause and the remaining sections were not affected. Secondly, more than one type of bottle could be made at the same time, provided that the shape and weight of the gob were exactly the same for each type of bottle. The other difference was that this machine was activated by compressed air and not electricity. The greatly increased flexibility of this machine effected considerable savings for the size of plants Dominion operated, where, unlike their opposite numbers in the United States, they had much shorter runs of each type of bottle, thus increasing the amount of downtime for changing the moulds.

After 22 years of sharing the Canadian bottle market with Consumers Glass, a new company, Canadian Knox Glass, was set up in Oshawa, Ontario, in 1939 by Knox Glass of Pennsylvania. It never became commercially viable and, in the spring of 1940, Dominion took it over and closed it down.

This period in the company's history was probably the most difficult that its sales department had to face. With a minor recession and a war, they could for the first time only sell what the company could produce, limited as that was by the scarcity of raw materials and skilled labour.

The company first contributed to the war effort by subscribing to the First War Loan (3¾ percent). In all, they subscribed over $6,000,000. It was now directly involved in and affected by the war, as indicated by the directors' report for 1941:

> . . . The business of the year was of record proportions and the accounts reflect the advantages of greater volume and higher furnace load factor. Selling prices to Customers remained at the pre-war general level notwithstanding the increased cost of materials, wages and general expenses to the Company.

Your Company has supplied a considerable volume of its product for war services and in addition its machine shops have produced equipment and parts for munitions to the full extent of the available capacity.

The employees of the Company have displayed skill and energy in meeting demands and have liberally supported war savings schemes. 231 members of the personnel have undertaken active military service.

Restrictions limiting the regular work of the machine shops were in force during the year and it is felt that some expense, which would otherwise have been incurred may have to be met at a later date. A reserve has accordingly been made against contingency.

It will be observed that the income and profits taxes provided for are approximately 3-1/3 times the amount of the dividends.

An interesting proposal was brought to the board by T.W. Bassett, vice-president and general manager. The federal authorities had been approached by the Navy, Army and Air Force Institute (NAAFI) re the question of increasing the quantity of bottles in which to ship beer to the Armed Forces abroad. Bassett attended meetings with R.C. Berkinshaw, chairman of the Wartime Industries Control Board, along with Messrs. Harrison and "Mac" Yuile (a director of Dominion Glass), who were the administrators of Glass and Glass Products. To supply the quantities of bottles indicated would require additional production capacity. To this end, Plant #3 at Wallaceburg was reactivated at an approximate cost of $50,000. Thousands of beer bottles were made and shipped during the war period. It was reported that a number of breweries were also de-mothballed, including the Old Comrade's Brewery in Tecumseh, Ontario. (As a regular NAAFI customer overseas, I felt that some of the beer was not up to Molson's Export standards.)

At the inception of the company, the Royal Trust Company and the Bank of Montreal, in Montreal, were appointed transfer agents and registrar, respectively, for the company's shares. On January 27, 1942, these appointments were duplicated in the principal offices of these two companies in Toronto.

As mentioned before, Mr. Offer was far more than just the secretary of the company. Over the past 30 years he had been deeply involved in management policy discussions and, through them, actually monitored many of the board's decisions. At his request, and to give him a greater feeling of freedom from his day-to-day duties, Fred N. Dundas, son of T.B. Dundas, was transferred from the Toronto sales office and appointed assistant secretary.

Over the war years, the availability of new forming machinery was extremely limited. Consequently, it was necessary to carry out a great deal of firefighting maintenance. When this was no longer adequate, the company arranged to buy some second-hand machines in the United States. In mid-1944, through priority rating, it had been permitted to get its name on the waiting list for two H-E I.S. five-section machines and an H-E Paste Mould Tumbler machine. A tumbler was first made like a bottle, but revolved in the mould, which eliminated the mould seam. The moile (that part of the bottle above the straight sides) was then cut off, a smooth lip being acquired by exposure to a jet of fire. About 1945 experiments were carried out to try to emulate the Corning-style Pyrex borosilicate ovenware under the trade name Oven Queen. No commercial production was realized and the project was dropped.

In December Mr. Morin, plant manager at Pte. St. Charles, retired at the age of 67, with 38 years of service. This retirement caused a chain reaction. J.H. Sephton replaced Morin; J.R. Mackenzie from Redcliff replaced Sephton as plant manager at Hamilton; and N.W. Meldrum replaced Mackenzie as Redcliff plant manager. At the directors' organization meeting, several staff changes were made at head office as well. Mr. Dundas replaced Mr. Offer as secretary and was also appointed assistant controller; Mr. Wallace replaced him as controller; and I was appointed assistant secretary. Offer was retained as consultant to the general manager.

The next period, 1946 to 1966, appears in Chapter 8 and follows the story of the company to the end of its existence as an independent company.

CONSUMERS GLASS

The second phase of the company's history started by following the trend in the industry of eliminating hand production, except for special orders. This was a further blow to the glassblowers, who were now practically eliminated from mass production. Even the machine-made ware was nearly all fully automatic.

The company was now using three makes of machines: three O'Neills, three Millers and six Lynchs. With the exception of one of the O'Neills, no boys were required to transfer the glass blank from the parison mould to the blow mould. Each type of machine had its own range of bottles. The 48 O'Neill produced small ware: the 42 O'Neill made large ware, including milk and wide-mouth jars (fruit jars). The Millers handled a wide range of bottles, from small ware through milks to gallon jars. The Lynch MT made milks and gallon jars; the JPM made fruit jars; the Lynch 10, small ware; the Lynch L-A, medium-sized ware; the Lynch R, large ware and jars. In addition there was a tumbler machine which pressed tumblers and glass lids for fruit jars, and a lid machine which pressed lids, ash trays, and other flat pressed ware.

In 1927 the company maintained about 400 moulds, some of which were for standard shapes, while others were for made-to-order bottles for specific customers. In the standard category were such items as round-shouldered prescriptions, London Ovals, St. Lawrence Ovals, Philadelphia Ovals, Rex Ovals and American Panels. Fruit jars included Canadian Jewel, Canadian Mason, Canadian Sure Seal, Corona, Jewel, Queen, Royal, Safety Seal, Victory. Other styles were for castor oil, cod liver oil, ketchup, honey, condiments, spirits and wines. Customers for special bottles included Yardley, Cheesebrough, Horlicks and A-1 Sauce. The company was now producing flint, green and amber glass to satisfy demand.

The year 1928 was one of financial reorganization. Canada Cement sold its controlling interest to Frank P. Jones and his associates. By the end of the year, Jones had 21,002 shares. By supplementary letters patent, the 5,000 $100 par common shares were converted into 10,000 shares of no par value. Capital was further increased from 10,000 to 40,000 no par value common shares. In addition, there was a $1.5 million bond issue.

Over the years, Consumers was always aware of the contribution made by its employees. The first tangible recognition of this was the granting of a Christmas bonus of two-weeks' pay for all employees with two or more years of service. This gesture was continued for many years.

In March 1928 Frank Jones and Lord Beaverbrook formed Sheet Glass Limited to reopen the British Window Glass Company plant in Queenborough on the Isle of Shippey, where the company made flat glass from 1920 to 1924 by the Fourcault process.[3] Glass was produced in the first half of 1929, but the losses were so great, it was shut down.

The glass industry, unlike many other industries in 1929, was not immediately affected by the collapse of the stock market. After-tax profit reached $261,950, most of which was due to the fact that the mass-produced products of Consumers and Dominion Glass were, by and large, for day-to-day use regardless of the state of the economy. As a result, it was in the 1932-1933 period that sales and profit hit bottom.

Until 1931 the company only produced and shipped from their Ville St. Pierre plant. Despite the Depression, expansion plans were in the works, additional land was purchased on the south side of the property and plans were set to establish the first off-premises storage facilities in Toronto. Plans even included the purchase of a new Bentley for the president, at a cost of $10,000. Ernie Brunning was appointed vice-president and general manager.

On the company's fifteenth anniversary, in 1932, it started to flex its muscles and become involved in more diversification. Many of the standard lines were broadened to better handle customers' demands. For example, the Canadian square bottle was now offered in the following sizes: 3 oz., 4 oz., 6 oz., 8 oz., 12 oz. and 16 oz. Insertable bottom plates were developed so that a standard bottle could be adopted for a specific customer by changing the bottom plate in much the same way that the old standard milk bottles could be related to a specific company by the use of a shoulder plate. An oblong ash tray (lettered C.G.C.) was developed with embellishment for the general public and as a corporate gift.

An attempted flyer in the transportation business saw plans being considered to operate a freighter service in the St. Lawrence and Great Lakes during the navigable season, to be replaced in the off-season by a fleet of trucks.

In 1932 Package Freighters Limited was incorporated, but the only action taken appears to have been the leasing of a piece of land on the Lachine Canal, on which a shipping shed could be built.

By 1934 the company was well established and expanding rapidly. An employee stock purchase plan was introduced. A renovation and expansion program was approved and, in a two-year period, nearly $150,000 was authorized. In 1935 annual production reached a quarter-million bottles — the equivalent of about ten carloads a day. The company was now purchasing 45,000 tons of raw materials each year. Supplementary letters patent converted the 5,000 preferred shares into ten common on the basis of one-and-a-half common shares for each preferred share. There were now 31,957 common shares outstanding.

A new 30-ton tank was built in April 1937, along with the necessary ancillary equipment. A Lynch forming machine was added to the production facilities. The addition of Brian Heward and C.G. Heward expanded the board to seven. The former served the company for the next 40 years, many of those in the capacity of chairman. After-tax profits now exceeded a half million dollars.

Production in 1938, at 38,452 tons, showed a threefold increase since 1926. One yardstick in glass production efficiency is the number of man-hours per ton of ware produced. Between 1926 and 1938 the figure dropped from 54 to 32.4. With the employee stock option plan well established, the board authorized an employee profit-sharing program in the form of a bonus.

Early in 1939 Frank Jones, the obvious spark plug during the company's formative years, died. In a letter opened after his death, he suggested, and the board agreed, that Brunning be made president and general manager. He left the employees of the company a very generous bequest, details of which were withheld until the following year. Applied Colour Lettering (A.C.L.) equipment was bought. (This is the permanent type of lettering, not glass-embossed, that appears on soft drink bottles in place of a label.)

The year 1940 was another banner one. Net profits were nearly $600,000. The common shares were split ten-for-one. The main product classifications were prescription ware, fruit jars, wines and whiskeys, ketchups, vinegars, sodas and milks. Man-hours per ton had dropped to 29.6. A Miller MT forming machine was added for milks. An experimental tank was built and, over the next five years, ways and means were sought for changing glass and colour by varying the furnace temperatures.

The terms of Mr. Jones' will established that employees who had been working for the company for a year or longer, and who earned less than $2,000 a year, were to receive 50 percent of one year's earnings. Other employees received varying amounts. The Employee Fund received $50,000 or ten percent of the remaining trust property.

It would seem that this new benefit, added to those already enjoyed by the employees, would have provided a satisfied work force. That was not so. For the first time in the company's history, the workers went on a seven-day strike, on May 5, for better wages. At the end of the month, the Fair Wage Board's Conciliatory Committee was established, with three men representing workers and three representing the company. On July 18, the Wage Board Commission published a new wage ordinance for the glass industry in Quebec. Thirty days later, it applied to the employees at Dominion Glass. Under the ruling, workers were divided into nine classifications: salaried foremen, office employees, messengers, salesmen, and supervisors who earned at least $30 a week; machinists; firemen; cooks; producer-operators; watchmen; girls; apprentices; truck drivers.

By 1941 the war effort was going all out. Brunning had been borrowed by Ottawa to be associate director-general of munitions. The industry was being operated under government controls and glass containers were rationed. Production was running at full speed. Lack of time and men made it impossible to make other than minor repairs. Government controls were lifted a year later.

In the year 1942 the company instituted a noncontributory pension plan to provide annuities for employees at retirement age, with sufficient years of service. Consumers became a public company in 1943, with 60,000 shares being offered on the Montreal Stock Exchange. Production was still running full out. Tank One operated for 504 continuous days, Tank Two for 567 days, and Tank Three for 742 days. Kilpatrick was chairman; Brunning vice-president and general manager; and George Milne secretary-treasurer. In 1945 the board comprised E.J. Brunning, O.B.E.; Brian Heward; C.G. Heward, K.C.; G. Ford Jones; J.A. Kilpatrick; Arthur Lyman; and F.K. Morrow, O.B.E.

Consumers' story is continued in Chapter 8 – Expansion and Development 1946-1966.

MID-WEST GLASS COMPANY LIMITED,
Winnipeg, Manitoba (1928-1930)

According to an article written in 1929, the idea of establishing a glass factory in Winnipeg was promoted by the Industrial Development Board. The board enlisted the services of a glass-oriented engineering firm, H.L. Dixon and Co. of Pittsburgh, Pennsylvania, to make a feasibility study for the location of a glass factory. As a result, a group of local businessmen, who were potential customers and/or suppliers, made an application for a charter. The key promoters were Shea's Brewery, Drewery's (brewery), Modern Dairies, Martin Paper Products, W.J. Holmes (who had a vested interest in a sand deposit on Black Island), and the Carter, Hall & Allinger Construction Company.

A federal charter for Mid-West Glass was granted on July 19, 1928, and the group of directors and officers was headed up by W.P. Dutton, who was president and general manager. Land was purchased on Sutherland Avenue, with easy access to a spur of the Canadian Pacific Railway. The plant was located in buildings already available, to which some necessary renovations were made.

Production facilities comprised two continuous glass melting furnaces, three Miller bottlemaking machines, and two thermal lehrs. Energy for melting the raw materials was in the form of gas, provided by the adjoining gas plant of Winnipeg Electric Railway Company. The forming machines were operated by compressed air and the thermal lehrs were brought up to operating temperature by gas jets, after which the temperature was maintained by the heat from the cooling bottles.

The plant was expected to produce 18 million containers a year, including milks, sodas, beverages and medicines, fruit and honey jars; also packer's ware, including jelly glasses and tumblers, lamp chimneys and various lines of pressed ware. One furnace was to produce flint glass, while the other would alternate between amber and green.

George Mendell, an experienced forming machine operator who had been working at Consumers Glass in Montreal, was secured by Miller Glass Company of Toledo, Ohio, to assist in the installation of the forming machines at Mid-West. When the plant started production on June 3, 1929, the company arranged with Miller to have Mendell stay on during the start-up period. He stayed until the plant closed down at the end of 1930.

Each tank was capable of supplying enough molten glass to operate two forming machines, or about 35 tons of glass every 24 hours. The flint tank made glass for the dairies, soft drink bottlers, fruit jars, etc., while the other tank was used for the brewery and distillery trades.

The forming machine equipment consisted of three Lynch LA machines, one Lynch R machine, and one Miller M machine. As examples of their production capabilities, Lynch L machines could produce 400 gross of beer bottles per day, and on the Miller M machine, about 150 gross per day; on the Lynch R machine, which periodically alternated with the Miller machine, about 150 gross per day; on the Lynch R machine, which periodically alternated with the Miller M machine and was used mostly for wide-mouth ware (fruit jars), they could make about 200 gross per day. One fruit jar that was definitely made at Mid-West was embossed "Mid-West Canadian Made" and came in three sizes — American pint, American quart and American half gallon. There were two styles of lids, one with an M in the middle of concentric circles and the other with a seven-point maple leaf. On the Lynch LA machine, daily production ran 100 to 200 gross, depending on size of item being made. It produced whiskeys and pharmaceutical bottles.

The plant manager was Walter Yingling, who had been with Ball Brothers in the United States. Mid-West had two continuous production runs, the first from June 1929 to February/March 1930, and the second from August 1930 to the end of that year. Following the second run, an attempt was made to melt the batch with electricity, but the operation was not a success.

During this period in the history of the Canadian glass industry, competition was overwhelming, particularly from the two conglomerates, Dominion Glass and Consumers, and any tricks of the trade were attempted to keep the plant going. Here was a case in point. A Mr. Robinson, a local engraver, was looking for blank pieces of glass tableware for wheel engraving (a style of decorating). Mendell and five glassworkers got together with Robinson to set up a small operation to make tableware on a side-lever press. Robinson supplied the financing and the others the glass know-how. They rented sufficient space on the Mid-West production floor to build a small L-shaped day tank, which could operate for 12 hours. There were four glassblowers and a mould maker, along with Mendell & Robinson. Using a lead oxide glass (very little lead used), they turned out the following pieces: plates (6, 8 and 10 inches), cups and saucers, breakfast sets, sugar bowls, spooners, creamers and butter dishes. The finished pieces were glazed or polished in a small oven. Robinson drew a design on the glass pieces with a crayon. A "wheat" pattern was popular. He would then lightly cut the pattern into the glass with a wheel. At the end of three months, Robinson decided that they had enough pieces and the operation was shut down.

Although the plant was supposed to have shut down permanently before the end of 1930, quoting from a letter sent to me by J.R. Mackenzie, vice-president, manufacturing, of Dominion Glass, dated January 8, 1965:

> . . . as far as production was concerned they produced satisfactory bottles during 1930 and 1931. Unfortunately their costs were high and most of their capital became tied up in large stocks of beer bottles, etc., forcing a shut down.
>
> Later there was a revival of interests in the Company and electric melting was introduced. This did not turn out to be entirely successful and the factory later closed down permanently. It is understood that the entire mechanical end of the business was sold to interests in Israel and sent to that country.

However, in a letter dated October 6, 1936, from Dominion's sales representative in Winnipeg, Frank E. Johns, to T.W. Bassett, general manager in Montreal, Johns states:

> You will be interested in learning that the Mid-West Glass Limited owes the Winnipeg Electric Company, $100,000.00 for Gas and $35,000 for rent. I understand that they never paid one cent of the Gas bill. The Winnipeg Electric have a lien on their machines, which they were trying to dispose of some time ago in the U.S.
>
> Some time ago I reported that this concern was finally closed up on September 30th (1936).

Despite the above, there is no extant proof that the company operated successfully after 1930. It was legally dissolved on December 16, 1980.

CANADIAN KNOX GLASS COMPANY, LIMITED
Oshawa, Ontario (1939-1940)

This was the second glass company to be established in Oshawa. The first one was Feldspar Glass in 1921. This company was established as a conventional bottlemaking operation by a seven-company syndicate of American glass companies, headed up by the Knox Glass Company, Knox, Pennsylvania.

A federal charter was issued on February 1, 1939. The buildings were rented on a piece of land on the southeast corner of Athol and Charles streets, with the office at 39 Charles Street. Other tenants on the property included General Motors of Canada. The key personnel, including R.R. Underwood, president, and W.M. Snyder, vice-president, had come from the parent company in the United States.

The following editorial in an April 1939 issue of the *Oshawa Daily Times* clearly indicated the mixed opinions that existed concerning the future of the company. The *Times* editor was commenting on an editorial that appeared on the same date in the rival *Oshawa Courier*.

> An article on the front page of the *Oshawa Courier* issued this morning would seem to give the impression that there is some doubt as to the Knox Glass Bottle Company (sic) getting into production in the near future. Indeed some people might read into

the article that there is a possibility that the company may not operate at all . . .

The *Times* has made inquiries . . . and is satisfied there is not a scintilla of evidence to justify the inference contained in this article . . .

The opinion of the editor of the *Times* was finally vindicated a year later. In a Scroll Cash Book, accounts receivable entries were found representing payments for glassware sold to customers. The first entry was July 5, 1940, and the last entry was July 29, 1942. Bills of lading, covering the forwarding of unused Customers Own cartons (COC) to Dominion Glass's Hamilton plant, revealed the following:

Brights	26 oz. Wine
Glenwood Products	6 oz. bottles
Stewart Hall	2 oz. fruit Aide
Canada Vinegar	12-24 oz. Western Vinegars
	12-24 oz. Lion Vinegars
	12-24 oz. Canada Vinegars
Duthie Mfg. Co.	7 oz. P & D Sauce
Wildroot	
A & P	16 oz. Mayonnaise
Betty's Ltd.	20 oz. bottles
M. Wintrob and Sons	

It was obvious that after the shutdown in 1940 finished ware was sold for another two years.

Purchasing department memos indicate that the company was using feldspar from Frontenac Floor and Tile Co., Kingston, and ground dolomite quick lime from Canadian Gypsum Co., Guelph, Ontario.

In May 1940 the offer by Dominion Glass to purchase Canadian Knox was accepted. Bert Macklin, a Dominion Glass engineer, was sent to Oshawa to make an inventory of the assets and, at the same time, arrange for their disposal. Here are extracts from the report:

Knox Glass Co. factory was a block or so south of the Genosha Hotel with a good railway siding.

There was one glass machine rather similar to our O'Neill 42 and another much heavier and similar to a modified Owens. There was also a rather big machine about 5 feet tall, for fine crushing.

The furnace had been shut down with the glass still in it and I had to break it all out and sell it for cullet.

The furnace was new and all blocks in good condition, so dug them out and shipped to whichever factory wanted them.

The big Owens type machine had been set up on a wooden platform about 30″ above the floor. It probably weighed 8 or 10 tons and it had been placed on the platform with the 4 wheels on and did not realize the whole weight rested on the 4 wheels. They at once broke through the platform floor. I had to rent a small crane from General Motors to lift it up and set it on the floor. It was tricky but we got it on a freight car and sent it down to Wallaceburg, where it was left in the decorating dept. for 2 or 3 years.

During the night, it was 14 below zero outside and 2 below inside and to keep my gang working I got hot coffee and in each cup gave a shot of Canadian Club (whiskey). When I sent in my expense account to Bill Jordan, Office Manager at Wallaceburg, he saw an item for Canadian Club and I had given no explanation.

I was never able to find out who was running the show at Knox but know that somebody was going around Oshawa selling stock because a first cousin of mine put up a thousand or two and he came again to try and get more with no results.

The agreed purchase price was $618,270, and the final agreement was signed on May 14, 1940. The land and buildings were sold to Alger Press Ltd. in November 1940, and the company was dissolved on August 25, 1971.

FOOTNOTES

[1] Minutes from directors' meeting of Dominion Glass Company, Limited, January 21, 1926, book 2, pp. 287-288.
[2] Ibid. October 21, 1926, book 3, pp. 14, 15.
[3] See Chapter 11 Flat Glass, "Fourcault process."

CHAPTER 8

Expansion
and Development
(1946-1966)

Dominion Glass: Employee Benefits; Warehouses in British Columbia and Toronto Area;
Trend to Mechanization due to Increasing Labour Costs; Energy Subsidiary in
Wallaceburg; Rearrangement of Management Group; Glass Plant in British
Columbia; Pint Beer Bottle Standardization; Final Stock Split Achieved 50
for 1 During Period 1946 to 1962; Baby Foods
Consumers Glass: Plant Approved for Etobicoke, Ontario; Rearrangement of Management;
New Management Team; Capital Improvement Program; Agreement with
Brockway Glass; Change in Trademark; Warehouses Across Canada; Iroquois Glass
Company Limited, Candiac, Quebec (1958), Changed its Name to Iroquois Glass Limited
(1958-1965) and Later to Iroquois (1965) Limited (1965-1967)

DOMINION GLASS

The United States, forced into the war in 1941, enjoyed a booming wartime economy and replaced the war-torn United Kingdom as the champion of democracy in the West. Canada's economy suffered from lack of labour and raw materials and was now faced with the task of getting back to normal.

As an indication of the company's success in the period 1946-1962, it split its stock 50-to-1 in this 17-year period. In the last quarter of the year. July 1 to September 30, the company had to close down due to a strike in the plant of the supplier of one of its basic raw materials.

In the post-war period, labour's demands for increased benefits were becoming more persistent. The second step in a plan to bring its employee benefits up to the level of comparable industry was taken in 1949 with the introduction of a voluntary and contributory retirement income plan.

In 1950, with the threat of domestic or foreign competition establishing itself in British Columbia, the company purchased eight acres of land in Marpole that would be suitable for an office, warehouse and, if need be, a plant. Two years later, a more suitable 19-acre property was acquired in Burnaby, and the first one was subsequently sold.

Amendments to the Income Tax Act in 1951 put a severe strain on the company's financial position, which had the effect of breaking the continuing trend of annually increasing profits.

The second adjustment to capital took place in 1953 with a further split of the stock on a two-for-one basis, the dividends being adjusted accordingly. In the same year, in reviewing the accounts, the directors were concerned by the fact that the labour portion of the cost of production was running at approximately 44 percent. This was higher than the average in the

Dominion Glass, Wallaceburg Plant, 1946.   Courtesy of Dominion Glass Company Limited.

heavy industry sector in Canada. As will be seen later in the manufacturing section of the company's operations, a long-range plan of mechanization was being effected to control and, if possible, reduce this percentage.

Mr. John Wallace died in September 1953. Wallace had served the company for over 50 years in various capacities, latterly as treasurer and controller.

An office and warehouse on the Burnaby property were completed in 1954, with ample room for the establishment of a production facility at the appropriate time.

The Toronto area accounted for an ever-increasing percentage of the company's sales, all of which had to be uneconomically serviced, primarily by Hamilton, but also from Wallaceburg and Montreal. The first step to alleviate this situation was the acquisition in 1954 of 20 acres of land in nearby Etobicoke. Before construction of a warehouse had started, a more suitable 20-acre property and the buildings thereon was purchased at $10,000 per acre, plus $60,000 for the buildings. It was located on the west side of Highway No. 27, between the Queen Elizabeth Highway and Highway 5 on Dundas Street and was known as the Toronto West warehouse.

The Wallaceburg plant in southwest Ontario (successor to Sydenham Glass in 1913) was right in the middle of an extensive gas and oil field that had been centered on Petrolia, where oil had been discovered in the 1880s. While the Wallaceburg plant had been economically supplied with all the energy it needed, in 1954 the company decided to establish a gas and oil subsidiary. The name of the new subsidiary was the Sydenham Gas & Petroleum Company Limited. The president and vice-president were T.W. Bassett and F.N. Dundas, at head office in Montreal. E.G. Davies, plant manager at Wallaceburg, was secretary and was responsible for the development of the operation, with W. Jordan, office manager at Wallace-

BUCKINGHAM PALACE

7th May, 1952.

Dear Mr Mayor,

     I am commanded by Her Majesty The Queen to thank you and the People of Wallaceburg, most sincerely for the magnificent gift of drinking glasses which you sent to her. They arrived in perfect condition and Her Majesty is very pleased to have them, both for what they are and because they will serve to remind her of her first visit to Canada.

Yours sincerely,

Martin Charteris

Assistant Private Secretary.

His Worship
   The Mayor of Wallaceburg,
      Ontario.

Wallaceburg's gift to Princess Elizabeth and the Duke of Edinburgh upon the occasion of their first visit to Canada in 1952; and their letter of thanks.

burg, acting as treasurer. A number of leases for the underground gas rights were obtained, but there was too much competition from the oil industry and the leases were all sold by 1960.

The first of the triumverate — Jim Mackenzie, Mac Yuile and Mervyn Offer — to go was Mervyn Offer, who died in January 1955. He had served the company for 42 years; his contribution was an enviable one and his imprint remained for many years. A further recognition of Offer's contribution to the company was the decision to strengthen the senior management group by adding the position of chairman and replacing the vice-president by a vice-president and secretary, and a vice-president, sales. At the directors' organization meeting, held at the conclusion of the 1955 annual general meeting, the slate of offices was established: chairman, president, vice-president & secretary, vice-president in charge of sales, treasurer, and assistant-secretary.

Before the end of the year, the original bylaws of the company, instituted in 1913, were replaced by a set that more accurately reflected current business practice.

The effect of the ongoing modernization program, started in 1946, was beginning to be reflected in the production and sales figures as shown in the following table:

	Production (tons)	Sales ($000s)
1946	128,735	12,988
1955	220,021	30,172
1956	262,240	33,620

Norman W. Meldrum, appointed General Manager and Director of Dominion Glass Company Limited in December, 1959.

Due to the prolonged absence of Mr. Bassett due to illness, Mr. Dundas was appointed executive vice-president in February 1956. In April 1956 N.W. Meldrum (ex-Redcliff) was appointed vice-president and assistant general manager, J.R. Mackenzie (ex-Redcliff) was appointed vice-president in charge of manufacturing, and I was appointed secretary. The following slate was appointed at the end of the year:

L.J. Belnap	– chairman of the board
T.W. Bassett	– president & general manager
F.N. Dundas	– executive vice-president
N.W. Meldrum	– vice-president & asst. general manager
I.R. Macdonald	– vice-president, sales
J.R. Mackenzie	– vice-president, manufacturing
J.E. Glithero	– treasurer
T.B. King	– secretary
A.G. Price	– controller

The next phase of the employee benefits program was established in 1957 with the introduction of a group hospitalization plan for salaried employees.

In 1958 approval was given for the construction of a glass plant on the Burnaby property at an estimated cost of $4,000,000.

Since the inception in 1951 of London Life's retirement income plan for salaried employees, the terms of retirement for each such employee had been arbitrarily established by management. To put this on an official basis, in 1959 the company established a formula for determining a consistent retirement allowance for salaried employees.

The second major loss from senior management ranks occurred on November 10, 1959, when Bassett, president and general manager, died. Bassett had come to Montreal from Ireland in 1910 and, through an introduction to Mac Yuile, obtained a job at the Diamond Flint plant on Delorimier Avenue in Montreal. In 1925, when the nonmechanized, noncontainer operations of the company were centralized in Wallaceburg, he had been appointed plant manager there. He moved to head office to replace the deceased J.W. King as general manager in 1937, became vice-president and director two years later, and was appointed president in 1956 to succeed L.J. Belnap, who had been appointed the first chairman of the company in that year. F.N. Dundas became president and N.W. Meldrum, vice-president and general manager.

The year 1960 was one for reflection. Profits were down as costs continued to rise disproportionately to the return on the sales dollar — due to the signing of several new collective employment agreements, as well as increasing foreign competition.

With a continuing dimunition of return on sales again in 1961, it was decided to introduce a modest price increase on the general line of products on April 1. This was the first price increase in four years. H. MacDonald, formerly general sales manager, replaced I.R. Macdonald as vice-president, sales. During the year, the Canadian brewing industry decided to implement a conversion program in Eastern Canada to a new design of standard pint bottles.

The final modification of the stock took place in May 1962, whereby the common shares were split five-for-one and the preferred shares became convertible into common shares on a one-for-one basis at any time until December 29, 1977.

The company made its first move into the plastics industry in 1962 by setting up an experimental operation for the production of plastic bottles at the Pte. St. Charles plant in Montreal. In 1965 production of plastic bottles started up in a new building on the Toronto West warehouse site, with Ron Mander as manager. Also in 1962, the company started to make jars for baby food, which heretofore had only been available in tin cans.

Over the next few years, the company increased its share of the market. ". . . As the oldest and largest glass manufacturer in Canada, the Company has recognized its responsibility in participating tangibly in Canada's Centennial year. To this end, the Dominion Glass Centennial Research Foundation was established in September to collect and document, in conjunction with the Canadiana Department of the Royal Ontario Museum in Toronto, objects of old Canadian glass, the majority of which were made by this Company and its predecessor Companies. This documentation will be published in a book entitled *Canadian Glass c.1825-1925*, which will appear late in 1966. It will be written by Mr. Gerald Stevens, a leading Canadian glass authority, who has been retained by the Company as a Research Associate to the Museum, for the Foundation. This will contribute greatly to Canada's recorded cultural history . . ."[1]

I was appointed to coordinate the company's input. As a further gesture to the Centennial celebrations to be held in 1967, the company over a three-year period financially supported the establishment of a permanent exhibit of old Canadian glass, set up in the Canadiana Department of the Royal Ontario Museum in Toronto with me acting as liaison between the company and the museum.

Mac Yuile, the second of the "Group of Three," died on November 6, 1963, with 64 years of service. Starting in 1899, in Montreal, he worked up to the position of general sales manager in 1924. He left the company in 1926 and was then appointed a director, which position he held until his death. Appropriately enough, Jim Mackenzie replaced Mac Yuile on the board.

During the year, metal containers made inroads into what have always been considered as traditional glass markets, mainly in the beverage field. To offset the continuing trend toward canned beverages, the company introduced a nonreturnable bottle for use in the soft drink industry in 1965.

With the advent of a federal old age security plan in 1966, the company modified its plan so that the combined pensions would be the same as the company paid before the government introduced its plan. Frank W. Ross, one of the original directors appointed in 1913, died on March 18, 1966. He had been an active participant on the board until a few years before his death. The year 1966 was the last in which the company enjoyed independent status.

The following is a list of directors and principal officers of Dominion Glass Company, Limited:

DIRECTOR	OFFICER	DIRECTOR	OFFICER
G.A. Grier 1913-15	president 1913-16	P.N. Thomson 1967-	chairman 1968-71; 1973-76
Sir C.B. Gordon 1913-39	vice-president 1913-16; president 1916-39	W.I.M. Turner, Jr. 1967-	
W. McMaster 1913-30	vice-president 1918-30	J.R. Yarnell 1967-73	
A. Kingman 1913-31	vice-president 1916-18	R.A. Irwin 1967-79	chairman 1971-1973
T.B. Macaulay 1913-29		P.B. Paine, Q.C. 1967-73	
F.W. Ross 1913-66		H.H. Lank 1967-76	president 1967-76;
D.A. Gordon 1913-19		E.A. Thompson 1967-76	chairman 1976-nd
Hon. L.G. Guest 1913-26			
Sir W. Wiseman 1913-26		J. Parisien 1968-75	treasurer 1968-
G. Stirling	treasurer 1913-1945	E.G. Blyth	
G.H. Grier 1916-26		P.E. Martin 1970-	
J. Baillie 1919-23		P. Desmarais 1973-	
R. King 1921-32		Hon. J.B. Aird, Q.C. 1973-80	
J. Wallace	treasurer 1945-53	P.D. Curry 1974-nd	
H.D. Herdt 1923-26	vice-president 1930-39	E.A. Galvin 1976-nd	vice-president 1970-75;
F.G. Daniels 1926-33		J.E. Souccar 1976-	president 1976-nd
R.H. McMaster 1926-38			
W. Molson 1926-53			
N.M. Yuile 1926-64			
J.W. King 1929-37	president 1939-55;		
Hon. D. Raymond 1929-63	chairman 1955-67		
K.T. Dawes 1931-67			
Hon. S.C. Mewburn 1931-56			
J.W. Hobbs 1932-51			
G. Lydiatt 1933-39			
T.B. Dundas 1937-38			
L.J. Belnap 1938-67			
T.W. Bassett 1939-59	vice-president 1939-55; president 1955-59		
F.G. Bush 1939-40	secretary 1913		
H.E. Sellers 1940-67			
M. Offer 1946-55	secretary 1913-45		
Col. K.R. Marshall 1951-62			
H.E.C. Brennen 1953-54			
H.M. Turner 1954-70			
I.R. Macdonald 1955-65	vice-president 1955-59		
J.E. Glithero	assistant treasurer 1953-55; treasurer 1955-68		
F.N. Dundas 1956-68	assistant secretary 1943-45; secretary 1945-56; treasurer 1953-55; president 1959-67; chairman 1967-68		
N.W. Meldrum 1959-67	vice-president 1956-67		
R.W. Cooper 1962-67			
R. Chagnon 1963-80			
J.R. Mackenzie 1964-67	vice-president 1956-68		
H.R. Crabtree 1966-78			
T.B. King 1966-67	assistant secretary 1945-56; secretary 1956-78		

CONSUMERS GLASS

The next 21 years was a period of expansion and development. With the war over and service personnel being integrated into peacetime occupations, it took a while for the industry to settle down. With so many companies trying to renovate their war-strained facilities, there was a shortage of construction materials and equipment. Added to this was a mid-summer strike in the soda ash industry, which curtailed production.

In 1947 an employee death benefit plan was added to Consumers' pension plan. A year later, on the death of J.A. Kilpatrick, Ernie Brunning was appointed president and general manager.

Profits were off 30 percent in 1949. New equipment and greater diversification were used to reverse this trend. At the same time, sales were returning to the pre-war pattern of being seasonal — that is, very strong from May to October and considerably weaker for the other half of the year. This clearly indicated that the bulk of the sales were dependent on the food and beverage markets, as well as on the ever-increasing home canning practice.

In the early fifties, although sales and gross profits showed moderate gains, government programs had a dampening effect. In 1951 there was a 20-percent federal tax increase and, a year later, the Old Age Security plan was introduced. As a result, 54 percent of the company's net income went for taxes. J.N. Jordan was appointed vice-president of operations.

In 1953 plans were approved to build a plant in the Toronto area, part of the cost of which was offset by the issue of $3-million five-percent first mortgage bonds. The $2-million renovation program at Ville St. Pierre was completed with the construction of furnace #4. Production statistics give a good picture of the product mix at that time. Total production was 1,445,918 gross of bottles from 534 moulds (in 1927 there were 400 moulds). Of these moulds, just 55 accounted for 70 percent of sales. This included beers, whiskeys, soft drinks and bottles for food packers.

There was a realignment of management in 1954 under the presidency of Brunning and vice-presidency of Brian Heward. J.N. Jordan was appointed vice-president and general manager, and G.F. MacRae replaced George Milne as secretary-treasurer. The new Toronto plant in Etobicoke was completed at a cost of $2.7 million and began production in mid-July. In the following year extra warehousing was built to help smooth out the seasonal peaks and valleys, while maintaining production throughout the year on a profitable basis.

In 1957 earnings dropped a quarter of a million dollars due to a five-week strike. The funds used to service the pension plan, which had been in force for 15 years, had to be augmented from current operations to the extent of $109,907.

The second realignment of management took place in 1958. Brunning was appointed the company's first chairman. Jordan became president and general manager. Three vice-presidents were appointed: C.G. Kemp, operations; J.A. Riendeau, sales; and G.F. MacRae, who was appointed vice-president and secretary-treasurer.

In order to cover the cost of doubling production capacity in Toronto — the building of a second 100-ton furnace — $2.5-million 5½ first mortgage Sinking Fund Bonds were issued in February. A summary of the year's shipments produced the following figures:

tomato, sauce, vinegar bottles	63,806 gross
narrow-neck standard bottles	19,509 gross
narrow-neck bottles made-to-order	201,161 gross
beer bottles (flint, green, amber)	93,867 gross
soda bottles	87,722 gross
wine and whiskey bottles	171,142 gross
wide-mouth jars	296,392 gross
milk bottles	22,605 gross

Total production was 956,204 gross, or 138 million jars and bottles.

The year 1960 was one of reorganization in senior management. Net income fell from $750,000 to $180,000. Brunning (chairman), Jordan (president) and Milne (director) resigned. Brian Heward temporarily took over as president and the board appointed a special committee to help him. A management consultant firm was retained to examine the company's operations. They proposed substantial management changes and a major capital improvement program. As a result, two new professional managers were hired to take over the day-to-day operations of the company. J.D. Mingay, a former insurance executive, was appointed president and D.R. Gormley, from the cotton industry, became vice-president. The other change in management was to replace the secretary-treasurer's position by temporarily appointing both a secretary and a treasurer. N.J.P. Melnick was appointed secretary and R.D. Morison, treasurer. Two years later, Bob Morison was appointed secretary-treasurer.

A capital improvement program, to be carried out over the next five years at a cost of $3.5 million, was built around a scheduled replacement of the current Lynch and Miller forming machines with Hartford-Empire Individual Section (HE "IS") forming machines, which were 50 percent more productive than the company's Lynch machines and 35 percent more productive than the present Miller machines. Dominion Glass had obtained exclusive Canadian rights to these machines in 1939 and retained their monopoly until the mid-fifties. One of the requirements of the two new top officers was to move the executive offices to Toronto, leaving the head office in Ville St. Pierre. This move was made in 1961.

Concurrent with the above major changes, a five-year agreement was reached with Brockway Glass of Pennsylvania, fourth largest glass container plant in the United States. This was a technical assistance agreement to be paid for by Consumers. In return, Brockway was given the option of buying up to 20 percent of Consumers' common stock (82,293 treasury shares) at prices ranging from $21 to $25 for the five-year period.

In 1961 the beer bottle conversion program took place. Since beer and ale bottlemaking began in Canada, literally hundreds of shapes had been developed for individual breweries. To make matters worse, each brewery could order their bottles to be made in flint, amber, or more than five shades of green. As a result, the cost of this selectivity for all but the largest brewers was becoming prohibitive. The resultant cost reductions were enjoyed by both the glassmakers and the breweries. Major sales increases in the industry and higher profits resulted. To complete Consumers' new image, their old trademark, an inverted triangle with a C in it ( ), was replaced in 1962 by a traditional triangle with round corners enclosing a white C on a red background ( ).

A year later, the stock was split four-for-one. In October a price increase was announced. It was pointed out at the time that its prices had climbed only 60 percent in 23 years, compared to a 140 percent increase in the index of wholesale prices in the same period. D.R. Gormley resigned from the board and as executive vice-president in 1964. A growing trend to market soft drinks in nonreturnable cans encouraged the glass companies to provide disposable soft drink bottles.

In order to comply with current accounting practices, the company changed its fiscal year end of August 31 to the calendar year end of December 31 as of 1965. Montreal employees dropped their affiliation with one of the traditional glass unions, the Glass Bottle Blowers Association, with headquarters in Philadelphia, and joined a provincially-oriented union, Syndicat National des Employes du Verre de Ville St. Pierre (CSN-CNTU). Consumers joined the Glass Container Council of Canada, a forum for Canadian glass manufacturers and their principal suppliers. V.S.B. Corbet was appointed vice-president, operations, and A.F. Griffiths vice-president, marketing and sales.

In 1966, the last year under review, net income exceeded the $1 million mark, at $1,266,230. The company sought new horizons by acquiring Brentwood Containers, a plastics manufacturing company. Pension plans were modified to provide for introduction of the Canada and Quebec government pension plans.

A brief summary of the company's contemporary history will be found in Chapter 12 – The Contemporary Scene (1967-1980).

Bernard T. Johnson, appointed president of Iroquois Glass Industries Limited in June 1966.

IROQUOIS GLASS COMPANY LIMITED,
Candiac, Quebec (1958-1967)

In 1951 Sogemines Limited was established by the Société Générale De Belgique of Brussels to represent its interests in Canada. On April 18, 1958, Iroquois Glass was federally incorporated as a subsidiary of Sogemines. The plant site was located in a comparatively new industrial park in Candiac, southwest of Montreal, on the south side of the St. Lawrence River. With the technical assistance of the company's associate, Verreries des Hamandes in Belgium, the plant was completed in just over eight months.

The facility started with two glass furnaces, which would serve six production lines. The potential capacity was 36,000 tons of glass a year. Not unexpectedly, the final cost of construction exceeded the estimate and a loan was received from the parent company. It was not until 1962 that a reasonable profit was shown, part of which had been realized by the extra business that became available to the Canadian glass companies when the brewers' industry agreed to the establishment of a standard amber (stubby) beer bottle to reduce costs.

Management started out as a Belgo-Canadian melange. The chairman, W.L. Forster, C.B.E., was a Canadian, with C.G. Dupriez as president and M. Lambot vice-president, production, both from Belgium. This sounded like a pleasant hands-across-the-water atmosphere, the best of two worlds. Unfortunately, in practice, as it turned out over the next few years, it was neither practical nor economically feasible to carry on a manufacturing operation in North America using European operating practices. In Canada, "action" was the key word and it was necessary to move quickly to survive. In Europe, on the other hand, from centuries of experience, "deliberation" perhaps best described the pace of business. It was once said that Iroquois was operated by transatlantic telephone, but this of course was an exaggeration. On May 20, 1958, the company's name was changed to Iroquois Glass Limited. The binational philosophy was reversed in 1961, and from then on the company became North American-oriented in its operations.

The product mix — amber, green and flint — was similar to that of the other two companies, Dominion and Consumers, i.e. beers, soft drinks, whiskey, wines, milks, foods and pharmaceuticals. With just the one plant in Candiac, their market was Ontario, Quebec and the Maritimes, the Maritimes being represented by agents.

By March of 1963 a third furnace (unit melter) had been added and there were seven production lines. This increased the capacity of the plant by one-third. For the first time, in 1964, there were retained earnings ($72,000). Two events occurred during the year which had an adverse effect, not only on the company's sales, but on those of its competitors as well. The use of cans for soft drinks was beginning to be felt, and secondly, a strike occurred at the Quebec Liquor Board in December, the effect of the latter being somewhat alleviated by increased sales to the breweries.

The year 1965 marked the end of Phase 1 of the company's operations and the start of Phase 2. Heretofore, it had been operating as a subsidiary of Sogemines. Now, it was about to be amalgamated with its parent and two other controlled subsidiaries, Inland Cement and Brockville Chemicals. Iroquois Glass now became Iroquois Glass (1965) Limited.

Two years later, Iroquois was up for sale. Dominion Glass made an offer for it but did not agree with the final figure set by Iroquois. On April 30, 1967, it was bought by Consumers Glass for cash and the issue of a series of debentures. It then became Consumers' Candiac plant.

FOOTNOTES

[1] Annual Report (1964), Dominion Glass Company, Limited, d. November 24, 1964.

CHAPTER 9

Authentication,
Attribution
and Excavations

Authentication and Attribution

Trade Names and Trademarks; Advertisements; Mould and Stock Inventories

Excavations: Burlington Glass; Nova Scotia glasshouses; Delorimier Avenue, Montreal, glass-houses; Hamilton Glass; Manitoba Glass; Saint Lawrence Glass; and Napanee Glass.

Although no dig took place at Jefferson Glass in Toronto, the information has been extracted from published material.

An alphabetical list of the pressed glass patterns and the companies to which they have been attributed will be found at the end of the chapter.

CHRONOLOGICAL LIST OF DIGS

Mallorytown Glass Works, Mallorytown, Ontario, 1953
Nova Scotia glasshouses, Trenton, Nova Scotia, 1964-66, '69, '71
Burlington Glass Works, Hamilton, Ontario, 1965-66, '68, '69
The Manitoba Glass Manufacturing Company, Beausejour, Manitoba, 1966, '73
Napanee Glass Factory, Napanee, Ontario, 1968
Hamilton Glass Company, Hamilton, Ontario, 1970, '71
The Saint Lawrence Glass Company, Montreal, Quebec, 1970
Delorimier Avenue glasshouses, Montreal, Quebec, 1973

As a result of the publication of Gerald Stevens' book *Canadian Glass c.1825-1925* in 1967, interest was renewed in the research of Canadian glass. Previously, a few glass buffs — including Dr. Lorne Pierce and his wife, Edith Chown Pierce, of Toronto; George MacLaren, Chief Curator of History, Nova Scotia Museum, Halifax; and Stevens himself, in conjunction with the Royal Ontario Museum in Toronto — had carried out research and were involved in a number of digs during the 1960s. The findings were published in books and occasional papers. One of the direct results of the publishing of Stevens' book in 1967 was the establishment of GLASFAX,[1] which body became a contributing factor in the continuing search for further information on Canadian glass. Perhaps the most important and still to be answered question is "How can one establish, beyond a reasonable doubt, the place of manufacture of a glass article?"

There are two levels of acceptability. The higher one, *authentication*, requires positive identification, without a doubt, of the place of manufacture. Whereas the lower one, *attribution*, can only be the assumption of an individual or a group that, all factors considered, the piece was probably made at a specific factory. Even the finding of a great number of shards of a specific pattern, or a particular bottle on a glass factory site, is not sufficient evidence to make a

Monogram,
DIG *trademark*

case for authentication. To add to the problem, there appears to have been some movement of cullet between certain factories, which might account for the presence of shards. Each individual must therefore set his or her own guidelines for deciding whether the extant shards satisfy the criteria of authentication or only attribution.

In order to assist the researcher in authenticating or attributing an article to a specific company or factory, here are some guidelines.

TRADE NAMES, TRADEMARKS

Many bottlemakers since the mid-nineteenth century have glass-embossed the names of their companies and/or trade names on their bottles. This was particularly true of fruit jars (e.g. Erie Fruit Jar, Hamilton Glass Works Clamp Jar, etc.). To a lesser degree, the same principle applied to some insulators (e.g. Dominion 9, 10, 16, 42, 614).

On the other hand, trademarks did not come into general use until the twentieth century — Consumers Glass 1917 and Dominion Glass 1928.

ADVERTISEMENTS

In the latter part of the nineteenth century, glass companies started to advertise their products in newspapers and trade magazines. In most cases, these were not illustrated but simply listed the types of glassware they were capable of producing. Even if they were illustrated, many were with drawings and not photographs. In the twentieth century, as advertising became more sophisticated, the chances of authenticating an article improved.

PRICE LISTS AND ILLUSTRATED CATALOGS

Traditionally, glass companies do not sell to the public as individuals, but only to bottlers, distributors and wholesalers for tableware and industrial ware. As a result, price lists and catalogs are not plentiful. About 1915 Dominion Glass, the only Canadian producer of tableware at that time, appointed Cassidys in Montreal as their distributors for this type of ware, details of which Cassidys included in their own catalogs. In this way, some distributor catalogs are valuable.

MOULD AND STOCK INVENTORIES

Mould inventories were prepared from time to time, usually as the result of significant changes in production operations. As an example, in 1925, when Dominion Glass made the decision to centralize all hand shop production at its Wallaceburg plant, a list of all the extant moulds, both for hand and machine production, was prepared and included some 5,000 items. For each item there was a mould number, which at that time also served as the stock number, the capacity and name of each style of bottle or other glass article was given, and an indication of whether it was used for hand operations or on a machine, the abbreviation for which was used. Here are three examples:

765 2 oz.	Almond Cream Hand
1508 26 oz.	Ginger Ale Hand, Owens AR
3393 #4	Cheese Jar Owens AN, Miller

Twenty years later, as the company settled down again after the end of World War II, the 1925 mould inventory was replaced by a stock inventory in which new stock numbers were assigned for each item. To differentiate the new numbers from the old ones, the letter V (V for Victory?) preceded each new number. These inventories were prepared semiannually as the result of stocktaking.

EXCAVATIONS

Over the last 35 years, archaeological and informal excavations (digs) have taken place at the sites of some of the former glass companies. A detailed and illustrated report of such an archaeological dig at the site of the former Burlington Glass Works, in Hamilton, in May 1966, appears in Stevens' *Canadian Glass c.1825-1925*. The following brief descriptions of some of the other digs that have taken place have been condensed from internally published GLASFAX newsletters. A list of pressed glass patterns, represented by the shards, appears at the end of the chapter. Illustrations of these patterns with further references appear in Appendix 3 Selected Pressed Glassware Patterns. For other types of glassware, such as bottles, industrial ware, etc., only the kinds of ware (e.g. prescriptions, beverages, inks, insulators, etc.) are listed in the brief descriptions.

The two most prolific glasshouses in Canada producing pressed glassware were Burlington Glass and Nova Scotia Glass.

BURLINGTON GLASS WORKS, HAMILTON, ONTARIO

As early as 1965 the Royal Ontario Museum sponsored a limited dig on this site. What they found clearly indicated the need for a formal archaeological dig. This took place in May 1966.[2] A year later, GLASFAX member Frankie Woodrow and her family did a series of digs on the same site.[3] They were joined by glass researchers John Sheeler and Peter Behn. A number of new patterns were found, as well as some bottle shards. In July 1968 Ms. Woodrow again spearheaded another dig, assisted by some GLASFAX members from the Hamilton area. The following colours were represented in the form of cullet:

1. Clear (flint)	6. Gem blue
2. Milk white	7. Amber
3. Yellow-banded green	8. Blue opal
4. Milk yellow	9. Amethyst (pale to dark)
5. Green (light to mid-green)	

Shards of salts and peppers were also found.[4]

In 1969, under the leadership of Helen Sutermeister, an archaeologist on the staff of the Royal Ontario Museum, a formal dig took place. A report of this dig, prepared by John Sheeler, was filed with the museum, but to date (1985) has not been published.

NOVA SCOTIA GLASSHOUSES, TRENTON, NOVA SCOTIA

In the 1960s and 70s a number of digs took place in this area where three glasshouses — Nova Scotia Glass, Lamont Glass and Humphreys' Glass — operated almost side by side. Because of the close proximity of the three houses and the fact that much of the ground had been worked over in the intervening years, the shards that were found have to be attributed to each of the companies according to their advertised product mixes.

The first formal dig took place in the summer of 1964 under the direction of the late George Maclaren, Chief Curator of History at the Nova Scotia Museum.[5] Some ten patterns were identified from the shards. Types of ware represented among the shards were goblets, fruit nappies, cake plates, spooners, compotes, butter dishes, water pitchers, cream pitchers, cheese dishes and sugar bowls. Excavation and research in 1965-1966 added nine more patterns.

Members of the Maritime district of GLASFAX, headed by Doris and Bob Wentzell and Mary and Wally Saunders, unearthed shards of three further patterns in 1969.[6] These were turned over to the Nova Scotia Museum. The third and final dig, also under the sponsorship of GLASFAX, took place in September 1971. A few more patterns were identified. In all, 36 patterns attributed to Nova Scotia Glass are on display at the museum.

DELORIMIER AVENUE GLASSHOUSES, MONTREAL, QUEBEC

In the southern part of the block — bounded by Parthenais, De Montigny (now De Maisonneuve), and Delorimier Avenue — four glass companies operated: Excelsior Glass (1880-1883), North American Glass (1883-1890), Diamond Glass (1890-1902), and Diamond Flint Glass (1903-1913). As these companies occupied the same property in succession, with expansion as required, and were all bottle and pressed ware operations, it is not possible to authenticate or even attribute glass articles to a specific company except through catalogs, inventories and glass-embossed bottles showing the company name and/or monogram.

In the summer of 1973 GLASFAX members spent countless hours doing a surface dig on the few areas that were not covered over by buildings or paved surfaces. In March 1976 GLASFAX Research Director Jean-Pierre Dion tabled a bilingual report on the 1973 dig.

The extensive quantity of shards dug up related mostly to bottles, but also included 28 pressed glass patterns for tumblers, lamps and chimneys, fruit jars, milk bottles and insulators. In all, 33 different patterns, including five new patterns and some not previously attributed to Montreal. Included in the shards were those relating to the following fruit jars: Crown, North American Glass, Excelsior, Diamond Glass, Diamond Flint Glass, The Imperial, Best, Gem, Mason and American Porcelain lined.

HAMILTON GLASS COMPANY, HAMILTON, ONTARIO

Hamilton Glass was known as the "green house," a term used to indicate that the company's primary production was bottles, whereas Burlington Glass was known as the "flint house," to identify it with the production of pressed glass.

The first dig under the sponsorship of GLASFAX took place on November 8, 1970, under the leadership of the late Jack Kingdon, assisted by Dave Parker, Larry Taylor and other members.[7] A large quantity of bottle shards, pieces of glazed furnace brick and chunks of cullet were found. No attempt was made to relate the shards to finished bottles. The same group returned in April of the following year.

From the shards it was confirmed that this was basically a bottleworks and that one of the principal products was fruit jars. Shards found definitely related to the following lines: THE DARLING; the NO DOT CROWN; the GEM, bearing the well-known name Rutherford & Co.; Hamilton Glass Fruit Jar; Bogardus balls for trapshooting; Dalleys Ink; and fruit jar lids and stoppers. Bottles had been made for the following products: baking powder, flavouring extracts, mustard, coffee, bird seed, soups, perfumes and carbonated beverages.

THE MANITOBA GLASS MANUFACTURING COMPANY, LIMITED BEAUSEJOUR, MANITOBA

In 1966 Mac Provick, a member of the Winnipeg district of GLASFAX, did a dig on this site.[8] Handblown bottles were found in amber and aquamarine, as well as a few whimseys. From the machine-made operations of the company (c.1912), Provick attributed the following products from the shards he collected: milk bottles (clear); handmade beer bottles embossed with trademarks from breweries in Winnipeg, Vancouver and Victoria; clear bright-green sodas and soft drink bottles with crown finishes; embossed shards from Blackwoods and E.L. Drewry, both of Winnipeg. There was evidence, although scanty, of fruit jars and lids having been made. Many shards of and whole ink bottles made for the Reliance Ink Company of Winnipeg were found, in two types — a small type in pale green glass, mouldblown, hand-finished neck with a fast-pitch screw thread, and a clear and larger type finished in the same way but with an ordinary thread. A proliferation of shards of handmade bottles for drugs and prescriptions were found in clear and bright green. Customers identified included the Western Sewing Machine Co. and the R.D. Rawleigh Medical Co., both of Winnipeg. A few clear shards suggested that some lamp chimneys had been made. Bright green shards of spirits bottles were found in abundance, including two complete flasks of the "Shoo-Fly" variety. Included in the whimsey shards were drapes, or chains, hammers, hatchets, beer mugs with handles, baskets, canes and chickens. Another item was a "calendar rack" made from tubular coloured glass and, in some cases, twisted.

On June 24, 1973, another dig was organized by GLASFAX District Director Ailsa Pearson and included district members and friends.[9] The site had been picked over so thoroughly that no complete articles were found. However, from the glittering spectacle of the ruins it was confirmed again that the three colours of glass used at the factory were green, turquoise and amber.

MALLORYTOWN GLASS WORKS, MALLORYTOWN, ONTARIO

There is very little known about this operation, which is still recognized as the first recorded glass operation in Canada. In 1953, shortly after Gerald Stevens and his wife moved there from Montreal, a surface dig was conducted with the help of some local people.[10] Several pieces of aquamarine-coloured glass were unearthed, along with pieces of a melting pot. Many pieces of tableware have been attributed to the works, but there is insufficient evidence to authenticate them.

THE SAINT LAWRENCE GLASS COMPANY, MONTREAL, QUEBEC

Despite the fact that this company operated for five years, almost no shards were found during a surface dig that took place in the fall of 1970 by a group of GLASFAX members.[11] The reason for this was the fact that the site and building had changed hands more than once and the ground had been turned over.

Chunks of cullet extracted were of many colours and hues — olive amber, clear light blue, cobalt, milk glass, milk glass marbled with green, starch blue and extremely deep dark cobalt. Some cased glass shards were found and a quantity of powder-blue cullet. A two-piece mould was also found.

The most important shard, of deep cobalt, was an almost complete lamp base which nearly exactly matched that shown in a photograph of three lamps belonging to Newt Coburn, a Montreal member of GLASFAX, at that time.

NAPANEE GLASS WORKS, NAPANEE, ONTARIO

This dig took place in the summer of 1968 under the direction of Helen Sutermeister, a trained archaeologist at the Royal Ontario Museum, assisted by members of GLASFAX and some local residents.[12] The findings were not plentiful. Although it was primarily a flat glass operation, a few unidentifiable bottle shards were found.

Perhaps the highlight of the report was Ms. Sutermeister's statement that the Royal Ontario Museum definitely disproved the theory held by Gerald Stevens that the Napanee candlesticks and the Napanee druggist jars were produced at this factory. There was absolutely no trace of either of these items having come from there, the only glass factory to operate in Napanee.

LIST OF SELECTED PRESSED GLASS PATTERNS AND THEIR ATTRIBUTIONS

PATTERN	1 BUR	2 NSG	3 DEL	4 JEF
Acadian		*		
Acorn	*			
Actress**	*			
Aegis	*			
Anderson*	*			
Arched Grape	*			
Ashburton*	*			
Athenian			*	
Barberry (Oval Berries)**	*			
Bead and Petal (No. 210)			*	
Beaded Arched Panels	*			
Beaded Band	*			
Beaded Flange**	*			
Beaded Oval and Fan No. 1			*	
Beaded Oval and Fan No. 2 (No. 320)				*
Beaded Oval Window	*			
Black-Eyed Susan	*			
Block*	*	*		
Boling	*			
Bowtie (No. 204)			*	
Buckle with Star*	*			
Buttons and Bows			*	
Canadian	*			
Canadian Thistle (No. 220)				*
Cardinal	*			
Cat's Eye and Fan	*			
Centennial			*	
Chain and Star Band	*			
Chain with Star*	*			
Clear and Diamond Panels	*			
Clear Fuschia	*			
Coin Dot**	*			
Colonial (No. 1600)		*	*	
Colossus	*			
Cord and Tassel*	*			
Cross		*	*	
Crossed Ferns with Ball and Claw**	*			
Crown		*	*	*
Curled Leaf*	*			
Currant**	*			

* Patterns that were also made by American companies that joined in 1891 to form the United States Glass Company.
** Patterns that were made by other American glass companies in the 1870s and 1880s.

PATTERN	1 BUR	2 NSG	3 DEL	4 JEF
Dahlia**	*	*	*	
Daisy and Button*	*			
Daisy and X-Band	*		*	
Deer and Dog	*			
Diagonal Band	*			
Diagonal Band and Fan	*			
Diamond*	*	*	*	*
Diamond Ray		*	*	*
Diamond Sunburst*	*			
Double Vine	*			
Eastern Star*	*			
Fan Band		*	*	
Filly*	*	*	*	
Flat Diamond*	*			
Floral				*
Flower and Quill	*			
Frosted Butterfly	*			
Frosted Ribbon*	*			
Frosted Stork	*			
Garfield Drape	*			
Geddes	*			
Gesner	*			
Gordon	*			
Gothic				*
Graduated Diamonds	*			
Grape	*			
Grape and Festoon with Shield*	*			
Grape and Vine				*
Hamilton	*			
Hamilton Grape	*			
Hobnail				*
Honeycomb	*	*	*	
Hops Band*	*			
Jacob's Ladder*	*			
Jewel Band	*			
Kalbach	*			
Kenlee				*

* Patterns that were also made by American companies that joined in 1891 to form the United States Glass Company.

** Patterns that were made by other American glass companies in the 1870s and 1880s.

PATTERN	1 BUR	2 NSG	3 DEL	4 JEF
Late Buckle*	*			
Lattice**	*			
Leaf and Dart*	*			
Leverne	*			
Lily of the Valley	*			
Lozenges	*			
Maple Leaf (No. 205)		*	*	
Minerva	*			
Newcastle	*			
New York* (see Honeycomb)				
Norman Star	*			
Nugget, Early		*	*	
Nugget, Late		*	*	
Oaken Bucket		*	*	
101	*			
1883		*	*	
Palmette	*			
Panelled Dewdrop**	*			
Panelled Diamonds	*			
Panelled Forget-Me-Not*	*			
Panelled Thistle			*	
Peerless*	*			
Picket*	*			
Pillar (see Crown)			*	
Pitcairn	*			
Pleat and Panel*	*			
Princess Feather	*		*	
Raspberry				*
Raspberry and Shield	*			*
Rayed Heart		*	*	
Ribbed Band				*
Ribbed Forget-Me-Not*	*			
Ribbon and Star				*
Rose Branches		*	*	
Sawtooth*	*			
Scalloped Lines**	*			
Seneca Loop	*			
Sheraton*	*			

* Patterns that were also made by American companies that joined in 1891 to form the United States Glass Company.
** Patterns that were made by other American glass companies in the 1870s and 1880s.

PATTERN	1 BUR	2 NSG	3 DEL	4 JEF
Square Marsh Pink	*			
Starflower	*	*	*	*
Stippled Swirl and Star (No. 200)		*	*	
Strawberry*	*			
Sunburst Medallion	*			
Sunflower	*			
Swimming Swan		*		*
Tandem				*
Tassel and Crest				*
Totem		*	*	
Tulip*	*			
Victoria Commemorative		*		*
Washington Centennial	*			
Way's Currant	*			
Westward Ho	*			
Woodrow (No. 1501)			*	

* Patterns that were also made by American companies that joined in 1891 to form the United States Glass Company.

** Patterns that were made by other American glass companies in the 1870s and 1880s.

FOOTNOTES

[1] See Author's Preface.

[2] John Sheeler, "The Burlington Glass Works, Its History and Products," GLASFAX *Newsletter*, "Report to GLASFAX 10th Anniversary Seminar," (June 11, 1977), p. 7.

[3] Frankie Woodrow, "Results of Research at the Burlington Glassworks 1967," GLASFAX *Newsletter*, (April 1968), three pages.

[4] Frankie Woodrow, District VIII Project. "Results of three-day dig at the site of the Burlington Glassworks, July 12-14, 1968", GLASFAX *Newsletter*, (February 1970), pages unnumbered.

[5] George MacLaren, "Nova Scotia Glass," Nova Scotia Museum *Occasional Paper* No. 4, Historical Series No. 1, (revised 1974), pp. 27-42.

[6] Wallace P. Saunders, "Nova Scotia Glass," GLASFAX *Newsletter*, (February 1971), three pages.

[7] Jack Kingdon, David Parker and Larry Taylor, "Report by Research Committee — GLASFAX District VIII", Report presented at the first GLASFAX Seminar, Hamilton, June 11-13, 1971, pp. 18-28.

[8] A.M. Provick, "Beausejour Glass Works," *Canadian Collector*, (January 1967), pp. 8-10.

[9] Ailsa C. Pearson, "Preliminary Report of dig at site of Manitoba Glass Works," GLASFAX *Newsletter*, (September 1973), p. 16.

[10] Gerald Stevens, *Early Canadian Glass*, (Toronto: The Ryerson Press, 1961), p. 6 and ff.

[11] W. Newlands Coburn, "St. Lawrence Glass Company," GLASFAX *Newsletter*, (June 1977).

[12] Helen Sutermeister, "Report on dig at the site of the former Napanee Glass Works in 1968," GLASFAX *Newsletter*, (April 1969), pp. 4, 5.

Catalog cover for pressed glassware, Saguenay pattern.

CHAPTER 10

Tableware and
Industrial Ware
in the Twentieth Century

Background
Centralization of Dominion Glass's Tableware
and Industrial Ware Production at Wallaceburg
Insulators
Independent Glass Producers, Toronto (1910-1912)
Macbeth-Evans Glass, Toronto (1913)
Jefferson Glass, Toronto (1912-1925)
The Wallaceburg Glass Company (1911-1930)
Desmarais and Robitaille, Montreal (1909-c.1923)
Corning Glass Works, Toronto (1945-1978)
National Pressed Glass, Brantford, Ontario (1965-1976)
Libbey-St. Clair, Wallaceburg (1978-   )

BACKGROUND

During the second half of the nineteenth century, many of the larger glasshouses made tableware and industrial ware, as well as bottles. The tableware, made from a formula that produced better than bottle glass but certainly nowhere near the quality of crystal, was developed to satisfy the demand for an inexpensive substitute for the more expensive crystal. In fact, several of the larger companies specialized in producing tableware and industrial ware. These were Burlington Glass (c.1874-1885), Nova Scotia Glass (1881-1890), and a succession of companies that occupied that sprawling plant site in Montreal commonly referred to as the "Delorimier site." It stretched eastward from Delorimier Avenue and north from de Montigny (now de Maisonneuve). These companies were Excelsior Glass (1880-1883), North American (1883-1890), Diamond Glass (1890-1902) and Diamond Flint Glass (1903-1913). At the turn of the century, with the availability of semiautomatic and automatic forming machines, a few hand shops were maintained for small orders of special items.

By 1925 Dominion had centralized most of its nonbottle production at its Wallaceburg plant. In 1936 these operations were known as the Tableware and Specialty division of the company, under the management of Lind Ayres. The plant however continued to service the needs of the soft drink bottlers, brewers, distillers and food packers in southwestern Ontario. The plant manager, Eddie Davies, known as "Mr. Wallaceburg," was very involved in community activities well beyond the town limits and was responsible for Wallaceburg becoming known as "The Glasstown of Canada."

16-piece Acadia tableware "Starter Set".
Courtesy of Dominion Glass Company
Limited.

TABLEWARE

Tableware is loosely defined as articles used in the serving of food and beverages. This includes cups and saucers, jugs, bowls, butter dishes, spoon holders, plates and nappies, serving dishes, soda fountain ware and kitchenware. It also applied to oil lamps at the beginning of the century and, after 1945, cookware (Pyrex-type).

By 1936 tastes in tableware had undergone great changes. The ornate and intricate patterns of the Victorian era were no longer popular and were replaced by much simpler patterns and shapes with cleaner lines. In the next ten years some half-dozen patterns were created. These were made in clear (the catalog called it crystal) or opal glass. In some lines the outside surface of the ware was sprayed with a coloured ceramic paste, which was then baked into the surface in a lehr. Another type of decoration was by the A.C.L. process (applied colour lettering), the Canadian rights for which had been obtained by Dominion. This process could only be used on cylindrical items such as bottles (to replace the label) and tumblers and on articles with flat surfaces. In simple terms, the design to be printed on the article was photographed onto a silk or metal screen. The screen was covered with a layer of ceramic paste. By moving the screen backward and forward under a fixed rubber blade, the paste was forced through the perforations in the screen and transferred onto the article which was underneath the screen. The design was then baked on.

The first tableware set to be developed was named Acadia. It was sold in a 16-piece "starter set," which comprised four each of a dinner plate, cereal or fruit bowl, and a cup and saucer. It came in the following colours: burgundy, chartreuse, forest green and grey. A few years later, the following pieces were added: salad plate, fruit nappie (shallow bowl), creamer, sugar and covered marmalade jar.

TWIN UTILITY DISH

ACTUAL SIZE

Utility dish, Cubist pressed glass pattern.
Courtesy of Dominion Glass Company Limited.

A popular sales gimmick at this time was the use of premiums to be given away with a product. Shortly before 1940 Proctor and Gamble, in the United States, used pink glass tableware in the Cubist pressed glass pattern, made by Jeanette Glass in Pennsylvania, as a premium to be included with one of their products. In 1949 their promotional program was started in Canada. The two pieces produced here were a mayonnaise bowl and plate identical to those made by Jeanette but made in Canadian moulds and in clear glass. Supplies of the pink ware were shipped to Wallaceburg and interspersed with Dominion's ware for the Canadian market promotion program. In the period 1953-1959 additional pieces produced were a sugar bowl, creamer, milk pitcher and fruit bowl. When Proctor and Gamble terminated this program, the six pieces became part of Dominion's SSL (standard stock line) list.

During World War II (1939-1945) an acute shortage occurred in the availability of low-cost everyday china for the Canadian table. Dominion decided that, as a good substitute, it could produce attractive luncheon and dinner sets and companion pieces in good quality glass that would be accepted, particularly by the younger generation, during and after the war. Dominion convinced the machine tools controller in Ottawa that mould equipment would have to be imported from the United States and obtained a priority rating. In spite of this priority, the first production from these moulds wasn't made until 1947.

Salt and pepper shakers, Swirl pressed glass pattern.   Courtesy of Dominion Glass Company Limited.

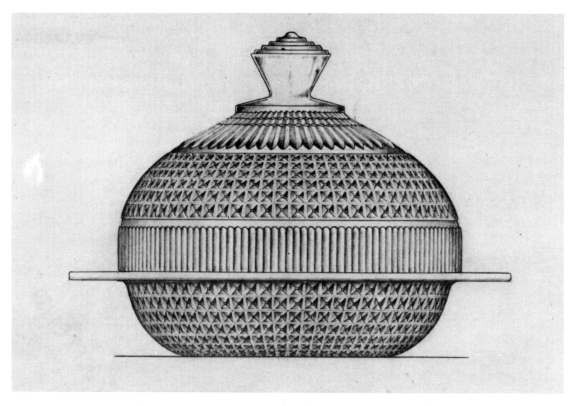

Butter dish, Hiawatha pressed glass pattern.   Courtesy of Dominion Glass Company Limited.

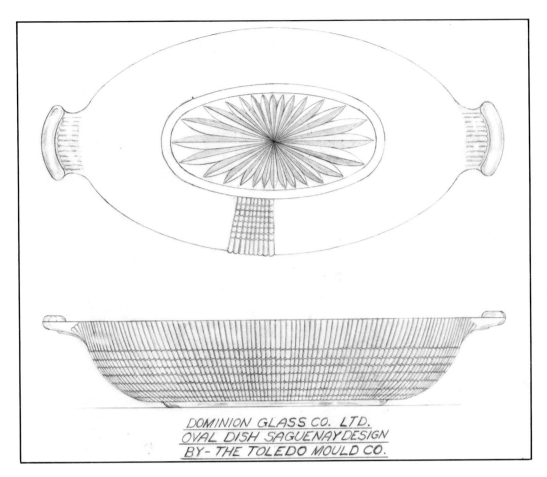

DOMINION GLASS CO. LTD.
OVAL DISH SAGUENAY DESIGN
BY- THE TOLEDO MOULD CO.

Oval dish, Saguenay pressed glass pattern.   Courtesy of Dominion Glass Company Limited.

The first pressed glass pattern was called the Swirl design, which was a modification of the old Stippled Swirl and Star design, without the stippling or stars. This was an extension of two items, a fruit nappie and a fruit bowl, that had already been made up as premiums for Lever Brothers a few years earlier. When the line was fully developed it included a creamer, sugar, covered sugar, covered butter dish, cup and saucer, sherbet, three sizes of plates, fruit nappie, fruit bowl, salts and peppers, two sizes of pitchers, two sizes of footed tumblers, and a regular tumbler.

In 1945 the company introduced two new patterns, Hiawatha and Saguenay. The former was produced for two years and the latter for five years. The Hiawatha line was first produced in clear glass and had five pieces: sugar, covered butter dish, sherbet and a plate. In addition to the above, the Saguenay pattern had a nappie, cup and saucer, and a plate. At a later date the Hiawatha pattern, sprayed in four pastel colours — green, blue, pink and yellow — included a covered butter dish, sugar, creamer, plate and sherbet.

In the 1950s an up-to-date line of pressed and blown kitchenware and other domestic items was developed, some of which is still available. In 1954 Rainbow Ware, a 16-piece luncheon set was introduced comprising four each of fruit juice glass, water glass, sherbet and plate. The sprayed-on colours were vivid blue, marigold, buttercup and robe red. The colours were ghastly. Later in the same decade, Wallaceburg started turning out two 16-piece luncheon sets. The patterns were now Snow Berry and Vineyard. Each set contained four each of two sizes of glasses, a sherbet, and a plate. In the Snow Berry set, the glasses and sherbet had gold banding around the rim. The ceramic paste decoration was frosty white to simulate acid etching.

DOMINION GLASS COMPANY
LIMITED
GLASS
INSULATORS

HEAD OFFICE: MONTREAL

FACTORIES AT
MONTREAL   TORONTO   HAMILTON
WALLACEBURG   REDCLIFF

Catalog cover, glass insulators.
Courtesy of Dominion Glass Company
Limited.

INDUSTRIAL WARE

Industrial ware includes all the other nonbottle items, such as insulators, streetlamp globes, lantern globes, lenses for railroad and ship lights, battery jars, fuse cases, percolator tops, bird seed cups, castor cups, ashtrays and other miscellaneous items. The most interesting and collectible item from this list is the insulator.

Insulators were made to be used with three different types of line service: electricity, telephone and telegraph. The earliest insulators were simply notched pieces of wood nailed to a tree, which kept the wires off the ground. These were superseded by glass insulators and porcelain insulators. In more contemporary times, insulators have been made of rubber and also of plastic.

In Canada the story of the insulator began with the coming of the telegraph in 1846, just ten years after the first railroad, the Champlain and St. Lawrence Railway, was completed. One of the earliest telegraph services was provided by the Montreal Telegraph Company, which was incorporated in 1847 and, for many years, was the outstanding service of its kind in Canada.

From 1850 to 1870 it expanded from 500 miles to 20,000 miles, and by 1881, when it was taken over by the Great North Western Telegraph Company, it had 30,000 miles of wire in the system. The Dominion Telegraph Company was started in 1868, and by 1880 serviced the area between Detroit, Michigan, and the Maritime Provinces. The two companies merged a year later. With the construction of the first transcontinental railroad by Canadian Pacific in the 1880s, the monopoly by Great North Western Telegraph ended. The government-operated railroad, Grand Trunk Railway, later to become Canadian National Railways, provided competitive service. About the same time, the Bell Telephone Company of Canada started to string their telephone lines along the highways and byways.

A review of recorded research has indicated that one of the earliest authenticated glass insulators was made in St. Johns, Quebec, by Canada Glass Works (Foster Brothers) in 1858. This was almost black glass and threadless, with "FOSTER BROTHERS ST JOHИ C.E. 1858" on the bottom of the single skirt, which had no drip points.

Starting in 1880 Bell Telephone purchased their insulators from Montreal-based Excelsior Glass (1880-1883) and then from its successor companies — North American Glass (1883-1890), Diamond Glass (1890-1902), Diamond Flint Glass (1903-1913), and Dominion Glass (1913-1976). The early insulators were made in three colours: light purple, light green and light blue. Many of these insulators have been found in the darker shades of these colours. This was caused by continued exposure to the sun, which, acting on the manganese oxide, one of the batch ingredients, changed the pale colours to very dark shades.

An undated Dominion Glass catalog of glass insulators, which must have been issued between 1913 and 1925 (Toronto Parkdale, which is listed as one of the operating plants, closed in 1925), illustrates the following insulators: No. 9 Pony, Double Groove Pony, Standard Telephone, No. 1671 Standard Telegraph, No. 1678 Extra Deep Groove Double Petticoat, No. 613 New Western Union Telegraph Double Petticoat, Heavy Telegraph Double Petticoat, Two-piece transposition, No. 2 cable, Stock No. 333 Standard Toll Line, Stock No. 334 Special Pony Drip Stock, and No. 365 New Heavy Telegraph (C.N.T.) Style.

During the Diamond and Diamond Flint Glass periods of operation (1890-1913) some of the insulators had a simple ◊ embossed on the skirt, while some of the others had various abbreviations for the users' names. The ◊ with a D in it was first used in 1928 when Dominion Glass adopted it as a trademark.

Many of the early small telephone companies imported their insulators from the United States, with such names as Brookfield and Hemingray. Other glass companies credited with producing insulators were Hamilton Glass (1864-1898); two of the Trenton, Nova Scotia, glasshouses, Nova Scotia Glass (1881-1890) and Lamont Glass (1890-1897); and in Sapperton, British Columbia, Crystal Glass (1906-c.1908). Production of insulators in Canada ceased about 1967.

SELECTED REFERENCES

*Cranfill, Gary G. Glass Insulators, A Comprehensive Reference. Sacramento, California: Spilman Printing Co., 1973.

McIntosh, Colin. Canadian Insulators and Communications Lines. Victoria, British Columbia: Canada Instant Print, n.d.

*Milholland, Marion and Evelyn. Most About Glass Insulators (3d rev.) plus 1976 Price Guide. Port Angeles, Washington: Pen Print, 1976.

Terrill, Francis M. Choice Insulators Priced. Portland, Oregon: Printing and Mailing Services, Inc., 1972.

Terrill, Francis M. Hemingray Insulators Prices. Portland, Oregon: Printing and Mailing Services, Inc., 1971.

*Woodward, N.R. The Glass Insulator in America. Houston, Texas: Privately Printed, n.d.

*(a must for serious collectors)

INDEPENDENT GLASS PRODUCERS, LIMITED,
Toronto, Ontario (1910-1912)

The story of Independent Glass is a good example of the extent to which a determined group of businessmen will go to establish and maintain a company. Unfortunately, it was a case of too little and too late.

The principals were John Lowden and his younger brother Robert, who had come from Montreal in 1879 and 1889, respectively, to establish druggists' agencies in Toronto; the third party was Richard Witt, a much-travelled German glassmaker; and the last was Walter Warren, a businessman in Toronto. Their credentials in the glass and related industries were impressive. John Lowden was appointed an agent in Toronto for Burlington Glass in 1890. This was the first recorded establishment of a glass manufacturer's sales office or agency in Toronto. Two years later he replaced his association with Burlington by becoming the agent for Erie Glass. In 1893 he added Diamond Glass to his list of principals. With the demise of Erie Glass about this time, he only represented the latter. Robert Lowden was involved in the druggist supply trade and joined his brother John as a traveller for Erie Glass. Richard Witt had been in the glass industry all his working life and had travelled extensively from his birthplace in Schleswick-Holstein to Norway, England, the United States, and eventually to Sydenham Glass in Wallaceburg. Researcher Gerald Stevens associated him later with Burlington.[1] In 1910 he was listed as living in Toronto, near Toronto Glass, in the Parkdale area. A year later he moved to the east end of the city, near the site of Independent Glass. The background of the fourth member, Warren, has been hard to trace. It has been assumed that he had worked his way up to the top of the Map and School Supply Co., whose lines included chemical apparatus and glassware.

The first concrete steps to form a company took place at a meeting on September 22, 1910, attended by the four principals. It would appear that Witt had approached Robert Lowden with the idea of forming a glassworks to compete with Diamond Flint Glass, then Robert encouraged his friend Warren to join, and only by persuasion did the older Lowden agree to become involved.

Letters patent were issued on October 19, 1910. The final version of the prospectus dated November 24, 1910, recorded the following list of directors and their appointments:

John Lowden	president
W.G. Lumbers	vice-president
Walter Warren	manager
Richard G. Witt	glassmaker
Robert W. Lowden	secretary

It should be noted that in the final prospectus, Lumbers, head of a wholesale grocery firm, had replaced R.W. Eyre as a director.

A parcel of land 700 feet long and 230 feet wide, bounded by Carlaw, Dickens, Thackeray and the Grand Trunk Railway, was purchased for $26,000. Building permits were then issued by the City of Toronto in December 1910 and February and March 1911 for the erection of a two-storey complex to house an office, factory and packing house for $23,500. The final cost given in June 1912 was $51,259. Financing during the construction period was still critical and was probably the basis for adding three more businessmen to the board: William C. Harvey, in the druggist trade; J. Percy Milnes, proprietor of Milnes Coal Co. Ltd., a natural supplier of energy; and Charles C. Dalton, owner of Dalton Brothers, a predecessor firm to the present Dalton's (1834) Ltd.

Production commenced in October 1911. Although no catalogs have been found, it would appear that, based on the operations of the principals running the company, the product mix included pharmaceutical ware and laboratory supplies.

A very crucial meeting took place on November 11. Costs of land and physical facilities were accumulating and far exceeding the original estimates. To make matters worse, investment in the company was still far below expectations and far short of their needs. Probably the greatest deterrent to achieving sufficient financing was the obvious influence Diamond Flint Glass was bringing to bear on prospective investors, particularly in view of the fact that Diamond was already in the late stages of reorganizing its far-flung operations into a new company (Dominion Glass).

There had to be something new and promising in the company's future prospects, something which had not been present earlier in the year and which was promising enough to more than offset the obvious distrust of potential investors and the certainty of retaliation from Diamond. Whatever the development was, it was good enough to elicit $47,000 from the nine directors, when all the other shareholders together had put up only $37,500. The new development appears to have been the signing of a technical assistance agreement with the Jefferson Glass Company, Follansbee, West Virginia, a maker of tableware and specialty items. Someone must have made the necessary contact with the American company and evidence suggests that it was Robert Lowden, the most enterprising and active member of Independent's officers. To support this as part of the additional investment identified, probably having been made at the November meeting, are two items:

Lowden, Robert W.	$1,500
Lowden, Robert W. Trust	5,000[2]

In my opinion, Robert probably was able to provide the $1,500 (less than any of the other directors), but it seems less likely that he could come up with an additional $5,000. Why could this latter amount not be in trust for Jefferson Glass?

From a taped conversation between Gerald Stevens and Arthur Shakeley, a glassmaker who had worked for Independent Glass, these comments have been extracted:

> . . . came to Canada in 1911 to 388 Carlaw Avenue (Independent Glass) . . . stayed three or four months, but they had trouble with the glass, so returned to U.S. . . .
>
> In 1912 heard from the union that the factory would start again, and came back . . .
>
> . . . moulds used in 1911 came from the Jefferson Glass company in Steubenville. (Jefferson Glass Co. started in Steubenville, Ohio, in 1900. In 1907 it moved across the Ohio River to a new and modern plant in Follansbee, West Virginia) . . . made here for only a year — moulds were known as the "Chippendale pattern." (Chippendale in Canada was known as "Colonial" or No. 1600.)

Word of the apparent agreement between Independent and Jefferson did not long remain a secret in the trade due to the high mobility of the glassworkers. By early 1912 Diamond Flint owned or controlled all major glass operations in Canada, with the exceptions of Humphreys' Glass in Nova Scotia and Independent Glass. With their advanced planning to reorganize well underway, Diamond would have had to set up a strong and effective plan to prevent this new development from jeopardizing their objective in the near future.

Matters came to a head in March 1912, when during an insurmountable cash crisis Independent sold out to Munderloh and Company, whose owner, Henry Munderloh, was a director of Diamond Flint Glass. Mr. Munderloh was an important member of the board because in Diamond's drive to monopolize the Canadian industry he was apparently the person through whom Diamond obtained control of the companies it acquired without its name being used.

Action was swift and decisive. On March 20, 1912, the number of directors of Independent was reduced from nine to seven, with the following constituting the new board: John E. Gordon (president), John Scott, Ernest Delorme, Samuel J. Frame, J.P. Milnes, John Lowden, and Robert Lowden. The first three were from Sydenham Glass in Wallaceburg, where, according to John Sheeler, the Munderloh firm held 97 percent of the stock. Frame was a clerk from the firm of Jenkins & Hardy, Chartered Accountants and Estate Agents, and the last three were retained from the former board. This could only mean that Diamond had convinced the shareholders of Independent that they would be best served if Diamond had an equal if not a controlling interest in Independent. Many carrots may have been offered, including a share exchange with Diamond which would help to recoup probable losses if Independent did not go for it.

On June 4, 1912, at a meeting of Independent, a decision was reached to "execute an assignment for the general benefit of the company's creditors to James Hardy" of Jenkins &

Hardy, Trustee. This had the same effect as "winding up." For details of the takeover, see Jefferson Glass. Notice of the cancellation of the company's letters patent were published in the Ontario *Gazette* effective March 2, 1959.

MACBETH-EVANS GLASS COMPANY, LIMITED,
Toronto, Ontario (1913)

This company was not incorporated to actually make glass in Canada but to act as a deterrent to the possible use of one of its glass formulas, which had been pirated by one of its former glassmen. To pick up the story, it is necessary to go back a few Years. The (American) Macbeth-Evans Company had a patent on the formula for Alba, a semi-translucent glass for illuminating ware. This had been developed by a Mr. H.A. Schnelbach of that company. Shortly thereafter, Schnelbach left Macbeth-Evans and, in conjunction with C.H. Blumenauer and D.J. Sinclair, successfully established the Jefferson Glass Company in Follansbee, West Virginia. It started to make Moonstone, which was very similar to Alba. This caused friction between the two companies. In order to avoid litigation between them, the latter agreed to pay a royalty on their Moonstone sales and, in return, Macbeth-Evans undertook to protect the patent against other glassmakers who might infringe upon it.

No further action took place and it was dissolved on October 15, 1924.

JEFFERSON GLASS COMPANY, LIMITED,
Toronto, Ontario (1912-1925)

The story of the conception and establishment of this company by Diamond Flint Glass illustrates the sensitivity of the Canadian glass industry to foreign competition. This appears to have been one of the early steps in the long-range plan of Diamond Flint Glass to reorganize its multi-plant operations in the form of a new conglomerate (Dominion Glass Company, Limited).

To put it in perspective, it is necessary to refer back to the story of Independent Glass. After a year's struggle, Independent started production in October 1911. Shortly thereafter, it made an arrangement with the Jefferson Glass Company of Follansbee, West Virginia, to receive technical expertise and a few tableware moulds. In March 1912, during an apparently insurmountable cash crisis, Independent sold out to Munderloh and Company, a general importer in Montreal. Munderloh was an important member of Diamond Flint's board and he was apparently the person through whom Diamond Flint Glass obtained control of the companies that it acquired. By this time Diamond owned or controlled every operating glassworks in Canada with the exception of Humphreys' Glass Company in Trenton, Nova Scotia, Manitoba Glass in Beausejour, Manitoba, and Independent Glass in Toronto, Ontario.

Diamond Flint's next step was to complete a ten-year agreement with Jefferson Glass in West Virginia, with the intention of forming a new company in Canada to be known as the Jefferson Glass Company (Limited) which would take over the assets of Independent Glass. The American company would get 13½ percent interest in the new company, in the form of paid-up stock, in return for which C.H. Blumenauer, president and treasurer, and H.A. Schnelbach, secretary and general manager, would undertake to promote "friendly" arrangements between the two companies.

At the September board meeting of Diamond Flint Glass, the company purchased Independent Glass from Munderloh for $110,000 cash and 240 paid-up shares of Diamond Flint Glass. On October 7, 1912, Jefferson Glass Company (Limited) received an Ontario charter with its head office in Toronto, but with permission to hold meetings outside of the province. Shortly thereafter, the newly formed Jefferson Glass acquired from Diamond Flint Glass the assets of Independent Glass, for which it paid 1,600 fully paid-up shares of Jefferson with the further condition that Diamond Flint Glass subscribe for and purchase 395 shares of Jefferson. The five remaining shares were to be issued to the incorporators of Jefferson.

The new company started operating at the old plant site, 388 Carlaw Avenue, Toronto, and shareholders' and directors' meetings were held there until 1915, when they were moved to the head office of Diamond Flint Glass and, after 1913 to Dominion Glass in Montreal.

The following directors and officers were elected: F.W. Ross, president; R. King, vice-president; A.H. Grier, N.M. Yuile, H.A. Schnelbach. All but Mr. Schnelbach were Diamond Flint Glass personnel. Miss C.H. Schnelbach was secretary until near the end of 1913, when Mr. Offer of Dominion Glass took over as secretary-treasurer.

With the incorporation of Dominion Glass Company, Limited in May 1913, Jefferson was treated as a semi-independent subsidiary, retaining its own directors and officers. The majority shareholder at the beginning was, of course, Diamond Flint Glass. However, with the start of Dominion Glass and its takeover of Diamond Flint Glass, this changed. The following was the list of shareholders for the years 1913-1915:

	1913	1914	1915
Diamond Flint Glass Company Ltd.	1,745	250	250
Jefferson Glass Company Follansbee, W. Va.	125	–	–
C.H. Blumenauer	42	125	125
D.J. Sinclair	42	–	–
H.A. Schnelbach	32	95	95
C.H. Schnelbach (Miss)	10	10	10
A.H. Grier	1	1	0
Ralph King	1	1	1
Frank W. Ross	1	1	1
N.M. Yuile	1	1	1
J.G. Schnelbach	–	10	10
J.K. Schnelbach	–	10	10
Royal Trust Company in Trust (for Dominion Glass)	–	1,496	1,496
George Lydiatt	–	–	1
	2,000	2,000	2,000

With the resumption of production late in 1912 or early in 1913, the business began to grow under the management of H.A. Schnelbach, who reported to Ralph King. King also chaired most of the directors' meetings until the mid-twenties.

In 1914 it was necessary to set up a ten-year bond issue for $150,000 to carry on the operations. A convenient arrangement was made with American Jefferson for them to handle any business that was beyond the capacity of the Canadian company. Early in 1915 George Lydiatt was transferred from Sydenham in Wallaceburg to assist Schnelbach in getting the plant back in operation after its shutdown a year before. The plant was operating again in the summer of 1915. Production included some electric light bulbs (20 shops) and lead crystal blanks for "cut" glassware. In order to assist the company in maintaining a profitable level of production, some of Dominion's nonbottle production requirements were transferred to Jefferson.

By 1917 the Schnelbachs had returned to the United States and business was slowing down. The following is a description of operations from 1922-1925 written by Benjamin H. (Dick) Dickson, accountant, who retired as office manager and works accountant at Dominion's Hamilton plant in 1962:

> This plant (previously Jefferson Glass Co.) made illuminating glassware. There were two furnaces, one was a continuous flint tank, and the other a pot furnace with eight pots for coloured ware. All the production was by hand shops and included a side-lever press, and an airhead machine which made Cartier's Paste Pots. There was a sandblast machine for Ball Globes. Also a cutting department for cutting designs on lead crystalware. There was also an acid etching department for etching fancy designs on lighting units. This plant made a lot of tableware, including fancy bowls. All decorated ware was fired in a kiln. Shades for table lamps were hand-painted and were assembled on stands for export to Australia. This plant was forced to close in 1925 because of the impact of cheap lighting

ware imported by Canada from foreign sources. The shades were nicely decorated but in cold colour which faded off after a few washings, whereas our production was kiln fired. There was also a swing to parchment lamp shades. Colours made beside flint were genuine ruby, moonstone (translucent), casolite, opal, blue, green, etc. Lighting reflectors or shades were made from "cased" glass, green on the topside and opal on the underside.

By the end of 1925 Jefferson had ceased production. This was part of an overall plan by Dominion to concentrate all its nonbottle production at their Wallaceburg plant, formerly called Sydenham. From the time of the takeover by Dominion Glass the directors and officers were:

Jan. 20, 1913	F.W. Ross	director-president
Jan. 20, 1913	A.H. Grier	director
Jan. 20, 1913	N.M. Yuile	director
Jan. 20, 1913	Ralph King	director
Jan. 20, 1913	H.A. Schnelbach	director
Jan. 20, 1913	Miss C.H. Schnelbach	secretary-treasurer
Sept. 10, 1913	Ralph King	director-vice president
Sept. 10, 1913	Mervyn Offer	secretary
Jan. 22, 1915	George Lydiatt	director
Sept. 8, 1915	T.B. Dundas	director
Nov. 11, 1915	W.A. Martin	general manager
Jan. 6, 1916	W.A. Bevis	treasurer
Oct. 5, 1916	W.A. Martin	director-general manager
Dec. 19, 1917	A.H. Grier	director
Nov. 10, 1918	F.J. Mayo	treasurer
Aug. 1, 1923	John Wallace	treasurer
Jan. 17, 1924	A.H. Grier	director-president
Jan. 17, 1924	G.W. Robertson	director
Dec. 17, 1924	Mervyn Offer	director-secretary
Dec. 17, 1924	T.B. Dundas	director

In 1929 the facilities were sold to Melesse Luzine and two years later were acquired by the Acme Paper Box Company. The charter was surrendered on August 20, 1941.

THE WALLACEBURG GLASS COMPANY, LIMITED,
Wallaceburg, Ontario (1911-1930)

NEW GLASS INDUSTRY FOR WALLACEBURG

FOR THE MANUFACTURE OF CUT GLASS

ONLY ONE OF ITS KIND IN THE DOMINION

LOCATED TEMPORARILY AT THE GLASS WORKS

This heading appeared over an article in the *Wallaceburg News* on March 13, 1913. The promoter of this operation was D.A. Gordon, managing director of Sydenham Glass. According to the article, this plant had no connection with Sydenham Glass, but it is only reasonable to assume that Sydenham was quietly trying to broaden the market for glass products by providing a line of lightweight cut glass, as opposed to the heavy crystal cut glass Jefferson Glass was making in Toronto. Like Henry Munderloh, a director of Diamond Flint Glass, D.A. Gordon was the director on the Sydenham board who worked on expansion and acquisitions. He was involved in this way with Ontario Glass in Kingsville, Ontario.

The company received an Ontario charter on May 13, 1911, after an affidavit had been produced stating that there was no conflict of names with the Wallaceburg Glass Works that had never actually got started. Mr. Gordon brought in J.F. Singleton, an experienced glassman from Bowling Green, Ohio, to set up and run the plant, which initially operated in the flint house (tableware operations) of Sydenham Glass, using that company's blanks (uncut finished articles) with a view to ascertaining whether a trade in thin-blown ware could be viable.

When Sydenham became the Wallaceburg plant of the newly incorporated Dominion Glass Company, Limited in 1913, Mr. Gordon wrote to the president of Dominion indicating that he had spent about $4,000 setting up the operation and asking if Dominion would be interested in taking it over. Dominion turned down the offer and, as a result, Gordon moved the operation into a brick building located at 330 Duncan Street, Wallaceburg, opposite Our Lady of Help Roman Catholic Church.

According to Bill Jordan, a long-time office employee of Sydenham and later Dominion Glass, Wallaceburg Glass made a fairly complete line of cut glass articles, including baskets, bonbons, stemware, water sets, cake plates, tumblers, bowls, candlesticks, sugars and creamers, some of which were produced in rose-coloured glass, just then coming into vogue.

The company was dissolved on May 1, 1961.

DESMARAIS AND ROBITAILLE (LIMITED),
Montreal, Quebec (1909-c.1923)

The company obtained a federal charter on January 27, 1909, for the purpose of amalgamating two retail houses, that of Desmarais and Sons and one operated by L.A. Robitaille, both of whom were vendors of church ornaments. With the establishment of the new company, their line of coloured glass goods — which included votive lights, decorative and sanctuary lamps, and other glassware used for religious purposes — was made by Diamond Flint Glass and its successor company, Dominion Glass.

Around 1923-1924, when Dominion was finalizing its long-range plan to centralize all its nonbottle operations at its plant in Wallaceburg, Ontario, it also decided to eliminate as many of the unprofitable lines as possible. This apparently included the line of church items, whose small orders precluded a satisfactory return.

A letter to me dated November 19, 1982, written by André Robitaille, son of one of the founding partners, states:

> . . . At that particular time (mid 1920s) usage of glass votive lights was not prevalent in Europe, so that when we could not find a supplier there, we had to find an alternative. (Even nowadays, most Catholics in Europe use votive candles rather than votive glass, so that one cannot find a European source without some difficulty).
>
> My father had made the acquaintance of a glass worker who was, as well as I can remember, from Central Europe - Tchekoslovakia, I believe, who had heard of our problem in finding a manufacturer of colored glass items, and who offered to set up a small glass workshop in which we could manufacture some . . .
>
> He maintained that the making of these colored glasses in the manner of an unsophisticated, small crafts shop, would present no problem, that he had all the formulas and that he knew how to construct ovens and could manage such a small glass workshop . . .
>
> He lived in Montreal North which was in those days, right in the countryside. He offered to erect a wooden workshop on his property for the fabrication of colored glassware; it would of course be Desmarais & Robitaille who would finance such an undertaking, with the provision that the land it would be built upon would remain his. Thus, Desmarais & Robitaille put at his disposal the necessary monies to cover the cost of erecting such a wooden structure. As I recall, it measured approximately 30' x 30', but do not remember its exact height . . .
>
> The oven occupied the central part of the building and was lit from below. I

seem to recall that he used soft coal as fuel but it might have been wood. On the upper level, some 10' higher, was the part of the oven in which the crucibles (6) were set. He had himself made the crucibles using heat-resistant clay, and the fire was lit. It soon became evident, however, that the unsurmountable problem which made our endeavour an unsuccessful one was the breakdown of one crucible after another; they developed cracks due to the clay's inability to resist the very high temperatures. I recall that our workman succeeded in making a small quantity of pieces — we had a few left, but I do not know what happened to them. A French-speaking engineer who worked for one of the local glass Companies came to see my father at the time, and he explained that our glass worker was a good workman but that he lacked the necessary technical knowhow to solve the problems which were bound to crop up . . .

There was talk of resuming the project, but as this involved a sizeable expenditure, my father put off making such a decision . . .

In the interim, the glass making Company (Dominion Glass) had heard that we had the intention of making our own glass and they came up with an offer we could not refuse — they sold us, at ridiculously low prices, all their stock balances of the very items (colored glass) they had previously been making for us on a regular basis. As there was a large quantity of these items involved, it somehow compensated for the capital outlay we had made to finance our unsuccessful venture in glass making . . .

I believe that shortly thereafter, we began to bring in colored glassware from a region of Tchekoslovakia where we could procure all we needed at affordable prices . . .

Desmarais & Robitaille still operate retail stores in Montreal and Ottawa.

CORNING GLASS WORKS OF CANADA LTD. (1945-1978)
CORNING CANADA INC. (1978-   ),
Toronto, Ontario

When some people hear the word "Corning" they immediately think of the handblown "Steuben" ware that is made in Corning, New York. However, the majority of people think of the famous "Pyrex" cookware and related products. In 1921 discussions were started between Alexander D. Falck, president of Corning Glass Works, Corning, New York, and A. Harold Grier, general manager of Jefferson Glass Company Limited, Toronto, Ontario, (subsidiary of Dominion Glass), to consider the former company establishing itself in Canada. Three possibilities were considered: the outright takeover of Jefferson Glass; joint operation of this plant with Dominion; setting up a Corning plant in Toronto. After a year of discussions, negotiations were terminated by mutual consent. It wasn't until 1945 that Corning opted for the third alternative. A federal charter was issued on June 8, 1945, creating Corning Glass Works of Canada Ltd. (as a private company).

The company took over a building from Research Enterprises Limited, located at 135 Vandershoof Avenue, in the Leaside district of Toronto. This plant went through three different phases:

1) 1946-1954 - glass production
2) 1955-1959 - warehousing
3) 1959 to present - glass finishing and Canadian distribution centre for consumer ware

Production started on June 22, 1946, and included Pyrex ovenware, baby bottles, handles, covers, and pumps for "Range Top" ware, all made from a borosilicate-based batch that produced glass with a low coefficient of expansion. Their line of Opal ware included Pyrex bakeware, "Corex" tableware, and trilight lamp reflectors made from white high-expansion glass. The tableware was also produced in blue and turquoise shades. A third of this production was for the Canadian market and the remainder for the United States.

In 1954 the Leaside plant shut down its production lines. There were plenty of export markets, although none had the hard currency to pay and the Canadian market was not large enough to keep the plant in operation. All the forming and machine shop equipment in the plant was shipped back to the United States.

By 1955 the TV market was booming and (American) Corning was the chief supplier of glass tubes for the TV industry. In Canada the TV manufacturers were Canadian General Electric in Toronto; Philips, adjacent to the Leaside plant; and Westinghouse in Hamilton, Ontario.

A new line of tableware, Pyroceram Cooking Ware (Corning Ware), with even more resistance to sudden temperature changes, was ready for the market by the late 50s. For the Canadian market, undecorated blanks of opal Pyrex glass were produced in the United States and then shipped to Leaside for decorating and ceramming (hardening) in a kiln. At the same time, Corning assumed the responsibility and control of consumer products in Canada, which had previously been handled by a distributor, John A. Huston Ltd., Toronto; as well, the Leaside operation became sales agent and distributor for the English firm of James A. Jobling & Co. Ltd., which was a Corning licencee and specialized in laboratory glass — Hysil, Quickfit Quartz, Emil, and also Corning Drainline glass piping.

In 1961, as an aftermath of the Cold War, and under contract to the Canadian government, Leaside set up production facilities to make dosiemeters (radiation measuring devices) for the Armed Forces for a two-year period. During the same period, a neck-sealing process for black-and-white TV tubes was set up at Leaside, the components being imported. With the growth of the colour TV business in Canada, RCA built a colour TV tube plant in Midland, Ontario, north of Toronto.

By 1965 there was sufficient volume for Corning to build a new plant. It was located in Bracebridge, Ontario, not far from the RCA plant in Midland. It was planned and designed in 1965 and started operations in 1967. The manager was Maurice G. Locklin. There was a 230-foot gas-fired melting furnace and the necessary forming and finishing equipment. Both black-and-white and colour tubes were produced, while the panels were brought in from the United States. When the plant started up, the black-and-white sealing operation was transferred from Leaside. The Bracebridge plant supplied all the requirements of the Canadian market and also exported coloured funnels and components to the United Kingdom as well.

In 1975 the market in North America for domestically produced colour TV sets decreased as Japanese imports began to make substantial inroads. As a result, RCA Midland began to import from its parent in the United States. At the same time, exports to the United Kingdom dried up. These events made it necessary to close the Bracebridge operation, the remaining Canadian market being supplied from the United States. (There is no duty on TV parts imported into Canada.) The plant was sold to Uniroyal in 1977. In November 1978 the name of the company was changed to Corning Canada Inc.

NATIONAL PRESSED GLASS LIMITED
Brantford, Ontario (1965-1976)

This private company was incorporated by Richard Kruger of Toronto to manufacture glass fuse bodies, percolator tops and related ware. It received an Ontario charter on April 15, 1945, with its head office in Toronto. Kruger was an entrepreneur in the real sense of the word. In the mechanical and electrical field he had the ability not only to produce saleable products but also to mechanize, to a high degree, many of the tedious and labour-intensive operations in this type of operation.

A one-storey building was erected in 1965 at 47 Morton Avenue East in Brantford, with a siding to the Canadian National Railway. The final cost was about $300,000. Original equipment consisted of an electric melting furnace and a Lynch MPD press, which pressed out the fuse bodies and percolator tops by inserting a plunger into the gob of glass in the mould.

National Pressed Glass Limited, Brantford, Ontario (1965-1976).   Courtesy National Pressed Glass.

Before the plant was operative, it was necessary to obtain additional financing. This was carried out through the issue of three separate supplementary letters patent in 1966.

At the same time Morton Leaseholds, of the same address, received an Ontario charter on July 15, 1966, to own the land on a leaseback arrangement with National Pressed Glass.

The plant started producing fuse bodies on a commercial basis in April 1967. To give some idea of the market Kruger had developed, the following table shows the potential North American market (75 percent of which was in the United States) and the firm orders after one year's production:

Customer	Total Maximum Requirements in Millions of Pieces	Total Maximum Annual Sales by N.P.G. in Millions of Pieces	Firm Orders To Date in Millions of Pieces	Price for Thousand
General Electric (US)	15	15	¼	$8.15 U.S.
Eagle Electric	25	25	5	$7.75 U.S.
Cable Electric	20	20	20	$7.75 U.S.
I.T.T.	18	18	18	$7.00 U.S.
Pierce Fuse Ltd.	10	10	10	
Canadian General Electric	17	nil	nil	
Total	105	88	53¼	

Unfortunately, Kruger's mechanical skills were not supported by adequate financing. In February 1969 he reported to the board that ". . . the company will be without cash in approximately two weeks . . ." Several alternative courses of action were proposed:

1. To remain as is and do nothing.
2. To sell 100% or less of the company to Consumers Glass Company.
3. To sell 100% or less to another Canadian company.
4. To await a proposal from a Mr. Saddler for a public underwriting.
5. To sell 100% or less to a U.S. company.

While discussions on the various options were taking place, the company became involved in a controversy with their auditors, Price, Waterhouse, over the interpretation of the sale of some of the company's inventory to Dorchester Electronics, another company which Kruger had developed for the manufacture of home entertainment units. The company claimed that it was a bona fide sale, whereas the auditors said that it was not a bona fide sale but simply a method of financing the company. The sale of inventory to a "third-party" in advance of the contract requirement was left as a sale. The auditors resigned in August 1969 and the 1968 year-end accounts were only published in September 1969 under the certificate of the new auditors, Millard, Rouse and Roseburgh.

Under course number three above, Kruger started discussions with Dominion Glass on October 9, 1969. As a result, an agreement dated January 30, 1970, was reached between Dominion Glass and Messrs. Kruger, Macaulay, Fisch, Fisch, Newell and Walker (acting as agents for all the shareholders of the company), whereby Dominion would buy all the outstanding shares of the company for $350,000. At a board meeting held on February 13, 1970, the directors of the company sanctioned the transfer of said shares to Dominion and at the same time arranged for the resignations of all the directors and officers. By resolution, the board was reduced to three members. At the following organizational meeting E.A. Thompson and E.G. Blyth of Dominion were appointed president and secretary-treasurer, respectively. R.P. Kruger was retained as the third member and was appointed vice-president and general manager.

In 1972 the company purchased from Hazel-Atlas Glass (a division of Continental Can in the United States) their customers' lists, moulds, drawings and process data for the manufacture of Type "C" (or safety) fuse bodies and percolator tops for about $60,000. This offer was taken up by the company in September and a second production line was set up at a cost of $949,000. This included a 15-18 ton electric furnace and ancilliary equipment. A 15,000-square-foot addition was made to the building. In 1974 glazing equipment was added for the fire finishing of the percolator tops, which gave them a lustre.

A new type of fuse, the "S", which was safety induced, was now being developed. (The amperage of the fuse was controlled by the depth of the socket in such a way that, for instance, a 15-ampere fuse would not fit into a 20-ampere socket.) In order that the company could carry out the necessary experimental work, a loan of $100,000 was arranged with the Ontario Development Corporation. One of the potential customers was General Electric, who were in the market for such a fuse. Although the process was eventually successful from a technical point of view, it was a failure economically.

In October 1974 Dominion acquired Dorchester Electronics and, by agreement, Kruger was required to split his time equally between National Pressed Glass and the Dorchester operation in Toronto. In January 1975 the board of National was increased to four with the addition of Ray Suutari of Dominion. At the same time, Thompson became chairman and was replaced as president by Kruger. His brother, Walter Kreuger (they elected to spell their surnames differently), was appointed general manager and Bob Spriggs was transferred from Dominion to take over the controller's position. Thompson resigned as a director and chairman in August 1975 and was replaced by Joe Souccar of Domglas. W.H. Shotton, vice-president, manufacturing, of Domglas, was added at the same time.

The year 1976 was one of reorganization for the company, as new products were sought. Packer tumblers, made in a press and capable of being capped and used as food containers, were added to the product mix. In February the company was merged with Plant Kimble Limited of Montreal (a recently acquired subsidiary of Domglas), and by supplementary letters patent dated June 25, 1976, National Pressed Glass became National Pressed Glass (1976) Ltd. Plant Kimble's equipment, which made glass vials and ampoules for the pharmaceutical trade, was leased to Interglass Inc. in Montreal. Later in the year, supplementary letters patent were issued to increase the capital from $1,250,000 to $4,000,000.

On December 13, 1976, Walter Kreuger left the company and was replaced by experienced glass technician J. Eugene Voros.

By June 1977 the company had achieved a pack to possible of 93.8 percent on "C" fuses, and the cost-sharing program with Dorchester was terminated. On March 31, 1978, National

Pressed Glass (1976) Ltd. was dissolved and the plant became a wholly-owned division of Domglas. The original name of the company, National Pressed Glass Limited, was struck off the register on November 27, 1979, but Domglas retained the use of the name National Pressed Glass. Dorchester Electronics was shut down in March 1980 because of unsatisfactory returns on investment.

LIBBEY-ST. CLAIR INC.,
Wallaceburg, Ontario (1878-   )

By 1975 imports of tableware from the United States, especially in the table-top lines, were making serious inroads on Dominion's (now Domglas) tableware lines. To offset this competition, Domglas hired a team, headed up by Phil Jacobs, to implement a new and aggressive marketing plan. The new organization was named the St. Clair division, after the nearby St. Clair River. Although a number of the old and successful lines were continued, the accent was now on the beverage-related items. New shapes and decorations were developed, modern packaging was adopted, and new colourful catalogs made up.

All this had the effect of improving Domglas's share of the market. Early in 1978 discussions began with the Libbey division of Owens-Illinois Inc. of Toledo, Ohio, a leading tableware producer which had been responsible for so much of the competition from American imports. While Domglas had been trying to offset the import competition, Libbey and other American tableware makers had been trying to gain a greater share of the Canadian market. On October 1, 1978, Libbey-St. Clair Inc. was incorporated to take over the St. Clair operations. As equal partners, the chairman alternated on an annual basis between the two principals, Domglas Inc. and Libbey Glass Company, with the directors and officers being drawn from both companies. At this time, the company had over a thousand different tableware and industrial ware machine-made items in their product mix. The crowning achievement was the successful establishment of a broad line of mass-produced machine-made one-piece stemware (goblets) in March 1981. This was a first for Canada.

FOOTNOTES

[1] Gerald Stevens, *Early Canadian Glass*, (Toronto: The Ryerson Press, 1961), p. 36.
[2] J.C. Stephenson, "The Story of Independent Glass Producers, (Limited)," typed draft August 25, 1975, p. 55.

CHAPTER 11

Flat Glass

Historical Background
Glassmaking Techniques
Cayuga Glass, Cayuga, Ontario (1835)
Canada Glass Works, St. Johns, Canada East (Quebec) (1845-c.1853)
Penetang Glass, Penetanguishene, Ontario (1879-1883)
Napanee Glass, Napanee, Ontario (1881-1883)
The Pilkington Group (1905 to date)
Canadian Libbey-Owens, Hamilton, Ontario (1920-1922)
The Canadian Pittsburgh Industries Group (1940 to date)
Federal Glass, Toronto, Ontario (1926)

HISTORICAL BACKGROUND

As indicated in Chapter 1, glass was not "invented" in the normal sense of the word but was developed over many centuries. Perhaps the invention of the blowpipe about 100 B.C. should be considered as the time at which flat glass was first made.

The first method was known as the *cylinder* process and was later replaced by the *crown* process. As the Roman Empire spread westward across Europe, so did the various crafts, including glassmaking. In medieval France, Lorraine was the centre for the manufacture of window glass by the cylinder process. Normandy specialized in crown glass (1706).

Roger Bacon, a medieval scientist living in England in the thirteenth century, experimented with the magnifying properties of convex glass lenses. Gutenberg's invention of the printing press in 1446 spurred on the development of reading glasses. In Holland, in 1590, two Dutch scientists, Jansen and Lippershey, developed the principle of the telescope. By sighting through two convex lenses, held in line, they found that distant objects appeared to be very close. The microscope was developed by another Dutch inventor, Van Leeunewhoek, in 1660.

As early as 1612, "green glass for windows" (no doubt an apt description) was being made in a coal-fired furnace in Southwark (SE London). The patron of glassmaking in England was Sir Robert Mansfield or, as he came to be known, Sir Robert Mansell. His operations were centered in Newcastle because of the plentiful coal deposits, the energy used at that time for melting the batch.

Within one hundred years, the centre of flat glassmaking had moved to Lancashire for easy access to the port of Liverpool. It was here, in St. Helens, that the Pilkington dynasty got its start in 1826. In the United States, flat glassmaking did not develop until after the War of 1812.

Flat glass making by the blown cylinder sheet glass process.   Courtesy Pilkington Glass.

A. HAND

1. *Blown cylinder sheet glass* (broad, green or spread glass)
   Process

Fig. 1 The molten glass gathered on a blowpipe was blown into an open wooden block or mould which dictated the ultimate diameter of the cylinder. Water sprinkled on the wood prevented the glass from scratching and the wood from burning. Fig. 2 After reheating at the "glory hole," blowing and rotating, the molten metal formed a flat-bottomed hollow vessel. Fig. 3 The glass was then alternately reheated and swung over a swing hole or trench so that a cylinder was formed. The diameter of the cylinder was kept constant by blowing. Fig. 4 When the cylinder had cooled, a longitudinal cut was made on the inner surface. The cutting tool was a diamond guided by a wooden ruler. Fig. 5 The split cylinder was replaced in a flattening kiln where, after reheating, it opened and flattened into a flat sheet of glass or lagre. A polissoir, a wood block on the end of a rod, soaked in water, was used to iron out any irregularities. The sheet of glass was then placed in an annealing kiln.[1]

Flat glass making by the crown process.
Courtesy Pilkington Glass.

2. Crown or bull's eye

Process

Fig. 1 The molten glass, gathered on the end of a blowpipe, was formed into a pear shape by rolling on a marver, a polished iron slab. Fig. 2 By reheating, rotating and blowing, a globe was formed. Fig. 3 When the globe was of sufficient size, a punty, or solid iron rod, was attached to it opposite the blowing iron, which was then cracked off. Fig. 4 The globe on the punty was reheated, then rotated at considerable speed so that centrifugal force acting on the edge of the opening caused the metal (molten glass) to be flung outwards, forming a flat disc or "table." This operation is known as "flashing." Fig. 5 The completed table with the bull's eye, or bullion, in the centre, where the punty was attached. Fig. 6 The completed tables were piled in a kiln for annealing.[2]

3. Plate glass

i. Cylinder process

Plate glass was first made in the same way as sheet glass, by the cylinder process, the differences being that only the purest supplies of sand, lime and soda were used and that red lead (or litharge) was also added (hence lead glass or lead crystal glass). It was made thicker than sheet glass so that it could bear grinding (using sand) and polishing (using rouge), by which means an even, lustrous finish was produced.

ii. Casting process

The French were the first to make plate by casting, though just who was responsible for this important development is far from clear. Both Bernard Perrot of Orléans and Louis Lucas de Nehou, an official at the Tourlaville glassworks near Cherbourg, where plate glass was already being made, lay claim to the honour. What is undisputed is that several Frenchmen of note, acting through one Abraham Thévart, were granted letters patent in December 1688, which gave them a monopoly of glass manufacture by the casting process for the French home market, and later for export as well.

> From *The Glassmakers* by T.C. Barker:
>
> ... In theory, the casting process was so much more straightforward than the complicated method of making a flat piece of glass by way of a cylinder, that it seems curious that plate glass was not made in this way long before the end of the seventeenth century. In practice, however, casting, grinding and polishing required a very large capital outlay, a strong deterrent to even the wealthier investors. Instead of the customary small glasshouse, a large casting hall was needed, complete with an extensive melting furnace in the centre, a number of sizeable annealing ovens round the walls, a casting table upwards of ten feet long and six feet wide, and cuvettes (or cisterns) in which the metal could be transferred from the furnace to the casting table, together with a crane to carry them ...

B. MECHANICAL

1. *Lubbers process* or drawn cylinder (1903)
(John H. Lubbers, glass flattener, Toledo, Ohio)

The American Window Glass Company introduced to the trade the first successful machine for blowing window glass cylinders. Lubbers' invention simply mechanized the hand process of blowing cylinders. A metal cone-shaped nozzle known as a "bait," suspended from a long, hollow tube, was dipped into the molten glass in the tank furnace and, by raising the bait and introducing air into the glass attached thereto, a long symmetrical cylinder was formed. It was then converted into sheets of glass by the same method used in the handblown cylinder method.

2. *Colburn process* (1906)
(Irwin W. Colburn, Toledo Glass Company)

An automatic device fed the batch into a huge continuous tank furnace, which melted and refined it. From the far end of the furnace, the glass poured into a rather shallow tub built of refractory material. It was most essential that the glass in this tub be kept at just the proper temperature, otherwise it would not be stretchable and pliant as the machine drew it up and over a bending roller in a continuous sheet. As soon as the sheet rose from the tub, two sets of knurled rollers gripped the sheet's outer edges and thereby kept its width constant and prevented the glass from narrowing into a stringy tail. Water coolers on either side of the sheet cooled the glass and hence gave it strength for the upward pull through about two or three feet of space separating the tub from the bending roller. After it was bent over the roller into a horizon-

Manufacture of window glass on the Lubber's Cylinder Machine.
Courtesy of Libbey-Owens-Ford.

Sheet drawing on the Colburn Machine.
Courtesy of Libbey-Owens-Ford.

tal position, the sheet was gripped along its edges by endless chains and pulled across several rollers into a long lehr. Here it travelled slowly and finally emerged at near room temperature. A worker then broke off its edges, which bore the marks of the knurled rollers and drawing chains, and another worker cut up the endless sheet into large pieces for the convenience of inspectors, pane cutters and packers.

The operation of such a machine doubtless appears quite simple to most casual observers, and as compared with the paste-mould and bottle machine processes, it actually is. The Colburn machine does not really form the sheet; the sheet is formed by the physical properties of molten glass as it is pulled from the tub. The machine only does the pulling and keeps the sheet at even width and thickness. The greater the speed of the machine, the thinner the sheet.

3. *Fourcault process*

This process, developed by Emile Fourcault in Belgium, about 1906, was similar to the Colburn process but, rather than drawing the glass up for a few feet and then bending it over a roller and into a horizontal lehr, the glass was drawn upwards all the way and into a vertical lehr.[3]

4. *Float process*

i. *Pilkington*
  England (1961)

The raw materials to make glass are melted in a tank, or furnace, and the molten glass moves in a continuous ribbon from this onto a bath of molten tin. The molten tin (half-a-million dollars worth) and the atmosphere around it are kept at precisely controlled temperatures. As the glass floats over the metal bath, it passes through three temperature zones. The first is the heating zone. Here, all irregularities on both surfaces of the glass are melted out. The next is the fire polishing zone, where the glass acquires its brilliant surfaces. The third zone through

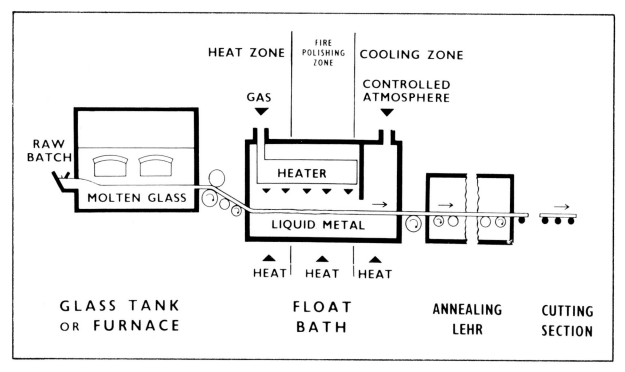

HEAT ZONE   FIRE POLISHING ZONE   COOLING ZONE

CONTROLLED ATMOSPHERE

GAS

HEATER

RAW BATCH

MOLTEN GLASS

LIQUID METAL

HEAT   HEAT   HEAT

GLASS TANK or **FURNACE**   **FLOAT BATH**   **ANNEALING LEHR**   **CUTTING SECTION**

Float Glass Process.

Courtesy of Pilkington Glass.

which the glass floats is the cooling zone, where the glass becomes hard enough to be touched without spoiling the fire-polished surfaces.

From the float bath, the glass moves to the annealing lehr for the final cooling, which is also done under precisely controlled conditions. This operation removes all stress or strain that may have been left in the glass ribbon. At the end of the lehr, the ribbon of float glass is cut on the automatic cutting line into the final sizes ordered by the customer.

ii. PPG Flat Glass process

United States (1963)

This process is similar to the Pilkington process except that it draws a ribbon of molten glass across the molten tin bath instead of pouring the molten glass onto it.

NINETEENTH CENTURY OPERATIONS IN CANADA

The first record which attempts to establish a glassworks in Canada centres on the Niagara Peninsula, between Hamilton and Niagara Falls, Ontario. The pioneer in this effort was John DeCow. His sponsor in the Legislative Assembly of Ontario was William Merritt, Member for the Niagara District. Merritt will be best remembered as the driving force behind the construction of the Welland Canal. He subsequently operated the Welland Canal Company. DeCow's first application, on February 20, 1828, was in the name of the Thorold Glass Manufacturing Company, after the town in which he lived. The bill did not get beyond the first reading. His second attempt, on January 14, 1829, was in the name of the Upper Canada Glass Manufacturing Company. It received approval from the Assembly on March 8, 1829, but was never returned from the Legislative Council, where it had been sent for consideration. A third attempt, on January 12, 1833, suffered the same fate. Before the end of the year, his fourth petition, although approved by the Council, was set aside by the Assembly. Over a year later, William Hepburn, an associate of DeCow's, filed a petition in the name of the Upper Canada Glass Company, to be based in the township of Cayuga, a short distance south of Hamilton, Ontario. The application was successful, the only provision being that the name be changed to the Cayuga Glass Manufacturing Company.

CAYUGA GLASS MANUFACTURING COMPANY
Cayuga, Ontario (1835)

An act to incorporate this company was passed on April 16, 1835, and stated that the bill would be forfeited if it was not in operation by January 1, 1838. The petitioners, headed up by William Hepburn and John DeCow, purchased a piece of land on which to build the factory.

Nothing appears to have happened, because DeCow (now known as Decew) on June 7, 1841, sought Merritt's support for the establishment of another glass factory. In his letter he states ''that there will be much difficulty and expense in its creation as it is the first glass factory.'' The letter also refers to the fact that there were 75 shareholders and that there would be substantially more subscribers if the bill were passed.

The petition was read in the Assembly on June 14, 1841, in the name of the Haldimand Glass Works Company, to be located in Cayuga, Haldimand County. While the Assembly was willing to give consideration to the bill, they would not accept DeCew's request for assistance from the public purse to get the enterprise going. After gaining approval from the various authorities, it was refused Royal Assent, with no reasons given. Undaunted, DeCew and his associates made two further attempts. On December 16, 1844, they sought to obtain renewal of the charter granted in 1835, but to no avail. On February 7, 1845, a motion was put forward to have the bill read a second time, but the vote was negative and the bill died.

No further attempts were made to secure a charter, and thus Mallorytown Glass Works still holds the honour of being recorded as the first works to produce glass articles in Canada.

CANADA GLASS WORKS
St. Johns, Canada East (Quebec) (1845-c.1853)

The honour of being the first fully operational glassworks in the Province of Quebec goes to the Canada Glass Works. It was also the first producer of window glass in Canada. Although it was operating at the same time as Ottawa Glass Works in Como, Quebec, and was created to produce the same product, flat glass, it actually got off to a better start.

The main reason was that it was established by an experienced glassworker, Frederick Smith, who had been in the flat glass business for 11 years. Since 1827 the Champlain Glass Works had been producing flat glass in Burlington, Vermont, on the east side of Lake Champlain, some 70 miles by water south of St. Johns. In 1837 Mr. Smith bought the company and, with various partners, the last of whom was William Henry Wilkins Jr., operated it for 13 years under the name Smith & Wilkins. Their main market was probably the surrounding area, but it must be assumed that they also shipped glass into southern Quebec via the Richelieu River. Because of the import duties of 20 percent for glass entering Canada, it seems highly probable that they decided to establish a Canadian operation that would eliminate this extra cost and would put them closer to the larger cities in Quebec — Montreal, Three Rivers and Quebec City.

The first indication appeared in a newspaper article titled ''Glass Works have recently been erected in St. Johns,'' by a Mr. Smith of Burlington. Within two months, a ready-made market for window glass was created as the result of two disastrous fires in Quebec City, a month apart, that levelled 2,000 homes and left 15,000 people homeless.

A partnership of Messrs. Smith and Wilkins of Burlington and Edwin Atwater of Montreal was established in the name of the Canada Glass Works. Atwater was a self-made man. Born in the United States, he came to Montreal as an artist. He opened a studio on St. Paul St. in 1842 and sold paints and oils. He took an active interest in civic affairs and was elected president of the Montreal Board of Trade in 1861, having previously been an alderman of the city from 1850-

1857. When the Montreal City and District Savings Bank was founded in 1846, Atwater was selected as a member of the first board of honourary directors and, shortly after, he was elected to the board of management. He was a director (1848-1875), vice-president (1852-1859) and president (1859-1861). Although the bank had originally been established to provide a means whereby citizens could deposit their monies with the assurance that a courteous welcome awaited them, it has to be assumed that they had a vested interest in the Canada Glass Works as well. Twenty-three years later, in 1868, senior members of the bank would become involved in another glass company.[4]

Land was leased and eventually acquired by deed of sale from the Honourable Charles William Grant, Baron de la Baronnie de Longueuil, by Frederick Smith of the Town of Dorchester (which had been proclaimed a municipality of the Parish of St. Johns on August 27, 1835). The deed used the old numbering system for the lots and included lots 376-379, plus lots 388-397, the boundaries of which were Glass (Gouin), Dormaray/Albert (Collin), St. Jean (Mercier) and Lemoine (Frontenac). Presumably, the other block to the north was acquired in 1844 or early 1845, as the factory started operations in May 1845. The boundaries of this block were Lemoine, Dormaray, St. Jean and the railroad right-of-way.

The 1847 map is very clear about the location of the first factory and the deed of sale of 1846 confirms this location. The map shows the entire block, but the deed refers to only the south block. The north block was adjacent to the right-of-way of the Champlain and St. Lawrence Railroad, and the factory would logically have been built as close as possible to the tracks. The railroad ran from St. Johns to La Prairie, on the south bank of the St. Lawrence River, opposite Montreal. It was built by brewer John Molson and opened in 1836, and was the first railway in what would become Canada. When all arrangements had been completed, Mr. Smith returned to Burlington.

No description of the buildings has been found for the period of the company's operations but it is assumed that Foster Brothers, who took over the dormant works about 1854, used the same facilities.

The *Canadian Economist*, September 12, 1846, reported:

> The glass manufactory noted as established at St. Johns has been in operation something more than a year. It has two furnaces and can turn out 100 half-boxes of glass a day.

The expression "100 half-boxes" referred to the method of shipping flat glass. According to the latest information I have, sheet glass was quoted in the U.S.A. as being in "boxes" (50 square feet per box) and occasionally "half-boxes" (25 square feet per box). There has been much speculation as to whether bottles were also made there, but so far there has been no hard evidence to support such a theory.

Also from the *Canadian Economist*, an advertisement which appeared regularly during 1846-1847:

"CANADA" WINDOW GLASS

The subscriber is now prepared to supply orders for all sizes and qualities of Window Glass, manufactured at the "Canada Glass Works" St. Johns C.E. to the extent of 10,000 boxes.

2nd May 1846   EDWIN ATWATER
                      193 St. Paul St.
                      Montreal

Production was graded for retailing into firsts, seconds, thirds, and sometimes fourths. The grading was dependent on the number of vesicles or air bubbles, grit, etc., in the glass, the lack of colouration, and the amount of distortion or ripples in the sheet. The thickness of the sheets was calculated by the number of ounces to the square foot — with 15, 21, 32, 36 and 42 ounces representing the standard thicknesses.

Up to the middle of the nineteenth century, the "crown" glass method was universally considered superior to the "blown cylinder" process, but was severely limited with respect to pane size. The latter process was used in this glass operation. In August 1849 Atwater made the following declaration, which indicated that the partnership headed by Smith had been expanded in 1846:

> I, the undersigned, of Montreal, do hereby certify that I have carried on and intend to carry on a Trade and Business as Glass Manufacturers at St. Johns aforesaid in partnership with Fred Smith and William Henry Wilkins of Burlington, Vermont, Jason C. Peirce, Chas. S. Peirce and Chas. Seymour of St. Johns and that the said partnership hath subsisted since the first day of August one thousand eight hundred and forty-six and the said Edwin Atwater and Fred Smith, Jason C. Peirce, Chas. S. Peirce, W.H. Wilkins and Chas. Seymour are and have been since the said day the only members of the said partnership and witness my hand at Montreal this thirtieth day of July, one thousand eight hundred and forty-nine.[5]

The following advertisement in the *Standstead Journal* suggests that the two operations, Smith and Wilkins in Burlington (Vermont) and Canada Glass Works in St. Johns, were supplying their respective markets with the same glass:

> . . . a fresh supply of Vermont and Canada Glass (any size of the above glass furnished to order) . . .

The works was obviously still in operation in 1849 when three new partners were added: Jason C. Peirce, Charles S. Peirce and Charles Seymour, all of St. Johns. Between 1851 and 1854, when Foster Brothers took over, the partners closed down both the American and Canadian operations, reportedly because of the high cost of fuel. It would be interesting to research the possibility that the window glass in some existing houses in Quebec City, replacing that destroyed in the fires of 1845, was made in St. Johns or Como.

PENETANG GLASS FACTORY
Penetanguishene, Ontario (1879-1883)

Located at the southeast end of Lake Huron's Georgian Bay, Penetanguishene (whose name is said to be derived from an Indian term meaning "white rolling sands") was the site of Royal Navy and military establishments in the period 1814-1856. The story of this endeavour is one of a typical group of small-town businessmen who put up their money to establish a glass factory in the hopes that it would bring additional prosperity to their city. Alas, it was not to be. The plant and equipment were completed, but no glass was produced on a commercial basis.

Twenty-six men set up a syndicate and appointed Philip Spohn, physician, Rev. Theopholus Frances Laboureau, priest, and James Wynne, wine merchant, to act as trustees for the company, popularly known as "The Glass Factory." Two acres of land were purchased from George Copeland, miller.

The following is an extract from Willa Mercer's article "The Penetanguishene Glass Factory" in the July/August 1971 issue of *Canadian Collector*. Mercer quotes:

> ". . . The Glass Works at Penetang are going up fast. Mr. R.R. Serson of Barrie has the superintendence of the job and it is doing well . . . This company (sic) have erected a building 250 feet long, and expect to start work within six weeks with 250 men . . ."

In March 1880 Richard Davis, a glass entrepreneur, arrived from Nova Scotia, where he had been involved with New Brunswick Crystal and Courtenay Bay Glass, and convinced the owners to assign the works to him. Some glass was probably made on an experimental basis, because an Orillia paper stated:

> We have been shown several specimens of the glass manufactured at Penetanguishene, which to all appearances is faultless, and so far as the material goes there is no doubt that the institution can be made a profitable enterprise . . .

Sources in Penetanguishene have stated that there had been some items from the works stored in the basement of the public library, but no trace of them has been found.

The following was extracted from the March 31, 1881, issue of the *Orillia Times*:

> ROUGH TREATMENT — On Friday Night, the manager of the glass works (Davis, by name) was set on by a crowd of disguised men who poured tar over him and then doused him with feathers. It is said that the outrage was committed by parties who allege that Davis has kept them out of their wages. The victim of the assault . . . denies that he owes anyone in the village, urging that he was only the agent of the projector of the works, and is in no way responsible for their not going on, or for any failure on the part of his principal to meet his obligations . . .

By 1883 the idea of establishing an operational glass factory was abandoned. The four trustees and 23 others who had invested in the operation sold a portion of the property and buildings to Peter Baldwin of Toronto for the sum of $1,000. The remainder of the property was signed back to George Copeland in lieu of the debt still owed by the trustees. The buildings might have been used for Baldwin's Door and Sash Factory. On April 25, 1885, Baldwin sold the property back to George Copeland for the sum of $700.

NAPANEE GLASS WORKS
Napanee, Ontario (1881-1883)

The man behind the Napanee Glass Works venture, John Herring, was born in Denmark, New York, in 1818. In September 1879 Herring and Mr. A.H. Roe, another community leader, made a tour of a number of glasshouses in the state of New York, across the St. Lawrence River. As a result, they decided that the establishment of a window glassworks in Napanee was viable, if the capital could be raised. Mr. Rathbun of nearby Mill Point offered to invest $50,000 if the work were established in his community. However, it was felt that by establishing it in Napanee the town would benefit economically. At a meeting in the town hall late in September 1879, a committee comprising Messrs. Herring, Roe, Pruyn, Gibson and Denison was formed to canvas the town for funding.

In March 1881 Messrs. Herring and Roe visited Pittsburgh, Pennsylvania (then the technical centre of the North American glass industry), to thoroughly investigate the process of flat-glassmaking. Before the end of the month, stock books for the glass company were opened in Napanee. A month later, a bonus of $5,000 in aid of the factory was considered on the assurance that the works employ at least 45 hands and pay out in wages $700 weekly for ten years. The company would then be eligible for a ten-year exemption from taxes. By the end of April, $27,000 had been subscribed and five acres of land north of the Grand Trunk Railway, facing on Selby Road, were donated by the owner, J.S. Cartwright of Toronto. On this land were erected a boarding house and several cottages to accommodate the 20 to 30 workers, most of whom were coming from Belgium and Germany. To the east of this, across a spur of the Napanee, Tamworth and Quebec Railway line, Herring acquired about 12 acres for the plant site for $950.

Extracts from the June 18 issue of the *Napanee Standard* give an idea of the magnitude of the job of establishing and furnishing the works:

> . . . about 215 carloads from Pittsburgh, Pennsylvania including 200 of coal have been purchased and are now on the way to Napanee. The materials for the furnace alone, fills three railway cars. It's made in sections in Pittsburgh ready to be put up in the company's buildings. The machinery for the flattening oven consists

essentially of an immense horizontal wheel, thirty feet in diameter which revolves during the process of flattening the glass. The thirty pots, in which are placed and melted the materials for making glass, are worth thirty dollars a piece. The works will possess facilities for making their own pots, when they get into operation. Among the purchases; one carload of miscellaneous apparatus, principally blow-pipes. Mr. Julius Seigsworth, a third generation glassman has been secured as foreman. The various buildings are as follows: The furnace building will be 90 x 90 feet. In the furnace are placed ten pots; the building, where are made the pots which require to be often renewed is 34 x 60 and two stories high. The flattening oven is contained in a building 50 x 120 feet connected with this building is the annealing furnace. The cutting room is 50 x 60 feet and here the sheets of glass are cut by diamonds to make sheets of two sizes, 3 x 5 feet and 4 x 6 feet. In this building also, the glass is boxed, branded and removed to the adjacent storehouse, which is placed next to the railway track. There will be two batch houses, each 32 x 40 on each side of the main building, 800 boxes, or two carloads of glass per week will be turned out.

On November 19, 1881, the *Standard* announced that "On Monday last, the work of blowing began at the Napanee Glass Factory." A few weeks later, the following story appeared:

> On Tuesday night a girl — one of the spectators — was flopping about in the insane style common to young females, fell against a cylinder of glass at Herring & Sons factory, knocking it down and half a dozen other cylinders. Of course there was a smash. A large hole in that day's profit for the blower, and a vigorous freshet of profanity. Visitors must bear in mind that the time of the blowers — who work by the piece — is money and if visitors can't witness the operations without being in the way, they cannot feel offended if they are excluded.

Early in December 1881 Finance Minister Sir Leonard A. Tilley and Lady Tilley visited the works and expressed their admiration for what they saw. In January 1882 there was a slowdown and temporary stoppage of operations due to the inefficiency of the tank teaser (furnace operator). He was replaced by Joseph Bowers from New York State.

Late in 1882 and during the winter of 1883, the glassworkers were getting out of hand, as the following extracts from the *Napanee Standard* indicate:

December 30, 1882, "A Brutal Blow".

> On Christmas evening, while Thomas Dunn, assisted by his brother, was carrying a trunk to the railway station, John Duffy, an employee at the Glass Works, assaulted him with an iron bar about two feet long by three quarter inch in diameter, with which he dealt him a blow upon his mouth, breaking off six teeth and otherwise injuring him seriously. If the blow had been delivered on the skull, at which it appears to have been aimed the victim would undoubtedly have been killed; but something caused Dunn to turn his head at the moment and he received the blow upon the mouth. An old quarrel between the men is said to have been the cause of the affair. The matter was investigated on Tuesday before the Mayor, by whom Duffy was committed for trial.

February 3, 1883, "Glass Works Troubles".

> Messrs. Herring have had difficulty of late in getting some of their hands to work steadily and regularly, and in consequence have suffered inconvenience, annoyance and damage. They have found it necessary on one or two recent occasions to bring some of the delinquents before the police court for deserting their employment. They have had five cases of this kind this week, one of which was disposed of by a heavy fine and the others are still pending. In the meantime the firm is bringing in new hands to supply the places of those who have left.

Total yearly wages were about $15,000 and raw materials added another $13,500 to the cost. Annual production was about $33,000, which represented about 160 boxes a day or 900 per week. Shipment was by rail and the rates from Napanee to various points in the province were unreasonably high. By comparison, carloads from Montreal westward were sent through about as cheaply as from Napanee, 200 miles further on, while it cost Herring about as much for freight from Montreal to Napanee as from Europe to Montreal, and in some instances considerably more.

The works were shut down in May, a month earlier than usual. This was due to the lack of satisfactory glassblowers and the need to make some changes in the furnaces which would effect a fuel economy. When the normal reopening time came in September, the works remained closed. Messrs. John Herring and Son petitioned for a bonus of $10,000 on condition that the works be reestablished and operated as a stock company, with a capital of $200,000. In October it was decided not to start up the works for the 1883-1884 season. The works remained closed for the next campaign (1884-1885). At a public meeting on July 18, 1885, called to consider the future of the glassworks, Herring offered to turn over his interests in the company to an acceptable buyer for $25,000. A subsequent canvassing of the townspeople elicited little encouragement.

In July Mayor Wilson received a letter from a former resident stating that a number of gentlemen in Montreal were looking for a suitable location at which to manufacture bottles and fancy glassware. A few days later, a letter was received from Messrs. R.J. Osborne and W.M. Hanson of Montreal in regard to the glassworks, in which the names of the officers of the new company were given and a request made that the town council decide at once as to what they would do with the premises, as interests in St. Johns, Quebec, had also made them an offer. The council was divided on what action should be taken. When called upon to express an opinion, Herring said he gathered from the communications that Mr. Yule's (Yuile's) glassworks had been destroyed by fire, that these 20 men were not very well satisfied with their employer, and that in retaliation they were going to form a joint stock company in opposition to him. (In 1886, the Yuile brothers were the principals of The North American Glass Company, Limited, which was operating in the east end of Montreal.) Mr. Hanson seemed to think that these men had lots of money and that they could establish and run a glass factory. Mr. Herring was not satisfied that this assumption was valid.

In the fall of 1886 a representative of the Montreal group visited Napanee to discuss the matter. No action appears to have been taken however. Herring died on October 21, 1896, at the age of 78, and will always be remembered for his contribution to the community. The plant site was purchased by Mayor H.L. Cook in 1888.

THE PILKINGTON GROUP

Background

The name Pilkington, or, as it was more familiarly known, Pilkington Brothers has had a long and illustrious history, not only in England, but also in Canada. It all started in St. Helens, England, in 1826, as a partnership between Messrs. Greenall, Bell, Bromilow and Barnes, and to their names that of Mr. Pilkington was added, operating under the name of the St. Helens Crown Glass Company. By 1848 it had become known as Pilkington Brothers, after William and Richard, who were then sole owners.

CANADIAN OPERATIONS

The beginnings of Pilkington in Canada are obscure, but records exist of sales to a customer in Halifax, Nova Scotia, in 1834. The company first established its own agents in Canada, in the early nineteenth century, in Halifax, Montreal and Vancouver, the centres of trade at that time. Sales were of a local nature. At Confederation, on July 1, 1867, and with the subsequent completion of the transcontinental Canadian Pacific Railway in 1885, not only did business pick up, but improved transportation and development of more land broadened the base of sales out of the three abovementioned agencies.

Warehouses were opened in the major cities across Canada from 1890 onwards and sales were expanded. Apparently, it was not uncommon in those days for an order to be received for a few small panes of glass packed in molasses. These were needed for the trapper's cabins and would have to be brought in by dog sled or carried on their backs. The panes were sealed into a flat tin of molasses, the glass travelling safely and the molasses forming a valuable part of the trapper's diet.

Pilkington produced in three locations in Canada, all in Ontario — Cayuga, Thorold and Scarborough. In Cayuga, the company became involved with the Canadian subsidiary of an American glass company which required someone to operate their process in Canada. With the termination of Canada Glass Works' flat glass operation in St. Johns, Quebec, about 1853, there was no flat glass production in Canada until the short-lived operation in Napanee.

WINDOW GLASS MACHINE COMPANY OF CANADA, LIMITED
Cayuga, Ontario (1905-1914)

The story began back in the 1890s when an American, John H. Lubbers, a glass flattener by trade, experimented with the cylinder or sheet process, successfully replacing the lung power of the glassblower with compressed air. This became known as the Lubbers process. This new process made it possible to blow much longer and larger cylinders, eventually achieving a length of 40 feet, 30 inches in diameter.

Lubbers took out some patents and attracted the interest of the giant American Window Glass Company. In 1903 that company set up a subsidiary, the American Window Glass Machine Company, to acquire Lubbers' patents and develop the process for commercial use. In the meantime, in England, Pilkington had kept themselves well informed on the development of this process, but decided to wait until it had been further developed before taking any action.

In 1905 American Window Glass Machine Company announced its intention of setting up a subsidiary in Canada to work this process. Cayuga, Ontario, south of Hamilton, was selected for the operation. The company obtained an Ontario charter issued on November 17, 1905, in the name of the Window Glass Machine Company of Canada, Limited. The Canadian company reached an agreement with the authorities in Cayuga whereby it received a 14-acre site tax-free for the following 30 years and, moreover, the town agreed to pay the cost of a siding from the nearby Grand Trunk Railway. The company, for its part, promised to build a factory which would initially employ 30 men and eventually 100. Building of the new factory started early in July 1906, and by the middle of February 1907 three machines had been installed and tanks and lehrs erected.

To protect their interests from importers, the promoters sought an increase in tariff from the current 15 percent. Of course, this raised the ire of the glass importers who sold hardware and paint as well as glass. It also precipitated a strong reaction by Pilkington, who also wished to protect their vested interests in their export trade to Canada. Pilkington was already operating in the Canadian market in keen competition with Belgian manufacturers, and the small benefits it enjoyed from the British preferential tariff, which had induced the company to invest more heavily in Canada, did not offset the cost advantages of manufacturing in Belgium. Pilkington succeeded in having the petition for a tariff increase quashed.

In 1907 an amendment to the English patent law required a patent to be worked within three years if it was to be valid in Britain. This provided the necessary impetus for the two companies, American Window Glass and Pilkington, to start negotiating. It was obvious by now that machine production was improving rapidly and was here to stay. In April 1909 a formal agreement was signed and a licence was granted to Pilkington giving it the right to work the drawn cylinder process (Lubbers) not only in Britain but also in Canada. The agreement also required Pilkington to establish a joint venture (with the Empire Machine Company in the United States) to exploit the new process outside of the United States, Canada and Britain. It was expected, erroneously, that the Belgians would be anxious to take up the process. However, perhaps because of their much longer history of sheet glassmaking, they were developing their own processes.

Pilkington set up an experimental machine (Lubbers) at St. Helens and, by 1910, had eight machines in commercial operation. In the meantime American Window Glass, because of excessive costs, ended up in the hands of a creditors' committee. Relations became strained between the two companies. According to T.C. Barker in *The Glassmakers*, the Window Glass Machine Company does not appear to have operated on a commercial basis, although some shards have been found. In 1909 Pilkington acquired it. In 1911 Pilkington decided that the process should be worked in Canada twice a year to satisfy the patent restrictions. Before this could be done, the patent office granted a year's extension before first use was required (1912).

By this time, the Americans were bringing pressure on Pilkington to work the process in Canada or they would do it themselves. This was contrary to the 1909 agreement. Secondly, and more seriously, American Window Glass threatened to export their glass to Canada. They actually went through with this latter threat, with the assistance of W.R. Hobbs and his Consolidated Plate Glass Company. As a result, the Cayuga operation was disbanded on October 19, 1914, whereupon the land and building reverted to local authority. On December 18, 1931, an affidavit declared that the Window Glass Machine Company of Canada, Limited had not been active for upwards of 15 years. However, due to a bureaucratic foul-up, actual dissolution did not take place until January 12, 1959.

PILKINGTON BROTHERS
Thorold, Ontario (1914-1924)

Even before the demise of the Cayuga venture, Pilkington had decided that they should operate the Lubbers process themselves on a commercial basis in Canada. In 1913, after looking at Windsor and Thorold, Ontario, for a site, they selected the latter, on the Welland Canal. Plans called for construction, on a site about two miles from Thorold, of a factory, houses for the factory workers and the warehouse manager, 12 single and 13 double houses, a recreation hall, school and a store. The self-contained community was named Windle Village, after the chairman of the board, Colonel Windle Pilkington. There was also a Pilkington Station on the Canadian National Railway line. With Thorold on the drawing board, Pilkington's central Canadian office was moved from Montreal to Toronto. In 1916 it was moved to Thorold.

Mrs. Kitty Beggington, one of the pioneers, recalled those early days:

My husband was sent out to Thorold in June 1914. In those days there weren't any posh hotels waiting for them but what we called the Bunk House, where single men and those waiting for their families to arrive lived. Meals were served to any employee who had purchased a meal ticket for 25 cents. In September of that year I, then aged nineteen, and my son Jack, eight months old, along with about a dozen other families, made that same journey to Thorold. When we arrived at our destination I wondered what on earth my husband had brought me to. The station consisted of two planks of wood and a sign. But things were made brighter for me because I knew all the familiar faces waiting to welcome me to Windle Village.

From *The World of Pilkington*, part two:

Transportation was one of the big problems these Pilkington pioneers had to face. If they did not live in the village, they had to catch the morning train at seven a.m. from Thorold, which by special arrangement stopped at the Pilkington station. A train was scheduled to return at six p.m. but was very unreliable. On the other hand, the wives living in Windle Village had to contend with the same unreliable train service or the good nature of some passing driver to get to the shops in Thorold. Soon, however, some enterprising businessmen decided that a profit could be made transporting people between the village and Thorold. The old cars they used for this "bus" service seated five but often carried ten or more, with some clinging to the running boards. The two-mile trip cost five cents, but the service was unreliable in the winter. Often, during heavy snows, you had to walk unless you were lucky enough to get a ride on a sleigh.

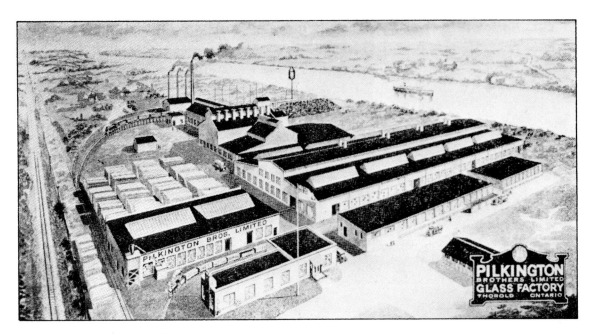

Pilkington Glass Factory, Thorold, Ontario.   Courtesy of Pilkington Glass.

By May 1914 the factory started producing rolled plate, using the old ladle-pouring method and three casting tables, one for window glass and two for rough cast. Drawn cylinder sheet was also produced on four Lubbers' machines, to which four more were added when the rolled plate operation was discontinued. Average production was about 250,000 ft. per week, with a maximum pane of 40 x 60 feet.

Production had barely settled down when the First World War began. As a result, imports from Europe began to diminish, which created a much greater demand for Thorold's output. Despite this, the factory continued to operate at a loss until 1918, when virtually no glass was imported. In that year the profit was $66,000 on sales of $464,000. In 1920 profits hit their peak at $83,000 on $789,000 of sales. With the cessation of hostilities in 1918, and the availability of cheap labour in the war-ravaged countries in Europe, production there slowly resumed, resulting in the dumping of glass into Canada at prices lower than it could be made here.

The Thorold factory operated off and on from 1922 to 1924, when it was finally closed down and sold, along with the village, to Welland Securities Limited for $225,000.

PILKINGTON BROTHERS (CANADA) LIMITED
Toronto, Ontario (1922-1945)

This company was granted a federal charter on November 23, 1922, with James Eustace Harrison as managing director and with its head office in Toronto. Like many glass companies of this era, they acquired interests in the paint industry, a natural adjunct to window glass. The timing for their move was perhaps a little more than coincidental.

Canadian Libbey-Owens Sheet Glass Company, Limited in Hamilton, Ontario, a subsidiary of Libbey-Owens Sheet Glass Company of Toledo, Ohio, had closed down in 1922 after two costly years of operating the Colburn process with little tariff protection from imports. Until 1946 no flat glass was produced in Canada, and Pilkington merely operated a distribution system for its glass products and paints. In 1946 a small partnership, Industrial Glass Works, started up in the outskirts of Montreal, Quebec. By 1950 it had been acquired by the Pittsburgh Plate Glass Company. This event and the fact that Pilkington was already experimenting with the revolutionary "float glass" process in England were probably the deciding factors in the reestablishment of their own production facilities in Canada.

On February 1, 1945, under a new name, Pilkington Glass Limited (a private company) was incorporated. They proceeded to acquire 34 acres of land in Scarborough, Ontario, on the eastern outskirts of Toronto, on which they built a sheet glass plant. This started up on November 1, 1951.

Much has been written about "float glass," the wonder of the 60s. The story started in England in the 1930s when plate glass was challenged by the development of two new products, Perspex and thick drawn sheet (TDS). The first, a product of Imperial Chemical Industries, was a clear plastic that, although useful for some applications, never became a serious contender because it scratched too easily and was too expensive. TDS, on the other hand, had the potential to compete with plate glass. Unfortunately, its market debut coincided with the start of World War II, which saw the almost complete elimination of imports and an unsatisfiable demand for replacement lights (panes) in the war-torn United Kingdom, which kept Pilkington and the rest of the flat glass industry operating at capacity.

Three steps were required to make cast plate glass. Firstly, it was necessary to cast it a third thicker than the finished product. The excess was then ground off to achieve the proper thickness and, finally, it had to be polished. A committee was set up, responsible for plate glass production up to 1939, and chiefly concerned with the reduction and even elimination altogether of the cumbersome and costly grinding and polishing operations after the war.

One of the engineers recruited was (Sir) Alastair Pilkington, who remarkably was not related in any way to the St. Helens' family. He was the second son of Mr. L.G. Pilkington, whose branch of the family had broken away at least 15 generations earlier. Despite the long-standing tradition of keeping the control of the company in the family, the board of directors finally agreed that this remote member of the family could be accepted as a potential director. He was offered a family traineeship in 1947, which exposed him to the company's operations firsthand. He soon recognized the company's overriding problem and began to work on its solution. By 1952 he was attending the manufacturing conference and was elected to the executive committee the following year at the age of 32. His solution was the successful implementation of the float glass process.

A provisional application for the first British patent in the float glass series was filed in December 1953 in the names of Alastair Pilkington and (much to his surprise) Kenneth Bicker-staff, in respect of his work on tin as a conveyor. Six years later, after much experimenting, the first public announcement was made on January 20, 1959, but no saleable glass was produced for 15 months from start-up. Development cost of 300,000 pounds and losses of 1,300,000 pounds were incurred before the process was established on a profitable basis in the fiscal year 1962-1963. The first foreign licence was granted to the Pittsburgh Plate Glass Company in the same period. By 1976, 21 licences had been issued.

In order to control the market and at the same time reap the greatest benefit from the invention, Pilkington placed limitations on the number and scope of licences it would grant. Licences would only be available to existing flat glass manufacturers, who could only convert their existing plate capacity to float. The licencee's export rights were limited to areas where the company had traditionally exported. Pilkington thus preserved the competitive status quo while protecting for itself locations where increasing demands from automobile manufacturers and builders might have made a float glass plant viable. Canada was a case in point. While Libbey-Owens-Ford produced more than enough float glass in the United States to equip Canadian-built cars, it could only export a small portion of its surplus to Canada, since Canada was not one of its established export markets. Over the 16-year life of the agreement, Pilkington expected to collect over $100,000,000 in royalties.

The year 1965 was an eventful one for the Canadian operations. A major development in Canadian-U.S. economic relations took place with the signing of the Automotive Products Agreement, which was designed to increase the Canadian content of automobiles made in North America. In effect, this opened up the entire North American automobile industry as a potential market for the high-quality glass produced by the float process. In anticipation of heavy demands on the company's working capital, Pilkington decided to get out of the paint business and concentrate on the manufacture of glass. This potential, combined with increasing demands for glazing of buildings, convinced Pilkington that they should establish a float glass plant in Canada. In November 1965 construction started on the Scarborough site, and by January 1967, after an expenditure of over $30,000,000, the plant with one line of float started production. An official opening took place on June 14, 1967. A second float line was started in 1969 and was operating in 1970, bringing total employment to about 900.

On November 14, 1978, the name was changed to Pilkington Glass Industries Limited, and in July 1981 the Canadian Foreign Investment Review Agency granted approval for the Ford Motor Co. (U.S.) to acquire a 51-percent interest in Pilkington's Canadian operation. The name was changed to Ford Glass Limited on February 8, 1982. In 1984 Ford acquired the remaining 49 percent of the company.

CANADIAN LIBBEY-OWENS SHEET GLASS COMPANY LIMITED
Hamilton, Ontario (1920-1922)

While Pilkington was enjoying limited success with its sheet glass operation in Thorold, Ontario, Irving W. Colburn, in Toledo, Ohio, was making great strides with his new flat drawn process, which drew a sheet of glass upwards from a tank of molten glass, over a roller, and into a horizontal annealing lehr.

In 1906 Colburn incorporated the Colburn Machine Glass Company and started experiments with his process. Lack of finances soon made further experimentation impossible. Michael J. Owens convinced Edward Libbey of Toledo Glass Company to buy out the patents. As a result, the Libbey-Owens Sheet Glass Company was formed in 1916. After establishing their operations in the United States, they sought licences in other countries. The first licence was granted to the American-Japan Sheet Glass Company in 1919, after which Libbey-Owens turned to Canada.

Ralph King, a director of Dominion Glass and manager of their Toronto and Hamilton plants, had for many years kept in touch with Edward Libbey and Michael Owens of the Toledo Glass Company — ever since the Owens bottle machine had been operated successfully on a commercial basis. Libbey had taken out a Canadian patent in 1908 and on subsequent improvements. In order to protect these patents, which would expire about 1920, they were anxious to have a factory built in Canada. Discussions ensued between Libbey and Owens, resulting in the decision to build a plant in Hamilton, Ontario. King then approached John W. Hobbs of Consolidated Plate Glass Company Limited, Toronto, who as a large glass distributor would naturally be interested. As a result, Canadian Libbey-Owens Sheet Glass Company Limited was incorporated in 1920 and, by agreement with Libbey-Owens Sheet Glass, operated the Colburn process on a royalty basis.

It was decided to build the factory in Hamilton (on Kenilworth Avenue). Unfortunately, Libbey-Owens insisted that they have charge of the construction, under the guidance of Owens, despite the fact that King was fully qualified to handle it himself. The plant was grossly overbuilt, costing more than twice the original estimate of $1,000,000. The tanks were constructed to use natural gas for melting. Unfortunately, no tests had been made of the local supply and, when production started up, the gas was found to contain too much sulphur. Consequently, the tanks and the firing ports had to be converted to the use of producer gas, at a cost estimated to be in excess of $100,000. Automatic cutting machines were installed, but these had to be converted to hand operations because of the expected resistance from the Glass Cutters Union.

The additional financing for the above operating changes was provided by Libbey-Owens in Toledo, Canadian Libbey-Owens, and the directors of the latter. The following directors and officers were appointed: Ralph King, director and president; John W. Hobbs, director and vice-president; William Ford, managing director; J.T. Richardson, director and secretary-treasurer; Seth B. Henshaw, director.

Although there is no present knowledge of when actual production commenced, it was reported at a directors' meeting on July 6, 1921, that No. 1 Tank was providing molten glass to the Colburn machine, which was producing flat glass 72 inches wide. The plant operated two machines on a regular basis through 1922 and then shut down shortly thereafter.

In Libbey-Owens' drive to broaden their market for the Colburn process, they licenced Mutuelle Mobilière et Immobilière of Belgium. Starting in 1925, La Compagnie International pour la Fabrication Mécanique du Verre (Mecaniver) arranged to have Canadian Libbey-Owens market their flat glass products in Canada.

In 1930 the Honourable R.B. Bennett became the Prime Minister of Canada, heading a Conservative government. In the middle of the Depression (1929-1933) unemployment was rampant and the government sought every avenue to relieve the situation. Bennett, accompanied by John W. Hobbs, visited the Hamilton operation with a view to increasing the tariff protection if the plant was reopened. On being referred to the parent company in Toledo, they suggested a level of duties based on import duties into the United States but slightly higher. The higher duties were submitted to the government in Ottawa and legislation was passed ratifying them. It would appear that Toledo really had no intention of restarting the Hamilton plant. When they were advised that the higher duties had been approved, they stated that they were not prepared to assist in further financing the operation. As a result, the government cancelled the legislation covering the increase.

This ended Canadian Libbey-Owens' operations as a producing company. The plant was leased and eventually sold. The company, however, has continued to operate in Toronto as a distributor for various types of flat glass imported from other countries.

CANADIAN PITTSBURGH INDUSTRIES GROUP

Seventeen years after Canadian Libbey-Owens ceased production in Hamilton, in 1922, a new independent company was formed in the Montreal area and became the base plant for what will be referred to as the Canadian Pittsburgh Industries Group.

INDUSTRIAL GLASS WORKS (1940-1946)
INDUSTRIAL GLASS COMPANY LIMITED
St. Laurent, Quebec (1946-1949)

Industrial Glass was the brainchild of Alexis Nihon. He had come from Belgium after the First World War to seek his fortune in Canada, variously as a butcher, grocer, vegetable importer and hardware merchant. With the onset of World War II, he anticipated that European and English imports would certainly be curtailed, if not stopped. Moreover, he realized that there was no flat glass being made in Canada at that time.

Together with some Belgo-Canadian friends, he established a partnership under the name Industrial Glass in St. Laurent, a suburb of Montreal, to make sheet glass for the local and eastern Canadian market. The plant was situated on Napoleon St. and started production in the summer of 1941, using a five-hundred-ton furnace (150 feet by 50 feet) which had a daily output of about 75 tons, and from which three Fourcault machines produced about 100,000 square feet of quarter-inch drawn glass. When in full operation, the factory employed 350 workers, with an annual production of $3,000,000. Although the plant burned down in 1945, it was immediately rebuilt.

In 1946 the company obtained a federal charter in the name of Industrial Glass Company Limited. By then, Nihon had bought out his partners and had 100-percent control. The war was over in Europe and, with the return of production, exports were resumed to Canada. This presented a very serious challenge for this small independent, which thus far had only had to share the Canadian market with American producers. To add to Nihon's problems, Pilkington was rumoured to be reassessing the potential of the Canadian market with a view to reestablishing a production facility there after an absence of 22 years. (Pilkington actually started a new facility near Toronto in 1951.) Whether all this proved too much for Nihon is not known, but in 1949 he sold out to Pittsburgh Plate Glass in the United States.

CANADIAN INDUSTRIAL GLASS COMPANY LTD.
(as a private company)
St. Laurent, Quebec (1949-1950)

This company was incorporated under federal charter. Lt. Col. W.E. Phillips, a legend in the Canadian flat glass industry, was appointed president and later became chairman. To manage the plant, Pittsburgh Plate Glass arranged to transfer Jean Peeters from its Belgian subsidiary to St. Laurent to manage the facility in November 1949. Peeters had been sent to Pittsburgh Plate Glass in Pittsburgh as a trainee but, with the outbreak of war in Europe, he had returned to Belgium to enlist in the armed forces. At the end of hostilities, he returned to Belgium. In 1950 the name of the company was changed to Canadian Pittsburgh Industries Limited to more readily relate it to the parent company in the United States.

CANADIAN PITTSBURGH INDUSTRIES LIMITED,
St. Laurent, Quebec (1950-1968)
Owen Sound, Ontario (1968-1975)

The first step was to replace the Fourcault process with the more advanced Pennvernon process. Three more machines were installed, with a capacity of 150 tons a day. A standard Pittsburgh melting furnace — 1,200 to 1,400 tons — drawing about 250 tons a day, could handle the requirements of four of these machines. The number of machines per furnace was eventually increased to ten. In 1953 the company altered the capital structure by designating the 200,000 shares as common shares, without nominal or par value and increasing the capital stock of the company by creating 70,000 nonparticipating redeemable preferred shares of the par value of $100 each.

The new company further consolidated its position in Canada by acquiring the Murphy Paint Co. in Montreal and the Hobbs Glass Co., a secondary glass manufacturer, in Toronto (1946). During this decade, most of Canadian Pittsburgh's production went to the U.S. By the early sixties, demand for sheet glass in Canada raised the question of the best way to expand production facilities. To this end, 72 acres of land were purchased in Owen Sound, Ontario, at the foot of Bruce Peninsula, on which a $22,000,000 plant was built, under the direction of Bob James, who had been recalled from Pittsburgh Plate Glass's subsidiary in Italy. Construction started in 1965 but, due to an 18-month strike in the building trade, the first glass didn't roll off the line until February 1968.

Jean Peeters was transferred from St. Laurent to become the first plant manager. The plant regularly employed 500-600, and produced sheet, tempered and insulating glass units. With Owen Sound running smoothly at the beginning of the seventies, St. Laurent was only used for experimentation and for additional production when demand exceeded the capacity of the Owen Sound plant. St. Laurent was eventually closed in 1975, and its manager was moved to Owen Sound to become assistant plant manager. The St. Laurent buildings were razed in 1978 and the property was sold.

With further diversification, the U.S. company changed its name to PPG Industries Inc. on April 1, 1968. On May 1, 1975, the Canadian operations were renamed PPG Industries Canada Ltd. and the Owen Sound operation became the CPI Division of that company.

At the same time, PPG had been experimenting with a variation of the float process. By 1970 it had successfully developed its own version, which it called the PPG Flat Glass process. The principal difference between the two processes was that, whereas Pilkington poured the molten glass onto the molten tin bath, PPG drew a ribbon of molten glass across it. The principal advantage was that, in the latter process, the ribbon of glass could be drawn much thinner than in the Pilkington process, and thus it gave PPG the opportunity to provide a broader range of thicknesses to the trade. They claimed better quality and cost advantages in the lower ranges (.050 to .125). Jean Peeters retired in July 1977 and was succeeded by Don Clarke.

LT. COL. W.E. PHILLIPS, DSO, MC, CBE (1893-1964)

No history of the Canadian flat glass industry would be complete without acknowledging its indebtedness to Eric Phillips. Coming out of World War I service as a Lt. Colonel, he started up the W.E. Phillips Company in Oshawa, Ontario, in 1922, dealing in picture framing accessories. In 1924, with the advent of the closed sedan as an alternative to the open touring car, he became involved in plate glass, jobbing for the automobile industry as well as the construction trade. In Canada, Phillips set up a partnership arrangement with Duplate Corp., under the name Duplate Safety Glass Company of Canada Limited, to mould flat glass provided by Pilkington Glass and PPG Industries Inc. It was operating successfully by 1930.

In 1933 Phillips, through Duplate, acquired the Canadian rights to the tempered glass process. Three years later, Pilkington and Pittsburgh Plate Glass jointly financed the construction of a new plant at Windsor, Ontario, to service the Chrysler Co. In 1938 Pilkington (Canada) and Duplate Corp. acquired the W.E. Phillips Co., retaining Phillips as chairman. In 1947 Phillips offered Pilkington 85 percent of his holdings in Duplate, but was turned down. However, Pittsburgh Plate Glass accepted it and Phillips was elected to the Pittsburgh Plate Glass board.

At the beginning of World War II, Col. Phillips became involved in the optical glass business as president of Research Enterprises Ltd., a C.D. Howe company. Other special war materials were also produced under the same roof. Various Duplate operations under his general direction made plastic parts and special tools. His efforts were recognized by a CBE.

In 1961 Col. Phillips resigned as president of Duplate, but remained as chairman of the board. At Christmas 1964, while convalescing at Palm Springs, California, from an earlier heart attack, he had a second attack and died at the age of 71.

FEDERAL GLASS COMPANY, LIMITED
Toronto, Ontario (1926)

This company was incorporated "(a) to manufacture, buy and sell both wholesale and retail and to import, export and otherwise deal in and with any and all of the following, namely, all kinds of plate and window glass, mirrors, signs, patterned glass, metal and glass store fronts, and all other and every kind of glass work whatsoever . . ."
No other action appears to have been taken.

FOOTNOTES

[1] Professor T.C. Barker, *The Glassmakers*, (London: Weidenfeld and Nicolson, 1977), p. 2.
[2] Ibid, pp. 56, 57.
[3] Ibid, p. 284.
[4] See Chapter 4, Early Canadian Glasshouses (c.1840-1878), "The Saint Lawrence Glass Company."
[5] Declaration deposited in Registry Office, Longueuil, Quebec, August 1849.

CHAPTER 12

The Contemporary Scene (1967-1980)

Dominion Glass (1967-1976)
Domglas Ltd. (1976-1978)
Domglas Inc. (1978-   )
Consumers Glass (1967-1980)
Ahlstrom Canada Limited, Scoudouc,
New Brunswick (1968-1979)
Ahlstrom Limited (1979-1980)
Domglas (Atlantic) Ltd. (1981)

DOMINION GLASS COMPANY, LIMITED
Montreal, Quebec (1967-1976)

In 1967 Expo attracted millions of people to Montreal. The company participated in a minor way by contributing to the building of the Pavillion of Economic Progress, where it maintained a pied-à-terre for its friends and associates. It was also a turning point in the history of the company. On Friday afternoon, May 26, after the close of the Montreal Stock Exchange, a group representing Power Corporation of Canada Limited and Bathurst Paper Limited (now Consolidated-Bathurst Inc.) advised Norman Meldrum, vice-president and general manager, and myself that in the next morning's *Gazette* there would appear an offer to purchase all outstanding shares of Dominion Glass — which they achieved over the next few years.

A comprehensive examination of the company was undertaken by management and outside consultants. As a result, a new management team was implemented over the next two years. L.J. Belnap, chairman of the board since 1955, was replaced by F.N. Dundas, who had been moved up from president, E.A. "Tommy" Thompson, formerly an officer of Domtar, became president. Ewart G. Blyth, previously chief financial officer, was appointed vice-president, finance and administration. W. Harry Shotton was recruited from American Motors to become vice-president, manufacturing, replacing Jim Mackenzie, who retired in December 1966 with 51 years of service.

With the retirement of Jim Mackenzie, a unique program of recognition was carried out in the company over the next 13 years. A series of commemorative bottles were made. Using a two-piece bottle mould, one half was engraved to produce a likeness of Jim Mackenzie and on the other half was engraved a listing of his numerous appointments during his years of service. A limited edition was produced and given to those present at his retirement dinner. Similar commemorative bottles were made and distributed on the retirements of: James A. Caskie, who started in 1924 and retired in 1972 as plant manager at Hamilton; George S. Mendell, who started in 1923 and retired in 1974 as manager, production development; Thomas B. King, who started in 1932 and retired in 1978 as corporate secretary; Gene L. Yachetti, who started in 1931 and retired in 1978 as manager, mould design and manufacture; Arthur G. Bowes, who started

Dominion Glass retirement bottles, from left to right, T.B. King (1932-1978), J.R. Mackenzie (1915-1966), G.L. Yachetti (1931-1978), J.A. Caskie (1924-1972), A.G. Bowes (1940-1979) and G.S. Mendell (1923-1974).

Photograph by Graetz, Montreal.

in 1940 and retired in 1979 as director, marketing services. These six employees had a combined service of 283 years, or an average of 47.

Capital expenditures for 1967 totalled $2,960,178, an increase of $1,282,617 from the previous year. An additional furnace and machine capacity was planned for the Burnaby plant at a cost of $5,000,000. Sales reached a new high of $57,895,917. The biggest contributor to this record figure was an 82-percent increase in the sales of no-deposit sodas. Due to an increase in demand for containers in southwestern Ontario, No. 2 furnace at Wallaceburg was doubled in capacity at a cost of $2,264,000. The company's year-end was changed from September 30 to December 31, to fall in line with those of Consolidated and Power.

Joe Souccar, a consultant and formerly with Atlas Steel, was named vice-president, marketing, to replace Bill Davidson, vice-president, sales, who died in October 1968 after 40 years of service.

Changes on the board are reflected in the following lists:

1966		1968	
L.J. Belnap	F.N. Dundas	R. Chagnon	[2]J. Parisien
R. Chagnon	T.B. King	H.R. Crabtree	E.A. Thompson
R.W. Cooper	N.W. Meldrum	[1]R.A. Irwin	H.M. Turner
H.R. Crabtree	H.E. Sellers, C.B.E.	H.H. Lank	[1]W.I.M. Turner, Jr.
K.T. Dawes	H.M. Turner	[2]P.B. Paine, Q.C.	[1]J.R. Yarnell

[1] Representing Consolidated-Bathurst
[2] Representing Power Corporation

Net earnings for the calendar year 1968 were 85 cents per common share, compared to two cents in the previous year. Bill Turner of Consolidated-Bathurst replaced Fred Dundas as chairman when Dundas retired after 33 years of service. Approval was given for the construction of a new plant in the Toronto area (Bramalea) at an estimated cost of $15,000,000. The plant was in operation in 1970. In the same year, the well-known trademark, the diamond D, which had identified the company's products over the past 40 years, was replaced by a new symbol to recognize the reorganized company. This symbol was in the form of a mould (purple) full of molten glass (orange) .

The year 1970 was one of substantial achievement. National Pressed Glass Limited (Brantford, Ontario), a producer of fuse plug cases and percolator tops, was acquired on January 1. Annual sales for Dominion Glass totalling $76,861,499 were adversely affected by British Columbia legislation which placed a mandatory refund of two cents on all beer and soft drink cans, bottles and plastic containers. Beer and ale were sold primarily in returnable bottles and this legislation had little effect on the company's sales to the brewing industry. In the soft drink industry, it was expected that some of the loss of one-trip bottle volume would be replaced by returnable bottle volume. Specialized facilities were installed at Wallaceburg to supply high-quality glass containers to the cosmetic and pharmaceutical industries.

During the previous three years (1968-1970), over $40,000,000 had been spent to increase the company's productivity and modernize its facilities. To reestablish a proper cash position, the company floated a $25,000,000 debenture early in 1971. A new central applied research and development department was set up at Bramalea by Dr. George Simmons, technical director, to consolidate the company's technical staff and facilities.

Environmental problems were becoming more prominent, particularly in the area of convenience-type packaging in paper, metal, glass and plastics. The word coined to describe this problem was "littering." Through the two applicable trade associations, the Glass Container Council of Canada and the Glass Container Manufacturers Institute Inc. in the United States, the North American glass industry contributed extensively in seeking a solution. The main thrust was to try to convince government authorities that littering could not be eliminated by changing the nature of the objects (the litter), but by educational programs directed to the general public (the cause of littering). Properly serviced public litter receptacles were advocated, as well as the need for practical and adequate anti-littering laws, and finally, an effective method of changing the behaviour of people who litter. Solid waste disposal programs were developed in the following years to establish effective reclamation and recycling arrangements. This all added up to a policy of Aggressive Ecology.

In February 1971 Paul Paine, executive vice-president and general counsel for Power Corporation, replaced Bill Turner as chairman of the board. Net income and production for the year was seriously affected by strikes at the four eastern plants (Montreal, Bramalea, Hamilton and Wallaceburg). They were finally settled by September 1971. In 1972 sales were up from $73,523,042 in 1971 to $93,015,785. Net income after taxes was $1,979,469, compared to a loss of $1,313,025 in the previous year.

In 1973, for the first time in the company's history, sales exceeded one hundred million dollars ($100,767,990). In the third quarter, the company sold its in-house plastics operation to Twinpak Ltd., at the same time acquiring a 50-percent interest. A second furnace was added at National Pressed Glass in Brantford.

In December 1973 Harry Shotton announced plans for the construction of a technical centre, which would be located in Sheridan Park Research Community in Mississauga, some 12 miles west of Toronto on the Queen Elizabeth Highway. The centre was originally planned to centralize the research, development and engineering capabilities of the company, as well as to set up an experimental glass forming unit at a later date. (This unit was later cancelled.)

In May 1973 the chairmanship of the company was relinquished by Paul Paine on his appointment as president of Montreal Trust Company. Bill Turner was appointed to replace him in that position and John B. Aird, Q.C., replaced Mr. Paine on the board.

Ever since 1925 the company had centralized the production of tableware and industrial ware at Wallaceburg. As part of a program to exploit these lines, in 1974 the company renamed this operation the "St. Clair division." At the same time a new logo was adopted for use on the production and packaging of its products. Phil Jacobs was appointed general manager and was responsible for introducing new and more attractive lines for the retail trade. This included production of coloured tableware for the first time.

During the summer of 1974 the technical centre at Sheridan Park was opened and the personnel working on research, development, engineering and technical projects in Montreal, Bramalea and Hamilton were transferred to this location. Later in the year, as part of a program to broaden the company's activities, Dominion purchased all shares of Dorchester Electronics Limited in Toronto, a manufacturer of home entertainment equipment. By the end of the year, all of the preferred shares and 95 percent of the common shares of Dominion had been acquired by Consolidated-Bathurst as the result of a public offer.

Despite the economic slowdown in 1975, there was an increase in consolidated net sales to $131,134,650. Two-year labour agreements were effected at five of the six glass container plants. Bramalea ratified an agreement a little later.

In August 1975 Mr. Thompson, while remaining as president and chief executive officer of Dominion Glass, was also appointed vice-president, packaging, of Consolidated-Bathurst Limited and president of Consolidated-Bathurst Packaging Limited. Mr. J.E. Souccar was appointed to the newly created position of executive vice-president of Dominion Glass, and Mr. R.J. Simpson was appointed to succeed Souccar as vice-president, marketing.

The company purchased the balance of 50-percent interest in Twinpak from Consolidated-Bathurst (TP) Limited in May 1976. National Pressed Glass was renamed National Pressed Glass (1976) Ltd. In the same month, the company changed its name to Domglas Ltd. and the French equivalent, Domglas Ltée. Mr. Thompson was elected chairman of the board, and Joe Souccar became president and a director.

In 1977, as the result of discussions with Diamond Glass in Royersford, Pennsylvania, it was agreed that the company would purchase a 25-percent interest in Diamond's holding company, D.G.H.C. Inc., for $2,000,000. The shares were registered in the name of Consolidated-Bathurst, but Domglas management was to be directly involved in the day-to-day activities.

In 1978 Domglas Ltd. was amalgamated with Consolidated-Bathurst (DG) Limited to become Domglas Inc. National Pressed Glass Ltd. and National Pressed Glass (1976) Ltd. were dissolved and the operation became a branch plant of Domglas. In May a joint 50-50 venture was created by the company and Owens-Illinois Inc., Toledo, Ohio, to take over the St. Clair division in Wallaceburg. The new name was Libbey-St. Clair Inc. As a result, and because of the reduction in container production at facilities in Wallaceburg, $7,716,000 was approved to rebuild and enlarge No. 2 furnace in Hamilton to handle the demand.

In October approval was granted to add a third furnace at Bramalea, at a cost of $9,500,000, to meet the increasing domestic and export demand for green glass, the latter demand for which was the result of the success Molson's Brewery was enjoying in exporting their products in one-way green beer bottles to the United States.

As the result of a continuing loss position, Dorchester Electronics was sold during 1980 for $4,260,000. In December a new building was erected in the Hamilton area, at a cost of $2,526,000, to house the central mould shop, the mould engineering group, the computer-aided design function and the Dot Pattern Works, which had previously been located on the Hamilton plant property.

CONSUMERS GLASS COMPANY, LIMITED (1967-1980)

In November 1966 the $6,000,000 expansion program undertaken at the company's Etobicoke plant was completed. This included a new furnace and related facilities. On May 26, 1967, Consumers' shares were listed on the Toronto Stock Exchange. The company issued $6,176,000 in debentures.

In 1967, in its 50th year of operations, the company attained record levels of sales and earnings. In April 1967 it acquired the Iroquois (glass) division of Sogemines Limited at Candiac,

Quebec, for $9,926,000, thus adding three glass tanks and ten IS Emhart glass machines. Iroquois had been turning out flint, amber, emerald and georgia green glass.

The year 1968 saw the breaking of ground at Lavington, British Columbia, for the first company plant in the West, estimated cost of which was ten million dollars. The company received a Gold Award from the Canadian Packaging Association for its work with rigid containers. The Glass Container Industry Research Association, of which both Dominion and Consumers were members, conducted some experiments in advanced glassmaking techniques at the company's plant.

The Lavington plant came on stream in 1969 and the company's program of expansion and diversification continued with a 38-percent interest ($2,398,000) in Glass Containers Limited, Australia, a new glass container company jointly established by Consumers and Australian interests, with V.S.B. Corbet, a Consumers vice-president, as managing director. Three plastics operations were also acquired.

To better control and report on its diversified operations, the company was reorganized into three divisions — glass, plastics and metals — in 1970. Some management changes were made in 1971. Mr. A.F. Griffiths resigned as executive vice-president and was replaced by R.D. Morison. At the same time, P.R. Holland became senior vice-president, sales and marketing. In June the Australian facility began production.

Effective January 1, 1973, R.D. Morison succeeded Don Mingay as president and chief executive officer. In 1974 net profits were down considerably due to a long strike at the Etobicoke plant and a slowing of the growth rate in certain segments of the glass container market.

The company purchased 80 acres of land in Milton, Ontario (near Toronto), for future manufacturing expansion, and an additional glass furnace was added at the Iroquois plant. The year 1974 saw a return to a more normal net profit after taxes — $6,617,000 (1973 - $920,000).

Because of Brockway Glass's interest (18.9 percent) in Consumers, a 1975 ministerial ruling under the Foreign Investment Review Act (FIRA) was obtained, certifying that Consumers Glass was a Canadian company. In conjunction with its operations, the company negotiated a favourable long-term agreement with its bankers, the Bank of Montreal, which provided $21,000,000 in term financing over a ten-year period.

In order to comply with the regulations of the Anti-Inflation Board in 1977, a justified price increase was delayed for one month and thus reduced net earnings by nearly half a million dollars.

The year 1978 was a banner one for the company. Consolidated net sales were $149,463,000, a 25-percent increase over the previous year. Consolidated net income (before extraordinary income of $1,862,000) increased to $8,903,000, compared to $3,876,000 in 1977. Construction started on a glass plant at the Milton, Ontario, site which would complement the already operating warehousing and distribution centre.

In 1979 dividends were increased from 20 cents to 25 cents per share. After reflecting a two-for-one share split earlier in the year, this increased the annual dividend from 80 cents to one dollar. Equity in the Australian operation was increased to 45 percent.

The Milton plant started up in May 1980, the first major addition to the company's glass division since the start up of the Lavington plant in 1969.

AHLSTROM CANADA LIMITED
Scoudouc, New Brunswick (1968-1979)

Glassmaking in the Maritime provinces has had its ups and downs over the last hundred years. With the exception of Humphreys' Glass, which started in Trenton, Nova Scotia, in 1890, and ended its days in Moncton, New Brunswick, in 1920, most of the others were short lived. There were several reasons for this situation. Glassware at competitive prices was being shipped in from the New England states, the demand for glassware in this part of Canada was somewhat limited and, finally, the transportation cost to service the trade in Quebec and Ontario was prohibitive.

In the first half of the twentieth century, both Dominion and Consumers made feasibility studies to determine the viability of operating a bottlemaking plant in the Maritimes, but neither could justify such an action.

Ahlstrom Canada was incorporated in 1968. It was a wholly-owned subsidiary of A. Ahlstrom Osakeyhtio, Helsinki, Finland, which for over 150 years has been a leader in the pulp and paper industry, with extensive interests in engineering and glassmaking. The name of the company recognizes its founder, Antti Ahlström.

The impetus actually came from the government of New Brunswick, who had sent a trade mission to Europe to try to attract labour-intensive industry to the province to bolster its struggling economy. Scoudouc was central to the Maritime provinces, with excellent rail and water transportation. The site of the plant was a former Royal Canadian Air Force base, which is now part of the Greater Moncton Industrial Park. The few remaining hangars were easily adaptable to warehousing for the company's products.

Both the provincial and federal governments provided financial assistance, supplemented by an advance of three-quarters of a million dollars from the parent company. Construction of the facility was completed in June 1969 and actual production started shortly thereafter, with one furnace and one Hartford-Empire "IS" six-section bottle-forming machine, the present world-standard machine.

The plant is laid out for straight line production. That is, raw materials are received and stored at one end, then mechanically fed into the furnace. At the hot end, the forming machines convert the gobs of molten glass into bottles. They, in turn, are transferred by conveyors into the open end of the long annealing lehrs. At the cold end, the packers select (inspect) the hand-cool bottles and pack them into previously set up cartons. The packed ware is then moved to the warehouses pending shipping instructions. Employment averages 200.

Through scheduled colour changes of the furnace, flint, green and amber ware was produced. Production over the years has been limited primarily to servicing the beverage industry — soft drinks, spirits, wine and beer — although some ware has been made for the food processors. The main raw materials were sourced as follows: sand by ship, via Shediac or Pugwash, from Belgium; soda from Allied Chemicals (Ontario); lime from Havelock Lime Works, Havelock, New Brunswick; miscellaneous chemicals were Canadian or came through Canadian agencies; cullet from recycled bottles was made on site. Energy for melting the glass batch was Bunker "C" oil, with propane as a standby.

In the first ten years, as the company achieved deeper market penetration, facilities were substantially increased. In 1971 a second furnace was added and enlarged three years later to handle increased demand. Three more I.S. machines were installed with their ancillary equipment.

In 1977 Jan Gube was sent out from Finland to replace Stephen Rigby, who had been vice-president and general manager. In his capacity as president, Gube became directly responsible for the day-to-day operations of the company. In step with improved operating techniques, costs were reduced by installing fully automatic (instead of hand) inspection, packaging and palletizing equipment.

At the same time, Brian Bezanson, a Canadian, was appointed controller. It is interesting to note that Brian was related by marriage to the famous Humphreys glassmaking family. His aunt, Helen Bezanson, was married to Gordon Humphreys of Trenton, Nova Scotia. It was Gordon's father, Benjamin, and his two brothers, Jock and Ephraim, who had founded Humphreys' Glass Works.

On August 20, 1979, the company's name was changed to Ahlstrom Limited. Under the new and dynamic leadership of Mr. Gube, a four-point expansion plan was set up:

1. No. 1 furnace, built in 1976, with a capacity of 90 tons a day, would require rebuilding within a year.
2. The two forming machines on this furnace were too small to operate economically under current operating conditions and were also in need of costly overhauls or replacement. More modern machines were being considered with the replacement of the furnace.

Domglas plant, Scoudouc, New Brunswick, formerly Ahlstrom Canada.   Courtesy Domglas (Atlantic) Limited.

3. Since it had not been possible to operate a glass plant economically for the small size and lack of growth in the Maritimes area, markets would have to be sought elsewhere. With the rest of Canada being well serviced by the other bottle manufacturers, and also because of the high freight rates to central Canada, the company was now looking to the success of Canadian beer export to the United States. To this end, a local Maritime brewery was in the process of installing considerable added brewing capacity to meet the increasing demand for this growing market. It was therefore planned that in conjunction with the upcoming rebuilding of No. 1 furnace, the necessary changes in production techniques would be incorporated to handle this new potential demand. The proposed investment would allow the company to continue to cover a 65-80 percent of the Maritime market for items like the standard nonrefillable 300 ml bottle, the nonrefillable 750 ml bottle, amber beer bottles, and a number of refillables. The production capacity would then be increased to handle this and other high-volume lines. It was hoped that there would also be some further penetration of the Ontario and Quebec markets.

4. To assist the company in staying abreast of all the latest technology, a long-term Trade Secret and Technical Assistance Agreement was signed with Owens-Illinois Inc. of Toledo, Ohio. (O-I is the largest glass bottle producer in the world, with some 21 plants in the United States and control of companies in 17 other countries.)

On December 3, 1981, the company was taken over by Domglas Inc. and renamed Domglas (Atlantic) Ltd. On January 1, 1982, it became the Scoudouc plant of the company.

Furnaces and hood in the studio of Harvey Littleton. The Glory Hole for reheating glass during working and before annealing is the second from right.   Courtesy of Harvey Littleton.

CHAPTER 13

Flameworking and Contemporary Glassblowing

Flameworking, Commercial (Lampworking)
Beaver Flint Glass (1896-1939)
Richards Glass (1912-1977)
O.H. Johns Glass, Toronto (1928-   )
Flameworking, Individual
Contemporary Glassblowing, Commercial
Altaglass, Medicine Hat, Alberta (1950-   )
Lorraine Glass, Montreal (1962-1974)
Chalet Artistic Glass (1963-1980)
Rossi Artistic Glass, Cornwall, Ontario (1981-   )
Continental Glass, Calgary (1963-c.1974)
Studio Glassblowing

FLAMEWORKING, COMMERCIAL

THE BEAVER FLINT GLASS COMPANY OF TORONTO (LIMITED)
Toronto, Ontario (1896-1939)

This company's proper place in the Canadian glass industry has been subject to discussion over the years. To the best of my knowledge, no hard evidence has surfaced to indicate that it was a primary glass manufacturer, i.e. glass articles made from raw materials, at least not on a commercial basis.

Stevens, in his book *Early Canadian Glass*, was of the opinion that the Beaver fruit jar, a collector's item (particularly a left-facing Beaver in amber glass), had been made there, but two well-recognized Canadian glass researchers, John R. Sheeler and John C. Barclay, both of whom live in southwestern Ontario, have conclusively established the fact that the Beaver jars were made at Ontario Glass and at Sydenham Glass around the turn of the century.[2]

Beaver Flint was a secondary manufacturer and used a flame to convert glass rod and tubing into articles for the pharmaceutical trade. The man behind the formation of this company was Robert William Lowden, stepson of John Lowden, the principal founder of Independent Glass, who had moved to Toronto from Montreal. The company received its charter in 1896. The display advertisement for Beaver Flint Glass, first appearing in Toronto directories in 1897, suggests this line of development:

> The Beaver Flint Glass Co. of Toronto (Limited)
> Manufacturers and Importers of
> Druggists', Chemists', and Scientific Glassware
> Specialties: Homeopathic vials, glass tubing, all styles of
> Glass Syringes, Screw cap vials, test tubes and
> Special Chemical Appliances.
> Office and Factory
> Cor. Winchester and Parliament Sts.
> Telephone No. 3110.

Speculation here would suggest that Robert had been strongly attracted to the glass business by his short interval as traveller for Erie Glass and had maintained that interest during the months following Erie's dissolution. Recognizing at the same time the value of a steadier, if less intriguing, base of commercial activity, he conceived the idea of combining the druggists' sundries business, with which he had become familiar during his first four years in Toronto, with a compatible line of pharmaceutical ware.

As will be seen from various entries in *Might's City Directory for Toronto*, the Lowden family had become deeply involved in the glass industry.

1899 LOWDEN
John/agent Diamond Glass Co. res. Scarboro
John S./traveller Beaver Flint Glass Co. res. Scarboro
Robert W./Manager and secretary-treasurer Beaver Flint Glass Co. res. 94 Winchester Street
Stuart C./Packer Toronto Glass Co. res. 27 Soho St.

1902 LOWDEN
John/(John Lowden & Son) Representing the Diamond Glass Co. Ltd.
John S./(John Lowden & Son)
Stuart C./clerk, Diamond Glass Co.

By comparing the information contained in the 1899 and 1902 Toronto directories listed above, the following pattern emerges:

(1) John (agent for Diamond Glass Co.) and John S. (traveller for Beaver Flint Glass Co.) had joined forces to become "John Lowden & Son," agents for the Diamond Glass Co. of Montreal and Toronto.

(2) Stuart C. Lowden (packer for The Toronto Glass Co.) was a clerk for Diamond Glass Co. and lived with John S. at 1942 Queen St. East.

(3) Most important of all, Robert W. Lowden (secretary-treasurer and manager of the Beaver Flint Glass Co.) was also the secretary-treasurer of J.G. Gibson Marble & Granite Co., Ltd., which was also located at the corner of Winchester and Parliament streets.[3]

The street addresses given for Beaver Flint appear to have been in conflict, but the answer is simple: the building was located at the corner of Winchester and Parliament streets, and the civic numbers 50-52 Winchester and 547 Parliament simply represent entrances on the two sides of the building respectively.[4]

Robert Lowden, through his Beaver Flint Glass, provided training and experience to several others who went on to play important roles in the Canadian glass industry. His nephew Stuart Lowden, John's son, worked as glassblower at Beaver before joining Toronto Glass Company's staff in 1899. Another nephew, John S., worked as traveller for Beaver before joining his father to form "John Lowden & Son" in 1901. A list of shareholders who were also employees, in 1906, includes the names of both Oscar H. Johns and James P. Richards. James Richards joined Beaver Flint Glass shortly after its formation, worked through several positions to become traveller by about 1905, and then left the company in 1912 to found Richards Glass Co. Ltd. Oscar H. Johns started with Beaver at about the same time as Richards did, as glassblower, became superintendent by 1910, left to become foreman at Richards Glass in 1916 and worked there until 1927. In 1927 he left Richards to start his own firm, O.H. Johns Glass Co. Ltd., took his son, Oscar Jr., in with him in 1929 and, like Richards Glass Co., succeeded in creating an organization which still exists today. Richards Glass Co. recently bought control of Johns Glass Co., but the two appear to have established separate enough identities that both names, at separate addresses, are still in current directories and telephone books.

In 1910, while continuing to manage Beaver Flint Glass, Robert Lowden, together with his stepfather (John) and Richard Witt, a glassmaker, established Independent Glass to manufacture glassware.

Beaver Flint Glass became increasingly a family, if not a one-man business, as the years passed. Mr. J.D. Wright died not long after the business started, with his estate holding a one-third share of the company's stock. Robert Lowden became managing director of Beaver Flint in 1910, and by 1925 was president and managing director. He was joined in 1925 by his daughter, Ina R. Lowden, as secretary, and in 1935 by a second daughter, Roberta, as secretary-treasurer. Mr. Lowden retired from an active part in the company and its associated companies early in 1939, and by mid-1942 the entire group was being liquidated, with the charter of Beaver Flint Glass being withdrawn on June 30, 1960.

THE RICHARDS GLASS COMPANY, LIMITED
Toronto, Ontario (1912-1977)

Richards Glass was formed in 1912 under an Ontario charter to establish a secondary glass operation to supply the druggists' trade. It was established by an Englishman, James P. Richards, who emigrated from England at the age of 13. One of his early jobs was with the famous Dr. A.D. Johnson, for whom he worked as general helper and assistant in the laboratory. It was here that he first became interested in glass.

Before setting up his own company, he spent several years with Beaver Flint Glass. Several glassworkers from Beaver Flint joined him in his new enterprise, including O.H. Johns, a master glassworker from Germany. For a period of time, Dominion Glass, which had been established in 1913 to take over the assets of Diamond Flint Glass, financially supported Richards Glass, holding 51 percent of the stock. They also appointed Richards Glass as a distributor for their druggists' and pharmaceutical lines of ware. One of the lines they made for Richards was the RIGO Oval, which was the Richards' trade name for their regular line of medicine bottles.

In 1929 several automatic glass-tubing processing machines and a gas-fired annealing oven were installed — the first in Canada.

In 1930 a division called RIGO Agencies was formed to handle such imported lines as Rolls Razors, MacLean's Toothpaste, Beecham's Pills, etc. The RIGO line was so popular that 24 glassworkers were employed full-time to meet demand. During World War II there was a great demand from the medical services for ampoules and suitable machines were installed. In 1943 Mr. Richards died and his son J. Stanley Richards assumed the presidency.

In 1968, when the facilities at Richards Glass became inadequate, Richards' manufacturing operations were transferred to O.H. Johns Glass (Johns Scientific). The name Richards Glass was changed to Stanrich Sales Inc. in 1977.

O.H. JOHNS GLASS CO., LIMITED
Toronto, Ontario (1928-   )

The proprietor of this company, Oscar Hugo Johns, who rated as one of the top five glassworkers in North America at that time, had come to Hoboken, New Jersey, on the conclusion of a five-year glassworking apprenticeship in Germany. His early years in America were varied. His first job was loading coal cars. He then took the job of a glassworker with a travelling road show. He eventually married the boss's daughter and settled in Toronto.

In 1928 he set up O.H. Johns Glass at 219 Broadview Avenue. His son Housson joined the company soon after and served as president from 1934 to 1970. In 1966 Paul Richards, son of Stanley Richards, joined the company as vice-president.

The company's early specialties included the flameworking of ampoules, blood drop counters, vials and medicine droppers. In 1932 a neon division was added, and for many years tube-bending and glass-housing contributed greatly to the growth of the company. The increasing popularity of plastic signs in the post-war period halted the growth of the neon business. This division was sold in 1966.

During World War II the company, in cooperation with the Department of Defense, manufactured, under special permit, spirit level vials for fire-control instrumentation on various pieces of war equipment, ranging from two-inch mortars to naval guns and turn-and-bank instruments.

In 1948 the company was appointed Canadian distributor for Chance Brothers' (England) cover glasses and Hysil laboratory glassware. Three years later John Sever became the first laboratory sales representative. Since then, the main thrust of production has been directed towards the manufacture and distribution of scientific glassware, instrumentation equipment and supplies. Customers include laboratories in hospitals, universities, government and industry.

FLAMEWORKING, INDIVIDUAL

One of the forums for North American flameworkers is the American Scientific Glassblowers Society, established in the United States about 1955. They held their first annual symposium outside of the United States in Ottawa in 1972. From a report on this symposium and from other sources, the following are a few of the people who have been identified as flameworkers in Canada: W.B. Griner, O.H. Johns, W.R. Eberhart, Len. Chodirker and E.J. Hookway.

WILLIAM BARNETT GRINER

Worked for Burlington Glass in Hamilton, Ontario, in the 1880s and 1890s. In 1893, together with several of his fellow blowers, he left Hamilton to form THE TORONTO GLASS COMPANY (LIMITED). In 1896 he resigned.

OSCAR H. JOHNS

Born in Germany, he came to America, where he did his flameworking with a travelling show out of the state of Michigan. In 1928, with his son Oscar Housson, he started THE O.H. JOHNS GLASS CO., LIMITED in Toronto, Ontario.

WOLFGANG R. EBERHART

Born in Vienna in 1926, at the age of 14 he was the only apprentice ever accepted by masterblower Franz Schuebel. While still in Europe, at the age of 17 he received his first degree in scientific glassblowing and seven years later he received a master's degree. He came to Canada in 1957 and four years later was a senior member of A.S.G.S. (Artistic & Scientific Glassblowers Society). His work is an example of ancient and modern glass craftsmanship, employing sophisticated flameworking techniques. A staff member of the University of Windsor (Ontario), he also maintains a studio.

LEN CHODIRKER

Started his apprenticeship as a flameworker in 1970 in Haifa, Israel, where he spent a year before returning to his home in Winnipeg, Manitoba. In 1973 he was in his third year of Science at the University of Manitoba. Since then he has been actively pursuing his trade, producing small animals in blob form.

ELMER JOHN HOOKWAY

Born in Toronto, Ontario, in 1889, he became interested in flameworking at the age of 15 when he was apprenticed to the Navarras Glassblowers, who worked for travelling shows around the world. After five years of experience he became associated with three Canadian glasshouses — O.H. Johns, Beaver Flint Glass and Richards Glass. In 1927 he formed his own company, Hookway and Rigby, with Walter Rigby and Thomas Gibson Kerr as fellow glassblowers. Two years later the name was changed to E. Hookway Scientific Glassblowing Co. During his lifetime, Hookway made many spectacular pieces, including a model steam engine, merry-go-round, a Ferris wheel and a "lampwork" ship floating on a spun glass sea. In 1952 he made a coronation coach, complete with horses, to commemorate the coronation of Queen Elizabeth II. He retired in 1955 and died in 1974.

CONTEMPORARY GLASSBLOWING, COMMERCIAL

ALTAGLASS
Medicine Hat, Alberta (1950-   )

According to a local newspaper, Altaglass started in 1950 near the Medicine Hat airport, later moving to its present location at 613 16th St. S.W., in the industrial area of the city. The principals are John Furch, master glassblower from Czechoslovakia, and Mrs. Margaret Stagg, who runs the operation. The number of workers vary from seven in the winter to 11 in the summer. Traditionally, glassblowing is curtailed in the summer months because of the heat, but because this is such a tourist attraction, the trend is reversed. Medicine Hat was chosen for the availability of a regular supply of natural gas.

The variety of shapes and objects produced is limited only by the imagination and skill of the glassblowers. However, the favourites have been vases, fish, baskets and free-form pieces, including paperweights. Most of the work is turned out in coloured glass comprising some 15 shades, including clear crystal, red, turquoise, amethyst and Caribbean blue.

The glassblowers contribute their own designs, which are converted into finished ware from a soda-lime batch, to which is added lead oxide to provide clarity. The hollow pieces, such as vases, fish and baskets, are blown on a pipe, whereas the art forms, such as centre pieces, swans and ashtrays, are gathered on a rod and pulled into the final form by tools.

Altaglass products are sold in most larger Canadian cities and, through satisfied customers, requests for pieces have been received from as far away as New Zealand.

LORRAINE GLASS INDUSTRIES LTD.
Montreal, Quebec (1962-1974)

The second company to start making artistic glass in Montreal in the twentieth century was Lorraine Glass. Under the leadership of Earl Myers in 1962, and with the assistance of the federal immigration department, a number of young master glassblowers and their families were flown out from the great glass centre in Murano, Italy, and settled in Pte. St. Charles, a district in southwest Montreal.

The company was incorporated in 1962. A building was erected at 275 Murray Street, with two five-ton tanks for clear soda-lime glass and eight pots for producing the various colours that would be used for a myriad of free-blown pieces of crystal art glass. Production started in 1963, using box lehrs, in which the finished pieces would be allowed to cool slowly to eliminate stress. These lehrs were later replaced with continuous lehrs which could handle 24-hour operations.

The design varieties and combinations of colours in the various pieces were unlimited. These included vases, baskets, centre pieces, bowls, animals, ashtrays and paperweights. In my opinion, the smooth flow of colour from, say, green through blue, then aqua and finally down to a clear crystal base, was certainly in the best traditions of Murano-made pieces. With a work force of about 30, production ran to about 10,000 pieces per month.

Lorraine's products were sold at stores throughout Canada and the United States, and through agents in Australia and New Zealand. To complete the cycle, a successful export business was developed for the European market, where the pieces compared favourably with local production. A certified piece of their production was deposited with the Royal Ontario Museum in Toronto in 1964. It was in the form of a multi-coloured rooster, after the style of the nineteenth-century chanticleer or cock.

In the late 1960s Lorraine started to supply glass components for the Canadian illumination and fixtures industry. Its success can perhaps be measured by the fact that the French government commissioned the company to provide all such glass fixtures needed for a new hotel they were building for the tourist trade in Guadaloupe, in the French West Indies.

The company ceased its manufacturing operations on a decision by the shareholders in December 1974. The year resulted in a loss on operations, and with increased costs of raw materials and natural gas, coupled with demands from the workers for higher wage rates, another unprofitable year was forecast. The furnaces were shut down in December and the work-in-process was finished off and eventually sold against undelivered orders. The standing glassmaking installations were demolished and the building was subsequently sold.

LES INDUSTRIES DE VERRE ET MIROIRS LIMITÉE
Montreal, Quebec (1958-1960)

MURANO GLASS INCORPORATED
Montreal (1960-1962)

CHALET ARTISTIC GLASS LTD./LA VERRERIE ARTISTIQUE CHALET LTÉE
Cornwall, Ontario (1962-1980)

ROSSI ARTISTIC GLASS INC.
Cornwall (1980-   )

This glass company had a chequered career. It started out in Montreal under the name Les Industries de Verre et Miroirs Limitée in 1958. Two years later, by supplementary letters patent, the name was changed to Murano Glass Incorporated. In 1963 a new company, Chalet Artistic Glass, was formed and the operation was moved to Cornwall, Ontario, where the proprietor, S.C. Heyes, and a team of Italian blowers operated a good shop, turning out semi-crystal art glass and stemware. The Cornwall operation was set up in an old building at the corner of Harbour and Edward streets which had belonged to Canadian Cottons.

In the mid-60s I joined a group of GLASFAX members from Montreal and Ottawa spending a day at the works, where we were allowed to watch the blowers at close hand as they created their attractive pieces. Two items of interest in this operation are worth remarking on. The first and most important was their method of guaranteeing that each time they made another run of a specific colour it would be identical to the original colour. To do this they would make a rod of the original colour and code it to each line of ware that used that specific colour. When a line was to be run again, a rod was made in advance which had to exactly match that of the original rod. Failing this, the molten glass in the pot would be thrown out and a new batch made for the next day's operation.

The other interesting item was that all unusable glass, whether from the pot or in the form of imperfect articles, was thrown out a window opening in the side of the building. This formed an increasingly large pile of multi-coloured glass. It could not be used again for cullet because of the mixture of shades and colours. However, for the researcher, it is acceptable evidence of the different colours that were worked in this factory.

In 1981 the Italian blowers took over the operation and renamed it Rossi Artistic Glass Inc.

CONTINENTAL GLASS MANUFACTURING LTD.
Calgary, Alberta (1961-c.1974)

This was one of many small operations established in the 1960s at the time of the renaissance of art glassblowing in North America. The principals were Josef Takacs, a glassblower, and his wife, Gisella. From 1961 to 1963 they operated as a partnership at 520-35th Avenue N.E., employing one or more glassblowers as required. They obtained an Alberta charter as a private company. At about the same time, they moved their operations to 215-35th Avenue N.E., where they remained until about 1974, when they appear to have ceased operations.

Their production consisted of handmade tableware items. I have two of their pieces — an elongated shallow bowl with curled finials at each end, made in flint with a greenish tinge, and an ashtray with elongated turned-up corners, in clear glass with streaks of white through the body.

For failure to file annual returns for the years 1974, 1976 and 1977, the provincial government removed the name of the company from the register on February 28, 1978.

John Littleton and his wife Kate Vogel producing a "Bagged Box" in their studio in Bakersville, North Carolina. Their glass furnace, glory hole, bench and annealing kiln were all constructed by them in the studio.

Photograph courtesy of Harvey Littleton.

STUDIO GLASSBLOWING

Quoting from Harvey Littleton's *Glassblowing — A Search for Form*: "... *There has long been a popular confusion about even the term 'glassblowing' which has been used to mean, as we do in this book, work with the blowpipe using molten glass from the furnace, as well as the traditional use of rods and tubes of glass manipulated in a flame, mainly for the production of scientific glassware...*"[1] The word *flameworking* is currently used to describe *lampworking*.

Glassblowing is the use of molten glass manipulated on a blowpipe for the production of hollow art glass or on a pontil rod for the production of solid art glass including paperweights. This is done either on a commercial scale by a group of glassblowers or in small groups (normally of not more than three) in a studio.

Littleton has been credited with having revived the glass art movement in North America. In 1962 he established a course on glassblowing as part of the arts curriculum at the University of Wisconsin at Madison, where he set up his first studio. Thus, for the first time, glass became the medium for the artist's studio as well as the factory. There are now glassblowing courses at more than 100 colleges and universities in the United States and Canada. In Canada, there have been courses at the Université de Québec à Trois Rivières, the Sheridan College of Applied Art and Technology (Mississauga, Ontario) and the Alberta College of Art and Technology, (Calgary, Alberta).

The movement started in Canada around 1965. Robert Held, who had studied under Mark Peiser at the Penland School of Arts and Crafts in North Carolina, set up a glass study program at Sheridan (Mississauga) four years later. About the same time, Martin Demaine, a former tobacco executive from the United States, set up a studio in a self-made log cabin in the wilds of northern New Brunswick, in Little Bartibogue. Like their predecessors, the glassblowers, these artists have been just as transient and literally "go where the action is."

The configuration of a studio varies according to the requirements of the particular glassblower, who in many cases builds his own equipment. However, there is a basic set-up for all of them. First of all, it is necessary to build a container in which to melt the raw material. In small operations, these are called pots and are made of refractory bricks that are held together with tie rods and angle irons. Normally there is one pot for clear glass and one or more pots for the different colours when a multi-coloured piece is being made. The energy may be natural gas, liquified petroleum such as propane or butane, oil or electricity. In large operations they use tanks, the bottom of which holds the molten glass. A separate pot is often used to keep the ends of the pipes and rods hot so that there is no adverse reaction when they come in contact with the hot glass.

The second item is a "glory hole." This has the appearance of a 40-gallon oil drum, lying on its side on a stand, with an opening at one end about a third the diameter of the drum. When working a piece of glass, it is necessary to reheat the unfinished piece from time to time when it has become too cool to be worked properly. The same source of energy is used for all these pieces.

After this, an annealing oven is required, in which the finished pieces are allowed to cool at a slow and controlled speed to eliminate any strains in the glass. These ovens are heavily insulated to retain the heat, which is controlled from an instrument panel. To complete the equipment, a simple bench with two extended metal arms is used by the glassblower to work the piece with the various tools.

The forum for studio glassblowers is the Glass Art Society, which was started in the United States about 20 years ago and includes among its members glassblowers from Canada and from around the world. A separate Canadian group was formed.

One of the biggest problems these artists face is the marketing of their pieces. Being self-employed and often working ten to 15 hours at a stretch, they have little time or inclination to establish proper sales outlets. Their pieces can be found in department stores, gift shops and other similar outlets. The most important outlet is probably Art Glass, in Montreal, whose proprietor, Mrs. Elena Lee, has espoused their cause over the last ten years or so and kept many of them going by her encouragement and enthusiasm. Unfortunately, industry and foundations have not seen fit to provide tangible support for these budding artists who, each in his or her own way, are establishing a distinctive form of Canadian art which will become the heritage of future generations.

FOOTNOTES

[1] Harvey K. Littleton, *Glassblowing — A Search for Form*, (Toronto: VanNostrand Reinhold Company, 1972), p. 6.

[2] See Chapter 4, The Establishment of the Canadian Glass Industry on a Permanent Basis (1878-1902), "The Ontario Glass Company Limited" and "The Sydenham Glass Company of Wallaceburg (Limited)."

[3] J.C. Stephenson, "The Story of Independent Glass Producers (Limited)," Toronto: typed draft d. August 25, 1975, pp. 23, 24.

[4] Ibid, p. 23.

APPENDIX 1

LIST OF GLASS COMPANIES
AND THEIR OPERATING DATES

Name of Company	Location	Operating Dates	Incorporation	Capital $	Remarks	Company Code
Thorold Glass Manufacturing Company	Thorold, Ontario	1828	–	–	1	TGM
Upper Canada Glass Manufacturing ompany	Cayuga, Ontario	1829	–	–	1	UCG
Cayuga Glass Manufacturing Company	Cayuga, Ontario	1835	Upper Canada April 16	48,000	2	CAY
Haldimand Glass Works Company	Cayuga, Ontario	1841	–	–	1	HAL
Mallorytown Glass Works	Mallory-town, Ontario	c.1839–1840	–	–		MAL
Caledonia Glass Works	Caledonia Springs, Ontario	1844–c.1850	–	–		CAL
Masson et Cie	Como, Quebec	1845–1847	–	–	2	MAS
Ottawa Glass Works	Como, Quebec	1847–1857	–	–		OTT
British American Glass Works	Como, Quebec	1857–c.1860	–	–		BAG
Canada Glass Works	St. Johns, Canada East (Quebec)	1845–c.1853	–	–		CGW
Canada Glass Works (Foster Brothers)	St. Johns, Canada East (Quebec)	c.1854–1860	–	–		FOB
Hamilton Glass Works	Hamilton, Ontario	1864–1880	–	–		HGW
The Hamilton Glass Company	Hamilton, Ontario	1880–1898	Ontario January 14	200,000		HAM
The Canada Glass Company (Limited)	Hudson, Quebec	1864–1877	Lower Canada October 26	Not known		CGC
St. Lawrence Glass Works	Montreal, Quebec	1867–1868	–	–		SGW
The Saint Lawrence Glass Company	Montreal, Quebec	1868–1873	Quebec February 1	50,000		STL
The Saint John Glass Company	Saint John, New Brunswick	1872–1873	–	–	2	SJG
Burlington Glass Works	Hamilton, Ontario	c.1874–1875	–	–		BGW

233

Name of Company	Location	Operating Dates	Incorporation	Capital $	Remarks	Company Code
Burlington Glass Company	Hamilton, Ontario	1875–1885	–	–		BUR
New Brunswick Crystal Glass Company (limited)	Crouchville, New Brunswick	1874–1878	New Brunswick April 8	50,000		NBC
Courtenay Bay Glass Works	Crouchville, New Brunswick	1878	–	–		CBG
St. Johns Glass Company	St. Johns, Quebec	1875–1877	Quebec December 10	10,000		STJ
The Excelsior Glass Company	St. Johns, Quebec	1879–1880	Quebec April 15	2,000		EXS
	Montreal, Quebec	1880–1883	–	–		EXG
The North American Glass Company	Montreal, Quebec	1883–1890	Quebec December 26	100,000		NAG
Penetang Glass Factory	Penetanguishene, Ontario	1879–1883	–	–		PEN
The Ontario Glass Burial Case Company (Limited)	Ridgetown, Ontario	1880–c.1883	Ontario May 14	25,000		OGB
Napanee Glass Works	Napanee, Ontario	1881–1883	–	–		NAP
The Nova Scotia Glass Company Limited	New Glasgow, Nova Scotia	1881–1890	Canada September 7	50,000		NSG
Dominion Glass Company (early)	Montreal, Quebec	c.1886–1894	–	–		DGM
Dominion Glass Company	Montreal, Quebec	1894–1896	Quebec October 22	100,000		DGC
The Dominion Glass Company (Limited)	Montreal, Quebec	1896–1897	Canada July 17	20,000		TDG
The Montreal Bottle and Glass Company	Montreal, Quebec	1887	Quebec January 22	20,000		MBG
The Diamond Glass Company (Limited)	Montreal and elsewhere	1890–1902	Canada June 27	10,000		DIG
Lamont Glass Company	Trenton, Nova Scotia	1890–1897	–	–		LAM
Humphreys' Glass Company	Trenton, Nova Scotia	1890–1917	–	–		HUT
Humphreys' Glass, Limited	Moncton, New Brunswick	1917–1920	Canada August 22	200,000		HUM
Humberstone Glass Works Company	Port Colborne, Ontario	1891	–	30,000	1	HGC
Lake Erie Glass Works Company of Port Colborne (Limited)	Port Colborne, Ontario	1891	–	–	1	LEG
Ontario Glass Company of Port Colborne	Port Colborne, Ontario	1892	–	–	1	OGC

Name of Company	Location	Operating Dates	Incorporation	Capital $	Remarks	Company Code
The Erie Glass Company of Canada (Limited)	Port Colborne, Ontario	1892–1893	Canada September 26	50,000		ERG
The Wallaceburg Glass Works Company (Limited)	Wallaceburg, Ontario	1893	Ontario May 8	3,000	2	WGW
The Toronto Glass Company (Limited)	Toronto, Ontario	1893–1899	Ontario September 15	50,000		TOR
Foster Glass Works	Port Colborne, Ontario	1894–1896	–	–	3	FGW
		1899–1900	–	–		FGW
The Sydenham Glass Company of Wallaceburg (Limited)	Wallaceburg, Ontario	1894–1913	Ontario November 7	50,000		SYD
The Beaver Flint Glass Company of Toronto (Limited)	Toronto, Ontario	1896–1939	Ontario August 6	20,000		BFG
The Ontario Glass Company Limited	Kingsville, Ontario	1899–1901	Ontario November 29	100,000		ONT
Diamond Flint Glass Company Limited	Toronto, Ontario and elsewhere	1903–1913	Ontario February 18	1,600,000		DIF
The Canadian Glass Manufacturing Company (Limited)	Montreal, Quebec	1905–1913	Canada September 19	25,000		CGM
Window Glass Machine Company of Canada Limited	Cayuga, Ontario	1905–1914	Ontario November 17	40,000		WGM
Crystal Glass Company, Limited	Sapperton, British Columbia	1906–c.1908	British Columbia June 14	150,000		CRY
The Manitoba Glass Manufacturing Company, Limited	Beausejour, Manitoba	1907–1912	Manitoba January 23	100,000		MAN
Desmarais and Robitaille (Limited)	Montreal, Quebec	1909–c.1923	Canada January 27	190,000		DRB
Welland Glass Manufacturing Company Limited	Welland, Ontario	1909	Ontario June 23	350,000	2	WEL
Independent Glass Producers, Limited	Toronto, Ontario	1910–1912	Ontario October 19	200,000		IGP
Jefferson Glass Company, Limited	Toronto, Ontario	1912–1925	Ontario October 7	200,000		JEF
The Wallaceburg Glass Company, Limited	Wallaceburg, Ontario	1911–1930	Ontario May 13	500,000		WGC
Alberta Glass Company Limited	Medicine Hat, Alberta	1911	Alberta May 23	150,000	4	ALB
The Richards Glass Company, Limited	Toronto, Ontario	1912–1977	Ontario May 31	40,000		RCG
Stanrich Sales Inc.	Toronto, Ontario	1977–	Ontario October 3	–		SRS

Name of Company	Location	Operating Dates	Incorporation	Capital $	Remarks	Company Code
Atlas Glass Works, Limited	Ville St. Pierre, Quebec	1912–1914	Canada August 16	300,000	4	ATL
The Premier Glass Company of Canada, Limited	Ville St. Pierre, Quebec	1914–1917	Canada May 9	3,000,000	4	PRE
Consumers Glass Company, Limited	Ville St. Pierre, Quebec and else-where	1917–	Canada October 4	1,000,000		CON
Macbeth-Evans Glass Company, Limited	Toronto, Ontario	1913	Ontario May 1	40,000	2	MAB
Dominion Glass Company, Limited	Montreal, Quebec and else-where	1913–1976	Canada May 15	8,000,000		DOM
Domglas Ltd./ Domglas Ltée.	Montreal and else-where	1976–1978	–	–		DGL
Domglas Inc.	Montreal and else-where	1978–	–	–		DGI
The Victoria Glass and Bottle Company, Limited	Victoria, British Columbia	1914–c.1915	British Columbia July 23	25,000		VIC
Canada Flint Glass Company, Limited	Toronto, Ontario	1919	Ontario May 23	10,000	2	CFG
Canadian Libbey-Owens Sheet Glass Company Limited	Hamilton, Ontario	1920–1922	Canada October 16	1,680,000		CLO
Feldspar Glass, Limited	Oshawa, Ontario	1921–c.1933	Ontario September 6	1,000,000		FEL
Pilkington Brothers (Limited)	Thorold, Ontario	1914–1922	Ontario February 28, 1895	–		PBL
Pilkington Brothers (Canada) Limited	Thorold, Ontario	1922–1945	Canada November 23	2,500,000		PBC
Pilkington Glass Limited	Scarborough, Ontario	1945–1971	Canada February 1	50,000		PGL
Pilkington Glass Limited/Vitrerie Pilkington Limitée	Scarborough, Ontario	1971–1978	Canada May 5	–		PGL
Pilkington Glass Industries Limited /Les Industries du Verre Pilkington Limitée	Scarborough, Ontario	1978–1982	Canada November 14	–		PGI
Ford Glass Limited/ Vitrerie Ford Limitée	Scarborough, Ontario	1982–	Canada February 8	–		FRD
Federal Glass Company, Limited	Toronto, Ontario	1926	Ontario May 14	40,000	2	FED
The O.H. Johns Glass Co., Limited	Toronto, Ontario	1928–	Ontario May 3	50,000		OHJ

Name of Company	Location	Operating Dates	Incorporation	Capital $	Remarks	Company Code
Mid-West Glass Company Limited	Winnipeg, Manitoba	1928–1930	Canada July 19	100,000		MID
Canadian Knox Glass Company, Limited	Oshawa, Ontario	1939–1940	Canada February 1	250,000		CKG
Industrial Glass Works	Ville St. Laurent, Quebec	1940–1946	–	–		IGW
Industrial Glass Company Limited	Ville St. Laurent, Quebec	1946–1949	Canada November 28	300,000		IGC
Canadian Industrial Glass Company Ltd.	Ville St. Laurent, Quebec	1949–1950	Canada May 31	2,000,000		CIG
Canadian Pittsburgh Industries Limited	Ville St. Laurent, Quebec	1950–1966	Canada February 24	2,000,000		CPI
Canadian Pittsburgh Industries Limited/ Les Industries Pittsburgh du Canada Limitée	Ville St. Laurent, Quebec	1966–1968	Canada June 3	–		CPI
	Owen Sound, Ontario	1968–1975	–	–		CPO
PPG Industries Canada Ltd./Industries PPG Canada Ltée.	Owen Sound, Ontario	1975–	Canada May 1	–		PPG
Corning Glass Works of Canada Ltd.	Toronto, Ontario	1945–1978	Canada June 8	2,000,000		COR
Corning Canada Inc.	Toronto, Ontario	1978–	Canada November 1	2,000,000		COI
Altaglass	Medicine Hat, Alberta	1950–	–	–		ALT
Iroquois Glass Company Limited	Candiac, Quebec	1958	Canada April 18	14,000,000		IRC
Iroquois Glass Limited	Candiac, Quebec	1958–1965	Canada May 20	10,000,000		IRQ
Iroquois Glass (1965) Limited	Candiac, Quebec	1965–1967	–	–		IRL
Les Industries de Verre et Miroirs Limitée/ Glass Mirrors Industries Limited	Montreal, Quebec	1958–1960	Quebec October 22	40,000		GMI
Murano Glass Incorporated	Montreal, Quebec	1960–1962	Quebec May 25	40,000		MUR
Chalet Artistic Glass Ltd./La Verrerie Artistique Chalet Ltée.	Cornwall, Ontario	1962–1980	Quebec April 17	–		CHL
Rossi Artistic Glass Inc.	Cornwall, Ontario	1980–	Canada December 1	–		ROS
Lorraine Glass Industries Ltd.	Montreal, Quebec	1962–1974	Quebec December 14	100,000		LOR

Name of Company	Location	Operating Dates	Incorporation	Capital $	Remarks	Company Code
Continental Glass Manufacturing Ltd.	Calgary, Alberta	1963–c.1974	Alberta July 19	20,000		CNT
National Pressed Glass Limited	Brantford, Ontario	1965–1976	Ontario April 15	40,000		NPG
National Pressed Glass (1976) Ltd.	Brantford, Ontario	1976–	Ontario June 25	–		NPL
Ahlstrom Canada Limited	Scoudouc, New Brunswick	1968–1979	New Brunswick February 2	1,100,000		AHC
Ahlstrom Limited	Scoudouc, New Brunswick	1979–1981	New Brunswick August 20	8,150,000		AHL
Domglas (Atlantic) Ltd.	Scoudouc, New Brunswick	1981–	New Brunswick December 7	–		AHD
Libbey-St. Clair Inc.	Wallace-burg, Ontario	1978–	Canada October 1	12,500,000		LSC

NOTES

1. Name not accepted.
2. Incorporated, no further action.
3. Leased by Diamond Glass (1896–1899).
4. Not completed.

APPENDIX 2

BOTTLE MARKINGS AND CLOSURES

INTRODUCTION

The following criteria are intended to provide general guidelines for establishing the company and approximate date of manufacture of a bottle. At the beginning of the twentieth century, when bottles began to be mass-produced by machine, the word "container" (which includes bottles, jars and narrow-mouth jugs capable of being sealed) slowly replaced the word "bottle." Unless otherwise indicated, the dates shown refer to the American industry, which ran about five years ahead of the Canadian one as far as development was concerned.

QUICK REFERENCE

A. PRODUCTION MARKS

In the 1970s Dr. Julian Harrison Toulouse, former chief engineer for Owens-Illinois Inc. of Toledo, Ohio, prepared a self-contained travelling kit of wooden moulds and explanatory notes on mould seams which he loaned to interested groups, including GLASFAX. Following tours of the various districts by GLASFAX, a write-up was included in the report of the proceedings of the GLASFAX Annual Seminar held in Montreal in 1977. The following material is extracted from this report and an article by Toulouse.[1]

    1. Mould Seams

    Summary: The seams on a bottle tell us much, and have been discussed as follows:
1. When there are no seams whatever:
    a. the piece may be freeblown without moulds, or
    b. it may have been blown in a shoulder height dip mould with hand-shaped shoulder, or
2. A seam disappearing at the shoulder means a bottle blown in a shoulder-height hinged mould.
3. Seams disappearing in the neck area may be blown in any mould, but the seam rubbed out with a hand-held finishing tool.
4. If a seam crosses the bottom the mould was a two-piece, hinged-bottom type.
5. A horizontal seam around the widest point, with two side seams going upward, means a three-part mould based on a dip mould bottom.

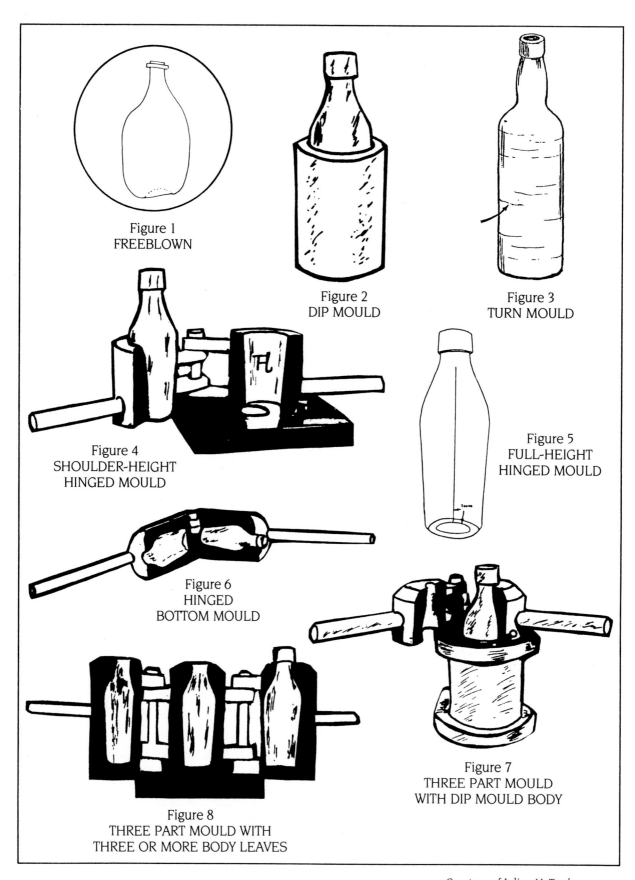

Figure 1
FREEBLOWN

Figure 2
DIP MOULD

Figure 3
TURN MOULD

Figure 4
SHOULDER-HEIGHT
HINGED MOULD

Figure 5
FULL-HEIGHT
HINGED MOULD

Figure 6
HINGED
BOTTOM MOULD

Figure 7
THREE PART MOULD
WITH DIP MOULD BODY

Figure 8
THREE PART MOULD WITH
THREE OR MORE BODY LEAVES

Courtesy of Julian H. Toulouse.

6. Three or more side seams from heel to finish means a three-part (or more) mould for decorative designs.
7. Circular seam symmetrical with bottom joining two or more side seams means a post-bottom mould.
8. Irregular, feathery, nonsymmetrical bottom seams usually mean a machine-made bottle from suction machine equipment.
9. Small diameter, *indented* into surface rather than extending, nonsymmetrical, on the bottom, usually is the valve mark of a press-and-blow machine.
10. Circular seam in heel-side wall tangent area means a cup-bottom mould.
11. Seams to top of finish, which is then ground to level, usually indicate hand-blown in blow-back mould, or snapped off by blow-over method.
12. Circular or oblong seams in side wall, not connected with other seams, are made by plated moulds.
13. Horizontal seams below finish area mean separate neck rings but do not prove machine manufacture.
14. One or more seams circling top of finish show machine manufacture.
15. 'Ghost seams' seams come from the use of a separate blank mould — hence indicate machine manufacture.

1.1 BOTTLES WITHOUT MOULD SEAMS

1.1.1 FREEBLOWN WITHOUT MOULDS (Fig. 1)
Offhand or freeblown bottles, the irregular shapes of which could be modified by various techniques and the use of tools.
RECOGNITION
Irregular shape; no mould seams.

1.1.2 DIP MOULD BODY – FREEBLOWN SHOULDER (Fig. 2)
A one-piece mould, straight-sided or tapered with the smaller diameter near the bottom of the mould, with a straight taper to the widest point at the open top of the mould, at the base of what will be the curve into the shoulder. When the moulded part had been completed, the bottle was withdrawn from the mould and the shoulder and neck were freeblown.
RECOGNITION
Regular shape. No mould seam unless caused by a slight blow-over at the base of the shoulder.

1.1.3 TURN MOULD (or Paste mould) (Fig. 3)
Two-piece mould in which the blower rotated the pipe as he formed the bottle. No lettering or decorative design could be used. The bottle had to be circular in cross section at all horizontal levels. It could have any vertical contour. The glass-contacting surface of the mould was covered with a "paste" of an organic fiber, in a binder that was evaporated by the heat of the baking process (part of the preparation of the mould). This surface was generally wetted between each blowing. The water flashed to steam, so the bottle "rode" on a cushion of steam.
RECOGNITION
No mould seams and faint striations on the body of the bottle.

1.2 BOTTLES WITH MOULD SEAMS

1.2.1 SHOULDER-HEIGHT HINGED MOULD (Fig. 4)
This mould could be lettered or decorated. It need not be tapered. Its side wall need not be a straight line, and the design need not be symmetrical or regular in any way. The mould was opened on its hinged support in order to remove the bottle.
RECOGNITION
Seam on side disappears at or just above the widest diameter.

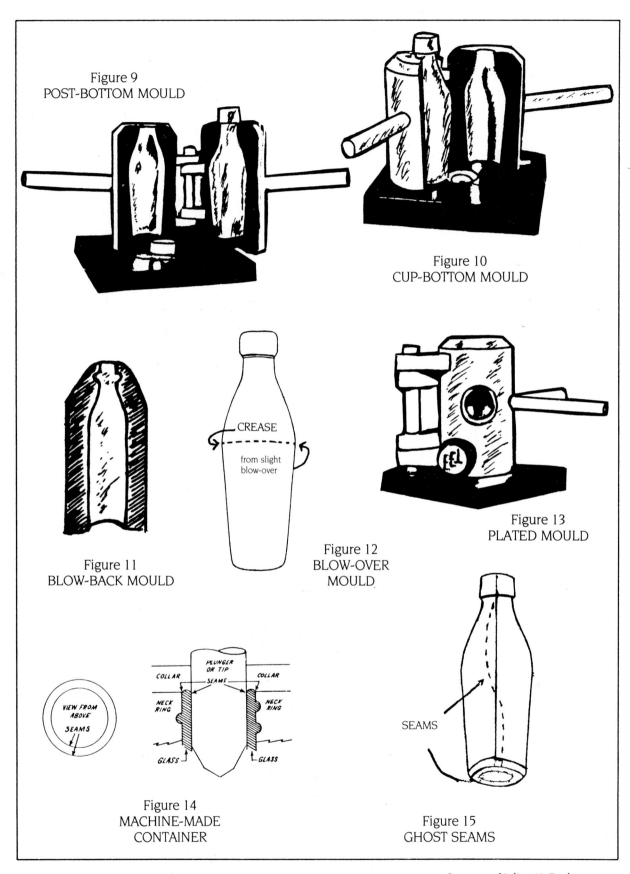

Figure 9
POST-BOTTOM MOULD

Figure 10
CUP-BOTTOM MOULD

Figure 11
BLOW-BACK MOULD

CREASE

from slight
blow-over

Figure 12
BLOW-OVER
MOULD

Figure 13
PLATED MOULD

VIEW FROM
ABOVE

SEAMS

PLUNGER
OR TIP

COLLAR   COLLAR

SEAMS

NECK
RING   NECK
RING

GLASS   GLASS

Figure 14
MACHINE-MADE
CONTAINER

SEAMS

Figure 15
GHOST SEAMS

Courtesy of Julian H. Toulouse.

242

1.2.2 FULL-HEIGHT HINGED MOULD (Fig. 5)

Any type of mould that is vertically hinged into two or more parts, having a "cup" bottom or "post" bottom or any other type in which the bottle's side seams go all the way to the base of the finish. The seam condition comes from any one of three treatments of the bottle after it has been removed from the mould.

a. ACTION OF A FINISHING TOOL

A hand-held jawed clamp that by rotation imparts the desired finish to the bottle and at the same time eliminates the seam on the upper part of the neck.
RECOGNITION
Seams disappear in the neck.

b. ACTION OF A PRESSING TOOL

The same finishing operation was carried out with a bench-mounted two-piece press. The clamping action of the press jaws on the neck of the bottle eliminated the seams at the top of the neck.
RECOGNITION
No striations in the neck area.

c. FLARED OR FIRED LIP

When a cork was to be the closure, a bottle could be finished either as a straight neck (often termed "sheared" even when not obviously trimmed with shears) or flared and fire-polished. In either case, the finish portion of the bottle was reheated in the glory hole. For a straight neck, only enough heat was applied to smooth the jagged edges caused by the crack-off. For the flared neck, the finish portion was heated sufficiently that the neck could be flared by a stick or tool, while being rotated in a snap at the chair.
RECOGNITION
No striations in the neck area. Finish smooth and polished.

1.2.3 HINGED-BOTTON MOULD (Fig. 6)

A two-piece mould hinged across the bottom.
RECOGNITION
A straight or arched mould seam across the bottom. In either case, the ends turned the heel and proceeded upwards towards the finish, where they could be modified by other conditions.

1.2.4 THREE-PART MOULD WITH DIP MOULD BODY (Fig. 7)

A dip mould used to make the body, on which is superimposed a two-piece horizontally or vertically hinged shoulder mould.
RECOGNITION
Lowest seam circled body at widest point. From this, two seams went up to the finish.

1.2.5 THREE-PART MOULD WITH THREE OR MORE BODY LEAVES (Fig. 8)

This type of mould was used when there was extensive embossing on the bottle. The bottom was generally of the "post" design but could also be of the "cup" design.
RECOGNITION
Three or more vertical seams from near the base to the finish.

1.2.6 POST-BOTTOM MOULD (Fig. 9)

Two-piece mould which closed around a post projection from the bottom plate.
RECOGNITION
A circular seam symmetrically located on the bottom of the bottle, either coincident with the bearing surface or with a slightly larger, but never smaller, diameter. Side seams joined the bottom circle.

1.2.7 CUP-BOTTOM MOULD (Fig. 10)

In contrast to the post-bottom mould, the part that shaped the bottom of the bottle was cut into the bottom plate as a small depression or cup.
RECOGNITION
Lowest bottle seam was a circle around the heel at, or just below, the tangent of the heel radius and the side wall.

1.2.8 BLOW-BACK AND BLOW-OVER MOULDS (Fig. 11 and 12)
   a. The blow-back mould could be of either the post- or cup-bottom type. As can be seen in the illustration, there is a small bulb-shaped part almost at the top of the mould. Here the glass was blown thinner and could be easily cracked-off prior to the grinding and/or fire-finishing of the top of the bottle. This was necessary to provide a good sealing surface for a mason jar or a smooth polished finish for other bottles.
   b. The blow-over was another method of accomplishing the same thing. The bottle cannot tell us which method was used. A small fraction of an inch of straight metal was designed into the mould above the top of the finish. When the bottle was blown to the extent that the mould was filled, and by keeping on blowing, helped somewhat by a wiping motion of the pipe across the top of the mould, the blower would balloon the glass above the mould and "pop" it free.
   RECOGNITION
   Seam went all the way to the top of the bottle, which was usually ground or fire-polished.

1.2.9 PLATED MOULD (Fig. 13)
   This seam is caused by the junction of the body mould part and a removable insert, called a plate, placed in a hole in the body mould part. It enabled the glassmaker to blow personalized bottles for a buyer whose needs were too small to justify the expense of a private mould. This same body mould could then serve many customers who would agree to the same arrangement. In addition to the personalized part on the plate, the mould might also carry standardized information common to all users, such as capacity, weight and product (if a product-oriented design).
   RECOGNITION
   A circular or oblong seam, on either or both side walls, not touching any other seam and appearing in round, oblong and panelled bottles.

1.2.10 SEPARATE NECK RINGS
   This horizontal seam is in itself not a proof of machine-made bottles. It only indicates that the neck rings (finish rings) were separate parts from the body mould, but it does not indicate that these neck ring halves opened separately from the body mould halves. The first such patent was by Robert Hemingray on Sept. 18, 1860, Pat. No. 30,063, and it was for a mould with a separate neck ring which opened by lifting, to make the groove for the fruit jar often identified as "Patent Sept. 18, 1860" and was often made with misdated lettering. Most of the patents that followed called for neck rings that were separable but bolted to the body mould so that the two operated as one unit.
   RECOGNITION
   A parting line (seam) between the finish and the body mould. This horizontal seam in itself is not proof of machine-made containers. That can only be determined if there are "cut off" or "shear" marks on the bottom.

1.2.11 MACHINE-MADE CONTAINERS
   a. SEAMS CIRCLE TOP OF FINISH (Fig. 14)
   With the exception of beverage and beer containers, which are often "fire-polished" to smooth the top of the finish, these seams appear. In machine production, a plunger guided by a collar starts the formation of the mouth or opening of the container. Both these pieces, when they came in contact with the parison of glass, left seams. This is clearly shown in figure 14.
   RECOGNITION
   One or more seams circle top of finish.
   b. GHOST SEAMS (Fig. 15)
   With the advent of hinged "blank" or "parison" moulds, a seam appeared on the blank of glass before it was transferred to the blow mould. By the time the container had finally been blown, there were actually two sets of mould seams on it. Faint ones left from the blank mould and normal ones made by the blow mould.
   RECOGNITION
   Irregular "ghost" seams beside the normal seams.

2.   OTHER MARKS

2.1   HAND OPERATIONS

2.1.1   PONTIL MARK
In the early days of glassblowing, a rough scar on the bottom of an article appeared as the result of breaking off the pontil rod from the article. In order that the article could stand evenly on a flat surface, the bottom was pushed up enough so that the rough scar was contained in this small concave area and therefore did not form part of the bearing surface.
RECOGNITION
Rough scar on bottom of article. In the better-quality articles, including paperweights, the pontil marks were ground out, leaving just a dimple.

2.1.2   SNAP CASE
Before the end of the nineteenth century, a "snap" or "snap case" was developed to eliminate the need for a pontil rod. It comprised a metal container or cage of the necessary size and shape on the end of a rod to hold the article while the finishing operation was carried out.
RECOGNITION
There was no scar or dimple.

2.2   MACHINE OPERATIONS
The introduction, over the turn of the century, of semiautomatic and automatic bottle-forming machines eliminated the blowpipe. There were two general types of machines for making containers — feeder machines and suction machines.
a. FEEDER MACHINES
The word "feeder" indicated that the gob of glass was transferred manually from the pot or tank to the semiautomatic machines and by gravity to the fully automatic machines.

2.2.1   VALVE MARK
The press and blow automatic machines, such as the Miller JP, MT, ML and the side-lever press, used a solid blank mould. In order to let the gas escape when the gob entered the blank, a valve was added to its bottom. The clearance between the valve and the blank (of glass) was sufficient to vent the trapped gases. The valves were always perfectly round and varied in diameter from about 3/8" to 1". Because there was a clearance between the blank and the valve, the glass would be pressed into this clearance.
RECOGNITION
A perfect but seldom centered circle on the bottom of the container.

2.2.2   BAFFLE MARK
The O'Neill, Lynch R, 10, and the Hartford-Empire (individual section) machines all had the same characteristics, in that the blank mould had a portion of its cavity in a baffle. (This was called the blank/baffle parting line.) Whatever the blank shape, be it round, oval or otherwise, at the blank/baffle parting line the baffle was made a few thousands smaller. This little ledge would not reheat out. Sometimes these so-called baffle matches were quite pronounced and at other times barely perceptible. This depended on how well the equipment was maintained and the thermal relation existing between the blank and the baffle.
RECOGNITION
A replica of the blank/baffle match on the bottom of the container.

b.   SUCTION MACHINES
CUT-OFF MARK
The only successful suction machine was the Owens machine. In this case, the gob of glass was sucked up into the blank mould on the machine from a revolving pot of molten glass. When sufficient glass had been sucked up, it was cut off by a knife, which sealed the bottom of the mould. The cutting action of the knife left a jagged scar as sharp as the edge of the blade. It took the shape of the blank opening.

Diagram showing glass container terms.
Courtesy C.E. Ramsden & Co. Ltd.

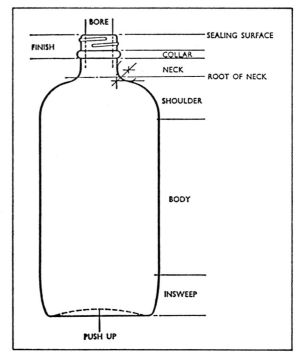

Bottle dating by mould seams (US).
Courtesy of Azor Vienneau. [2]

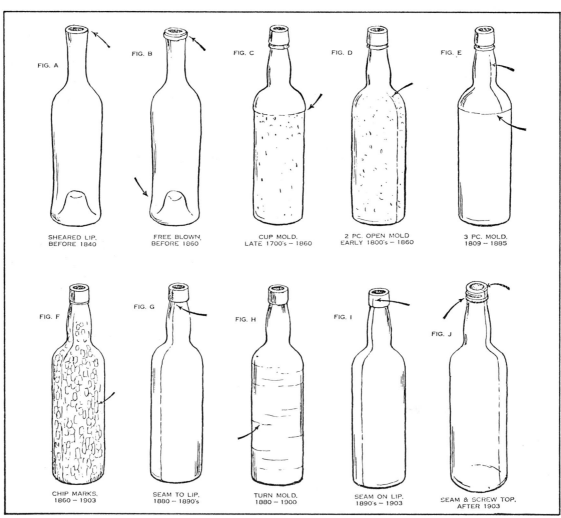

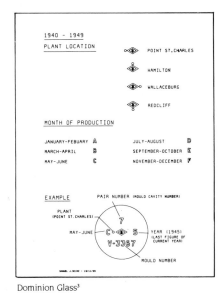

Dominion Glass[3]

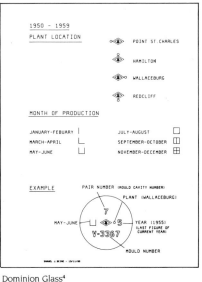

Dominion Glass[4]

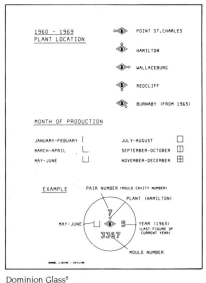

Dominion Glass[5]

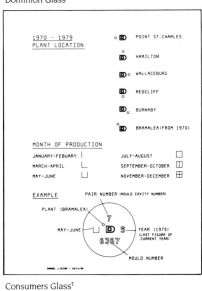

Consumers Glass[6]

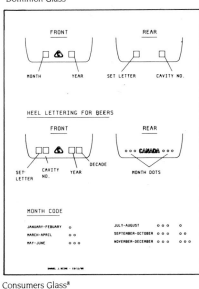

Consumers Glass[7]

Consumers Glass[8]

Bottom plate markings.

B. PRODUCERS' MARKS

1. TRADEMARKS

These are logos and/or symbols that are embossed on the body or bottom of a bottle to provide specific information.

PRE-1917

In Canada, until 1917, the only way of identifying the maker of a bottle was if the company embossed a logo or symbol (the latter being in a monogram containing the initials of the company, e.g. Diamond Glass, Diamond Flint Glass, North American Glass).

CONSUMERS GLASS

In 1917, on incorporation, the company adopted the letter C in an inverted triangle ▽ as its trademark. In 1962 the triangle became upright with round corners ⬧. Other trademarks for mason jars authenticated or attributed to the company were Canadian Jewel, Canadian Mason, Canadian Sure Seal, Corona, Jewel Jar, Queen, Royal, Safety Seal, Sure Seal and Victory.

DOMINION GLASS

Although incorporated in 1913, the company did not adopt its D in a diamond ◇ trademark until June 27, 1928. There were two reasons for adopting it. The first one was to distinguish its bottles from those made by other glass companies. The other one was much more intriguing. With the enactment of Prohibition in the United States in 1923, production of spirituous liquor fell into the hands of bootleggers.

About the same time, a family had established a distillery in the Province of Saskatchewan. Made under normal conditions, their product was far superior to that produced illegally in the American "stills." As a result, and with some international connivance, their superior product was appearing in unmarked bottles in the mid-west United States. However, it was too good to last, and about 1927 the American authorities required that all glass containers entering the United States from Canada have embossed on them the country of origin. As a result, the company adopted the Diamond D trademark.

Another story of the post-Prohibition era shows the ingenuity of people who wanted to "make a buck." In the second half of the thirties, there was still a great deal of "rum-running" across the Canada-United States border. In this case, the venue was the St. Clair River, which joins Lake Huron and Lake Erie. About halfway between the two lakes is Port Lambton, Ontario, and a stone's throw across the river, Algonac, Michigan, both of which were ports of entry for their respective countries. The story went something like this. On dark, stormy, foggy nights, a small boat, even a row boat, would appear out of the gloom at the Port Lambton wharf and would take out papers for a boatload of liquor for Cuba or some other destination outside of continental North America. They would then disappear into the night, and somewhere out in the river or in the marshes a quiet transshipment would take place.

Other trademarks authenticated or attributed to Dominion through takeover of predecessor companies or taken out directly included: Bee Hive, Best, Canadian King, Carrols, Crown, Dyson, Gem, Ideal, Imperial, Mason Fruit Jar, Perfect Seal, Safety Valve and Schram.

IROQUOIS GLASS

In 1958, on incorporation, the company adopted an I superimposed on a G ⊄ as its trademark. This mark was phased out after 1967, with the company's takeover by Consumers Glass.

AHLSTROM GLASS

In 1968, on incorporation, the company adopted the letter A as its trademark. This mark was phased out after 1981, with the company's takeover by Domglas.

For trademarks of other glass companies refer to:
Dr. J.H. Toulouse. *Bottle Makers and Their Marks*. New York: Thomas Nelson Inc., 1971.
A.G. Peterson. *400 Trademarks on Glass*. Takoma Park, Maryland: Washington College Press, 1968.
American Glass Review, Glass Factory Directory Issue. Clifton, New Jersey: Ebel-Doctorow Publications Inc. (Annual).
Punt Marks. Windsor, Connecticut: Hartford Division, Emhart Corporation, 1982.
Glass Industry Club, Brussels, Belgium.
Glass Manufacturers Federation, London, England.

2.   STOCK NUMBERS AND MOULD NUMBERS
It is not the intention here to present exhaustive guidelines on the matter, but rather to use the Dominion Glass system as an example with the understanding and knowledge that the other three container companies — Consumers Glass, Iroquois Glass and Ahlstrom Glass — used systems similar in principle but tailored to the degree of complexity of their product mixes.

Container production falls into two categories 1) SSL (standard stock lines), these are plain, unembossed containers available to any customer, and 2) MTO (made-to-order), these are made to a customer's specific requirements as to shape, size and embossing. They are more expensive than the equivalent SSL container.

2.1   STOCK NUMBERS

During the last 30 years of hand bottle production (1883-1913), numbers appeared on the bottom of many bottles. These were considered as stock numbers and were used by Dominion Glass and its predecessor companies. When Diamond Glass was formed in 1890 and was later succeeded by Diamond Flint Glass in 1903, both companies had taken over a number of smaller companies, each of which unfortunately were allowed to retain their own series of stock numbers. As a result, the numbers on the bottoms of bottles could refer to any one of these former independents. Example: stock number 131 represented five different bottles within the Diamond Flint group: Sydenham, 16-ounce Philadelphia Oval; Toronto, 4-ounce Wide-Mouth Round, 8-ounce Wide-Mouth Round; Montreal, 3-ounce Round; Hamilton, 4-ounce Round. Unless one has access to these companies' stock lists or catalogs, it is almost impossible to identify the location of production.

In the year 1926, a Record of Mould Equipment was prepared to overcome the above problem. This not only referred to containers, but also to all other types of glass products. There were over 5,000 items in the record. It is interesting to note that the moulds for these items were still identified as stock numbers. By this time the majority of the bottles were made by machines of various types. As a result, the first series of mould numbers were set up and, over a period of time, replaced the stock number on the bottom of the bottle. Since then, however, stock numbers have been used for ordering and inventory records.

Here are random extracts from the Record of Mould Equipment (1926).

STOCK NO.	PRODUCT	PRODUCTION STYLE
1 to 7	Acme Oval 1/2-1-2-3-4-6-8 oz.	Hand, Owens AR
551	Metal polish 4 oz.	Olean
722	Pyramid mucilage 2 oz.	O'Neill
1152	Improved gem pint	Teeple Johnson
1908	Window prism	Press
2311	Footed lamp #106	Press
2420	Nutmeg chimney	Hand
2458	Short Trilite globe	Hand
3072	#34 Heinz Tumbler 10 oz.	Miller
4553	Dental chair cuspidor	Press
4614	Ford lens 8 in.	Side-lever press

2.2   MOULD NUMBERS

Numerical or alpha-numerical numbers appearing on the bottom of the container to identify the mould for each type of bottle.

By late 1945 this series had progressed into the 9900s, but obsolete numbers left so many gaps in the series that a new series was begun. The new series was identified by prefixing the number with the letter V. The letter following the mould number indicated which of several successive sets of moulds was involved. The first set bore the mould number with no suffix; successive sets show -A, -B, etc.; Z is followed by -AA, -BB, etc. This suffix proved confusing to some customers and no longer appears on the bottle. The digit located by itself above, below or over to the side is the "pair number," indicating a particular mould in a set.

3. PLANT AND DATE OF MANUFACTURE

3.1 DOMINION GLASS
About 1934 the company decided to add two more symbols to the bottom of the bottle for quality control purposes. These symbols identified the plant and date of manufacture respectively. The year was divided into six two-month periods, i.e. January-February, March-April, etc. The coding appearing on page 256 of Stevens' *Canadian Glass c.1825-1925* does not appear to have been adopted. The symbols were modified every ten years to reflect the decade to which they referred.

3.2 CONSUMERS GLASS
In 1962, when the company's trademark was changed from ▽ to ◭ , symbols to identify the plant and date of manufacture were added.

3.3 IROQUOIS GLASS
This was a one-plant operation and therefore this information was not indicated.

3.4 AHLSTROM GLASS
This company was a one-plant operation and therefore no plant identification was required. As the company only operated for 13 years as an independent, the year of production was not identified. There were two principal production lines.

BEERS
A dot system was used to identify the month of manufacture . . . each dot represented two consecutive months, i.e. January-February, March-April, etc.

SODAS
A cross-box ⊞ system was used to identify the month of manufacture.[10]

C. PRODUCT IDENTIFICATION

1. EMBOSSING
Embossing is the art of cutting logos and symbols into the mould so that the design will appear in relief on the finished container. The development of this technique was popularized by John Mason, a New Yorker, who in 1858 developed the mason jar (fruit jar) for preserving fruit and vegetables.

2. LABELLING

2.1 REPLACEABLE LABELS
With the exception of fruit jars and certain well-known soft drink containers, glass embossing was replaced by the much cheaper glued-on label, the purpose of which was to identify the contents and the name of the bottler. The date of such a bottle could then be generally established through reference to trade lists of the various bottlers that used labels.

2.2 PERMANENT LABELS

2.2.1 APPLIED COLOUR LETTERING (A.C.L.)
A.C.L. was first developed in the United States in the early thirties for the coloured decoration of plain tumblers and was later adapted to containers. Dominion Glass obtained the exclusive Canadian rights for this process in 1936 from the developers, Solar Laboratories. They also had the right to sub-licence the process to others in Canada.[11]

2.2.2 PLASTI-SHIELD
Special labels, using impact-modified polystyrene extruded foam, attractively printed, are purchased in a continuous roll. The labels are cut and placed over the container by special equipment. They are then heat-shrunk and adhere tightly to soft drink bottles, juices and wine coolers. The plasti-shield type offers added protection to the bottle in filling, handling and transportation.[12]

2.2.3 DECALS

Decals have been applied to glassware in a limited way, but mostly to identify tableware manufacturers.

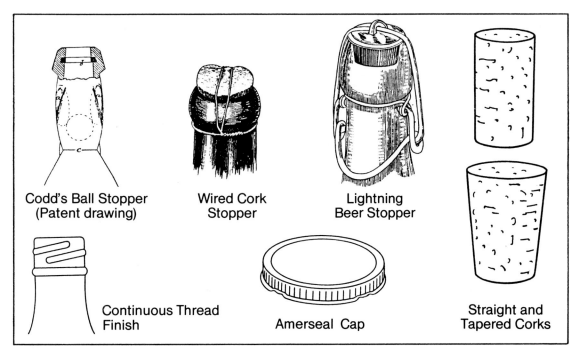

Codd's Ball Stopper
(Patent drawing)

Wired Cork
Stopper

Lightning
Beer Stopper

Continuous Thread
Finish

Amerseal Cap

Straight and
Tapered Corks

A selection of closures used over the years.   Courtesy of Alfred Lief.

D.   CLOSURES

The finish of a bottle indicates the type of closure that will be used to seal it (i.e. cork, screw cap, etc.).

Over the years, bottles have been sealed by whatever means were at hand — a stone, rag, piece of wood or other material. With the increased demand for wines and ales in England in the middle of the seventeenth century, straight and tapered corks for the wines and tied-on corks for the gaseous ales became the normal closures and remained so for the next 200 years. The second half of the nineteenth century and the first quarter of the twentieth century saw great changes in this practice.

In 1810 a Parisian confectioner, Nicholas Appert, successfully invented a method of processing fresh food by a sealed cooking process. This led to the invention of the "sealer" by John L. Mason in the United States in 1858. This was a high-shoulder wide-mouth jar with a threaded finish that was capable of taking a screw-on zinc cap. This "fruit jar" or mason jar, in its hundreds of variations, is still being produced. In 1869 Louis R. Boyd improved on the zinc lid by providing a glass liner, which reduced the incidence of contamination.

In the 1870s soda water or flavoured "pop," which had been invented in England in the first half of the nineteenth century, became popular in the United States. This conceived the Codd ball stopper in 1873 and the Hutchison stopper in 1879. In the 1880s the idea of pasturizing beer to eliminate bacteria was developed. Because of the pressure generated during the pasturizing process, the old French idea of the seventeenth-century wired-on corks for champagne was used. Bernardin invented a metal cap and neck band in 1880, and Putnam invented his Lightning Beer stopper during the same decade. By the 1890s pop had become so popular that it was necessary to find a cheaper closure than the existing ones. William Painter, a Baltimore machinist, came up with the solution in 1892. He developed the crimped Crown Cork for bottles filled under pressure.

In the first quarter of the twentieth century, the trend was to package more and more food products in glass. Starting with this period, the closuremakers worked closely with the bottlemakers and normally established the specifications for the finish of the bottle. Two new types were then developed: the Amerseal, which overlapped the finish of the bottle and engaged lugs embossed on the bead around the finish (1906), and the second and more useful one, the Screw Cap (S.C.) type, whereby a threaded metal (and later plastic) cap engaged matching threads on the finish of the bottle to make the seal. There have been many variations of this type of finish since then, particularly in the spirits and wines trade. The Continuous Thread (C.T.) is probably the most widely used of this type.[13]

REFERENCES

Toulouse, J.H. *Fruit Jars*. Camden, New Jersey: Thomas Nelson & Sons, 1969.
Lief, Alfred. A *Close-up of Closures – History and Progress*. New York: Glass Container Manufacturers Institute, n.d.

FOOTNOTES

[1] Dr. Julian H. Toulouse, "A Primer on Mold Seams," *Western Collector*, (November-December, 1969).
[2] Azor Vienneau, *The Bottle Collector*, (Halifax: Petheric Press, 1969), p. 14.
[3] Illustration prepared by Mould Design and Manufacture division of Domglas Inc., Hamilton.
[4] Ibid.
[5] Ibid.
[6] Ibid.
[7] Ibid.
[8] Illustration prepared by Consumers Glass.
[9] Julian Toulouse, *Fruit Jars*, (Don Mills, Ontario: Thomas Nelson & Sons Canada Limited, 1969), p. 514.
[10] Letter d. March 29, 1982, from Brian Bezanson, formerly controller of Ahlstrom Canada Limited, to me.
[11] A.C.L. is made of a "glass frit"-based paste and when fired into the surface cannot be removed.
[12] Description prepared by T. Rab, Engineering Department, Domglas Inc., November 5, 1985.
[13] Alfred Lief, A *Close-up of Closures - History and Progress*, (New York: Glass Container Manufacturers Institute, n.d.).

APPENDIX 3

SELECTED PRESSED GLASS PATTERNS

The patterns illustrated in the following pages have been selected to reflect, as closely as possible those that have been attributed to Canadian glass factories or have been found in Canada.

Regular production of pressed glass in Canada was only established as the result of the introduction in 1879 of a protective tariff of 30 percent on imported glassware. This resulted in a 45-year period (1880-1925) during which four Canadian companies were established to produce pressed glass. Three of these companies — Burlington Glass (1874-1885), Nova Scotia Glass (1881-1890), and Jefferson Glass (1912-1925) were eventually taken over by the fourth which operated under a variety of names before becoming Dominion Glass in 1913. Details of the operations of these companies will be found in Chapters 3, 4, 6 and 10.

Evidence to support the authentication or attribution of pressed glass patterns to specific companies in Canada has come from company catalogs and digs on the factory sites. Catalogs have been found for Dominion Glass and two of its predecessor companies and for Jefferson Glass. However caution must be observed in using such evidence for authentication because some of them list or illustrate not only those lines the company produces but also what lines they are capable of producing. In the same manner the finding of many shards of a particular pattern on a factory site concedes attribution but not necessarily authentication.

Again, the patterns themselves give no acceptable proof that they were original Canadian patterns with the possible exception of the Maple Leaf pattern which has been assumed to be Canadian because of its very motif and the fact that it does not appear to be attributed to any non-Canadian company. As will be seen most of the other patterns illustrated have already been documented, in some cases under a different name in connection with an American company.

Hundreds of pressed glass patterns have been recorded in both Canadian and American references. Some have had several names. In other cases the same pattern has had an American name as well as a Canadian one. To assist the reader, the names selected for each illustrated pattern is the one deemed to be the most familiar to Canadian collectors and researchers. From the lack of more detailed evidence, no dates have been given for the production of each pattern within the operating dates of each site quoted above.

The material that follows has been extracted from *Glass Manufacturing in Canada: A Survey of Pressed Glass Patterns* by permission of the authors Barbara Lang Rottenberg and Judith Tomlin, who are solely responsible for its contents. This paper was published in 1982 by the National Museum of Man, in its Mercury Series as History division paper no. 33.

At the end of the appendix will be found keys to the dig locations and source material.

ACADIAN

Relish dish, length 24.3 cm., width 13.5 cm.

Dig: Nova Scotia

Reference: (16) pp.16, 25.

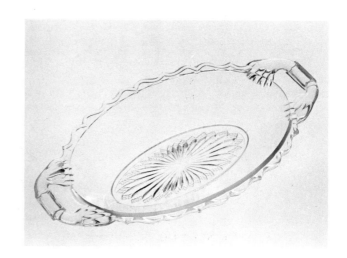

ACTRESS

Bread tray, length 32.3 cm., width 23.5 cm.

Dig: Burlington

References: (9); (11) p.278; (17) pp.102-103; (19) p.228.

   Revi lists an attribution to the La Belle Glass Company of Bridgeport, OH, c.1885. Adelaide Neilson, an English-born Shakespearian actress appears on this plate.

AEGIS

Jug, height 23 cm.

Dig: Burlington

References: (9); (11) p.278; (17) pp.122,123.

Metz lists this pattern as "Bead and Bar Medallion".

ANDERSON

Jug, height 23 cm.

Dig: Burlington

References: (9); (11) p.278; (19) p.276

A pattern produced by the O'Hara Glass Company of Pittsburgh, c.1870.

ATHENIAN

Covered comport, height (with lid) 28 cm.

References: (3); (5)

BARBERRY (OVAL BERRIES)

Jug, height 22 cm.

Dig: Burlington

References: (9); (11) p.278; (19) p.236.

A McKee & Brothers, Pittsburgh, pattern, c. 1870, reissued by the same firm in 1894.

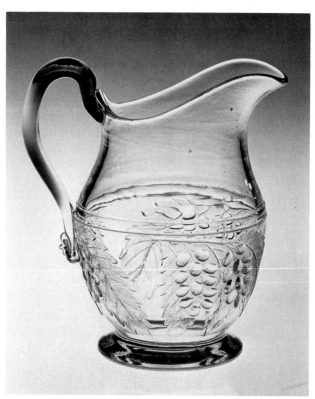

BEAD AND PETAL

Butter dish, height 10 cm., diameter 18.5 cm.

References: (1); (12).

Known as pattern no. 210 in the above catalogs; another common name is "Crocus".

BEADED OVAL AND FAN NO. 1

Sugar bowl, height (with lid) 19 cm.

Dig: Delormier

References: (8); (12).

BEADED OVAL AND FAN NO. 2

Jug, height 19 cm.

Reference: (12).

Listed in the Jefferson catalog as No. 320, this pattern was also advertised by Butler Brothers, American wholesale distributors of general merchandise, in their 1910 catalog, under the name "Crown Jewel".

BEADED OVAL WINDOW

Jug, height 26 cm.

Dig: Burlington

References: (9); (11) p.278; (17) pp.158, 159.

Also called "Oval Medallion" by Metz, who notes that it was produced in the United States in a variety of colours.

BLACK-EYED SUSAN

Cheese bell, height 16.8 cm., diameter 21.3 cm.

Dig: Burlington

Reference: (9)

No American reference to this pattern has been located to date. (1982)

BLOCK

Goblet, height 14.3 cm.

Dig: Burlington

References: (9); (17) pp.164, 165; (19) p.148.

Also known as "Clear Block" and attributed to the Duncan & Heisey Company of Pittsburg, c.1890.

BOLING

Goblet, height 14.7 cm.

Digs: Burlington and Delormier

References: (8); (9); (17) pp.156, 157; (20) p.214.

Stevens named this pattern "Cross". "Boling" appears to be the American name.

BOWTIE

Comport, height 18.5 cm.

Dig: Delormier

References: (10) p.15; (12).

Not to be confused with the American pattern of the same name as illustrated in Metz, *Much More Pattern Glass*, pp.116, 117.

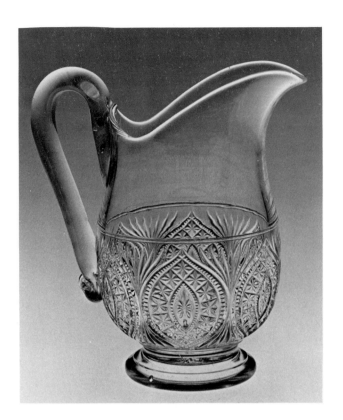

BUCKLE AND STAR

Jug, height 24 cm.

Dig: Burlington

References: (9); (11) p.278; (19) p.88.

A Bryce Brothers pattern of the 1880s, reissued by the United States Glass Company after 1891. Originally named "Orient".

BUTTONS AND BOWS

Jug, height 23 cm.

Digs: Delormier and Nova Scotia

References: (8); (16) p.33; (17) pp.200, 201.

Metz calls this pattern "Beaded Swirl".

CANADIAN

Covered comport, height (with lid) 21 cm.

Dig: Burlington

References: (9); (11) p.279; (17) pp. 111, 112.

CARDINAL

Creamer, height 14.5 cm.

Dig: Burlington

References: (9); (11) p.279.

CAT'S EYE AND FAN

Covered comport, height (with lid) 28 cm.

Dig: Burlington

References: (9); (11) p.278; (13) p.173.

CENTENNIAL

Covered comport, height (with lid) 25.5 cm.

Digs: Delormier and Nova Scotia

Reference: (16) pp.28, 29, 31.

This pattern was named by MacLaren in 1967 in honour of Canada's Centennial.

CHAIN WITH STAR

Plate, diameter (at handles) 34 cm.

Dig: Burlington

References: (9); (11) p.278; (17) pp.116, 117; (19) p.87.

    A Bryce Brothers Company pattern produced in Pittsburgh, c.1890.

COLONIAL

Goblet, height 15.3 cm.

References: (10) p.14; (12); (13) p.121.

    This pattern was produced for many years under the name "Chippendale" by the American Jefferson Glass Company (parent of the Canadian company).

COLOSSUS

Goblet, height 16.3 cm.

Dig: Burlington

References: (9); (1) p.278; (17) pp.176, 177.

   Also known as "Lacy Spiral" in the United States.

CORD AND TASSEL

Goblet, height 14.2 cm.

Dig: Burlington

References: (9); (11) p.278; (19) p.110.

   Design patented for the Central Glass Company, Wheeling, WV, in 1872.

CROSSED FERN
WITH BALL AND CLAW

Creamer, height 12.8 cm.

Dig: Burlington

References: (11) p.278; (17) pp.70, 71; (19) pp.27, 28.

An Atterbury & Company pattern patented in 1876 and also known simply as "Crossed Fern".

CROWN

Comport, height 17.7 cm.

Digs: Delormier and Nova Scotia

References: (16) pp.12, 27, 31, 33, 37; (17) pp.196, 197.

Metz calls this pattern "Notched Bar" and notes that it was listed in McKee catalogs of both 1894 & 1917. She also indicates that it is Canadian in origin. The pattern has long been known as "Pillar" as well, a name associated with at least one other American design.

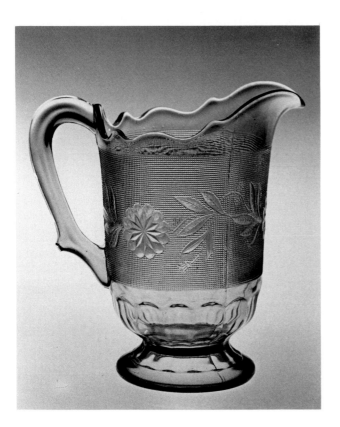

DAHLIA

Jug (amber), height 22 cm.

Dig: Burlington

References: (9); (11) p.278; (19) p.106.

The pattern is attributed to the Canton Glass Company, Canton, OH, c.1885. Shards found at the Burlington site were pale amber in colour.

DAISY AND X-BAND

Bowl, diameter 14 cm.

References: (10) p.12; (12); (17) pp.150, 151.

Metz calls this pattern "Hawaiian Lei".

DEER AND DOG

Sugar bowl, height (with lid) 24 cm.

Dig: Burlington

References: (9); (11) p.278; (14) pp.315, 316, plates 99, 101.

Produced in both clear and etched styles with the finial in common.

DIAMOND

Goblet, height 15.3 cm.

Digs: Delormier and Nova Scotia

References: (8); (16) pp.5, 39.

DIAMOND RAY

Comport, height 16.5 cm.

Digs: Delormier and Nova Scotia

References: (16) pp.8, 28, 29, 35.

    The comport illustrated has a foot in the "Crown" pattern which is typical of footed dishes in "Diamond Ray"; this is also known as a "Pillar Variant" pattern.

DOUBLE VINE

Plate, diameter 27.2 cm.

Dig: Burlington

References: (9); (14) p.645; (17) p.31.

    A variant of "Bellflower", a pattern produced from the 1830s by many American companies.

FILLY

Goblet, height 14.8 cm.

Di*g*: Burlington

References: (3); (9); (11) p.278; (19) p.87.

    A Bryce Brothers Company pattern made in Pittsburgh, c.1875, and reissued after 1891 by the United States Glass Company.

FLAT DIAMOND

Goblet, height 15.5 cm.

Di*g*: Burlington

References: (9); (11) p.278; (17) pp.198, 199; (19) p.287.

    A Richards and Hartley Flint Glass Company pattern, c.1875, originally named "Pillar".

FLORAL

Cake comport, height 17 cm.

Dig: Nova Scotia

Reference: (16) pp.28, 32.

A variant of a pattern called "Marsh Pink", shards of which were found on the Burlington site.

GARFIELD DRAPE

Goblet, height 15.8 cm.

Dig: Burlington

References: (9); (11) p.278; (17) pp.114, 115.

This pattern commemorates the 1881 assassination of the American president, James A. Garfield.

GESNER

Jug, height 23.4 cm.

Dig: Burlington

Reference: (11) p.278.

Pattern named for Dr. Abraham Gesner, the Nova Scotian inventor who first discovered kerosene.

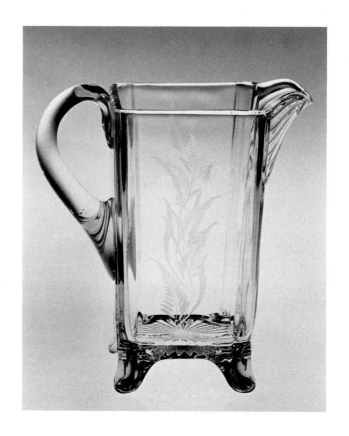

GOTHIC

Goblet, height 14.8 cm.

Dig: Nova Scotia

Reference: (16) p.27.

GRADUATED DIAMONDS

Goblet, height 14.5 cm.

Dig: Burlington

References: (9); (11) p.278.

To date this pattern has only been found in goblet form.

GRAPE AND FESTOON
WITH SHIELD

Goblet, height 15.9 cm.

Dig: Burlington

References: (9); (11) p.278; (19) p.138.

Pattern attributed to Doyle and Company, Pittsburgh, c.1870.

GRAPE AND VINE

Jug, height 22 cm.

Dig: Nova Scotia glass companies site, Trenton, N.S.

References: (16) pp.5, 27-30; (17) pp.80, 81; (18) pp.198, 199.

Metz calls this pattern "Ramsay Grape" and speculates in second book that it might also have been made in Canada.

HAMILTON GRAPE

Bowl, square 18.5 cm.

Dig: Burlington

References: (9); (11) p.278.

Also known as "Beaded Grape".

HONEYCOMB

Goblet, height 14.6 cm.

Digs: Burlington and Delormier

References: (8); (9); (11) p.278; (17) pp.42, 43.

Different versions of this pattern also known as "New York", were produced by a variety of American companies over many years.

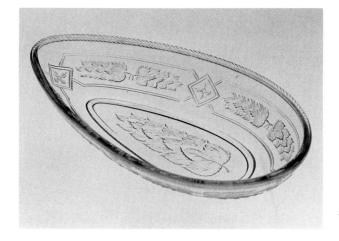

HOPS BAND

Relish dish, length 22.3 cm., width at widest point 12.8 cm.

Dig: Burlington

References: (9); (11) p.278; (19) pp.210, 214.

This pattern was patented for the King & Son Company of Pittsburgh in 1871 and originally called "Maple".

JACOB'S LADDER

Relish dish, length 25 cm., width 14.3 cm.

Dig: Burlington

References: (9); (11) p.278; (19) p.83.

Patented in 1826 by Bryce, Walker & Company of Pittsburgh as "Imperial", this pattern is also called "Maltese" in a Bryce Brothers catalog of 1885. It was still being produced in 1907 by the United States Glass Company.

JEWEL BAND

Bread tray, length 32.4 cm., width 23.5 cm.

Dig: Burlington

References: (9); (11) p.278; (15) p.50, plate 30.

An alternate name for this pattern is "Scalloped Tape".

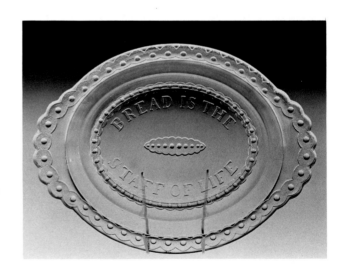

KALBACH

Goblet, height 15.2 cm.

Dig: Burlington

References: (9); (11) p.278; (17) pp.166, 167.

KENLEE

Goblet, height 15.5 cm.

Dig: Nova Scotia

References: (16) p.27; (18) pp.125, 126.

   Metz calls this pattern "Ribbon Band with Pendants".

LATE BUCKLE

Creamer, height 15.5 cm.

Dig: Burlington

References: (9); (11) p.278; (19) p.88.

    A pattern from Bryce Brothers Company of Pittsburgh, c.1880, originally called "Jasper".

LEAF AND DART

Creamer, height 16.5 cm.

Dig: Burlington

References: (9); (11) p.278; (14) p.456; (19) p.288.

    Produced by Richards and Hartley Flint Glass Company (later the Tarentum Glass Company) of Pittsburgh, c.1870, under the name "Pride".

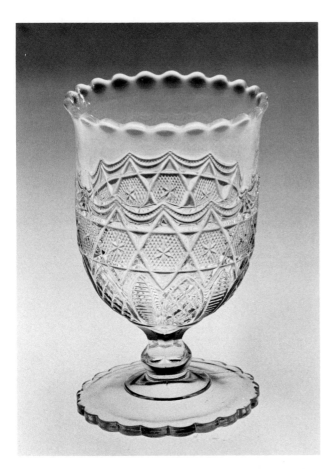

LEVERNE

Spooner, height 13.5 cm.

Dig: Burlington

References: (9); (11) p.278; (17) pp.118, 119.

LILLY OF THE VALLEY

Jug, height 18.2 cm.

Dig: Burlington

References: (9); (11) p.278; (17) pp.58, 59.

MAPLE LEAF

Creamer, height 10 cm.
Sugar, height (with lid) 16.5 cm.

Dig: Delormier

References: (2); (11) p.278; (12).

    This pattern is listed in the Diamond Glass catalog as No. 205. It comes in green, blue, opalescent and milk glass as well as clear.

MINERVA

Jug, height 24 cm.

Dig: Burlington

References: (9); (11) p.278; (17) pp.108, 109.

    Possibly made by the Boston and Sandwich Glass Company, Sandwich, MA., C.1870-80.

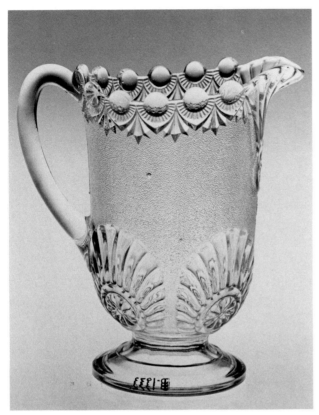

Figure A

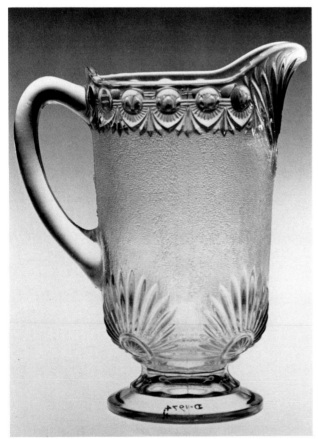

Figure B

NUGGET

Figure A – jug, Early Nugget, height 21 cm.
Figure B – jug, Late Nugget, height 23 cm.

References: (2); (11) p.274; (12); (19) pp.59, 61.

"Early Nugget" was produced by the Fostoria Glass Company of Moundsville, W, c.1900, when it was called "Victor". It may also have been produced in Canada prior to this date. "Late Nugget", illustrated in the Jefferson Glass Company catalog, is also known as "Shell and Jewel" in the United States.

101

Plate, diameter 29 cm.

Dig: Burlington

References: (11) p.278; (17) pp.188, 189.

PALMETTE

Goblet, height 15.5 cm.

Dig: Burlington

References: (9); (11) p.278; (14) pp.356, 357.

PANELLED DEWDROP

Goblet, height 15.5 cm.

Dig: Burlington

References: (9); (11) p.278; (17) pp.190, 191; (19) p.98.

Metz calls this pattern, which was patented in 1878 for Campbell, Jones and Company of Pittsburgh, "Beaded Pearls".

PANELLED FORGET-ME-NOT

Covered comport, height (with lid) 30 cm.

Dig: Burlington

References: (9); (11) p.278; (19) p.89.

Produced in Pittsburgh, first by Bryce Brothers, c.1875, under the name "Regal", and then by Doyle and Company, c.1880. Reissued by the United States Glass Company after 1891.

PANELLED THISTLE

Celery vase, height 14 cm.

References: (12); (19) p.92.

PEERLESS

Goblet, height 15.8 cm.

Dig: Burlington

References: (9); (11) p.278; (17) pp.168, 169.

Produced by the Richards and Hartley Flint Glass Company of Pittsburgh, c.1875.

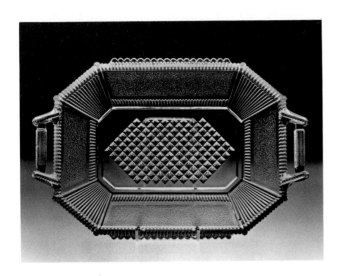

PLEAT AND PANEL

Bread plate, length 33.5 cm., width 21.5 cm.

Dig: Burlington

References: (9); (11) p.278; (19) pp.87, 88.

A Bryce Brothers Company pattern, c.1882, originally called "Derby". Reissued after 1891 by the United States Glass Company.

PRINCESS FEATHER

Plate, diameter (at handles) 29 cm.

Dig: Burlington

References: (9); (17) pp.126, 127.

Produced by Bakewell, Pears & Company, Pittsburgh, c.1870, under the name "Rochelle".

RASPBERRY

Plate, diameter (at handle) 28.5 cm.

Dig: Nova Scotia

References: (16) pp.27, 34, 39.

   This is a simplified version of the ''Raspberry and Shield'' pattern without the shield.

RASPBERRY AND SHIELD

Creamer, height 15 cm.

Digs: Burlington and Nova Scotia

References: (9); (16) pp.27, 28.

RAYED HEART

Footed jelly or bon bon dish, height 14 cm.

Reference: (4)

The example illustrated is in blue-green glass shading to opalescent on the edge of the bowl.

RIBBED BAND

Covered comport, height (with lid) 26.5 cm.

Dig: Nova Scotia

References: (16) pp.27-30; (17) p.137; (18) pp.198, 199.

Metz calls this pattern "Pleated Bands" and identifies it as Canadian.

RIBBON AND STAR

Goblet, height 15 cm.

Dig: Nova Scotia

References: (16) p.12; (19) pp.144, 149.

Patented for Duncan and Miller Glass Company of Pittsburgh in 1887 when it was called "Zippered Block". Reissued by the United States Glass Company after 1891.

SHERATON

Wine glass, height 9 cm.

Dig: Burlington

References: (9); (11) p.278; (19) p.92.

A Bryce, Higbee and Company pattern, c.1885, originally named "Ida".

STARFLOWER

Jug, height 18.5 cm.

Dig: Nova Scotia

References: (9); (16) pp.27-31; (18) p. 199

American names for this pattern are "Quantico" and "Dewdrops with Flowers".

STIPPLED SWIRL AND STAR

Covered comport, height (with lid) 28.5 cm.

Dig: Delormier

References: (2); (4); (12).

This pattern is listed in all of the catalogs cited as No. 200.

SUNBURST MEDALLION

Goblet, height 15.5 cm.

Dig: Burlington

References: (9); (11) p.278; (17) pp.128, 129.

SUNFLOWER

Creamer, height 12 cm.

Dig: Burlington

References: (9); (17) p.61; (19) p.29.

   An Atterbury and Company, Pittsburgh, pattern, c.1881, originally named "Lily".

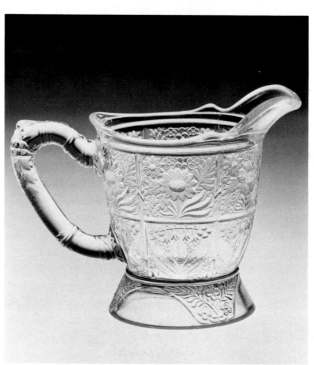

SWIMMING SWAN

Covered jar, height (with lid) 14.5 cm.

Digs: Delormier and Nova Scotia

Reference: (6).

TANDEM

Goblet, height 14.5 cm.

Dig: Nova Scotia

Reference: (16) pp.8, 34.

TULIP

Celery vase, height 18.4 cm.

Dig: Burlington

References: (9); (11) p.278; (19) p.88.

A Bryce Brothers, Pittsburgh, pattern reissued after 1891 by the United States Glass Company.

VICTORIA COMMEMORATIVE

Plates, diameter (at handles) 29.8 cm.

Digs: Delormier and Nova Scotia

Reference: (16) pp.32, 34.

Three different versions of this pattern are to be found – two with medallions of the young Victoria, and one with an illustration of the old queen superimposed on the young.

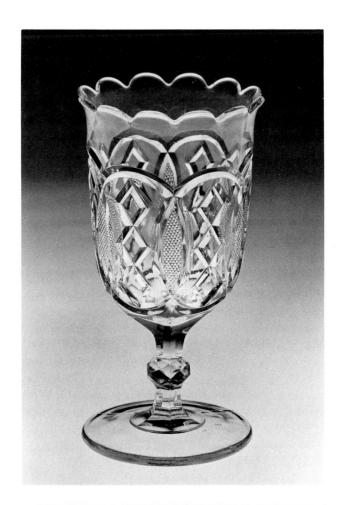

WASHINGTON CENTENNIAL

Celery vase, height 19.3 cm.

Dig: Burlington

References: (9); (11) p.278; (17) pp.112, 113.

A Gillinder and Company pattern originally designed for the Philadelphia Centennial Exposition in 1876.

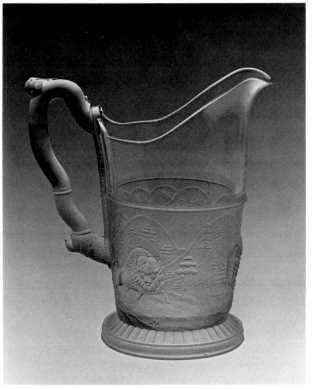

WESTWARD HO

Jug, height 24.5 cm.

Dig: Burlington

References: (9); (11) p.278; (19) p.170.

A Gillinder and Sons, Pittsburgh, pattern of the late 1880s.

WOODROW

Comport, height 20 cm.

References: (12); (17) pp.218, 219.

The American name for this pattern is "Galloway".

DIG LOCATIONS

Burlington — Burlington glass site, Hamilton, Ontario

Delorimier — Delorimier Ave. site, Montreal, Quebec

Nova Scotia — Nova Scotia glass companies sites, Trenton, Nova Scotia. Current theory attributes these patterns to the Nova Scotia Glass Company.

REFERENCES

(1) Diamond Flint Glass Company catalog
(2) Diamond Glass Company catalog c.1902
(4) Dominion Glass Company catalog c.1913
(5) Dominion Glass Company catalog c.1915
(6) GLASFAX *Newsletter*, 1971, p.5
(7) GLASFAX *Newsletter* No. 3 "The Delorimier Dig" (unpublished internal publication, 1971)
(8) GLASFAX *Newsletter* No. 10, 1976
(9) GLASFAX *Newsletter* "Report, 10th Anniversary Seminar" (unpublished internal publication, 1977)
(10) Janet Holmes, "Canadian Glass Patterns" in *Canadian Antiques Collector*, Volume 5, No. 1, January 1970, and No. 5, May 1970
(11) Janet Holmes, "Glass and the Glass Industry" in *The Book of Canadian Antiques*, Donald B. Webster, ed. (Toronto: McGraw-Hill Ryerson, 1974)
(12) Jefferson Glass Company catalog No. 21
(13) Minnie W. Kamm, *The Kamm-Wood Encyclopedia of Antique Pattern Glass* (Watkins Glen, N.Y.: Century House, 1961)
(14) Ruth Webb Lee, *Ealy American Pressed Glass* (Wellesley, Mass.: Lee Publications revised 1958)
(15) Ruth Webb Lee, *Victorian Glass*
(16) George MacLaren, *Nova Scotia Glass* (Halifax: Nova Scotia Museum, revised 1974)
(17) Alice Hulett Metz, *Early American Pattern Glass* (South Orleans, Mass.: Heritage Antiques, 1965)
(18) Alice Hulett Metz, *Much More Early American Pattern Glass* (South Orleans, Mass.: Heritage Antiques, 1965)
(19) Albert Christian Revi, *American Press Glass and Figure Bottles* (New York: Nelson, 1964)
(20) Gerald Stevens, *Canadian Glass c.1825-1925* (Toronto, Ont. Ryerson Press, 1967)

SELECTED GLOSSARY

ACID ETCHING — A method of decorating a glass article by use of hydrofluoric acid. The surface of the article is coated with wax, gum or varnish. The design is then drawn through this covering with a stylus, allowing the glass to be exposed to the acid. After a few minutes the covering is removed and the design remains.

AMERSEAL — A *closure* that has four inside projections that engage lugs on the glass bead and seals on the top.

ANNEALING — Controlled cooling of glass. — *furnace*: a small furnace where glass articles were cooled slowly to eliminate strains. — *oven*: (see *leer, lehr*).

APPLIED COLOUR LETTERING (A.C.L.) — A method of decorating a glass article by the *silk screen process*.

ART NOUVEAU — Glass articles taking the form of flowers or other foliage, or decorated by foliate or floral design, e.g. Tiffany ware, Carder ware. Late nineteenth century.

BASE — The bottom portion of a *paperweight*.

BATCH — The mixture of raw materials which, when melted, produce glass.

BLANK — The shaped body of glass, not yet a *container*, that comes from the blank mould. — *mould*: the first of a series of two moulds in which the *gob* of glass is converted into a *blank* and where preliminary shaping as well as the formation of the *finish* takes place.

BLOWER — (See *glassblower*.)

BLOW-AND-BLOW PROCESS — (See *flow process*.)

BLOWING-IRON — Former English name for a *blowpipe*.

BLOW MOULD — The second of the two *moulds* in which the *container* is blown into its final shape.

BLOWPIPE — A hollow iron tube 2-6 feet long, wider and thicker at the end at which the *gather* is made.

BOTTLE — A *narrow-mouth* (NM) *container* (i.e. prescription ware, beverage ware, etc.) (see illustration p.246).

BROAD GLASS — (See *cylinder glass*.)

BULL'S EYE — A circular scar in the centre of a piece of *crown glass* where it was *cracked-off* from the *pontil*.

CAMPAIGN — The working life of a *tank furnace* or other melting unit from one major repair to another.

CANE — 1) A solid glass rod of multiple cased layers stretched when hot to the desired diameter. 2) A small slice or segment of a *cane*.

CARBOY — A large *narrow-mouth bottle* with a nominal capacity of five gallons and upwards for acids, solvents, corrosives and other similar liquids.

CARNIVAL GLASS — A commercial quality *pressed glass* with an applied iridescent coating, usually of orange-brown but also of blue, mauve and greenish colours. It was a commercial attempt to compete with expensive iridescent Tiffany and Steuben "Aurene" glass. This glass, which was largely an American product, was so named because it was often tawdry in later years and was given as prizes at fairs and carnivals. In production about 1900-1935; reproduced in glossy, harsher tones from the late 1960s onwards.

CARRY-IN BOY — A boy, usually an apprentice, who carried the finished articles to the *annealing* operation.

CASED GLASS — Glass article containing two or more layers, usually of contrasting colours.

CAST GLASS PROCESS — Molten glass is poured onto a flat table.

CATHEDRAL GLASS — A rolled glass, one surface of which has a definite pattern or texture.

CHAIR — Wooden bench, with extended arms, at which the *gaffer* works.

CLOSURE — Any article or mechanism capable of sealing a *container*.

CODD'S BALL STOPPER — The *bottle* was made with a groove inside the neck. A glass ball was inserted, and then a ring of cork or rubber was fitted into the groove. Gas pressure within made the seal, holding the ball against the obstructing ring. To break the seal one had to thrust in a finger or stick to dislodge the ball.

COLBURN PROCESS — A method of manufacturing *sheet glass* by drawing the ribbon of glass horizontally from the melting furnace.

COLOURANT FOREHEARTH — (See *forehearth.*)

CONTAINER — A *bottle* if it has a narrow mouth or a *jar* if it has a wide mouth.

CONTINUOUS THREAD — (C.T.). Shallow cap of metal or other material with a single continuous thread and a screw-thread *finish* on the *bottle* to match.

CORK (Ck) — A *closure* consisting of a straight or tapered piece of cork inserted in the mouth of the *bottle.*

CRACK OFF — After an article has been affixed to the *pontil*, the *blowpipe* is cracked off.

CRIZZLING — A glass disease often due to excessive borax in colourless glass. The glass breaks down into thin layers which show as internal cloudiness and minute patterns of cracks. Sometimes droplets of alkaline liquid form on the surface; this state is referred to as "weeping" or "sweating."

CROWN — 1) *Closure.* A metal cap having a corrugated flange to crimp into a locking position on the *bottle* bead. 2) *Paperweight.* That part of a *paperweight* above the *motif.* (see also *dome*). 3) — *glass process.* A *gob* of glass is *gathered* on the end of a *blowpipe* and then formed into a pear shape by rolling it on a polished iron slab. After reheating, a globe is formed by rotating and blowing into the blowpipe. When it has reached a certain size, a *pontil rod* is attached to the globe opposite the blowpipe, which is then *cracked off.* After a second reheating, the globe on the pontil rod is rotated quickly enough that centrifugal force acting on the edge of the opening causes the molten glass to be flung outwards, forming a flat disc.

CRYSTAL GLASS — A loosely used term to describe *lead* glass.

CULLET — Broken glass used in the *batch* to accelerate the melting process.

CUT GLASS — A glass article whose surface is decorated with *cuttings* applied by an abrasive wheel.

CUTTING — A method of decorating glass by cutting it, either by hand or machine, on metal or abrasive wheels or discs.

CYLINDER GLASS PROCESS — Hand: Molten glass was *gathered* on a *blowpipe* and blown and shaped into a cylindrical form. By constant working, blowing, reheating and swinging the mass back and forth over a pit, these cylinders could be formed up to 12-15 inches in diameter and 4-6 feet long. *Machine:* In both cylinder processes the cylinder was cut and flattened to form window panes. A pipe was lowered into the molten glass and this solidified on the tip. Compressed air supplied through the pipe formed a cylinder which was drawn up until it was 30" in diameter and 40' long.

DAY TANK — (See *tank furnace.*)

DECOLOURIZING — The process of masking impurities in the raw materials to produce colourless glass by the addition of manganese, selenium or arsenic to the *batch.*

DECORATING LEHR — (See *lehr.*)

DEMI-JOHN — A large bladder-shaped *narrow-mouth bottle* with a nominal capacity of one to ten gallons.

DIG — Excavation of the site of a former glass operation or dump for *shards* of glass.

DOME — Refers to the shape of a *paperweight* and should not be confused with *crown.* A dome is cylindrical, tapering slightly towards the rounded top.

EMBOSSING — A method of superimposing lettering and/or a design on a glass article by cutting the lettering or design into the *blow mould.*

ENGRAVING — A method of applying a design to a glass article by the use of a wheel, diamond point or acid.

FACET — A plane cut on the exterior of a *paperweight* or other glass article. (See also *punty*.)

FEEDER — 1) — *machine*. A glass-forming machine (e.g. O'Neill, Miller, Lynch, etc.) which is fed from a continuous stream of glass cut into suitably sized *gobs* by the *feeder mechanism*. 2) — *mechanism*. Mechanical device on end of *forehearth* for converting the molten glass into *gobs* of glass of the right weight and size to make a bottle in a *feeder machine*.

FILAGREE — Threads or ribbons of opaque or coloured glass in a random pattern.

FINISH — The upper portion of the neck of a *container*.

FIRE — 1) In the nineteenth century, the period of time from the start of glassblowing in the fall to the shutdown in the spring for the summer break. 2) — *polishing*. A process for removing mould or tool marks by reheating.

FLAMEWORKING — The working of glass rods and tubes heated in a flame to produce glass articles.

FLASHING — A single-colour metallic stain brushed or sprayed on the exterior of a glass article for decorative purposes. The better pieces were then baked to ensure permanence.

FLAT GLASS — A generic term for glass used for residential and commercial construction.

FLINT GLASS — 1) A colourless glass, developed in England late in the seventeenth century, which used powdered calcined flints in place of sand (see also *lead glass*). 2) A twentieth century term used to describe colourless glass made from sand, lime and soda ash. 3) A term used to designate a good quality of colourless glass using lead.

FLINT HOUSE — Common term used in the nineteenth century to describe a *pressed glass* operation as opposed to a bottlemaking operating (*green house*).

FLINTS — Stones which, when calcined and powdered, were used in place of sand as the principal raw material (seventeenth century) (see also *flint glass*).

FLOAT GLASS PROCESS — 1. *Pilkington*. Molten glass is poured onto the molten tin bath, passing through three zones: heating, *firepolishing* and cooling. It then passes through an *annealing lehr*, where the glass is further cooled under precisely controlled conditions. 2. PPG. A ribbon of glass is drawn across the molten tin bath rather than poured onto it.

FLOW PROCESS — 1. *Blow-and-blow*. For *narrow-mouth bottles*, a process in which air pressure is used in both the *blank mould* and *blow mould*. 2. *Press-and-blow*. For *wide-mouth jars*, a process in which a *plunger* is used in the *blank mould* and air pressure is used in the *blow mould*.

FOREHEARTH — 1) Long box-like, fire brick-lined channel for conveying the molten glass from the furnace to the *feeder mechanism*. 2) *Colourant* —: forehearth into which coloured *frit* has been added to convert *flint* (clear) glass to coloured glass.

FOURCAULT PROCESS — A method of manufacturing *sheet glass* by drawing the ribbon of glass up vertically from the melting furnace to a *lehr*.

FREE-BLOWN — Glass article formed by blowing and manipulating with tools, without the use of a *mould*. (See also *handblown*.)

FRIT — This is produced by heating raw materials in an oven until some or most of the carbonates and other volatile matters are eliminated. Coloured frit is used in the *silk screen process* for decorating and in a *colourant forehearth*.

FRUIT JAR — A type of *wide-mouth jar* with a metal *screw cap* securing a *glass lid*, for storing preserves (cooked fruit or vegetables).

FUMING — The coating of the surface of glass with a thin spray of metallic chloride, creating a wrinkled and iridescent surface.

FURNACE — (See *tank furnace*.)

Gaffer. Master *blower*, head of *shop*.

GARLAND — A continuous string or line of *canes* often intertwined in a *paperweight* other than a circle.

GATHER — A *gob* of glass of a size that will be used for or on one *container* that is removed from the *pot* or *furnace* on a *blowpipe*, as for blowing, or on a *pontil*, as for a *laid-on ring*. Gatherer. Assistant to *gaffer*; accumulates the *gather* on the *blowpipe*. Gathering. The *glasshouse* term for the operation of forming a *gather* on the end of a *blowpipe* or *pontil* by placing the end in a pool of molten glass and slowly rotating it until the desired quantity through the cooling action of the *blowpipe*, has gathered into a ball at the end of the *pipe*.

GLASS — An inorganic product that is neither a solid nor a liquid, but has the random disordered structure of a liquid and the rigidity of a crystalline solid. It is commonly made by fusing together carefully selected silica sand mixed with soda ash, potash, lead or lime and other components at very high temperatures.

GLASSFORMING MACHINE — 1) "Semiautomatic." A machine to which the *gob* of glass is manually transferred. 2) "Automatic." A machine to which the *gob* of glass is automatically transferred, either by suction or gravity.

GLASSHOUSE — Nineteenth century term for a glass operation.

GLASS LID — Part of the sealing mechanism on a *mason jar*.

GLORY HOLE — A small *furnace* or opening in the side of it for the frequent reheating of a glass article in the forming or finishing stage.

GOB — 1) Hand operations. A portion of glass separated from the *gather*. 2) Machine operations. Feeder machine — a portion of glass severed from the *forehearth* by the *feeder mechanism*. Suction *machine* — a portion of glass sucked up from the *revolving pot*.

GREEN HOUSE — Common term used in the nineteenth century to describe a bottlemaking operation as opposed to a *pressed glass* operation (*flint house*).

GROSS — Quantity measurement for *containers* (144).

GROUND — That portion of a *paperweight* between the *motif* and the *base*.

HALF-BOX — Quantity measurement for *flat glass* (25 square feet per box).

HAND — 1) — *blown*. Article formed by blowing and manipulating with tools, with the aid of a mould (see also *free-blown*). 2) — *shop*. A team of glassworkers headed up by a *gaffer* and assisted by a *gatherer*, *mould boy*, a *servitor* and additional workers as required.

HUTCHISON STOPPER — A loop of heavy wire which protruded from the mouth of the *bottle*. The lower end, with a rubber gasket attached, went past the neck. After filling, the gasket was pulled up against the shoulders and was firmly kept there by the carbonation.

INDUSTRIAL WARE — Glassware for commercial use, such as lantern globes, insulators, street globes and other similar illuminating articles.

JAR — A *wide-mouth* (WM) *container* (i.e. mason jar, food packer, etc.).

JUG — A large *narrow-mouth bottle*. 1/2 gallon or larger.

LAID-ON RING — An added portion of glass around the neck of a *jar*, completely blown except for the tooling of the *finish*, formed by rotating the *jar* while a thin stream of glass is flowing from a small *gather* on the *pontil*.

LAMPWORKING — Former name for *flameworking*.

LATTICINIO, LATTIMO — Italian words for "filagree." Threads or ribbons of opaque white or coloured glass giving the effect of intersecting lines or latticework.

LEAD GLASS — 1) An alternative name for *flint glass* produced in the late seventeenth century. 2) A colourless glass using red lead instead of lime. (See also *flint glass*.)

LEER — An early term for a *lehr*. — *pans*: iron pans in which the finished articles were placed during *annealing*; metal pans were preceded by earthenware containers.

LEHR — A long tunnel-shaped oven with a moving metal belt for *annealing* glass articles. *Decorating* —: a lehr for baking in the *applied colour lettering* or *spraying* decoration.

LIGHTNING BEER STOPPER — A vulcanized rubber plug centred on the bail, which could be lifted out of the bottle or clamped in with a flick of the eccentric.

LIGHTWEIGHTING — The process of producing *bottles* containing less glass to save on material, space and transportation costs, at the same time increasing production speeds and number of *bottles* from a ton of glass.

LUBBERS' PROCESS — The mechanization of the *cylinder process (hand)*.

MADE-TO-ORDER — (MTO). A glass article made to a customer's specifications and for his exclusive use.

MAGNUM — A *paperweight* whose diameter measures over 3¼ inches.

MARVER — A table of marble, other stone or iron, on which the *gather* on the *blowpipe* can be rolled in order to both shape it for better blowing and to chill the surface of the glass.

MASON JAR — (See *fruit jar*.)

METAL — An alternative term for molten or cold *glass*.

MILLEFIORI — Italian word for "a thousand flowers." The term is used for *cased glass* which has a *motif* of glass *canes* with various coloured patterns.

MINIATURE — A *paperweight* which is two inches or less in diameter.

MOILE — That part of a bottle shape that is cut off at the top of the straight sides to convert the remainder into a tumbler.

MONOGRAM — *Embossed* arrangement of letters on *mason jars* and other food packers to identify maker.

MOTIF — The internal decoration of a *paperweight*.

MOULD BOY. A boy who opens and shuts the mould in a *hand shop*.

MUFFLE — A small *furnace*.

NARROW-MOUTH BOTTLE — (NM). (See *container*.)

OFF-HAND BLOWN — (*See free-blown*.)

OVERLAY — Term applied to Victorian *cased glass* in which the outside layer(s) was partially cut away to form a pattern. It was also used to describe a glass of more than one layer.

PAPERWEIGHT — A hand-formed, solid piece of glass usually globular in shape and containing a decorative *motif*.

PARISON — (See *blank*.) — mould: (see *blank mould*).

PATÉ DE VERRE — A paste formed by the fusion of powdered glass or *frit* heated in a mould.

PATTERN GLASS — 1) Flat glass (see *cathedral glass*). 2) Tableware (see *pressed glass*).

PEDESTAL WEIGHT — A *paperweight* whose base is extended to form a pedestal, which may enclose a *latticinio* design.

PIPE — (See *blowpipe*.)

PLATE — A metal insert with lettering and/or a design that fits into a round or oval opening in a plate mould for a *standard stock line container*, to cater to the customer who only orders small quantities of *embossed* glassware.

PLATE GLASS PROCESS — 1. Hand. (See *cast glass process*.) 2. *Machine*. A continuous ribbon of molten glass passed through a *lehr*, grinding process and polishing process.

PLUNGER — A mechanically moving element that, in the *blow-and-blow process*, extends only enough into the mouth of the *bottle* to determine the inside diameter at the opening but, in the *press-and-blow process*, extends well into the *parison* for the *jar* it helps to form.

PONTIL — rod: a solid iron rod on which a *gob* is *gathered* but on which the *gather* cannot be blown; — mark: a jagged scar on the bottom of a glass article resulting from the *cracking-off* of the pontil from the base of the article. — scar: (see *pontil mark*). bare —: the method of sticking the *pontil* to the bottom of the article without the use of a bit of hot glass as an intermediary.

POT — 1) *Clay or melting* —: large clay pot, either open-top or hooded, in which the *batch* is melted. 2) *Revolving* —: saucer-shaped refractory bowl from which *glass* is sucked up into the *blank mould* of a *suction machine*, i.e. Owens. 3) *Furnace* —: a centrally heated chamber in which two or more glass melting *pots* are located, each with its own opening for *gathering gobs* of glass.

PRESERVING JAR — (See *fruit jar*.)

PRESS-AND-BLOW PROCESS — (See *flow process.*)

PRESSED GLASS — Glassware formed by pressure between a *plunger* and a mould.

PRUNT — A small blob of glass, plain or designed, attached to a glass article.

PUCELLAS — A metal tonglike tool for shaping glass articles.

PUNTY — A concave cut on the exterior of a *paperweight* or other glass article (see also *facet*).

PUTNAM'S LIGHTNING FASTENER — A *closure* in which a bail goes over a groove in the *glass lid* and is held on the jar by a neck wire. An eccentric lever acts as a pivot.

SANDBLASTING — A method of frosting the surface of a glass article by applying a jet of fine sand under pressure. If a pattern is desired, that part of the surface to remain clear is covered by a protective coating.

SCREW CAP — (S.C.). A generic term to denote any type of threaded *closure*. (See *continuous thread.*)

SEALER — (See *fruit jar.*)

SERVITOR — The *glassblower* who is first assistant to the *gaffer.*

SHARD — A piece of broken *glass.*

SHEET GLASS — A generic term for glass, produced by a variety of manufacturing processes, which has natural fire finished surfaces. But because the two surfaces are never perfectly flat and parallel, there is always some distortion of vision and reflection.

SHOP — (See *hand shop.*)

SILK SCREEN PROCESS — A design is photographed onto a framed silk or, more likely, metal screen. A quantity of glass *frit*, suspended in a medium, is put onto the screen and is distributed over it by the back-and-forth movement of a flexible blade, forcing the *frit* through the photographed design onto the article. The article is then *annealed* in a *decorating lehr.*

SNAP — A spring cradle-type device which replaced the *pontil* as a holding tool. S*napper-up boy*: boy who handled the *snap.*

SODA-LIME GLASS — Glass made from the basic raw materials sand, lime and soda.

SOUTH JERSEY TRADITION — Type of glassware evolved by Caspar Wistar in southern New Jersey (USA) in the eighteenth century.

SPRAYING — A method of decorating in which the colour is sprayed onto the article and then baked in a *decorating lehr.*

STANDARD STOCK LINE — (SSL). A glass article, usually a *container*, that is not *embellished* and is available to any customer.

STOPPER — Any *closure* that enters into, and seals within, the mouth of the *bottle*, regardless of how it is held.

STUDIO GLASSBLOWING — Hand-blowing glass articles in a small shop by a team of one or two glassblowers.

SUCTION MACHINE — A glass-forming machine which sucks up a *gob of glass* into the *blank mould*, forms the *finish* and the general shape of the *container*. It is then transferred to the *blow mould*, where the finished *container* is created by the use of compressed air, e.g. Owens machine.

SULPHIDE — Ceramic bas-relief portrait or medallion, usually white, in a *paperweight.*

TABLEWARE — Glass articles associated with eating and drinking. May also include other table-related items, such as lamps, ashtrays, etc.

TANK — 1) *Day* —: a *furnace* from which glass is intended to be drawn for blowing only during the daytime; during the night the melting and refining of the raw materials into glass takes place 2) — *furnace a furnace*, the walls of which are made of fired clay blocks and in which the *batch* is melted. The fire is in a separate side structure, from which flames will pass over the raw materials to be melted. 3) *Continuous* — *furnace*: a *furnace* that is intended to be used for glass-blowing "around the clock." In contrast with the *day tank*, which has small ports around all sides, if desired, for workman's use either for hand or semiautomatic machine glass blowing; the continuous tank has means for introducing the *batch* material at a slow and steady rate at one end, approximating the rate at which *glass* is withdrawn at the other end. Melting and refining go on continuously as the mixture flows from one end to the other.

TURN — period during which a *hand shop* worked.

WEIGHT — (See *paperweight*.)

WETTING OFF — Marking the neck of a hot *bottle* with water so that it can be easily *cracked-off* from the *blowpipe*.

WHIMSEY — A noncommercial object created either for pleasure or to demonstrate the ability of a glassblower.

WHITTLE MARKS — Assumed to be the marks left on the surface of wooden moulds by whittling with a knife; this defect is actually the result of trying to blow into shape glass that was too chilled for the purpose.

WIDE-MOUTH JAR — (WM). (See *container*.)

YOKE — 1) Wire in *Putnam's lightning fastener* which engages the groove in the *glass lid*. 2) Y-shaped support on which to rest the *blowpipe* or *pontil* when *gathering* a *gob* of *glass*.

SELECTED BIBLIOGRAPHY

Barclay, John C. *Canadian Fruit Jar Report*. Kent Bridge, Ontario: published by the author, 1977.

Barker, Prof. T.C. *The Glassmakers*. "Pilkington: the rise of an international company 1826-1976." London, England: Weidenfeld and Nicolson, 1977.

Bird, Marion, and Douglas Bird. *North American Fruit Jar Index* and *Supplement to North American Fruit Jar Index*. Orillia, Ontario: published by authors, 1968, 1969.

Bird, Marion, Douglas Bird and Charles Corke. A *Century of Antique Canadian Glass Fruit Jars*. London, Ontario: published by the authors, 1971.

Bradbeer, Alan, and Dorothy Bradbeer. "The Crystal Glass Company: British Columbia's First Glass Factory." *Canadian Collector*, May/June 1976, pp. 104-06.

Burns, Doris W. *Paperweights and How to Collect Them*: A *Primer*. Montreal: published by the author, 1979.

Canadian Collector. Toronto: Bi-monthly.

Coburn, W. Newlands. "The First Quebec Glass Factory. La première verrerie du Québec." *Canadian Collector*, May/June 1974, pp. 93-97.

Collard, Elizabeth. "The St. Lawrence Glass Co.; Glasshouse to Pottery." *Canadian Collector*, September 1970, pp. 12-13.

Fauster, Carl. *Libbey Glass since 1818: Pictorial History and Collector's Guide*. Toledo, Ohio: Len Beach Press, 1979.

Foster, John Morrill. *Old Bottle Foster & His Glass Making Descendants*. Fort Wayne, Ind.: Keefer Printing Company, 1972.

Gilhen, John. "Telephone and Telegraph Insulators: The End of an Era." Halifax: *Nova Scotia Museum, The Occasional* 3, no. 3, summer 1976, pp. 26-35.

GLASFAX *Newsletter*. Ottawa: Internal publication of GLASFAX. 1, no. 1 (1967).

Hamilton, Alice. *Manitoban Stained Glass*. Winnipeg: University of Winnipeg, 1970.

Himel, Susan, and Elaine Lambert. *Handmade in Ontario*: A *Guide to Crafts and Craftsmen*. Toronto: Van Nostrand Reinhold, 1976.

Holmes, Janet. "Canadian Glass Patterns." *Canadian Collector*, January 1970, pp. 10-12.
 "Canadian Glass Patterns." *Canadian Collector*, May 1970, pp. 14-17.
 "Ottawa Glass Works, Como, Quebec." *Journal of Glass Studies* 14, pp. 164-5.
 "Glass and the Glass Industry." *The Book of Canadian Antiques*, ed. Donald B. Webster. Toronto: McGraw-Hill Ryerson, 1974.

Holscher, H.H. *Hollow and Specialty Glass*. Toledo, Ohio: Owens-Illinois Glass Company, 1965.
 "Feeding and Forming," reprint from *Handbook of Glass Manufacture*.

Illmann, Alberta. "Canadian Glass Pitchers." *Spinning Wheel* 22, September 1966, p. 16.
 "The Canadian Glass Insulator." *Western Collector* 7, no. 8, August 1969, pp. 384-86.

Journal of Glass Studies. Corning, New York: Corning Glass Centre.

Kaellgren, Peter ed. A *Gather of Glass: Glass Through the Ages in the Royal Ontario Museum*. Toronto: Royal Ontario Museum, 1977.

Kennedy, Jr., Donald. "Manitoba Glass Works." *Canadian Collector*, November/December 1971, pp. 64-67.

King, Thomas B. "History of the Canadian Glass Industry." *Journal of the Canadian Ceramic Society* 34, 1964, pp. 86-91.

Kingdon, Jack, Dave Parker and Larry Taylor et al. *The Hamilton Glass Works — c.1865-1912*. Hamilton: Report at the first GLASFAX Seminar, June 11-13, 1971.

Lief, Alfred. A *Close-Up of Closures. History and Progress*. New York: Glass Container Manufacturers Institute, 1975.

Littleton, Harvey K. *Glass Blowing*: A *Search for Form*. Toronto: Van Nostrand Reinhold Company, 1971.

MacLaren, George. "The Trenton Glass Works: Humphreys' Glass Works: the Lamont Glass Works; the Nova Scotia Glass Company." Halifax: *Nova Scotia Museum Newsletter* 2, April 1958, pp. 47-55.

"Nova Scotia Glass." Halifax: *Nova Scotia Museum, Occasional Paper 4*, Historical Series no. 1, 1965.

"Some Thoughts on Canadian Glass." *Canadian Collector*, November 1970, p.27.

McIntosh, Colin. *Canadian Insulators and Communication Lines*. Victoria, British Columbia: published by author, n.d.

McNally, Paul. "Table Glass in Canada." Ottawa: Canadian Government Publications, *History and Archaeology* no. 60, 1982.

Meigh, Edward. *The Story of the Glass Bottle*. Stoke-on-Trent, England: C.E. Ramsden and Company Limited, 1972.

Mercer, Willa. "The Penetanguishene Glass Factory." *Canadian Collector*, July/August 1971, pp. 34-36.

Metz, Alice Hulett. *Early American Pattern Glass* (Book 1) Chicago, 1958.

Much More Early American Pattern Glass. Columbus, Ohio: Spencer-Walker Press, 1965.

Milholland, Marrion, and Evelyn Milholland. 4th ed. *Most About Glass Insulators*. Seguim, Washington: published by the authors, 1976.

Miller, George L., and Catherine Sullivan. "Machine-Made Glass Containers and the End of Production for Mouth-Blown Bottles." Ottawa: Parks Canada, *Research Bulletin* no. 171, 1981.

Moody, B.E. *Packaging in Glass*. London: Hutchison of London, 1964.

Munsey, Cecil. *The Illustrated Guide to Collecting Bottles*. New York: Hawthorn Books Inc., 1970.

National Early American Glass Club. *Bulletin*.

Nelson, Celia. "Historic Hudson Old Cavagnal". 3rd. ed. Hudson, Quebec: Hudson Historical Society.

Ontario Bottle Magazine, St. Catherines, Ontario. 1, no. 1, January 1976.

Pacey, Antony. "A History of Window Glass Manufacture in Canada". *Association for the Preservation of Technology Bulletin*, Vol. XIII, no. 3, 1981.

Parkland Bottle Collector. Spy Hill, Saskatchewan: published by Parkland Bottle Collectors Club, no. 1, February 1971.

Peterson, Arthur G. *Glass Salt Shakers: 1000 Patterns*. DesMoines, Iowa: Wallace-Homestead Book Co. 1974.

400 Trademarks on Glass. Takoma Park, Maryland: Washington College Press, 1968.

Pierce, Edith Chown. *Canadian Glass, A Footnote to History*. Toronto: privately printed, 1954.

Provick, A.M. "Beausejour's Glass Works." *Canadian Collector*, January 1967, pp. 7-10.

Reifschneider, John Charles. "Recollections of Beausejour and the Manitoba Glass Works 1909-1911." *Manitoba Pageant* 22, no. 4, summer 1976, pp. 4-13.

Robinson, Beth. "Glass: A Classic Field for the Collector." *Canadian Collector*, April 1966, pp. 8-9.

Russell, Loris S. *Lighting the Pioneer Ontario Home*. Toronto: *Royal Ontario Museum Series What? Why? When? How? Where? Who?* University of Toronto Press, 1966.

"Confederation Lamps." *Canadian Collector*, March 1967, pp. 9-11.

A Heritage of Light Lamps and Lighting in the Early Canadian Home. Toronto: University of Toronto Press, 1968.

Rottenberg, Barbara Lang, and Judith Tomlin. *Glass Manufacturing in Canada: A Survey of Pressed Glass Patterns*, Mercury Series #33. Ottawa: National Museum of Man, 1982.

Ryder, Huia. "New Brunswick Glass." *New Brunswick Museum Art Bulletin* 6, no. 3, March 1962.

Scoville, Warren C. *Revolution in Glassmaking Entrepreneurship and Technological Change in the American Industry, 1880-1920*. Cambridge: Harvard University Press, 1948.

Séguin, Robert-Lionel. "La Verrerie du Haut Vaudreuil." *Bulletin des reserches historiques*, 61, pp. 119-28.

Sheeler, John. "The Burlington Glass Site." *Canadian Collector*, April 1968, pp. 7-9.

    "The Burlington Glass Site." *Canadian Collector*, May 1968, pp. 11, 12.

    "The Burlington Glass Site." *Canadian Collector*, June 1968, pp. 18-20.

    "The Burlington Glass Site." *Canadian Collector*, July 1968, pp. 14-15.

    "Burlington Glass Site." *Canadian Collector*, August 1968, pp. 8, 9.

    "Burlington Glass Site." *Canadian Collector*, November 1968, pp. 10-12.

    "Burlington Glass Site." *Canadian Collector*, January 1969, pp. 12, 13.

Shepherd, Elizabeth. "Canadian Glass Collecting." *Canadian Collector*, July/August, 1977, pp. 45-47.

Smith, F.R., and R.E. Smith. *Miniature Lamps*. 1st. ed. Toronto: Thomas Nelson and Sons, 1968.

Spence, Hilda, and Kelvin Spence. A *Guide to Early Canadian Glass*. Toronto: Longmans Canada Limited, 1966.

Stevens, Gerald. "Early Canadian Glass." Kingston, Ontario: *Historic Kingston*. Transactions of the Kingston Historical Society, 1953-54, no. 3, pp. 57-69.

    Early Canadian Glass. Toronto: Ryerson Press, 1961.

    Early Ontario Glass. Toronto: *Royal Ontario Museum Series What? Why? When? How? Where? Who?* University of Toronto Press, 1965.

    Canadian Glass, c.1825-1925. Toronto: Ryerson Press, 1967.

Thompson, John Beswarick. "Vaudreuil Glass Industry." *Canadian Collector*. November/December 1972, pp. 39-42.

    Cavagnal 1820-1867. 4th ed. Hudson, Quebec: Hudson Historical Society, 1980.

Thuro, Catherine M.V. "Lomax Lamps." *Canadian Collector*, November/December 1975, pp. 26-30.

    Oil Lamps: The Kerosene Era in North America. DesMoines, Iowa: Wallace-Homestead Book Co., 1976.

Toulouse, Julian H. *Fruit Jars*. Toronto: Thomas Nelson and Sons (Canada) Limited, 1969.

    Bottle Makers and Their Marks. Toronto: Thomas Nelson and Sons (Canada) Limited, 1971.

Unitt, Doris, and Peter Unitt. *Bottles in Canada*. Peterborough, Ontario: Clock House, 1972.

Urquhart, O. *Bottlers and Bottles, Canadian*. Toronto: published by S. and O. Urquhart, 1976.

Vallières, Jean. "Le soufflage du verre: art perdu et retrouvé." Québec, Québec: Ministère des Affaires culturelles, *Collection Civilisation du Québec*, série arts et métiers, published by Les Éditions Leméac, Inc., 1979.

Vienneau, Azor. *The Bottle Collector*. Halifax, Nova Scotia: Petherec Press, 1969.

Watson, George, and Robert Skrill. *Western Canadian Bottle Collecting*. Nanaimo, British Columbia: Hume Compton, 1971.

Watson, George, Robert Skrill, and Jim Heidt. *Western Canadian Bottle Collecting — Book 2*. Nanaimo, British Columbia: Evergreen Press, 1972.

Webster, Donald B. "New Form of Pattern Glass for Collectors." *Canadian Collector*, June 1970, pp. 22, 24.

Westward Collector Quarterly, 1, no. 1, 1973. Nanaimo, British Columbia: Western Collector Publishing Limited.

Wilson, Kenneth M. *New England Glass and Glassmaking*. An Old Stourbridge Village Book. New York: Crowell Co., 1972.

Index

Leverne pattern 176, A3
le Virir, William 14
Libbey, Edward D. 20, 107, 213
Libbey, Glass Co. (US) 20, 104
Libbey-Owens-Ford (US) 212
Libbey-Owens Sheet Glass (US) 211, 213, 214
Libbey-St. Clair 104, **196**, 220
Lid press 153
Lilly of the valley pattern 176, A3
Little Bartibogue N.B. 231
Little Egypt (Egypt Road) Trenton, N.S. 78
Littleton, Harvey K. 225, 231
Lockhart, W.A. 55
Locklin, Maurice G. 193
Lockwood, Herbert 118
London Glass Co. of Virginia (US) 18
Lorraine (France) 197
Lorraine Glass **229-230**
Losch, John 94
Lowden **family**
    Ina, R. 227
    John 226, 227
    John S. 93, 186, 187, 226, 227
    Robert W. 93, 186, 187, 225, 226
    Roberta 227
    Stuart C. 226, 227
Lowden & Son, John 226, 227
Lozenges pattern 176
Lubbers, John H. 200, 209
Lumbers, Walter G. 186
Lumsden, A. 88
Luzine, Melesse 190
Lydiatt **family**
    George 90, 94, 95, 104, 113, 133, 164, 189, 190
    James 90, 92, 93
    James Jr. 90
Lyman, Arthur 137, 138, 141, 155
Lyman, Benjamin 44, 49
Lyman, Dr. S.J. 49, 50
Lyman Bros. & Co. 49
Lymans Ltd. 136
Lynch (forming machine) 132, 141, 143, 146, 153, 154, 155, 166, 193

McAllister, John 55
Macaulay, R.W. 195
Macaulay, T.B. 164
MacBeth-Evans Glass **188**
MacBeth-Evans Glass Co. (US) 188
McCallum, W.J. 142, 143
McDermott, Alex 54
MacDonald, Hugh 163
Macdonald, Ian R. 162, 163, 164
MacDonald, William 50
MacDonald, William F. 78
McGavin, John C. 122
MacGillivray, Joseph H. 80
McGinnis, William 26
McGregor, Alexander 115
MacGregor, P.A. 73
McIntosh, Colin 185
McKay, William D. 82

McKearin **family**
    George 34
    Helen 34
McKens(z)ie, B.E. 92
Mackenzie, James R. 130, 152, 156, 161, 163, 164, 217
McKibbin, W. 117, 118
McKinlay, John P. 105, 106
Macklin, Bert 143, 157
MacLaren, George 78, 83, 169, 172
McLarens Cheese Co. 63
McMaster **family**
    Ross H. 134, 164
    William 134, 164
MacNaughton **family**
    Alexander 43
    Johnny 43
McNichol, Charles 26
MacPherson, James 47, 49
MacRae, G.F. 165
Magoun, Joseph 27
Malcolmson **family**
    Herbert H. 85
    John C. 85, 87
Mallory **family**
    Amassa W. 35, 36
    Andrew W. 35
    Daniel 34, 35
    David 35
Mallorytown, Ont. 34
Mallorytown Glass **34-36**, 169, 173, 203
Mander, Ronald E. 163
Manitoba Glass 27, 112, 113, 115, **121-123**, 134, 137, 140, 146, 169, **172-173**, 188
Mansfield, Robert. See Mansell, Sir Robert
Mansell, Sir Robert 15, 197
Maple leaf pattern (No. 205) 176, A3
Marshall, Col. K.R. 164
Martin, H. 104
Martin, Paul E. 164
Martin, R. 120
Martin, W.A. 190
Mason (fruit jar) 139, 172
Masson, Damase 39, 40
Masson et Cie **39-40**
Matthews, George 43, 44
Matthews, Major J.S. 119
Mayer 143
Mayo, F.J. 190
Medicine Hat, Alberta 112, 113, 123, 125, 229
Meigh, Edward 11, 15
Meldrum, Norman W. 152, 162, 163, 164, 217, 218
Melnick, N.J.P. 166
Mendell, George S. 140, 143, 155, 156, 217
Mercer, Willa 205
Merritt, William 89, 202, 203
Mewburn, Hon. Sydney C. 164
Meyer, Ernst R. 98
Mid-West Glass **155-156**
Mid-West Canadian made fruit jar 150
Midland, Ont. 193
Midland Glass Co. (US) 25
Miller, Edward 96